THE WORLD
STORMRIDER GUIDE

LOW PRESSURE

THE WORLD STORMRIDER GUIDE

LOW PRESSURE LTD
Unit 2 Efford Farm Business Park
Bude Cornwall EX23 8LP
Tel +44 (0)1288 359867 **Fax** +44 (0)1288 359869
E-mail enquiries@lowpressure.co.uk
Web www.lowpressure.co.uk

LOW PRESSURE – Europe
Tel/Fax +33 (0)5 58 77 76 85

First published in 2001 by **LOW PRESSURE LTD**

Compilation of all weather and swell data YEP 2000©

Creation of all zone maps YEP/Low Pressure Ltd 2000©

Creation of all other maps, graphic arrangement, pictogramms,
text and index Low Pressure Ltd 2000©

A catalogue reference for this book can be obtained from the British
Library. ISBN Softback: 0 9539840 0 1

Reproduction in the UK by Permanent Publishing
1 Stert Street Abingdon Oxon OX14 3JF

Printed in the UK by Bath Press Ltd
Lower Bristol Road Bath BA2 3BL

THE WORLD
STORMRIDER GUIDE

LOW PRESSURE

Written and Researched by
Antony 'Yep' Colas
Zone Map Creation: Julia Ratsimandresy
Photo Editor: Laurent Masurel

Information Compilation
Zone Maps: Laurent Lafitte Jérôme Laigneau
Nautical Charts: Hugues Gosselin – Mapmedia
Swell Statistics: Pascal Dunoyer Vincent Loaec
Weather Statistics: Dom Léoture

Publishing Directors
Ollie Fitzjones Bruce Sutherland Dan Haylock

Editor
Bruce Sutherland

Editorial Assistance
Stuart Butler Alex Dick-Read Ollie Fitzjones
Craig Jarvis Drew Kampion

Design and Production
Dan Haylock Graham Waldron

Photo Editors
Laurent Masurel Dan Haylock

Proof Reading
Vik Sell

Advertising
Simon Mahomo

Photographic Contributors
Javier Amezaga Rodrigo Barraza Cedric Barros
Vincent Biard Nick Bothma Rod Braby John Callahan
Sylvain Cazenave Chris Chapman Eric Chauché
Philippe Chevodian Andrew Christie Kiki Commarieu
Lionel Corbel Emmanuel Daubrée Sean Davey
Philippe de Marsan Christophe Dimulle Alessandro Dini
Tom Dugan Alfredo Escobar Marc Fénies Javier Fernandez
Steve Fitzpatrick Tony Fleury Rob Gilley Chuck Graham
Dan Haylock G J de Konig Gecko Andrew Hobson
Phil Holden Heather Holjes Paul Kennedy Alex Laurel
Fred le Leannec Paul Maartens Laurent Masurel Dick Meseroll
Stéphane Mira Tara Moller Bill Morris Thierry Organoff
Louis Powell Kristen Pelou Geoffrey Ragatz Ben Rak
Jim Russi Garth Robinson Steve Ryan Cory Scott
Bradley Seaman Mike Searle Wallace Summers
Hisayuki Tsuchiya Tungsten Willy Uribe Joao Valente
Chris Van Lennep Flavio Vidigal Alex Williams
Peter Wilson Yep

Editorial Contributors
Sebastien Barth Biloute Lena Blain Jérôme Boggio-Pasqua
Tony Butt Alex Dick-Read Felip Patrice Galand Gil Erik Hesse
Russell Hill Craig Jarvis Drew Kampion Denis Lartigau
Eric Marmora Todd Mazur Noriyuki Mochizuki Ricardo Nuñez
Robert Parker Fred Ralaiminatroa Fabrice Ratti
Vincent Stuhlen Bruce Sutherland Steve Thompson
Graham Walker Jody Wood

Special Thanks
Mary Alegoet Laurent Masurel Nicolas Dejean Philippe Lauga
Latif Benhaddad Benoit Duthu Gibus de Soultrait
Tiki Yates Tim Rainger Camillo Gallardo Marc Hare
Kore Antonson David Simms Stephen Jenkins
Alex Dick-Read Jim Peskett and all at Permanent Publishing
Andrea Dillon Sheila Jake Shani and Marla Fitzjones
Louise Aedan Anna Ella and Jamie Millais
Sue John Mathew and Adam Haylock

This page – Blacks, San Diego, California

Cover – Heinere Paez at home in Tahiti PHOTO: ROB GILLEY

The World Stormrider Guide

Foreword

In 1989, after extensive travelling across Asia, Africa, Australia and the Pacific the seeds of **The World Stormrider Guide** were sown on a cold, dusty building site in London. All I wanted to do was travel and surf, and had spent a couple of years painting houses for fast cash but it wasn't ideal. Stuck in traffic while trying to get some more work, my non-surfing friend, Camillo Gallardo, casually suggested I write a world surf guide as a way to fulfil my dream. That was it. I started work on **The World Stormrider Guide** straight away, painting during the day and scribbling notes at night. It didn't take long to realise that the world is a big place. It broke down nicely into continental chapters and Europe seemed the ideal place to start. Very little information existed, surf spots were always hard to find and people were never too keen to tell. I soon realised that there was a big black hole when it came to European surf travel information. Whilst most well-travelled, experienced surfers knew of Europe's waves, most average surf trippers had not considered its potential as one of the prime surf locations in the world! Guides existed for Australia, New Zealand, South Africa and California but the great waves of Europe had been overlooked. **The Stormrider Guide: Europe** 1st edition was released in June 1992 and Low Pressure was up and riding. As the team grew over the following years a second and third edition were produced and during that time a great many people turned up, interested in what we were doing. Among these was Antony 'Yep' Colas, a hardcore French surfer whose past years had been devoted to a similar cause, studying maps, looking at swell patterns, and writing travel stories. Antony helped compile and translate **The Stormrider Guide: Europe** and also talked about the idea of a world guide. Low Pressure got sidetracked (in the nicest possible way) with a couple of Snowboard Guides and **The World Stormrider Guide** was again, regrettably put aside. Whilst creating surftrip.net, a website for up-to-date surf travel information, Antony Colas gathered and compiled information and statistics on 80 of the planet's primo surf zones, furthering the concept of the world guide. Eventually, Low Pressure and Yep joined forces and after two years work, with masses of help from hundreds of super cool surfers, here is **The World Stormrider Guide**.

Ollie Fitzjones

Note – We have always tried our hardest to show local surfers respect for their secret spots, balanced against the fact that all surfers love to travel. Bear this in mind on your next trip. We hope you enjoy your yourselves.

Mentawai boat trip

As the World shrinks and frontiers retreat in the face of a frenzied search for perfect, uncrowded surf, take a moment to reflect on what it means to be a global surf traveller.

The unrivalled exhilaration that comes from riding a pearl of pure oceanic power is essentially the same, regardless of geographical location. Travelling becomes the attraction, where the path is awash with the ebb and flow of cultures. This journey is best undertaken with an open mind that embraces respect and rejects prejudices.

The 80 zones that follow are a fraction of the World's true wealth, yet each one is a gem in the crown of Planet Surf.

SEAN DAVEY

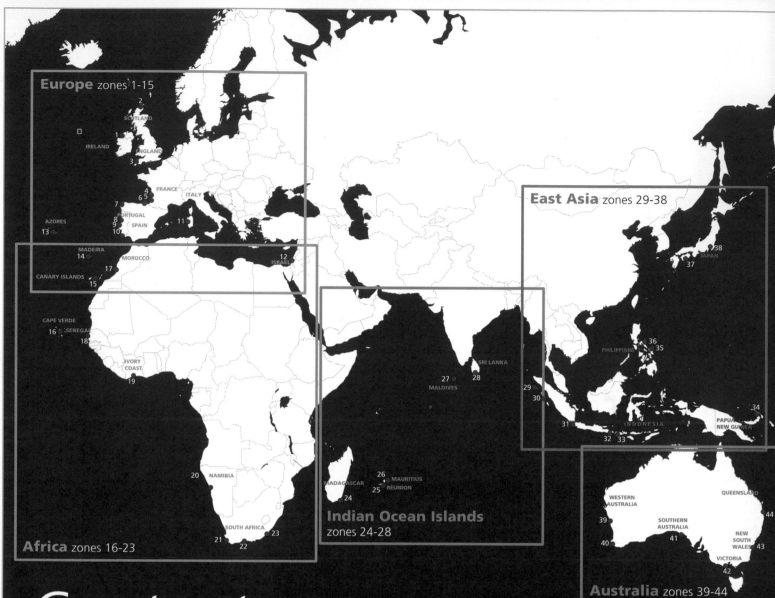

Europe zones 1-15

East Asia zones 29-38

Africa zones 16-23

Indian Ocean Islands zones 24-28

Australia zones 39-44

Contents

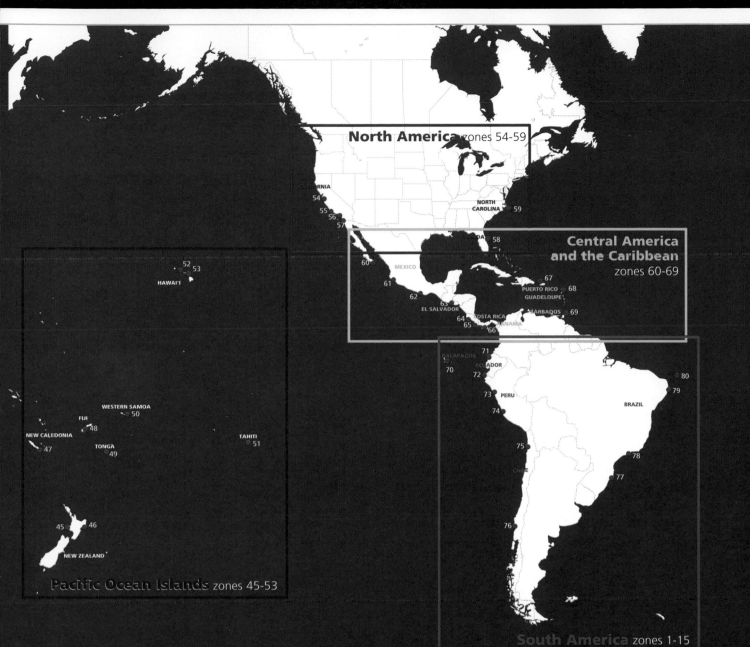

North America zones 54-59

Central America
and the Caribbean
zones 60-69

Pacific Ocean Islands zones 45-53

South America zones 1-15

LAURENT MASUREL

SEAN DAVEY

Meteorology and Oceanography

I. The World's Oceans

Oceans and seas cover 71% of the Earth's surface, representing about 362,000,000km² (140,000,000mi²). Surrounding this immense blanket of water is an estimated 400,000km (250,000mi) of potentially surf-exposed coastlines. Not all of this extensive global coastline receives rideable waves, with about 20% of this figure being hardly ever exposed or too cold to surf. Another 20% of the world's coastline suffers from low consistency, whereby surfable waves are rare in any given month of the year. Then there is the world average (40%) where waves occur more frequently than monthly but may not break more than once every week. This leaves the world's surfing population with only 20% of the global coastline to scour for high consistency waves, meaning places with surf more or less on a daily basis. These assessments of low (monthly), medium (weekly) and high (daily) consistency are far too precise in the unpredictable realm of surfing ocean waves, but help shed some light on the geographical possibilities and limitations that face the global surf traveller. Bearing these simplified statistics in mind, the southern hemisphere contains more of these highly consistent shores because it is dominated by water and hosts only two entire continents, Australasia and Antarctica.

The Atlantic Ocean 82,000,000km²

The Atlantic is the world's second largest ocean with 22% of the global sea area, but it's only half the size of the Pacific. Bisected by the Equator, the greatest distance from east to west in the North Atlantic is Morocco to Florida – 7,200km (4475mi) and 9,600km (5965mi) from Guinea to Brazil in the South Atlantic. The average depth is 12,000ft (3,660m) and the deepest point of 28,374ft (8,648m) is in the Puerto Rico Trench.

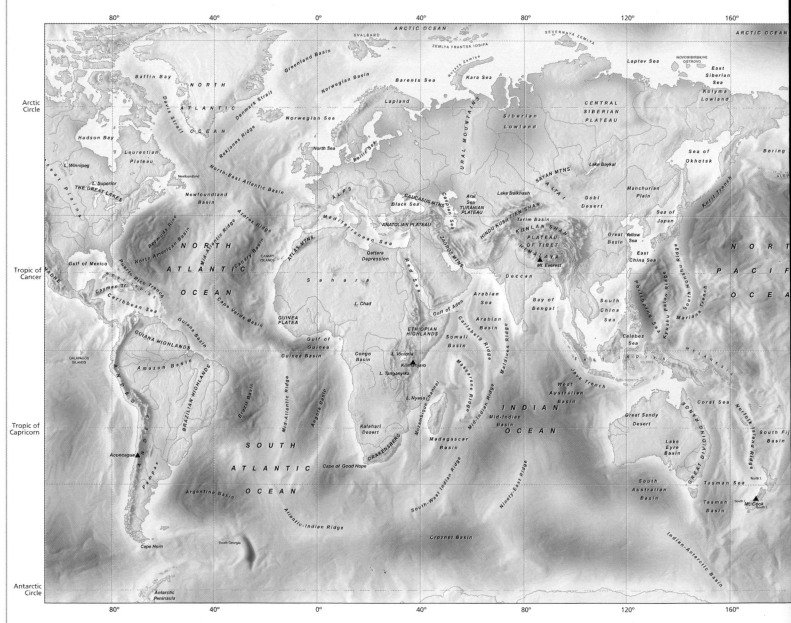

The North Atlantic is the windiest and roughest ocean, with strong winter westerlies of over 55kmh (35mph), generating a band of seas greater than 15ft (5m) between Nova Scotia and the UK. There is significant seasonal variation with much milder conditions occuring in summer. The NE trade winds blowing from the sub-tropical highs around 30°N towards the Equator are sustained throughout the year but weaker than those in the North Pacific. An extensive area of light winds or doldrums dominates the equatorial regions apart from a weak SW monsoon that is experienced in the Gulf of Guinea, around July.

The South Atlantic is the smallest ocean and is unusual because it has a complete lack of tropical storm activity. The barrier provided by the Andes produces a slight reduction of strength in the SE trade winds and a marked reduction of waves in the south-west throughout the year. Overall, the Atlantic trades are the weakest of all oceans. The strongest swells occur in winter and spring, produced by the westerlies in the 30° to 60° zone, sending the biggest waves to the eastern shore of the basin.

The Indian Ocean   73,000,000km²

Representing 20% of the global sea area, the Indian Ocean is quite similar in size to the Atlantic Ocean. The major difference is its southern hemisphere location, with little area located north of the Equator. The average depth is a little under 13,000ft (4000m), while the Java Trench bottoms out at 24,441ft (7,450m).

The low latitude of the westerly flow can clash with the icy polar easterlies, creating unpredictable and gusty winds. These winds have the greatest fetch of anywhere on the planet, leading to the term the 'Roaring Forties', which produce large ocean swells, resulting in regular 'fully arisen seas'. Peak mean waves of over 15ft (5m) are observed in July/August and unlike the northern hemisphere, the seasonal change is minimal. The Asian/Australasian monsoon dominates the eastern half of the Indian Ocean throughout summer (Dec-March), when strong NW winds blow throughout Indonesia and northern Australia, while NE winds flow towards India. In the western half of the Indian Ocean winter (July) there is a SW monsoon, which reaches its greatest intensity around Somalia (Somalia Jet). The remainder of the sub-tropical to equatorial zone is mostly influenced by SE trades.

The Pacific Ocean   165,000,000km²

Accounting for 45% of the global ocean coverage, The Pacific Ocean is the largest body of water and single biggest feature on the planet Earth. It is also the deepest ocean with an average depth of 13,800ft (4,200m), plunging to the unequalled depth of 35,826ft (10,920m) at the Mariana Trench. The widest point in an east-west direction is 17,700km (11,000mi), extending almost halfway round the world and it stands 11,000km (7,000mi) tall from north to south.

In the winter, the northern half of the North Pacific is raked by high winds of over 55kmh (35mph), usually blowing from the west. These winds can generate sustained seas of over 15ft (5m) to pound the western shores of North America and Hawai'i. The tropical band of the western North Pacific is under the influence of the Asian Monsoon. Strong E trades extend to the Equator in January and generate seas of up to 10ft (3.2m). Generally light winds are experienced in the eastern Equatorial Pacific throughout the year and wave height is maintained by swell propagation from both the North and South Pacific westerlies.

The South Pacific experiences strong westerlies flowing between the 35° to 60° mid-latitudes throughout the year. This broad corridor extending from New Zealand to Cape Horn, reaches maximum activity from June to September, when the S to SW swells primarily affect the central and eastern Pacific. In the tropics, the trade winds are less extensive and weaker than the North Pacific, so this area relies on long distance oscillations from the mid-latitude westerlies in either hemisphere.

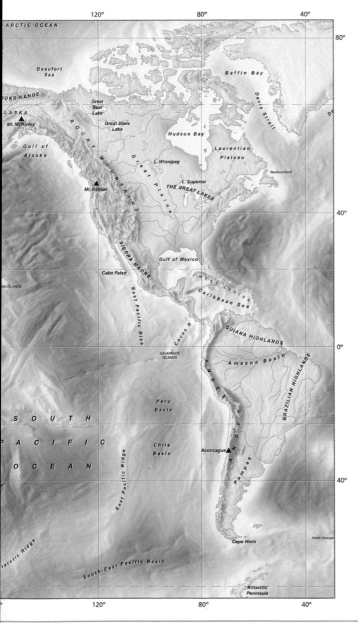

Top 10 low latitude closed/semi-closed seas (Mkm²)	
Mediterranean Sea	2.5
South China Sea	2.3
Caribbean Sea	1.9
Gulf of Mexico	1.5
East China Sea	1.2
Yellow Sea	1.2
Japan Sea	1
North Sea	0.6
Red Sea	0.4
Black Sea	0.4

II. The Creation of Wind

The Earth's weather is a complex system designed to redistribute the heat energy that the Sun delivers. The Sun's rays strike the equatorial regions with more concentration, causing the surrounding air to be heated. This lighter, hot air rises in updrafts, then travels towards the poles, high in the atmosphere. When it cools, the air becomes denser, sinks down to sea level and returns towards the Equator, replacing the warm air and completing the heat exchange process. These parcels of air are measured by barometric pressure, whereby the warmer, lighter packages of air are known as high pressures and the colder, denser air is called an area of low pressure. The air in a high pressure is attracted to areas of low pressure and rushes towards it, creating winds. The rotation of the Earth deflects the wind from taking a direct route to the poles, a phenomenon known as the coriolis force. In the northern hemisphere, this causes the air to spin clockwise around a high pressure and anti-clockwise around a low pressure. The winds spin in the

The Jet Stream

The two polar jet streams meander gently from north to south. Beneath them large frontal systems form along the boundary between polar and tropical air masses.

High level Jet Stream

Meandering waves called Rossby waves

Meanders produce rotating frontal weather system

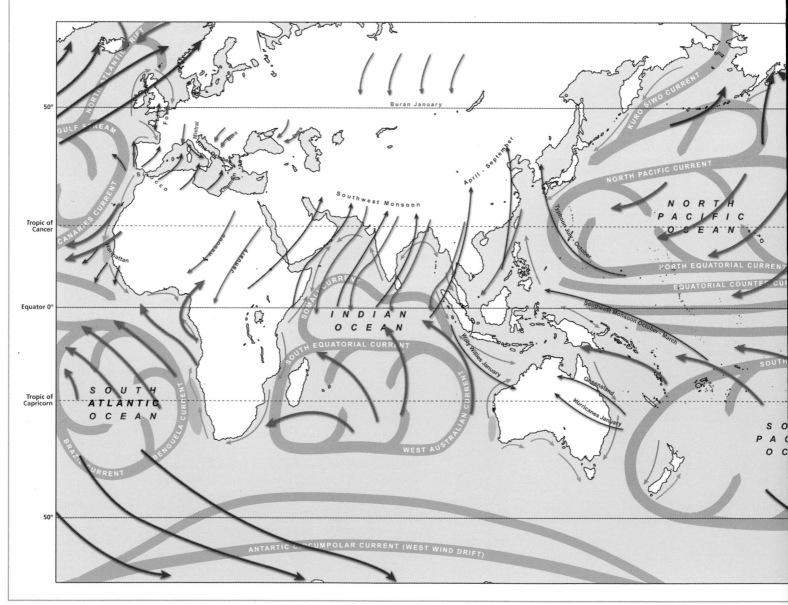

opposite direction in the southern hemisphere and these rotations are mirrored by the ocean currents. The coriolis effect is also responsible for bending any wind (or pressure system) in the northern hemisphere to the right of its direction of travel. This right turn will be regardless of which way it is flowing between the Equator and the poles and will be a left arc for winds south of the Equator. This produces the NE and SE trade winds that blow towards the Equator from each hemisphere and also angles the mid-latitude westerlies from the NW and SW respectively. Besides these two dominant bands of circulating winds, there are polar cells at the extremities of the planet and doldrums directly over the Equator.

A low pressure or depression will strengthen when a warm air mass collides with it and slides over the top, lowering the barometric pressure and creating instability which makes the air spin faster. These mid-latitude systems become more energetic in the winter when the temperature difference between the Equator and the poles increases. A primary influence on the west to east movements of these weather systems is the flow of air in the upper atmosphere

Wind strength measured with the Beaufort Scale

Force	Strength	km/h Speed	mph	Land Actions
F0	calm	0-1.5	0-1	Smoke rises vertically
F1	light air	1.6-6.3	1-3	Smoke drifts slowly
F2	light breeze	6.4-11	4-7	Wind felt on face; leaves rustle
F3	gentle breeze	12-19	8-12	Twigs move; light flags unfurl
F4	moderate breeze	20-29	13-18	Wind moves dust and paper; twigs move
F5	fresh breeze	30-39	19-24	Small trees sway; wavelets on inland waters
F6	strong breeze	40-50	25-31	Large branches move; whistling in telegraph lines
F7	near gale	51-61	32-38	Whole trees sway; difficult to walk against wind
F8	gale	62-74	39-46	Twigs break off trees; very difficult to walk
F9	strong gale	75-87	47-54	Roof tiles blown down
F10	storm	88-101	55-63	Trees uprooted; considerable damage to buildings
F11	violent storm	102-117	64-73	Widespread damage to buildings
F12	hurricane	118+	74+	Devastating damage

called the jet stream. The jet stream moves at much higher speeds than the surface air and dictates the speed, intensity and trajectory of surface weather systems. A jet which takes a polar heading will create surface low pressures that deepen, while a jet leading towards the Equator will cause the low to fill and fizzle out.

The most violent of all low pressures are formed over warm, tropical oceans when huge differences in temperature get a storm spinning extremely fast. Massive amounts of water vapour are drawn up into the vortex of these destructive tropical storms that are known by different names around the world. Hurricane is used in the Atlantic and north-eastern Pacific, Typhoon is the word for the north-western Pacific and Cyclone is favoured in the South Pacific and Indian Ocean.

Land and sea breezes are a small scale version of the global convection currents governed by heat. During the day, the land quickly heats up and hot air starts rising. This brings in cool air from the sea in the form of the afternoon onshore sea breeze. At night when the land cools, the flow is reversed and the offshores blow. These are the forces that drive the monsoon, which is basically a powerful land or sea breeze depending on the season.

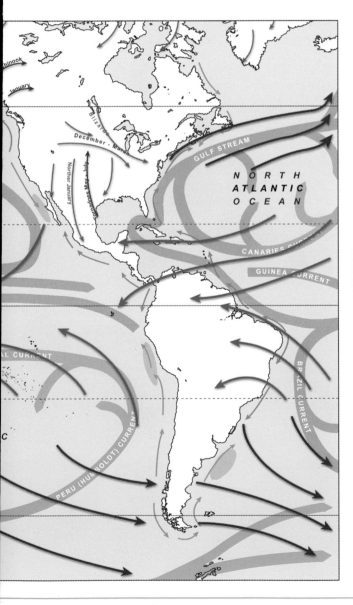

Wind Types

There are 3 types of winds:

Westerlies
Blow in the mid-latitudes (30° to 60°) and produce the ground swells. The rotation of the Earth causes them to blow more NW in the northern hemisphere and more SW in the southern hemisphere.

East Trades
Blow in the sub-tropical latitudes (5° to 30°) and produce constant small windswell. They tend to blow more NE in the northern hemisphere and more SE in the southern hemisphere.

Doldrums
Areas of light winds in the equatorial belt (5°N to 5°S). Occasional squalls may produce a rare small swell.

Wind direction is a reference to the wind's compass point of origin: i.e. the direction it is blowing from and not blowing to.

Currents and Upwelling

These vast moving belts of water, convey warm water from the Equator and return cold water from the poles. Like a big heat exchanger, currents (and winds) keep the Earth evenly distributed with warmth. Surface currents are mainly wind driven and can move extremely quickly (from 10km/6mi up to 220km/136mi per day) while deep ocean currents barely move (3ft/1m per day) and work on differences in ocean density and salinity. Open ocean, wind driven, surface currents form large round circulation patterns known as gyres. As with the wind, they circulate in a clockwise direction in the northern hemisphere and anti-clockwise in the south. While the wind is the major motivating force, the currents do not follow the exact same path, because the coriolis effect steps in to alter the current's course. Northern hemisphere currents will swing to the right (clockwise) of the dominant wind direction, while it's left and anti-clockwise south of the Equator. Wherever there is a cold current heading back to the Equator combined with trade winds blowing away from the land, the phenomenon of upwelling occurs. Warmer surface water is driven offshore and colder water rises up from depth to replace it. This colder water is usually rich in biological species, which is fortunate because these areas of upwelling are almost exclusively situated next to deserts.

Key

Warm Current

Cold Current

Warm Local Current

Cold Local Current

Areas of Upwelling

III.The Creation of Swell

The main creator of rideable waves is wind blowing over the surface of the water. The wind comes in different strengths and goes by different names but essentially, it always has the same affect on wave creation. Wind blows across the surface of the globe from the four points of the compass and everything in between, but it also changes direction in the vertical plane, exerting a downward pressure on the surface of the sea. At first, this produces ripples on a calm surface, which are then easier for the wind to get a grip on and increase their size. This two part process starts with the ripples or capillary waves, which are still small enough to be pulled back down by surface tension. As the ripples grow, small disturbances of rotating air form between the ripples adding more height to the waves, which in turn creates more uniform pockets of turbulence between the quickly growing waves. Surface tension is no longer strong enough to restore the rippling disturbance and gravity now attempts to push the waves back down. This

Diagram showing the stages of development of open ocean swells.

3. The following wind adds more energy to the waves and makes them grow.

2. The agitated sea modifies the flow of air causing more turbulent fluctuations which further agitates the sea's surface.

1. Turbulent fluctuations in the wind cause the surface of the sea to become bumpy and agitated while surface tension tries to restore it.

self-perpetuating cycle increases wave height exponentially until gravity limits further growth and the wave reaches saturation point. The wave height can also be limited by white-capping, where storm force winds literally blow the tops off the cresting waves. The main factors that determine the size of the waves will be the strength and duration of the wind plus the fetch, meaning distance over which the wind blows.

Propagation, Dispersion and Grouping

Once the wind has done its job and the waves begin to travel or propagate away from the source, they organize themselves into lines of swell. As the swell fans out, the waves lose some height, which happens at a set rate. This is called circumferential dispersion, and the further a swell travels, the more this process will cause it to spread out. The width it spreads out is directly proportional to the distance it has travelled. For every doubling of the propagation distance, the height reduces by about one-third, which doesn't include other height reducing factors like white-capping and opposing winds in the propagation path.

Radial dispersion is the term used to describe how swell cleans itself up into the orderly lines that surfers love to see hitting their local beach. This revolves around wave speed, which is governed by how far apart each wave is, known as wavelength. The longer the distance between two crests, the faster the waves will travel across the open ocean. When the swell is first created, many different wavelengths will be mixed in together, producing messy, disorganised waves. As the swell starts to propagate away, the faster waves with the longer wavelengths will progressively overtake the slower, shorter wavelength swells. Given enough time and distance, the faster swells will hit the coast first, bringing the clean, well-spaced corduroy lines that produce quality surf. The shorter wavelength swells will arrive later with less organisation and power, and some of the weaker, choppy waves won't even make it at all. Differences in wavelength are also responsible for the creation of sets. Technically referred to as wave grouping, sets are the result of two different swells travelling in the same direction and merging together. When the peaks of two different wave-trains coincide, a larger wave will result. However, when the peak of one wave-train coincides with the trough of another, a cancelling out effect occurs, resulting in the dreaded lulls at the beach. There are other complicated influencing factors and most non-surfing oceanographers are theoretically dismissive of wave grouping, indicating that further research is necessary to understand why sets occur.

When Swell Travels Away From the Storm
Swells with a longer wavelength travel faster and overtake shorter wavelength swells.

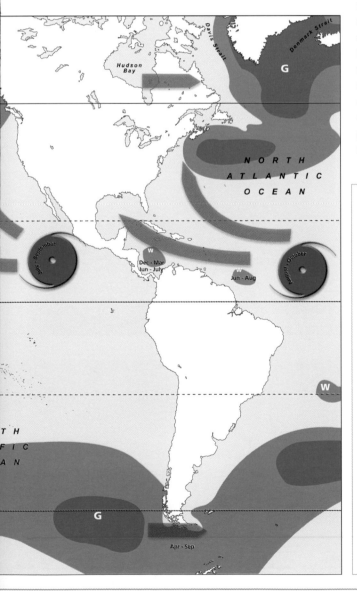

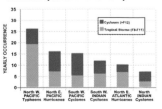

Swell Types

There are 3 types of swells:

Groundswell

Produced by mid-latitude depressions between 30° and 60°. These low pressures travel from the west to the east so therefore send out more W swells than E. As with the winds in these latitudes, the swells will have the tendency to swing towards the Equator. Groundswells are the most consistent, powerful and sizeable of ocean swells and are capable of travelling vast distances.

Open Ocean Swell over 15ft

40% of the time

30% of the time

20% of the time

G = Groundswell
W= Windswell

Windswell

Result from strong, regular winds with enough fetch and duration to create rideable waves. Windswell is most prevalent where the east trades blow and its direction is totally governed by the wind. Strong winds can also produce surf in seas (Mediterranean, China, Carribean, Arabian), gulfs (Mexico, Persian) and even lakes (Great Lakes). Windswells are usually short lived, messy and disorganised, with little in the way of discernable swell lines.

Tropical Storm Swell

Hurricane, Cyclone or Typhoon Swells
Born in sub-tropical latitudes (10° to 30°), these depressions often travel from east to west. This produces more E swells than W but any swell direction is possible. Tropical storms only form at certain times of the year when the temperature contrasts between air and sea are at a maximum. These unpredictable, seasonal swells can produce a significant amount of sizeable waves as the storms can be slow moving. Hurricanes, cyclones and typhoons are given people's names from pre-determined alphabetical lists that alternate between male and female.

Tropical Storms spin anti-clockwise in the northern hemisphere and clockwise in the southern hemisphere

time of year

direction of travel

Worldwide Cyclone/Hurricane Activity

Swell direction is always a reference to the swell's compass point of origin: i.e. the direction it is arriving from and not rolling to.

IV. The Creation of Surf

Speed, Shoaling and Refraction

Wavelengths are also a major factor in determining the speed of waves. A straightforward equation is used for the velocity of deep water waves. Speed is equal to the wavelength divided by the time it takes for two waves to pass a fixed point (period). This means that a well spaced, long period, big swell will travel at up to 40kmh (25mph).

As waves approach the coast and come in contact with the sea floor, they slow down, but only lose a little bit of energy to friction. The excess speed or velocity energy is channelled into making the waves higher, which happens

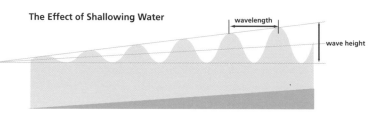

The Effect of Shallowing Water

wavelength

wave height

As waves propogate into shallow water they slow down, the wavelength is shortened and the wave height rises

when they start to feel the bottom at depths around one half of their wavelength. Unlike open ocean swell, the shallower the water, the slower a wave will travel. As they slow down, they squash together, forcing the period to shorten, as it must remain constant throughout the swell. Similar to traffic approaching a bottleneck, this slowing and bunching is termed shoaling, it increases wave height and the effect is more pronounced the steeper the shelf. If a section of one swell starts to feel the bottom while an adjacent section does not, then it will start to refract (bend) the swell. Depending on the swell direction, refraction will bend the swell one of two ways. If an obstacle (reef) is situated next to deep water, and a swell hits it straight on, then the part of the swell that hits the reef will slow down while the rest of the swell line will maintain speed. This faster travelling section will start to bend in towards the reef, resulting in concave refraction. The energy gets concentrated towards

the peak, making the wave bigger, more sucky and bowly, but it often makes the wave shorter or far smaller on the inside. Convex refraction describes what happens at many classic pointbreaks, especially if they are at right angles to the prevailing swell direction. As a swell line hits the tip of the point, the bulk of the swell will continue on its way while only the part right on the point will be slowed and start to break. The breaking part of the wave then tries to catch up to the faster advancing swell line, which creates a fanned out appearance. Convex refraction spreads the wave energy over a wider area, so power and size will be less than in a concave set-up but the wave will be a long, walled-up type ride and sometimes even get bigger down the line.

Concave Refraction – St. Leu, Réunion

SYLVAIN CAZENAVE

Convex Refraction – Steamer Lane, Santa Cruz

ROB GILLEY

Global Wave Model known as the WAM, predicts wave size and direction for up to six days. Dark blue is flat while the red colours are over 30ft (10m). The northern hemisphere shows a strong pattern of seasonal variation.

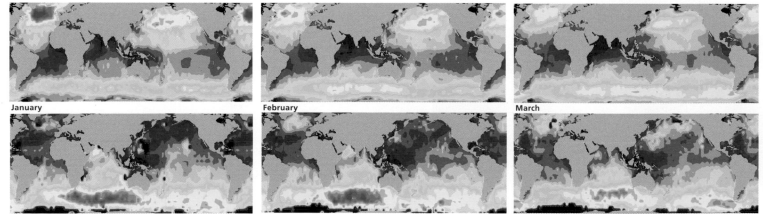

January

February

March

July

August

September

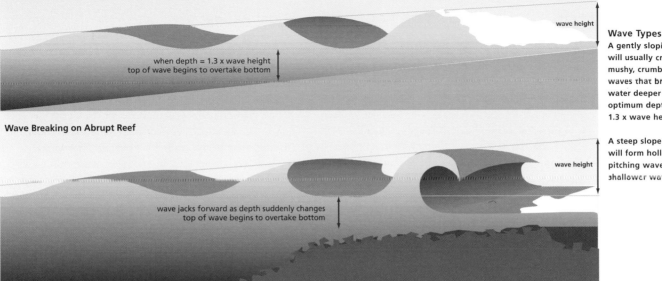

Wave Breaking on Gently Sloping Beach

wave height

when depth = 1.3 x wave height
top of wave begins to overtake bottom

Wave Breaking on Abrupt Reef

wave height

wave jacks forward as depth suddenly changes
top of wave begins to overtake bottom

Wave Types
A gently sloping beach
will usually create
mushy, crumbling type
waves that break in
water deeper than the
optimum depth of
1.3 x wave height.

A steep slope or reef
will form hollow,
pitching waves in
shallower water.

Breaking Waves and Bathymetry

Waves will break when the bottom part of the wave is slowed down so much that the top of the wave overtakes it and spills forward. A simple equation is used, stating that a wave will break in water at a depth of 1.3 times the wave height. This equation can be affected by other factors such as wind, swell type and beach slope. An offshore wind will hold up and delay the top of the wave from overtaking the bottom, resulting in the wave breaking in shallower water. Onshore winds have the opposite effect and can push the waves over before they reach the critical depth. Different types of swell may break in different depths of water. Fast lined-up groundswell will get to shallower water before breaking while short wavelength, choppy windswell is more likely to crumble in deeper water. A gently sloping beach will cause waves to break prematurely while a steep slope makes them overshoot their normal breaking depth. Combining all these factors, a small, onshore, windswell wave, on a flat beach would break in very deep water, while a large, groundswell in an offshore wind, on a steep reef would break in very shallow water.

Bathymetry refers to sea floor features like reefs and points (that are part of the refraction process). Two other important bathymetric features from a surfer's point of view are beaches and rivermouths. Beachbreaks need a certain shape of sandbar to provide a good forum for rideable waves. If the sand under the waves was totally flat and featureless, then when swell arrived it would almost certainly close-out. An ideal sandbar formation will be vaguely triangular with slightly deeper water on either side of the bar. This is formed when a wave breaks on a bar and starts pushing water towards the beach, picking up sand along the way. The water starts to get pushed sideways until it loses forward momentum and looks for a way back out to sea. This is where rips and currents form, aiding the circulation of water and sand. The rip gouges out a handy paddling channel and deposits more sand out towards the peak for more swell to focus upon. Rivermouths work on the same principle whereby sand is constantly deposited at the sandbar, and are far more reliable for well shaped bathymetry.

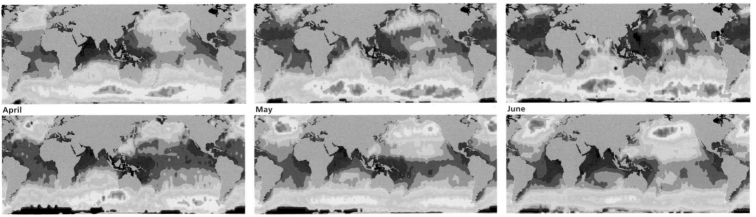

April

May

June

October

November

December

v. Tides

Tides are the result of the Moon's gravitational force producing a bulge in the sea, directly in line with the Moon's position. An equal bulge forms on the opposite side of the Earth to balance the planet out during orbit. The two bulges are the high tides and the areas in between are the low tides. The Earth spins on its axis and every point on the ocean's surface will experience at least one of these bulges every day. Throughout the time it takes for the Earth and Moon to go round each other (a lunar month), the Moon has four phases: opposition, quadrature, conjunction and quadrature (again). The Sun has a smaller gravitational pull on the oceans, which also produces bulges. So when the Sun and the Moon are lined up (in opposition or conjunction), their bulges are added together, making the tides bigger, known as spring tides. When the Sun is at an angle of 90° to the Moon (quadrature), they create bulges at right angles to each other. The water is evened out over the Earth's oceans, producing neap tides.

Tidal Range

Depending on latitude and underwater topography, tidal ranges (heights) vary massively from one region to another. Most seas have minimum tides whereas places like Nova Scotia's Bay of Fundy can experience a depth difference of 50ft (16m) between low and high water. Micro-tidal range means that spring tides never exceed 6ft (2m). Even this small amplitude will affect most spots, especially shallow reefs, but the tide won't be the key factor. Under 3ft (1m) will be insignificant and between 3ft-6ft (1-2m), some sensitive spots won't work on all tides. For meso-tidal range, spring tides will oscillate between 7ft (2.3m) and 13ft (4.3m), meaning a tide table is essential. Many tide sensitive spots will only work for about one third of the tide (low, mid or high). Europe, North Brazil, Panama and East Canada experience macro-tidal ranges over 14ft (4.6m) for spring tides. This results in extremely unstable surf conditions, where tide will be the main priority, rather than the swell and wind.

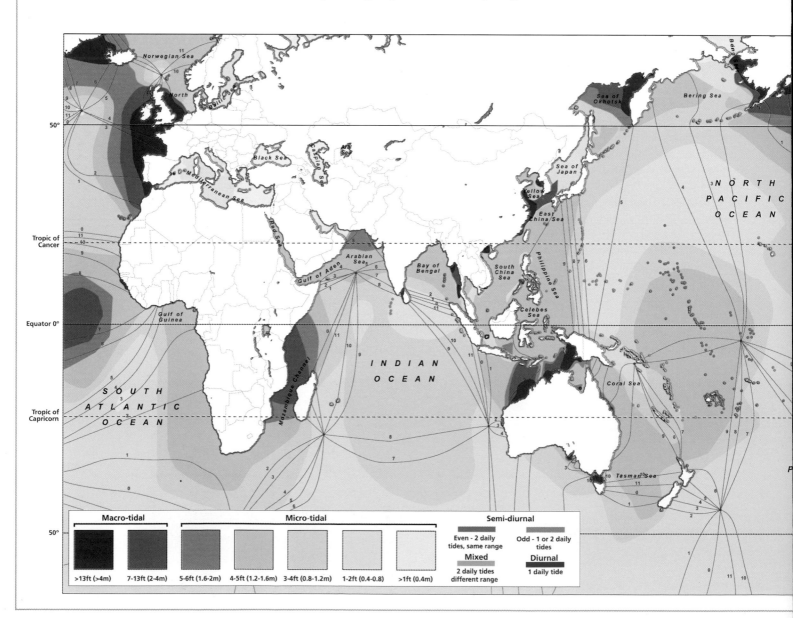

Tide Cycle

A tide cycle is made of outgoing (ebb) and incoming (flow). Because the moon phase is 24hr50min, the average length of a tide is 12hr25min. High and low tide times move forward every day and the tide increases and decreases in increments of twelfths. 50% of the tide occurs during the 3rd and 4th hours. The graph below represent a semi-diurnal type, from low tide to high tide and back down over twelve hours.

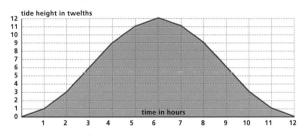

tide height in twelfths

time in hours

Tides make a difference

Tidal Types

Because of the Earth's rotation, different latitudes and uneven underwater topography, there are four types of tides. Semi-diurnal 'even' is the most commonly occurring, with two high tides and two low tides every day that are of the same range. Semi-diurnal 'odd' also has two tides but the daily range is different. Diurnal refers to areas that only have one tide per day. Mixed tide describes those tropical latitudes where some days have two tides and some days only one.

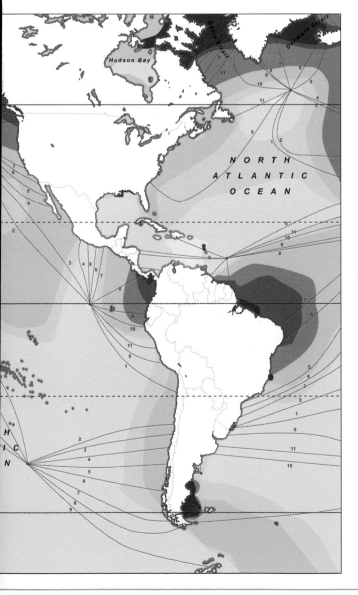

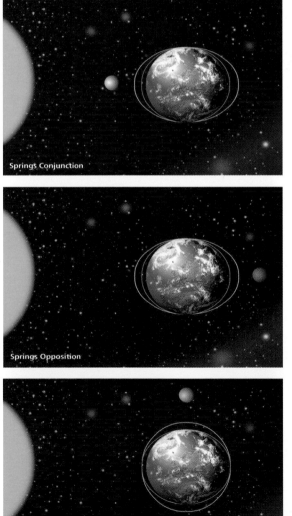

Springs Conjunction

Springs Opposition

Neaps Quadrature

Springs and Neaps

Larger tides (spring tides) occur when the gravitational pull of the Moon and the Sun are combined in line. Smaller tides (neap tides) happen when the Sun and the Moon are at right angles to the Earth evening out the bulge.

DON'T DESTROY WHAT YOU CAME TO ENJOY...

Les Alcyons

Europe

Meteorology and Oceanography

Facing the world's stormiest ocean, Europe receives surf from North Atlantic low pressure systems that track from Nova Scotia through Iceland and on to the British Isles and Scandinavia. In the summer months (June-Sept) these lows tend to take a more northerly path, around Iceland and on to Norway. Winter brings a more southerly trajectory, sometimes pushing depressions as far south as the Iberian Peninsula from their usual formation point off Nova Scotia. This high latitude storm track between 35° and 70° is super consistent and its exact path is dictated by the upper atmosphere jet stream. Low barometric pressures are a feature of North Atlantic lows and when the jet stream is straight lining, they appear back to back through the winter months. These regular, strong, weather systems are a godsend to

European surfers because there are no other reliable swell sources. Europe's high latitude discounts any southern hemisphere swell reaching it and hurricane swell usually requires a west to east path off the US East Coast. This can translate to summer flat spells in many parts of Europe, but there is always something going on somewhere. Ireland, Scotland and Norway will benefit most from remote, northern lows, while Portugal can pick up even the slightest wind or groundswell oscillation. Winter can produce some of the biggest waves in the northern hemisphere (outside of Hawai'i), mostly in France, Spain, Portugal and Madeira. Northern Europe and the British Isles also get some sizeable swell but it tends to be stormy and messy due to their proximity to the deep lows.

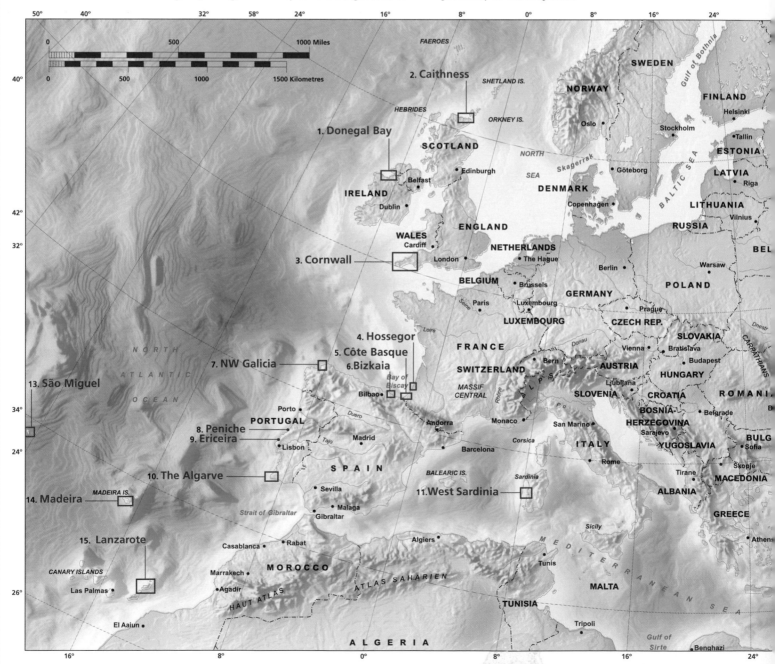

One factor that is a common curse for all of Europe is the dominance of the onshore W-NW winds on most exposed coastlines. However, the clockwise rotation of the Azores High can protect Europe, keeping the lows moving to the NE and giving perfect surf conditions, particularly in the south.

Considering the latitude, water temperatures should be much lower but the Gulf Stream blankets the western shoreline of Northern Europe resulting in temperatures which greatly exceeds those found on a similar latitude on the US East Coast. The British Isles are cold instead of icy, while France and Spain remain cool in winter and warm in summer. Portugal offers mild winter temps (16°C/66°F) but never gets warm in summer because it is influenced by the cold Canaries Current. The Atlantic Islands, once referred to as Macaronesia, are also surrounded by this colder water.

The bulk of Europe's tides are semi-diurnal even and in the macro tidal range. This means big tides, twice a day. The tremendous tidal range (up to 20ft/6.6m), which peaks around the English Channel, contributes much to unstable surf conditions in already unpredictable weather patterns. Some waves don't exist at low tide while others can't feel the bottom at high.

The surf in the Mediterranean Sea can be influenced by the North Atlantic winter storms, if they come in low enough over the Iberian Peninsula. Far more reliable is the Mistral wind – the main swell producer in the western Med. When this strong wind whistles out of the Rhône Valley into the Mediterranean, a W-NW windswell is produced, bringing short, slow, often windy waves up to 4-6ft (1.3-2m). The Mistral primarily affects Sardinia, Corsica and Northern Italy. Many strong winds can have enough fetch to build rideable waves, such as E winds in the Adriatic. The eastern Mediterranean is a fairly large body of water with dominant NW winds favouring Israel as the most consistent shore. Long flat spells are a feature of the Mediterranean basin shores.

Notably, this large and extremely deep sea has virtually no perceptible tidal change being classified as micro-tidal, with a range of around 1ft (0.3m).

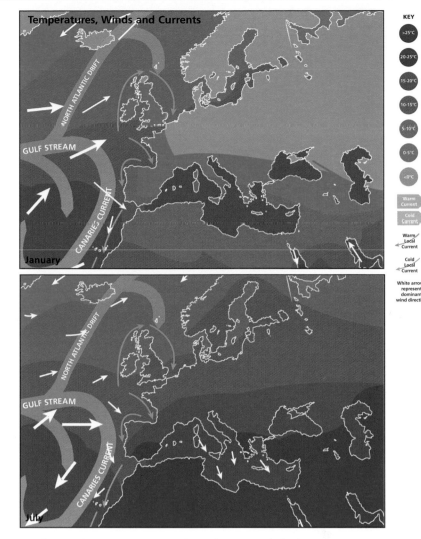

Temperatures, Winds and Currents

NORTH ATLANTIC DRIFT

GULF STREAM

CANARIES CURRENT

January

NORTH ATLANTIC DRIFT

GULF STREAM

CANARIES CURRENT

July

KEY

>25°C
20-25°C
15-20°C
10-15°C
5-10°C
0-5°C
<0°C

Warm Current
Cold Current
Warm Local Current
Cold Local Current

White arrows represent dominant wind direction

COUNTRY INFORMATION

	IRELAND	SCOTLAND	ENGLAND	FRANCE
Area (sq km/mi):	84,444/32,604	78,789/30,420	130,000/50,193	551,500/212,935
Population:	5.2M	5.2M	48M	60M
Waveriders:	7,000	1,500	30,000	55,000
Tourists (per yr):	4M	2M	18M	73M
Language:	English, Irish	English, Gaelic	English	French, Basque
Currency:	Punt (IR£)/Pound (£)	Pound Sterling (£)	Pound Sterling (£)	French franc (ff)
Exchange:	$1 = Ir £0.8	$1 = £0.7	$1 = £0.7	$1 = 7ff
GDP (per yr):	$17,000	$18,138	$18,138	$25,000
Inflation:	2%	3%	3%	2%

	SPAIN	PORTUGAL	ITALY	ISRAEL
Area (sq km/mi):	492,000/189,961	92,000/35.521	301,268/116,320	20,770/8,130
Population:	40M	10.5M	58M	5.8M
Waveriders:	30,000	50,000	15,000	10,000
Tourists (per yr):	47M	11M	36M	1M
Language:	Spanish, Catalan	Portuguese	Italian	Hebrew, Arabic
Currency:	Peseta (ptas)	Escudo (Esc)	Italian Lira (L)	New Israeli Shekel
Exchange:	$1 = 180 (ptas)	$1 = 210esc	$1 = 2,000L	$1 = 4.1NIS
GDP (per yr):	$14,000	$15,200	$20,000	$14,000.
Inflation:	4%	2%	2%	8%

1. Donegal Bay

IRELAND

Easkey Left

ALEX WILLIAMS

Summary

+ GREAT UNCROWDED REEFBREAKS
+ POWERFUL SWELLS
+ PREDOMINANT OFFSHORES
+ COOL PEOPLE.

– RAINY CLIMATE AND COLD WATER
– WINDY CONDITIONS
– BIG TIDAL RANGES
– FAIRLY PRICEY

North-West Ireland (Eire) is one of the most consistent surf destinations in Europe. A steady supply of storms forming along the jet stream provide the region with regular swells, which hit a contorted coastline, offering numerous, quality surf options. However, positioned so close to the most turbulent corner of the North Atlantic, North-West Ireland is also prone to some vile weather conditions and short period windy swells. So travelling surfers won't sit around waiting for long, but will have to endure a few

SYLVAIN CAZENAVE

less-than-perfect days before scoring the epic waves Eire undoubtedly receives. The awesome landscape and warm, welcoming inhabitants mean that an Irish surf trip is always something more than just a frenzied hunt for waves.

The 2 main surf spots in the Donegal Bay area are Bundoran

in the north and Easkey in the south, but there is far more in between to explore. The bay is open to the NW and catches whatever juice is out there. The coastline here alternates between deep indents, broad beaches and small headlands, offering a good variety of waves. Problems do occur if the N winds kick in, cutting your options down considerably. Muckros beach faces south and is one of a few quiet possibilities on the northern shore of Donegal Bay. The west facing beaches of the bay start at Rossnowlagh, which has a fun, longboard-ish beachbreak and the biggest surf club in Ireland. Just south, Tullan Strand is a high quality beach with numerous good peaks, the most popular of which is a left breaking at the foot of the cliffs at the south end. It attracts crowds from nearby Bundoran and like everywhere in the region, respect for local surfers is extremely important here – they're some of the friendliest locals on the planet if you're polite and not greedy. Bundoran town is a swell-magnet with superb waves in the right conditions. The best spot is The Peak; a long, hollow left reefbreak, that works at low tide. It also

TRAVEL INFORMATION

Local Population:
Donegal Co. – 130,000
Coastline: 310km (194mi)
Time: GMT
Contests: Masters (Sept) National

Getting There – No visas needed. Most visitors will travel through London before flying on to Dublin, Belfast, Sligo or Knock (Donegal's Airports). There are car ferries from Scotland, Wales, England and France. Scotland and N. England ferries are Stranraer – Belfast and Cairnyan – Larne. From Wales services include Holyhead – Dublin, Fishguard – Rosslaire and Swansea – Cork. From France you can go from Le Havre/Cherbourg – Rosslaire and Le Havre/Roscoff - Cork. A number of UK and Irish bus companies also run services from London and other UK cities.

Getting Around – Apart from rare motorways, Irish roads are very slow and require patience: 50km/h (30mph) being an average driving

speed. Fuel is pricey at $1.30/l. Rental cars cost $250/wk. Buses are cheap and will carry boards. Cycling is a great way to see Ireland – fix up a board rack, buy a tent, waterproofs and you'll love it.

Lodging and Food – Ireland is not a budget destination. B&B's cost at least $30/dble. 'The Strand' in Strandhill is a good option for surfers. There are campsites everywhere, but Ireland's wet climate can make this a miserable experience. Pub meals are $10-15. Irish society is centred around the pub, so add the cost of drinks into your budget.

Weather – Ireland is known as the Emerald Isle for good reason - the land is very green, thanks to the high rainfall. Despite the northerly latitude, the water is not that cold because of the Gulf Stream. It rarely snows in the winter and freezing temperatures only occur at night. Winter is a hardcore time to surf in Ireland: you will need a 5-4 wetsuit, boots, hat and gloves. Summertime sees periods of settled warm

weather and long daylight hours. A 3-2 fullsuit is ideal in summer/early autumn.

Nature and Culture – Western Ireland is a stunning patchwork of lonely valleys, lakes and mountains, scattered with cottages and old castles. It is possible however that your most enduring memory of Ireland will be of the nights spent in the local pub, drinking Guinness and listening to the traditional music. Check out the 'Surfer's Bar' in Rossnowlagh and 'The Ould Bridge Bar' in Bundoran.

Hazards and Hassles – Wind and rain. Reefbreaks can be treacherous. Easkey left has a lot of seaweed that can become tangled around leashes. There are no lifeguards at most surf spots. Tidal ranges are large. Hassles in the water are rare, but travel in small groups and show respect.

Handy Hints – There are surf shops in Rossnowlagh, Bundoran, Strandhill (Byrne Bros) and Easkey. Gear is expensive.

WEATHER STATISTICS	J/F	M/A	M/J	J/A	S/O	N/D
total rainfall (mm)	82	57	62	87	100	100
consistency (days/mth)	17	13	12	16	17	18
min temp (°C/°F)	3/37	4/39	8/46	12/54	9/48	5/41
max temp (°C/°F)	8/46	10/50	14/57	17/62	14/57	9/48

offers a short right. It's here that the international contests are held and being right in the middle of town you should expect crowds and some localism. Immediately south is Tullaghan, a rivermouth, where long rights wrap around a point. The swell needs to be large and care should be taken of the rocks on the inside. Close by is Mullaghmore Back Strands which needs a bigger swell, but offers excellent protection from westerly winds. Like so many spots here, just finding your way down the maze of lanes and the long paddle-out keeps crowds down. Big wave chargers should take note of the dredging lefthander on the other side of the cliffs which reputedly holds swell up to 20ft (6.4m). Nearby Streedagh Strand is a long beach with many different peaks, and the SW end gives some shelter from the full brunt of the swells. The last village on the peninsula is Ballyconnell, from where a thousand and one narrow country lanes lead to unknown possibilities. You may be rewarded with perfection but be prepared to get very lost. Strandhill is the major surf town in Sligo. The west facing beachbreak produces quality peaks at high tide. Check the Lighthouse reefs to the north, and while in Strandhill, you will probably hear talk of the 'The Bar' to the south of town, a powerful sandbar wave that involves a ten minute paddle to reach. The

Kilcummin
ALEX WILLIAMS

Reef near to Bundoran
PHIL HOLDEN

beginner's favourite near Strandhill is Dunmoran Strand, a mellow beachbreak hidden in a secluded cove. On the south side of the bay is Easkey which has numerous reefs along an accessible stretch of rocky coast. Here a SW wind is offshore and the waves stay clean in the regular gales which come in from that direction. Easkey holds size, some of its peaks are extremely hollow and it has everything a traveller could hope for from Ireland: a word class right pointbreak, an excellent left, a castle, a surf shop, a school, a friendly village, and pubs with good Guinness. Don't miss it. Beyond Easkey lies a number of superb spots for big swells – the trick is to find them.

Most of the lows crossing the North Atlantic will hit the Irish coastline. There are two standard weather scenarios, the most likely being that a low pressure system will travel E-NE across the Atlantic and Ireland, giving anything from 6ft-20ft (2-6.4m) W swells. As the system passes over, the wind will usually swing around to the NW and N but the first half of the storm will provide clean, offshore winds and sizeable surf on the north facing beaches. The second common scenario is a high pressure system extending over the North Atlantic, Britain and Ireland. In this case there's little hope of finding surf in most of Europe, but if you're in north-west Ireland you're in with a better chance than anyone of getting the clean, northerly swells from high latitude storms passing over Iceland towards Norway. Dominant winds are W-SW year round and are often dead S in the winter while spring and summer see frequently shifting but lighter breezes. Spring is a good time to be in Ireland, despite the cold water. The tidal range can reach 12ft (4m) and most spots will be stable for two hours at low tide and high tide. Never underestimate the tide factor.

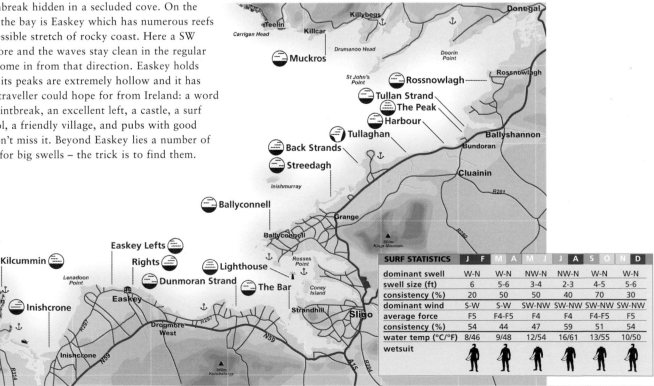

SURF STATISTICS	J F	M A	M J	J A	S O	N D
dominant swell	W-N	W-N	NW-N	NW-N	W-N	W-N
swell size (ft)	6	5-6	3-4	2-3	4-5	5-6
consistency (%)	20	50	50	40	70	30
dominant wind	S-W	S-W	SW-NW	SW-NW	SW-NW	SW-NW
average force	F5	F4-F5	F4	F4	F4-F5	F5
consistency (%)	54	44	47	59	51	54
water temp (°C/°F)	8/46	9/48	12/54	16/61	13/55	10/50
wetsuit						

2. Caithness

Thurso East

ALEX WILLIAMS

Summary
+ QUALITY REEFS
+ THURSO EAST
+ UNCROWDED WAVES
+ HIGH LATITUDE SURFING
+ FANTASTIC SCENERY

− COLD WATER
− WET AND UNSTABLE WEATHER
− WINDY CONDITIONS
− HARD ACCESS

ALEX WILLIAMS

Sandside Bay

ALEX WILLIAMS

Scotland is better known for its Highlands, whisky, lochs and bagpipes than for surf, but there's little doubt that all three of Scotland's coasts receive excellent waves. With the improvements in wetsuit technology these days, more and more surfers are braving the cold to seek out Scotland's thick, heavy barrels, in uncrowded line-ups. The west coast is one of the remotest surf zones in Europe, fully deserving its reputation as the 'Wild West'. Offshore from Cape Wrath, the NW corner of Scotland, the Inner and Outer Hebrides take the brunt of the massive westerly swells. The drier east coast enjoys swell from both North Atlantic and North Sea storms, and enjoys a predominantly offshore wind. The remote Orkney and Shetland Islands further north, see the occasional hardcore surfer and are known to hide a few lonely but perfect set-ups.

The north coast county of Caithness is the most famous surf zone in Scotland, where regular offshore winds clean up the heavy swells, which break hard onto flat, flagstone reefs. The most famous wave is Thurso East; a world class righthander which has been likened to a cold water Nias. The mellow take-off is followed by a long tubular section over a kelp-covered reef and the wave walls up all the way through to the end section. A decent N swell is needed to kick Thurso East into life and the worrying dark brown colour of the wave comes from peat river water, which is not a dangerous pollutant. Nearby, the pollution riddled and aptly named Shitpipe is a peaky wave favouring extremely hollow rights. These two spots alone will keep

TRAVEL INFORMATION

Local Population:
Caithness – 28,000
Coastline: 140km (88mi)
Time: GMT
Contest: regional

Getting There – No visa is necessary. Most visitors will travel through London and take a connection to Glasgow or Edinburgh. This can be expensive. Driving from London to Glasgow takes 8 hours followed by 7 hours to Thurso. Trains are faster, but more expensive than coaches and buses.

Getting Around – Apart from the A9, Scottish roads are slow, 70km/h (40mph) being an average speed. Most of the coastline is private property, so be polite and respectful to the owners and their land. Fuel costs $1.30/l. Rental cars cost $250/w, coaches are cheap and will take

boards (except for National Express coaches). Car ferries do a regular run to the Orkney's.

Lodging and Food – Scotland is not a budget destination. B&B's will cost at least $25/dble or $40/dble for a hotel room. For B&B in Thurso try Mrs Christie or Mrs McDonald. Ask at the tourist office on Riverside Road. Caravans for rent in summer ($180/w/4p). A meal shouldn't cost more than $12-15.

Weather – Extreme weather is renowned. Although the Gulf Stream can warm things up a little snow is frequent in the winter with freezing temperatures occurring four or five months of the year. Late summer and early autumn are good times to visit. The east coast is drier but the water is colder. Scotland is generally very windy, especially in the west. Take a 6-5-4mm fullsuit with hood, boots and gloves in winter and a 4-3mm in summer/early autumn.

Nature and Culture – Scotland is one of the least densely populated areas in Europe. The predominantly flat peat lands that dominate the countryside around Caithness make it less impressive than the Highlands to the west. There are numerous castles (Sinclair, Old Keiss, Old Wick), stone rows and circles, burial cairns and a wide variety of rare wildlife.

Hazards and Hassles – Rain, wind and ice-cream headaches. The reefbreaks are all heavy, spooky places to surf. Remember that big tidal ranges greatly affect the surf. Sea-kayaks and wave skis are popular.

Handy Hints – Good Vibes in Thurso has a large range of equipment. Take a semi-gun for Brimms Ness and Thurso, which will also help counter the extra neoprene you'll be wearing. Near constant daylight in June-July is a magic experience.

WEATHER STATISTICS	J/F	M/A	M/J	J/A	S/O	N/D
total rainfall (mm)	48	40	50	80	60	57
consistency (days/mth)	11	10	11	11	12	12
min temp (°C/°F)	1/34	3/37	8/46	11/52	8/46	3/37
max temp (°C/°F)	6/43	9/48	15/59	18/64	14/57	8/46

East Strathy

ALEX WILLIAMS

SURF STATISTICS	J F	M A	M J	J A	S O	N D
dominant swell	NW-NE	NW-NE	NW-NE	NW-NE	NW-NE	NW-NE
swell size (ft)	7	6	4	3	5-6	6-7
consistency (%)	30	60	60	50	70	40
dominant wind	S-NW	SW-W	SW-W	S-N	SW-W	S-NW
average force	F5	F4-F5	F4	F4	F4	F4-F5
consistency (%)	66	56	53	69	63	67
water temp (°C/°F)	5/41	6/43	10/50	15/59	12/54	8/46
wetsuit						

North Atlantic low pressures inevitably touch somewhere on the Scottish coastline. The most frequent scenario is when a low pressure system forms around Greenland, travels across the Atlantic in an E-NE direction, which produces major westerly swells up to 20ft (6.6m). This will enable the north-facing, sheltered spots to turn on, with offshore SW winds and solid waves. The summer scenario is when a high pressure system covers the North Atlantic and the British Isles, pushing the low pressures into higher latitudes, therefore passing over Iceland and Norway and producing lined up northerly swells. The east coast is often offshore with dominant winds from the W-SW year round, although summer sees much lighter, variable wind. Swells from the appreciably colder North Sea are usually N to NE but short fetch, short duration E to SE swell can be good for many spots. Autumn is a good time to visit, with regular swells and reasonable water temperatures. The tidal range can reach 12ft (4m); most spots will be stable for two hours at low and high tide, with the reefs generally being better at mid to high tide.

most people happy. If it's flat drive west to Brimms Ness, a Nordic word for 'surf point'. There are three excellent reefs here, all of which pick up far more swell than Thurso. The Bowl is the scariest wave - a square, righthand barrel for experts only. The Left (aka The Cove), is gentler but all break in fairly shallow water. It's quite a walk through the fields, (on private land, so show respect), and it's only worth going there if the wind is non-existent or light. Sandside is a good beachbreak, but the Dounreay nuclear reprocessing plant looms over the beach and the water is none too clean. A cluster of leukaemia cases in the area, plus discoveries of small sand-sized nuclear particles or 'hotspots' both on the beach and underwater, means surfers should be worried, although many still consider the lefthand pointbreak at the western end of the bay worth the risk. A safer bet may be to head to Melvich, a good rivermouth beachbreak, again accessed through private property. Here, like many parts of this rugged coast, you might find yourself surfing alongside seals and schools of salmon. East of Thurso, at around the halfway point to Dunnet Bay, is a rock called 'The Spur' which produces an occasional classic left. Dunnet Bay itself has 5km (3mi) of decent beachbreak and a righthand reef facing NW. From here to Gills Bay is a set of reefs that favour mid-to-high tides. Check spots like Ham, Kirk o' Tang or Tang Head. Gills Bay is a beachbreak that has rights and lefts - you park at the graveyard and walk. Once you reach the east coast, you can check most spots from the road. The harbour at Skirza is the place to hit when NE swells are pumping. It is yet another classy pointbreak with long lefts and hollow sections. Sinclair's Bay is a huge beach full of peaks - check Keiss at the northern end. For a scenic session underneath an old Scottish castle, try Ackergill rights on rare SE swells.

ALEX WILLIAMS

Brimms Ness

Brimms Ness

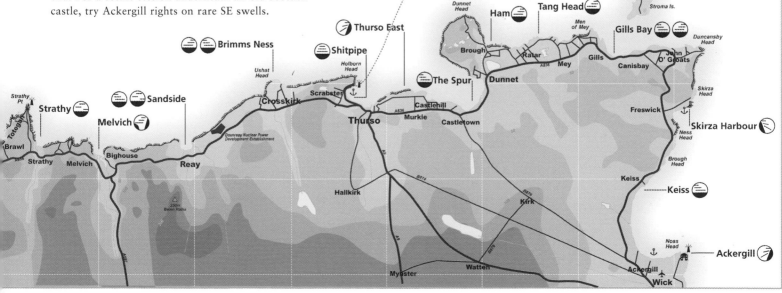

3. Cornwall

North coast view from Porthtowan to Chapelporth

ALEX WILLIAMS

Summary

+ North and South facing coastlines
+ Variety of beach aspects
+ Good nightlife
+ Friendly local surfers

– Cold water
– Cool and wet climate
– Crowds
– Pollution
– Expensive

ESTPIX

Minsey, Porthtowan

ALEX WILLIAMS

For travelling English speaking surfers, a European surfari will usually begin in England. No language barriers and the international transport links that London provides are the main reasons, but what many surfers fail to realise is that England receives waves on all its coasts. The most consistent surfing area of this long coastline is Cornwall, in the far south-west where year round swells batter a mixture of small, rocky bays and long, sandy beaches. A system of coastal paths runs the entire length of the Cornish coast, offering extensive views of the beaches, reefs, and points.

Bude is the most northerly of Cornish resorts, with wide open, west facing beachbreaks in abundance. Crooklets and Summerleaze in the centre of town get crowded, shifting, quality peaks. Widemouth Bay has consistent sandbars and a few rocky outcrops can throw up some decent waves at higher tides. Heading south, the coast twists and turns along high cliffs, which hide a few fickle breaks. Polzeath receives plenty of swell, but like many Cornish beachbreaks, can be a bit fat

and slow until the swell gets overhead. When there's a SW storm, the horseshoe shaped, north facing bay of Harlyn is offshore and attracts plenty of surfers when everywhere else is blown out and/or closed out. When the swell is small, Constantine Bay will be catching it all, where a mixture of good, low tide reefs and powerful high tide beachbreaks keep a large local crew busy. Watergate Bay is a 3km (2mi) beach with plenty of softer style peaks for beginners to enjoy, particularly at the

TRAVEL INFORMATION

Local Population:
Cornwall – 490,000
Coastline:
6,028km (3,767mi)
Time: GMT
Contest: WQS (Aug)

Getting There – No visa. Most visitors will arrive in London (Heathrow, Gatwick, Luton or Stansted). It's at least 4-5 hours drive to the beach. Trains run to Newquay, Falmouth and Plymouth and are cheaper if booked a week in advance. The coach is cheaper ($50/o-w), although the carrier National Express have a no surfboards policy! Bodyboards are OK if the coach is not full.

Getting Around – Rental cars cost $150/w and car transport is essential. Traffic keeps to the left. Many foreigners buy cheap campervans to travel down to Europe. There are regular car ferries to France from southern England including Plymouth to Roscoff.

Lodging and Food – England is an expensive destination, in particular London. B&B's are everywhere, expect to pay $25-$40/dble. Fistral Beach hotel is quality at a price. The Backpackers in Newquay or Fistral are good deals and surfer friendly. A pub meal costs $10-$15 and daytime 'greasy caffs' are cheaper.

Weather – England's weather is notoriously famous for its wind, rainy spells and unpredictability. Despite the northerly latitude it's not that cold because the Gulf Stream warms up the coast. It rarely snows in the winter and freezing temperatures only occur at night. The best time to be a surfer in Britain is during the autumn, particularly October, when the air and water temperatures are still reasonable, swells consistent and the winds are offshore. In the middle of winter you will need a 5-4mm wetsuit with boots, gloves and maybe a hat, as the water drops to 7-9°C (45°-49°F). A 3-2 steamer is ideal in summer as the water touches 20°C (68°F).

Nature and Culture – North Cornwall is backed almost entirely by National Trust land, with little development marring its windswept beauty. There are many festivals in summer around Newquay. Cornwall and Devon are summer holiday hotspots in Britain. Resorts such as Newquay, Bude and Torquay become jam packed and very lively.

Hazards and Hassles – Rocks, cold water, strong riptides, sewage and summer crowds. Cornwall suffers from intense traffic jams during holidays, the roads are notoriously thin and travelling times are longer than expected.

Handy Hints – You don't need a gun. There are a myriad of surf shops and board manufacturers like Ocean Magic. Boards: Nigel Semmens, Fluid Juice, Zuma Jay. A board costs $450. If you're travelling via London, visit Low Pressure surf shop (23 Kensington Pk Rd, Tel 020 7792 3134), where they can advise you on all aspects of surf travel.

WEATHER STATISTICS	J/F	M/A	M/J	J/A	S/O	N/D
total rainfall (mm)	90	63	62	75	87	115
consistency (days/mth)	12	9	9	10	11	15
min temp (°C/°F)	4/39	5/41	9/48	13/55	11/52	6/43
max temp (°C/°F)	8/46	11/52	16/61	19/66	17/62	10/50

southern end. South of this, Newquay town beaches afford good protection from strong SW winds and big winter swells. Newquay is England's surfing capital, where there are more surf shops, surf schools, pubs and discos than anywhere else in Cornwall. Fistral Beach is an all tides, all swells, super consistent spot. There are a variety of rippable waves, like the south end lefts, the North and Little Fistral peaks or the mysto big wave spot – 'The Cribber'. Competition is fierce amongst the many

SURF STATISTICS	J F	M A	M J	J A	S O	N D
dominant swell	SW-NW	SW-NW	SW-NW	SW-NW	SW-NW	SW-NW
swell size (ft)	7	6	4	2	5-6	6-7
consistency (%)	40	70	70	60	80	50
dominant wind	S-NW	S-NW	S-NW	SW-NW	S-NW	S-NW
average force	F5	F4-F5	F4	F4	F4-F5	F5
consistency (%)	65	56	61	59	63	66
water temp (°C/°F)	9/48	10/50	12/54	16/61	14/57	11/52
wetsuit						

Fistral, Newquay – Surf City, UK.

locals and the hundreds of others, drawn to Fistral by its reputation as England's premier surfing beach and international pro-surfing tour venue.

Small swells are perfect for the Perranporth stretch, which spreads the inevitable summer crowds to the northern corner of Penhale, where huge sand dunes flank the beach. The southern end has a rivermouth break with heavy rips but rewards for constant paddlers.

Next stop south is St. Agnes, which is offshore in the south-westerlys and the lefts can be awesome in a decent swell. Low tide at Chapel Porth and high tide at Porthtowan produce various quality beachbreaks that are powerful but usually over subscribed to. St Ives has a flexible array of beaches with Gwithian providing small swell action while the northerly aspects of Porthmeor and Carbis Bay deal with the bigger swells. St Ives is also an artisans' community and home to the Tate Gallery, which has previously exhibited historical surfing artefacts and memorabilia. Sennen Cove catches any swell going, so if it's flat here, then it's flat everywhere. Rounding Land's End onto Cornwall's southern coastline, the focus is set firmly on Porthleven, a rare world class reef offering hollow, powerful rights that are always crowded if the swell is overhead and the wind is from the north.

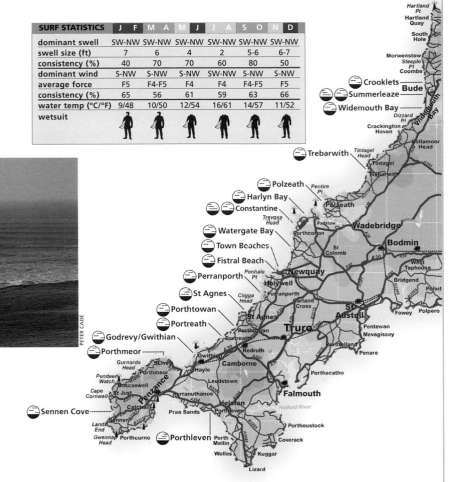

PETER CADE

North Atlantic depressions usually start deepening off Nova Scotia, reaching their lowest pressure just to the south of Iceland. Cornwall receives SW-W swells, but smaller NW swells are blocked out by Ireland, which explains summer flat spells. Autumn and winter are best, and the west coast is the most consistent with regular 2-12ft (0.6-4m) swells and S to SW winds. Britain's long continental shelf drains the swells of some power, which is noticeable on the beaches but not at the reefbreaks. The south coast, though consistent, is rarely classic as the SW swells are often accompanied by onshore, SW winds. The SW swell/NW wind combo in Porthleven works about 20-30 times a year. Prevailing winds are S-NW with more W in the summer time. The tide factor can reach 15ft (4.8m), 'pushing' the swell on the incoming tide, and totally dictating break choice, especially if it is a reef! Tide tables are available at most surf shops.

ALEX WILLIAMS

Porthleven

Harbour wall at Portreath

ALEX WILLIAMS

4. Hossegor

FRANCE

SPAIN

La Gravière

LAURENT MASUREL

Summary

+ TOP-QUALITY BEACHBREAKS
+ HOLLOW CONSISTENT WAVES
+ EMPTY BEACHES
+ CRAZY SUMMER PARTIES
+ BEAUTIFUL SCENERY

– NO SHELTERED SPOTS
– FREQUENT ONSHORES
– BEACHBREAKS ONLY
– COLD WATER IN WINTER
– NO QUALITY ACCOMMODATION

The 230km (145mi) of coastline called the Côte d'Argent is the longest uninterrupted stretch of sandy beach in Europe. Here, swells are focused on to the coast by the Gouf, a deep water canyon, which juts in towards the coast off Hossegor, and are shaped by well-defined sand formations into top quality beachbreaks. Aside from the many small rivers and streams which flow into the Bay of Biscay and shape the sandbars, there are some unusual formations called 'baines' – circular lagoons of sand in the line-up, created by currents refracting and eddying off the Gouf. These bathymetric features combine to yield perfect, super-hollow beachbreak surf when conditions (swell,

YEP

LAURENT MASUREL

tide and wind) are right. On the downside, there are few paddle-out channels along the Côte d'Argent, so swells over 6-8ft (2-2.6m) tend to close out. Also, decent sandbars are likely to be washed away by major storms, so continual surf checks are necessary to see which banks

TRAVEL INFORMATION

Local Population:
Hossegor – 8,000
Coastline: 5,500km (3,500mi)
Time: GMT+1hr
Contests: WQS (Aug)
EPSA + Local

Getting There – Visa: Brazilian, South African, and Japanese nationals all need visas. Paris is 8-10 hours away on an expensive toll highway. Fuel costs about $1/l. It takes 5 hours by TGV bullet train from Paris, boards cost $30 to take on the train. Biarritz airport, 40 minutes from Hossegor, is a 1hr flight from Paris (Air France). Tickets are expensive.

Getting Around – The road network is efficient, although roads get very busy in the summertime. There are many beach car parks. The RDTL bus service is only reliable in summer. Good bike trails cover the region. Fines for driving along the sandy forest trails.

Lodging and Food – Hotel choice in Hossegor is slim. La Centrale in Hossegor has a couple of beach hotels (Amigo, Hotel de la Plage). Expect to pay $30/dble. Most travellers rent flats, stay in their vans, or pitch a tent at campsites, which

are plentiful and open May to October. Book in advance during summer. A typical restaurant bill is $20, not including wine.

Weather – It rains about 1,500mm annually in the south of Les Landes (1 day out of 2). This is less than the Basque coast further south, where the Pyrénées mountains greatly influence the weather. It can be raining in Biarritz and only overcast or even sunny in Hossegor. Mid-summer will be light until 10.30pm, winter gets dark at 6pm. Stable weather from March to October. May and June are good months despite the cooler water. March-April can have occasional lukewarm spells with afternoon temperatures around 20°C (68°F), but spring is usually windy with low pressures from Iberia producing squalls, rain and choppy swells. Take a 5/4/3 fullsuit for winter, a 3/2 for mid-season, and a shorty or boardies for the warmer days.

Nature and Culture – The Côte d'Argent is an endless beach skirted by sand dunes and thick forests, so it's easy to find relative wilderness as an antidote to the busy towns. At the beach, most women are topless and full nudity is common along many stretches of the coast.

Golf, sailing, water slides at Atlantic Parc, a skate park in Le Penon, plus crazy summer parties are some of the distractions. Rockfood is the most popular tourist bar. Winter is mellow.

Hazards and Hassles – Beware when the surf gets big and stormy - rips are common and extremely powerful; many visitors drown every year. The water is not as dirty as the Basque coast, but Capbreton harbour does throw out some unpleasant surprises. In the winter, beaches often get covered in rubbish washed up by big storms. Hossegor is a small town with a large surf community, so respect the locals - they are amazingly tolerant, although things are beginning to change. Look out for thieves and vandals (often protective local surfers) when parking in forest spots.

Handy Hints – There is a thriving surf industry growing up around the Zone Pédebert where you can easily get boards repaired or find a shaper. Most surf shops are open year round. Gear is expensive. You need a gun only for serious La Gravière or La Nord. Try to learn some French; it will be appreciated. Driving and parking are tricky during the summer, when the whole of France is on holiday.

WEATHER STATISTICS	J/F	M/A	M/J	J/A	S/O	N/D
total rainfall (mm)	132	126	105	84	130	134
consistency (days/mth)	14	13	12	12	14	14
min temp (°C/°F)	5/41	7/44	12/54	16/61	13/55	6/43
max temp (°C/°F)	12/54	15/59	20/68	24/75	22/72	14/57

are working best. Add to this the fact that these breaks are heavily influenced by the tide and you have a situation where every day is a new day along the Côte d'Argent. Hossegor, France's most renowned surf spot, is located at the southern boundary of this coast. Here, a combination of a steep beach slope and the trench of the Gouf funnelling swell energy straight in, create ideal conditions for powerful, hollow waves. Quality breaks stretch northwards from La Piste (Capbreton) in the south. Located directly in front of a half a dozen World War II bunkers, La Piste is at its best when clean, mid-sized swells produce fast, heavy barrels. Capbreton's town beaches, defined by four protruding rock jetties, offer peaky, fun surf when it's big or blown-out along the more exposed beaches. This is one of the area's few sheltered spots in heavy conditions, but it's always busy, regardless of size. North of Capbreton is the town of Hossegor. 'La Centrale' is the first low tide, mid-size spot you reach north of the river. However, if it's big, the challenging outside bank of 'La Nord' can be ridden up to 12-15ft (4-4.8m) – but it needs to be clean. Next up is La Gravière, an outstanding shorebreak that holds 12ft (4m) Puerto Escondido-like barrels, which are mostly rights and better at high tide. The line-up can look messy, but the waves are extremely powerful. Next door Les Cul-Nuls, 'bare bums', has similar power but fewer surfers. The further north you go the more the banks become suited to small swells. Les Estagnots or Bourdaines are the most popular surfing beaches – both have huge car parks. To the north, Le Penon is the last seaside resort with easy access to the waves. After that, if you want to surf, you'll have to do some scenic but inconvenient walking through the forest which conveniently minimises the crowds.

Since tides play a big part at all these spots, your visit to the Côte d'Argent should allow for a few days to check out which banks are working best and when. As a general rule, if the swell is big, high tide is best in the southern end of the zone; when it's small, the low tide sandbars to the north generally break better. Beaches to the north of Hossegor tend to get less crowded, especially during the summertime. Spots up here are spread out among the pines and, while they are generally qualitative clones of the Hossegor beaches, they lack the packs of wave marauders. As for the zone south of Hossegor, it's jealously guarded by local surfers; this is also the area with the famously lively nightlife that attracts travellers, so expect to pay to play.

LAURENT MASUREL
La Centrale

The Côte d'Argent faces west, and consequently receives very consistent high latitude W-NW swells, which can reach up to 15ft (4.8m). However, the angle of the coastline is not so good for the area's dominant NW winds. As a cold front approaches, winds usually clock around from the SW to WNW, and storms, even in summer, are common. As storm cells pass over, the surf can remain blown out for several days with wet and windy conditions making the whole place a little depressing. On the other hand, when a high pressure system sits over the land, you will enjoy light offshore winds in the morning (about a third of the time), followed by a moderate NW seabreeze that blows from noon until dusk. Tide ranges can reach 14ft (4.6m) on spring tides and any sandbar can go from ugly mush to perfect peak in the space of an hour. Tide tables are essential on this stretch of coast, where tides rule!

SURF STATISTICS	J F	M A	M J	J A	S O	N D
dominant swell	W-NW	W-NW	W-NW	W-NW	W-NW	W-NW
swell size (ft)	7-8	6-7	5	3	6	7
consistency (%)	50	60	80	70	90	60
dominant wind	W-NW	W-NW	W-NW	W-NW	NE-E	W-NW
average force	F5	F5	F4	F3	F3	F5
consistency (%)	36	37	38	39	31	40
water temp (°C/°F)	12/54	13/55	17/62	21/70	18/64	15/59
wetsuit						

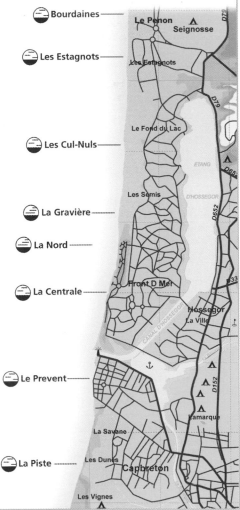

Bourdaines — Le Penon — Seignosse D79
Les Estagnots — Les Estagnots D79
Les Cul-Nuls — Le Fond du Lac
ETANG
Les Semis D652 D'HOSSEGOR
La Gravière —
La Nord —
Front D Mer
La Centrale — Hossegor La Ville
CANAL D'HOSSEGOR D33
Le Prevent — D152
Lamarque
La Savane
La Piste — Les Dunes Capbreton
Les Vignes

SYLVAIN CAZENAVE
Gary Elkerton, Cul Nuls

5. Côte Basque

FRANCE

SPAIN

Anglet Jetties

LAURENT MASUREL

Summary

+ VARIETY OF CONSISTENT WAVES
+ UNCROWDED IN OFF-SEASON
+ CULTURAL INTERESTS

− WET CLIMATE YEAR ROUND
− POLLUTION AND CROWDS IN JULY-AUGUST
− COLD WATER IN WINTER
− EXPENSIVE

The Côte Basque has been a popular tourist destination since Napoleon III chose it to launch the craze of sunbathing in the 19th century. Surfing in France began in 1956, when the first surfboards arrived in the luggage of a Californian surfer and filmmaker named Peter Viertel. He was amazed by the quality of the waves that he found on the Côte Basque and surfing caught on quickly, due, in no small part to the Basque people's love of the ocean.

The river Adour marks the northern border of the Basque Country and this surf zone starting with the beaches of Anglet. Before the major jetty was built between 1971 and 1973, La Barre was considered a world class spot amongst the surf travellers of the 60's. Now a sheltered spot for big swells only, a recent extension of the jetty has further reduced the surf potential but not the pollution. North of the jetty is Boucau, a localised

MARC FENIES

Fred Robin, Biarritz Grande Plage

STEPHANE MIRA

spot that holds big lefts. To the south of La Barre are 4km (2.5mi) of good beachbreaks, well exposed to swell and sheltered from sideshore winds by numerous jetties. Les Cavaliers gets the biggest surf and is usually the cleanest when the summer afternoon sea breeze kicks in,

TRAVEL INFORMATION

Local Population:
Côte Basque – 175,000
Coastline: 35km (21mi)
Time: GMT+1hr
Contests: LB (early Jul), WQS (early Aug)

Getting There – Citizens of Brazil, South Africa and Japan need visas. Paris is 8-10 hours away on an expensive toll road. Unleaded fuel costs about $1/l. It's a one hour flight with Air France from Paris. Ryan Air fly cheap from London. Tickets are expensive. It takes 5 hours by TGV bullet train from Paris and boards are charged an extra $25.

Getting Around – The road network is very efficient, although the N10 road running down the coast of Aquitaine and the Basque Country is busy. There are car parks close to most spots. The bus service is only reliable in Anglet, Bayonne and Biarritz. The train stops in Bayonne, (for Anglet and Biarritz) Guéthary and St-Jean de Luz. Cycling around here is tough, because of steep hills, rain and traffic.

Lodging and Food – Many hotels, from budget up to 4-star. On the N10, you can expect a double from $25, but the average in town is $35, especially in high season. Campsites are plentiful from May to September but beware of the wet climate. Typically, a restaurant bill is $20 not including wine. Hypermarkets have a huge selection of cheap food for self-caterers.

Weather – Due to the proximity of the Pyrénées mountains, it rains about 1500mm annually on the French Basque coast (1 day out of 2), which is less than the Spanish Basque country, but more than Hossegor. Summer stays light until 10pm, in the winter it's dark by 6pm. The weather is reasonably stable from March to October. March and April can experience occasional afternoon temps around 20°C (68°F), while May and June are much warmer months, despite the cooler water. Same wetsuit requirements as Hossegor

Nature and Culture – There is an aquarium in Biarritz and a surf museum is on its way. The Longboard Surf Festival occurs in mid-July. If

you are in the area in early August, then don't miss the Fêtes du Bayonne. There are more festivals in October. Bars and nightclubs are very lively in peak season. The combination of sea and high mountains found in the Basque Country make this area one of the most beautiful and enjoyable places in the world. Local sports that are well catered for include golf and mountain sports in the Pyrénées, whilst Pelote and Courses de Vaches are interesting spectator sports.

Hazards and Hassles – Jetty rocks and shallow reefs can be threats. River run-off and tourist crowds equate to bad summer pollution, especially after storms. In the winter, beaches get covered in rubbish washed in by big storms. Driving and parking tricky during July/August.

Handy Hints – This is a well developed area with everything you will need. Some surf shops are open year round and in general gear is expensive - you will need a gun to surf the reefs when they're big. Try and learn some French, as it will be appreciated.

WEATHER STATISTICS	J/F	M/A	M/J	J/A	S/O	N/D
total rainfall (mm)	132	126	105	84	130	161
consistency (days/mth)	14	13	12	12	14	16
min temp (°C/°F)	5/41	7/44	12/54	16/61	13/55	6/43
max temp (°C/°F)	12/54	15/59	20/68	24/75	22/72	14/57

Lafiténia

COURTESY QUIKSILVER

Gibus de Soultrait. Avalanche

THIERRY ORGANOFF

while Chambre d'Amour offers less powerful waves. Once you pass Biarritz lighthouse, you hit the first of the rocky headlands that are a feature of this chic city. There are good beachbreaks that need a moderate sized swell and lower tides to get going. Grande Plage, in the heart of Biarritz, produces powerful peaks that are protected from south-westerly winds. Côte des Basques is the next spot to the south; it is a meeting point for longboarders since the waves are mellow and sheltered from afternoon NW seabreezes. Towards the south is Bidart, with some sand-covered reefs that work on small swells but close-out when it's big. On these big days you need to head to Guéthary, where three major reefs are to be found. Furthest east are the consistent rights of Parlementia, which are often compared to Sunset Beach and can hold 12-15ft (4-5m) surf. Second is Alcyons, on the other side of the channel, which is the best lefthand reefbreak around. Outside Alcyons is a serious big wave spot named Avalanche that's been ridden up to 18-20ft (5.8-6.4m). Next to Guéthary and surrounded by campsites is Lafiténia, the best righthand pointbreak on the French Basque coast. Boils and whirlpools in the take-off zone are an outstanding feature of this wave along with the inside barrel section. In the bay of St-Jean de Luz a major swell is needed to turn on the reefs. One of these reefs, Sainte-Barbe, offers a fast, powerful take-off next to the jetty at the north end of the bay. If conditions are out of control with large swells and strong winds, then Hendaye Plage offers protection and rideable surf. It is always crowded with beginners from the various surf schools that operate in the smaller waves.

The coastline faces due west around to due north, catching the bulk of the very consistent North Atlantic swells. Unfortunately, it is not so well orientated for the dominant NW winds. When a low pressure approaches the coast, winds usually blow from the SW before turning WNW. Big storms are common and the surf can remain blown out for several days. Combine this with rain and cooler temperatures and it can get a little depressing! On the other hand, when a high pressure covers the country you will be blessed with sunny skies and in the mornings, light offshore breezes (about 1/3 of the time). In the afternoons it's usual for a light to moderate NW seabreeze to kick in. Tidal ranges can reach 14ft (4.5m) on spring tides, at which time very few spots work properly. Get a tide table.

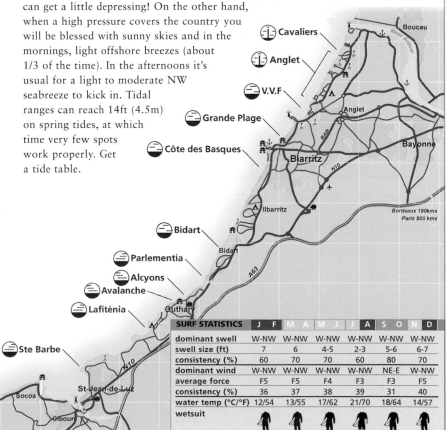

SURF STATISTICS	J F	M A	M J	J A	S O	N D
dominant swell	W-NW	W-NW	W-NW	W-NW	W-NW	W-NW
swell size (ft)	7	6	4-5	2-3	5-6	6-7
consistency (%)	60	70	70	60	80	70
dominant wind	W-NW	W-NW	W-NW	W-NW	NE-E	W-NW
average force	F5	F5	F4	F3	F3	F5
consistency (%)	36	37	38	39	31	40
water temp (°C/°F)	12/54	13/55	17/62	21/70	18/64	14/57
wetsuit						

6. Bizkaia

PORTUGAL
SPAIN

Summary
+ Heavy tubing waves
+ Fabulous scenery
+ Easy access

− Lack of wave choice
− Inconsistent
− Windy and subject to tides

Mundaka with Izaro Island

Tucked into the corner of the Bay of Biscay, Mundaka is a dream lefthand barrel and possibly the best rivermouth wave in the world. A scenic road leads to the pretty fishing village of Mundaka, located at the very end of an estuary or 'ria'. This Basque village is now a celebrated surfing spot and attracts waveriders from all over the world.

A deep channel at the end of the ria has helped to create a long triangular sandbank with the perfect angle for catching the NW swells. The more rain there's been, the stronger the rivermouth flow, which in turn improves the quality of the sandbar. Thicker, longer and heavier barrels will result when the swell hits 4-6ft (1.3-2m), the wind is from the S and the tide is low incoming. Conditions such as these will create a long barrelling tube with rides

The church on the point

Bakio

of up to 150-200m. From the word go the wave sucks up hard, making for steep challenging take-offs straight into a sick barrel section. The ensuing long, fast wall allows a few turns if you are going close to warp speed. The final two sections of the wave can vary in quality depending on the sandbar, but frequently they offer hollow cylinders with less crowd pressure. These sections can be trickier with higher pockets and difficult to make sections.

TRAVEL INFORMATION

Local Population:
Bilbao – 500,000
Coastline: 3900km (2430mi)
Time: GMT+1hr
Contest: WCT (Sept)

Getting There – Visas required for Japanese, South African and Brazilian citizens. Bilbao is about 400km (250mi) north of Madrid. It takes 2h from the French border, using the expensive toll roads. The other option, the N634 road, is packed with slow moving trucks. Fuel is cheaper in Spain than France (75c/l). There are car ferries to Santander and Bilbao from the UK.

Getting Around – Mundaka has a train station, with track leading to Bilbao (45min) and San Sebastian (2h). The drive to Mundaka is

spectacular but the narrow twisting roads are full of crazy drivers and the parking in Mundaka is never easy. Rental cars from Bilbao Airport cost from $275/w (ATESA).

Lodging and Food – Mundaka campsite is open from May to October. There are 3 hotels, starting from $27/dble in low season. Farm guest houses are a good option in this area. Tapas bars are a great Spanish institution.

Weather – Bizkaia province is subject to a changeable climate with numerous storms produced by high latitude lows travelling from W to E. The mountains rising up directly behind the coast produce plenty of rain. On average one day out of two sees rainfall, mainly in the autumn and winter.

Nature and Culture – If there's a lack of swell the bars are entertaining and busy. From July 7th-14th the nearby city of Pamplona plays host to Spain's biggest street party, the Fiesta San Fermin with the famous Running of the Bulls. Urdaibi Valley is a UN protected biosphere with caves and monasteries worth visiting.

Hazards and Hassles – You have to be fit to survive a Mundaka session, the clean-up sets, impact zone, long paddles and the rips quickly tire you out. Some guys wear helmets when it's packed. Localism used to be very severe, now it's just a very competitive line-up. Avoid weekends, noon and the best tide.

Handy Hints – Guns can be bought quite cheap at Mundaka surf shop, owned by Craig, an Aussie that settled here. Early risers will get more space.

WEATHER STATISTICS	J/F	M/A	M/J	J/A	S/O	N/D
total rainfall (mm)	105	82	78	75	125	140
consistency (days/mth)	15	13	13	12	14	17
min temp (°C/°F)	7/44	9/48	12/54	16/61	13/55	9/48
max temp (°C/°F)	12/54	15/59	19/66	22/72	19/66	14/57

Getting to the line-up is easy by paddling out from the harbour steps with the river flow that runs between the rocky cliffs and the take-off zone. This huge current can swiftly take you beyond the first peak and out to sea, making it difficult to hold position in the line-up. If you get caught in the impact zone, ride the white water in and paddle to the edge of the river, which will quickly deposit you back at the take-off zone. This is also true when it's big (rather than trying to paddle back out around the shoulder). The bigger the tidal range, the harder the rip will be pulling on the outgoing tide and the bigger the tubes will be on the incoming tide. When the tide hits that magic point, between low and mid, the line-up will always be packed with locals from the surrounding area or Bilbao, French Basques and various international travellers. For the visiting surfer, mid tide and rising may be a better option, as the line-up will be far less hectic. However, like any jewel, perfect Mundaka is not easy to come by. The days when the right tide, right wind, and a good sized NW swell all come together are few and far between. To get 4-6ft (1.3-2m) waves at Mundaka, the beaches open to maximum swell have to be around 10-12ft (3.2-4m).

Unfortunately, this zone is pretty much limited to one world class spot with little else around. Nearby Bakio, further west along the spectacular coast road, holds

Peter Mel, Mundaka

ALEX WILLIAMS

Meñakoz

F.MUÑOZ

The Cantabrican Coast faces north: not too good for small westerly swells, it is however, ideal for the numerous, big NW swells. Many of these larger swells are accompanied by the low pressure system that produced them, which means offshore SW winds if the system is coming through the more southerly latitudes. Good conditions at Mundaka rarely last for more than two days, as the large swells required drop off. Unless there's a North Atlantic low pressure measuring less than 980Mb, then there's no chance of waves. Therefore, this classic wave is only rideable about 50 days a year. The Urdaibi Valley funnels SW winds into a more southerly direction. When a high pressure covers the country, the wind will frequently turn N-NE in the afternoons. Tide heights vary from 6-12ft (2-4m) and greatly effect the wave quality. The BBK bank gives out free tide tables!

SURF STATISTICS	J F	M A	M J	J A	S O	N D
dominant swell	NW-N	NW-N	NW-N	NW-N	NW-N	NW-N
swell size (ft)	5-6	4-5	3-4	2	4-5	5-6
consistency (%)	70	70	55	40	70	70
dominant wind	W-NW	W-NW	W-NW	W-NW	NE-E	W-NW
average force	F5	F5	F4	F3	F3	F5
consistency (%)	36	37	38	39	31	40
water temp (°C/°F)	12/54	13/55	15/59	19/66	17/62	14/57
wetsuit						

consistent, quality peaks breaking over a sand and rock bottom. Further towards Bilbao is the challenging big wave spot, Meñakoz, where 20ft (6m) rights are possible. Sopelana has consistent waves as it will pick up swell of any size or direction from west to north.

There are other spots that you'll pass while travelling the Mundaka - Bakio road – they only work at low tide and with major swells when Mundaka will also be breaking. On the other side of the ria, driving through historical Gernika, is Laga beachbreak, a fairly average wave from where you have a perfect view over Izaro Island. The huge rights here would be perfect for tow-in surfing, but are as yet untested.

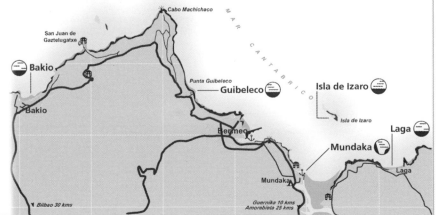

PORTUGAL SPAIN

7. North-West Galicia

ALEX WILLIAMS

Summary
+ **180° SWELL WINDOW**
+ **MULTIPLE SWELL/WIND OPTIONS**
+ **BEAUTIFUL COUNTRYSIDE**
+ **CAMPERVAN FRIENDLY**

- **UNSTABLE CLIMATE**
- **LACK OF SUNSHINE**
- **NO WORLD CLASS BREAKS**
- **COOL WATER YEAR ROUND**
- **LONG DRIVES AND HARD ACCESS**

Valdoviño

Galicia's landscape of steep forested hills hidden behind clouds of misty drizzle earned it the "end of the world" nickname from the Romans. Since then, the Celtic inhabitants or Gallegos, have been left alone in this un-Spanish corner of Iberia. Plunging valleys cut across the landscape, leading to large inlets and estuaries called "rias". Similar to fjords, these flooded valleys deeply punctuate the coastline, and effectively filter the consistent North Atlantic swells.

Galicia has mainland Europe's largest swell window and the jagged coastline means somewhere will always be offshore.

Despite the heavy industries around La Coruña, the small student city of Ferrol and its environs have remained fairly untouched. To the north, Doniños is an exposed and consistent west

DAN HAYLOCK

Santi Dias, Doniños

GECKO

facing spot. There are four major reefs and some sandbars, offering powerful beachbreaks best from low to midtide. It gets busy with groms outside of school times, but mornings or weekdays are uncrowded. SW winds destroy Doniños but are offshore at Playa de San Jorge (Xurxo), the next bay north. It's a multi aspect crescent

TRAVEL INFORMATION

Local Population:
Ferrol – 82,000
Coastline: 3,900km
(2,438mi)
Time: GMT+1hr
Contest: WQS (Sept)

Getting There – Citizens of Japan, South Africa and Brazil need visas. If you fly into Madrid, Coruña is 600km (375mi) to the NW, plus a further hours drive to Ferrol. Iberia places a heavy tax on surfboards. It's possible to get expensive flights straight to Santiago de Compostela, (two hours from Ferrol). It takes at least 10 hours to drive from the French border.

Getting Around – The wind and swell changes a lot, so you are going to do a lot of driving in order to find optimum conditions. Rental cars from Coruña airport are $275/w (ATESA). National roads are good, but the coastal C646 is slow, as everything from lorries to donkeys use the road.

Lodging and Food – There are dozens of campsites operating in the summer (May-Oct), although in some of the more remote areas of Galicia, a camper van will prove useful. There are a few pensions (B&B) in Valdoviño and Doniños but don't expect a lot of choice (±$25/dble). Ferrol has some top end hotels costing around $140/dble. As with the rest of Spain, seafood is plentiful and reasonably priced.

Weather – Galicia is the most exposed 'provincia' in Spain and is the windiest, rainiest and cloudiest part of the country. This has earned it the nickname "Green Spain" and it's often compared to Ireland. Temp variations are minimal throughout the year, with mild winters and gentle summers. Autumn and winter are the rainiest times but the good news is the rainfall never lasts long. The weather can change many times during the day. The water is quite cold and upwelling so a light fullsuit in summer and a 5-4-3, boots and gloves in winter.

Nature and Culture – The region of Galicia to the south of Coruña is extremely picturesque. Ferrol has lots of bars and clubs for a large student population. Undoubtedly though, the cultural highlight of a visit to Galicia is the famous pilgrimage town of Santiago de Compostela.

Hazards and Hassles – The strong rips in the rias, cold water and the unpredictable weather patterns are your main cause for concern. Most spots are fun beachbreaks, which tend to get busy near the main towns. The atmosphere in the water is generally cool.

Handy Hints – There's many traditional parties in the summer, the most popular one is held in Santiago de Compostela in late July. Even though the surf gets big, it's not the sort of place you'll need a gun. A camper van is the best way to see and surf Galicia with plenty of free camps, especially out of season.

WEATHER STATISTICS	J/F	M/A	M/J	J/A	S/O	N/D
total rainfall (mm)	99	80	50	38	75	130
consistency (days/mth)	17	14	11	8	12	18
min temp (°C/°F)	7/44	8/46	12/54	15/59	13/55	8/46
max temp (°C/°F)	13/55	16/61	19/66	23/74	21/70	14/57

of sand with a long left in the southern corner and peaks all the way to the northern end. Ponzos, on the east side of the Cobas Peninsula, holds many different peaks and is best checked on SE to SW winds. One of these spots, La Mina, will form good rights in front of some ruins if the swell is small and clean. By Galician standards, Campelo is crowded in summer because it is consistently good in varying conditions and smaller swells, it handles some north in the wind but doesn't like high tide. Valdoviño is a run down resort that is worth checking in winter as the main beach faces north and offers some protection

ALEX WILLIAMS

Vilarrube, inside Ria de Cedeira

from big westerly swells and wind. Percebelleira Island, at the north end of the beach has the best quality waves. Around the corner is Pantin, the most famous spot in Galicia, where regular international contests are held. The cliffs protect Pantin from a NE wind and the sandbanks usually throw up some long, but disorganised rights. It works on all tides but low to mid is usually best. Multiple peaks spread the regular crowds. Most people stay in vans at nearby campsites. If you want to get away from the crowds at Pantin, try the nudist beach at Baleo, the little cove is nice but the sandbars are not usually very good. In case of a huge swell, Vilarrube inside the Ria de Cedeira can have small but long rivermouth rights in beautiful surroundings.

Jutting out into the Atlantic, Galicia gathers any swell from the SW to the NE. The Ferrol coastline faces NW and gathers the brunt of these year round swells. Straight NW swells average 4-15ft (1.3-5m) in winter and 2-10ft (0.6-3.2m) in the summer. The lows track further north across the Atlantic in the summer, so swells tend to be from a more northerly direction, whereas the winter sees more W swell. Many weather systems hit Galicia, so the climate tends to be wet and

windy. Up to 200 swells a year buffet its coast but they are frequently disorganised and messy. The dominant wind is a strong W, more NW in summer and then SW in winter. The ideal surf conditions are a moderate W swell breaking into light east winds. Tidal ranges vary from 6-12ft (2-4m), and play a big part in deciding where and when you will be surfing - a tide table is a must. Use extra caution when surfing the many rias or rivermouths, where incoming low to mid tides tend to offer the best conditions.

SURF STATISTICS	J F	M A	M J	J A	S O	N D
dominant swell	SW-NW	SW-NW	NW-NE	NW-NE	SW-NW	SW-NW
swell size (ft)	6-7	5-6	4	2-3	5	6
consistency (%)	70	70	60	50	80	70
dominant wind	SW-NW	SW-NW	NW-NE	NW-NE	NW-NE	SW-NW
average force	F4-F5	F4-F5	F4	F3-F4	F4	F4-F5
consistency (%)	69	76	58	62	46	72
water temp (°C/°F)	12/54	13/55	15/59	18/64	17/62	14/57
wetsuit	🌊	🌊	🌊	🌊	🌊	🌊

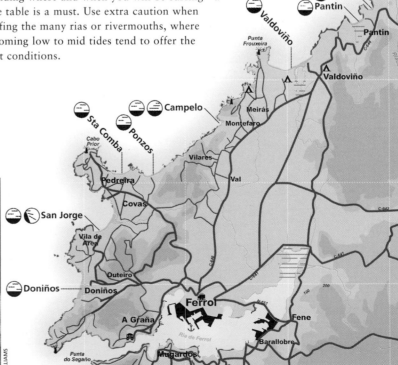

ALEX WILLIAMS

Pantin

8. Peniche

PORTUGAL

SPAIN

Supertubos

JOÃO VALENTE

Summary
+ WIDE SWELL WINDOW
+ FLEXIBLE WIND AND
  SWELL COMBINATIONS
+ QUALITY BEACH AND REEFBREAKS
+ RELATIVELY CHEAP

− SUMMER ONSHORES
− COOL WATER YEAR ROUND
− SMELL FROM FISH FACTORY

Portugal sits on the western edge of Europe's continental shelf, enticing deep ocean swells to break unimpeded on its sunny shores. The Portuguese coast is wide open to the consistent W-NW swells that pound Europe from October to April. The climate is the most pleasant on Europe's Atlantic seaboard, but the water remains cold year round. This coldness doesn't transfer to the friendly people who have an affinity with the sea through their age-old traditions of seafaring and fishing. Both these themes are strong in Peniche, which is home to one of Portugal's biggest fishing fleets.

Whereas most of the Portugese seaboard faces due west, with few headlands for wind and swell protection, Peniche is on a small peninsula at right angles to the

Consolação left

JOÃO VALENTE

Guillerme Herdy, Supertubos

JOÃO VALENTE

Portuguese coast. This peninsula used to be an island, until a causeway was built in the 12th century, and rarely holds much surf. Sand dunes to the north link this peninsula to the smaller Baleal peninsula, offering 5km

TRAVEL INFORMATION

Local Population:
Peniche – 20,000
Coastline: 1793km (1120mi)
Time: GMT
Contest: National (May)

Getting There – Australians need visas. Peniche is 1h30 drive from Lisbon and its international connections to most major cities. TAP, the national airline, is surfboard friendly. It takes at least 12 hours to drive from the French border. Fuel is cheaper than Spain. Departure tax on international flights is $14.

Getting Around – Main roads are usually well surfaced but busy and the driving can be very dangerous. The main IC1 road contains a mixture of fast drivers and slow horse-drawn carts, creating chaos. Portugal has the second worst road safety record in Europe. Buses are cheap and take surfboards for free. Local car rentals (Auto Jardim) are $180/w. Many beaches are down muddy or sandy dirt roads where it's easy to get your car stuck.

Lodging and Food – Unless it's high season (June-Sept), finding quartos (rooms) or flats in Baleal/Peniche is easy; ask at the tourismo or try the 'pensãos' on Rua Jose Estevao in the old town. Particularly recommended are the Residencial Maciel and the Residencial Marisqueira, both around $25/dble. Many camper vans stay in Baleal car park. There is a surf camp/school - Cantinho da Baia in Baleal. A meal costs around $7 if you can resist the pricey appetisers. Don't let the fish factory stench put you off the national dish of grilled sardines.

Weather – The climate in Portugal is very pleasant year round. Ericeira and Peniche are in the middle of the country, between the dry Algarve and the damp regions north of Porto. The wettest season is November until April. There is snow in the Serra da Estrela (the snow resorts are only reliable in February). The best climate occurs during spring and autumn, even though mid-summer rarely gets too hot on the coast. The Nortada (north winds) always cool things down and conspire with the cold Canaries Current to prevent the water from

ever reaching boardshorts temperature. A light 2/2 or 3/2 steamer will do except in mid-winter when a 4/3 and boots are necessary.

Nature and Culture – Don't miss Obidos, the fortified city to the west. Take a trip to the Berlenga Islands; a bird filled National Park, with nice beaches and snorkelling.

Hazards and Hassles – Apart from rocks and a bit of localism at Molho Leste and Lagide, the atmosphere in the water is cool. The stink of fish being processed in the factory near Supertubos is as heavy as the wave. Waves on the south side of the peninsula break harder than the more crumbly waves on the north side. There are lots of surf schools at Baia and Baleal.

Handy Hints – There are 2 good surf shops in Peniche. Bodyboarding is as big here as in the rest of Portugal and it's the bodyboarders who control the line-ups. There are no real big wave spots here, so you won't need a gun. A board costs $250. This zone links up with Ericeira, one hour to the south.

WEATHER STATISTICS	J/F	M/A	M/J	J/A	S/O	N/D
total rainfall (mm)	90	80	30	4	31	100
consistency (days/mth)	10	8	4	1	6	10
min temp (°C/°F)	8/46	11/52	14/57	17/62	15/59	9/48
max temp (°C/°F)	15/59	19/66	23/74	28/82	25/77	16/61

(3mi) of beachbreaks, with a N to SW exposure. Further north, the zone starts off with a stretch of straight NW facing beachbreaks, backed by fields of crops, making access difficult. These beaches pick up the summer N swells, so check spots like Praia del Rei, Praia de Bom Successo and Praia aos Belgas, which is a well known swell-magnet for the Peniche area. Sand covers a reef at Baleal, known as Lagide. This left is a top quality break, especially when strong S or SW winds are blowing out all the other spots. It's a fairly long ride with big, open walls to carve up, but it's best to avoid low tide, because urchins are plentiful. This is a consistent and always crowded wave. Many surf schools are based here, learning on the N facing beach of Lagide or the 3km (2mi) beach between Baleal and Peniche. It's only an average quality beachbreak where the middle peaks should be the more powerful. Peniche town itself is hardly the most attractive of places, although there are some nice fish restaurants beside the harbour, sporting good views across to the Berlenga Islands (no reported surf spots). Of more interest to surfers is Molho Leste, beside the harbour, which creates a wedgy, fast, tubing right when it's big. This is Peniche's most localised wave, with bodyboarders controlling the small take-off zone. To reach the best beachbreak in Portugal, just follow your nose and the foul smell of the fish processing plant will lead you down a short dirt road to Supertubos. The dominant N wind is offshore, so all you have to do is wait for a big NW swell or a rare SW swell and higher tides to taste the amazing barrels, that are best going left. Once again this spot is owned by bodyboarders, the standard of whom is incredibly high. The crowds and the acrid stench blowing into the line-up can diminish the experience but essentially, the name says it all. Consolação lefts are rare, but the righthander on the other side of the castle can be an outstanding pointbreak. Protected from the prevailing N winds, Consolação needs more swell than Supers and low tide.

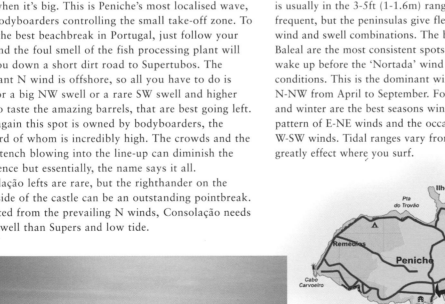
JOÃO VALENTE
Consolação right

Portugal is the European yardstick for year round consistency, and Peniche stylishly handles the regular SW-NW swells. Average swell size is around 6-7ft (2-2.3m) in winter, peaking at 12-15ft (4-5m) and summer is usually in the 3-5ft (1-1.6m) range. Storms are pretty frequent, but the peninsulas give flexibility with different wind and swell combinations. The beachbreaks north of Baleal are the most consistent spots in the summer, but wake up before the 'Nortada' wind in order to get clean conditions. This is the dominant wind, blowing from the N-NW from April to September. For this reason, autumn and winter are the best seasons wind wise, with a standard pattern of E-NE winds and the occasional storm bringing W-SW winds. Tidal ranges vary from 4-12ft (1.3-4m) and greatly effect where you surf.

SURF STATISTICS	J F	M A	M J	J A	S O	N D
dominant swell	SW-NW	SW-NW	W-NW	W-NW	SW-NW	SW-NW
swell size (ft)	5-6	5-6	4	3	4-5	5-6
consistency (%)	80	70	60	40	80	80
dominant wind	W-E	W-N	W-N	NW-N	W-N	W-E
average force	F2	F2	F2	F2	F3	F3
consistency (%)	71	54	65	55	51	73
water temp (°C/°F)	13/55	14/57	16/61	18/64	17/62	15/59
wetsuit						

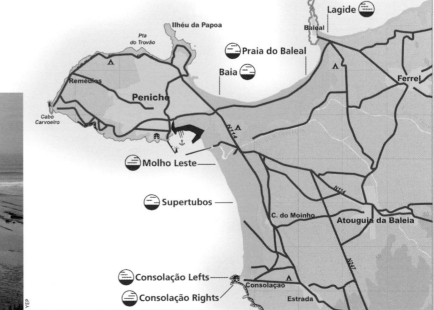
Baleal Reef
YEP

Ilha das Pombas

Lagide

Ilhéu da Papoa

Pta do Trovão

Baleal

Praia do Baleal

Baia

Remédios

Ferrel

Peniche

Cabo Carvoeiro

Molho Leste

Supertubos

C. do Moinho

Atouguia da Baleia

Consolação Lefts

Consolação Rights

Consolação

Estrada

9. Ericeira

PORTUGAL

SPAIN

Ribeira d'Ilhas

JOÃO VALENTE

Summary
+ SUPER CONSISTENT
+ WORLD CLASS REEFS AND POINTS
+ RELATIVELY CHEAP

– FEW SHELTERED BREAKS
– LIMITED WIND OPTIONS
– COOL WATER YEAR ROUND

As with Peniche, Ericeira has no shortage of Atlantic swell to play with. Numerous classic reef set ups, rocky headlands and small rivermouth bays shape the swells into world class waves such as Coxos. Ericeira can be considered the centre of Portuguese surfing with its concentration of classy breaks a mere 30km (19mi) from Lisbon. It doesn't quite have the wind protection of Peniche and big, stormy swells tend to favour the south facing coast of Lisbon, but for consistent quality and challenging waves, Ericeira rules.

Big wave contestants

JOÃO VALENTE

JOÃO VALENTE

São Lourenço in the north is a rivermouth bay with a heavy right point that's rideable up to 12ft (4m). It has been likened to Sunset Beach, Hawai'i, especially when W

TRAVEL INFORMATION

Local Population:
Ericeira – 30,000
Coastline: 1793km (1,120mi)
Time: GMT
Contests: WQS (early Sept)
WCT (mid Sept)
GOB (late Aug)

Getting There – (See 8.Peniche). The only difference is a shorter 30min drive from Lisbon.

Getting Around – (See 8.Peniche). The Ericeira area is now linked with a new highway from Lisbon. Sunday driving in Portugal is mental and it's a good day to stay off the roads.

Lodging and Food – Apart from high season (June-Sept), finding quartos (rooms) or flats in Ericeira/Ribamar is easy. The Turismo keeps accommodation lists or ask at the restaurants. Ericeira has a wide variety of pensãoes and hotels starting at $20-$25/d. A meal is ±$6 if you can resist the more expensive seafood.

Weather – (See 8.Peniche).

Nature and Culture – Ericeira is a typical fishing/tourist town with pastelerias, pretty streets and churches. It's lively year round because of its proximity to Lisbon, but still fairly low key. A Saturday night out in Lisbon's Barrio Alto district can be interesting, as thousands of people pour onto the streets to drink themselves stupid. Don't miss Sintra, and the majestic castles of the old Royal City nearby.

Hazards and Hassles – The rocky ledges and reefs are more dangerous than the locals, but the area is getting increasingly overcrowded. Some of the remote car parks are tempting for thieves. Sitting out storm surf conditions is a regular occurrence.

Handy Hints – There are a couple of surf shops in Ericeira town. Semente Surfboards in Ribamar is Portugal's biggest board shaper. The factory shop stocks boards costing around $250. Bodyboarders in Portugal outnumber stand up surfers in most line-ups, except for Coxos and Ribeira d'Ilhas. Peniche is a one hour drive to the north. There are plenty of automatic cash dispensers throughout the country.

WEATHER STATISTICS	J/F	M/A	M/J	J/A	S/O	N/D
total rainfall (mm)	90	80	30	4	31	100
consistency (days/mth)	10	8	4	1	6	10
min temp (°C/°F)	8/46	11/52	14/57	17/62	15/59	9/48
max temp (°C/°F)	15/59	19/66	23/74	28/82	25/77	16/61

Coxos

CHRISTOPHE DIMULLE

Tadeu Pereira, Pedra Blanca

JOÃO VALENTE

Reef

LIONEL CORBEL

swell rogue sets punish the unwary. Coxos is Portugal's undisputed pointbreak king. This barrelling world class right, breaks close to a rocky ledge in a small bay and 4-6 second barrels are the norm when it's firing. The rocks are sharp, so getting in and out of the water is as difficult as mastering this powerful beast of a wave. Coxos doesn't handle high tide or crowds very well. On the other side of the bay is Crazy Left which gets very hollow, but is a rare, dangerous wave. The next bay south, Ribeira d'Ilhas, is a major contest venue due to its reliability and slightly better wind protection than the surrounding waves. Long, righthand point waves, or scattered powerful peaks, break along the beach. There is always a wave worth surfing, unless it's really big or hard onshore. A new water treatment plant has vastly improved the rivermouth water quality. South of Ribeira d'Ilhas is the aptly named 'Reef' which is an insane, barrelling righthander. Swells here jack up out of deep water and slam onto a shallow ledge producing 6ft (2m) barrels when there is only 3ft (1m) of swell. The wave eventually closes out on a rocky ledge and is for experts only. Next door to this is Pedra Blanca (White Rock), an awesome lefthander which gets extremely hollow, making it a very popular bodyboarding wave, and always crowded. Low tide is very shallow and the rocky bottom is sharp and uneven. Once you reach Ericeira town, the wave quality decreases, although Praia do Norte can have some good rights. Praia do Peixe offers short rides inside the harbour and the only shelter around

here when it's out of control. Furnas is a right point in the town centre, which needs big N/NW swell but it's rarely lined-up. South of town, the rivermouth at Foz do Lizandro will work in S-W swells and São Julio beachbreaks catch any swell going. Further south are many more spots worth checking if you like mellow waves and no crowds.

Ericeira's swell and wind synopsis is similar to Peniche, but the wind options are less flexible. All the breaks require E or even SE winds for due offshore so the summer Nortada is obviously bad news. Winter storms can mean some driving around to find places offering shelter from the wind and swell, which means Peniche or Lisbon. Autumn, with its more easterly airflow is the best bet, but Ericeira can turn it on at any time of the year. Low tide can be suicidal on some reefs.

SURF STATISTICS	J F	M A	M J	J A	S O	N D
dominant swell	SW-NW	SW-NW	W-NW	W-NW	SW-NW	SW-NW
swell size (ft)	6-7	6	4-5	3	5	6
consistency (%)	60	60	60	50	80	70
dominant wind	W-E	W-N	W-N	NW-N	W-N	W-E
average force	F4	F4	F3-F4	F3-F4	F3-F4	F4
consistency (%)	71	54	65	55	51	73
water temp (°C/°F)	13/55	14/57	16/61	18/64	17/62	15/59
wetsuit						

São Lourenço — São Lourenço

Ribamar

Coxos

Crazy Left — Palhais

Pontinha

Ribeira de Ilhas

Reef

Pedra Blanca — Cabo São Sebastião

Praia do Norte

Mafra 7kms

Praia do Peixe — Ericeira

Furnas

Fonte Boa da Brincosa

Foz do Lizandro — Foz do Lizandro

São Lourenço

JOÃO VALENTE

PORTUGAL

SPAIN

10. The Algarve

Zavial

MARC FENIES

Summary

+ UNCROWDED BREAKS
+ REEFS AND BEACHES
+ WIDE SWELL WINDOW
+ WARMEST EUROPEAN CLIMATE

− NO WORLD CLASS SPOTS
− COOL WATER
− WEST COAST ONSHORES

Castelejo

ALEX WILLIAMS

Marlon Lipke, Carrapateira

MARC FENIES

The Algarve is the south-western corner of the Iberian Peninsula and is an intoxicating mix of Atlantic and Mediterranean influences. It was the last major European surf region to be explored and although it doesn't contain the classic reefs of central Portugal, the potential for good, uncrowded waves is high. The countryside is a gently undulating mesh of forests and small fields, leading down to an undeveloped coastline of high cliffs and long empty beaches scattered with rocks. The small, lively town of Sagres is well located to take advantage of the wide swell window of Cape St. Vincent, where the west and south coasts meet.

About 40km (25mi) north of Sagres is Arrifana, a superb cove with good shelter from big swells and N winds. Treacherous rights peel around the northern headland of this classic big wave spot, that doesn't even begin to start breaking until it's over 6-8ft (2-2.6m) on the open beaches. It remains rideable up to 12-15ft (4-5m) and naturally, is only for experienced big wave surfers. On the other side of the channel is a very

TRAVEL INFORMATION

Local Population:
West Algarve – 30,000
Coastline: 120km (75mi)
Time: GMT
Contests: Junior (Oct)
WQS (Oct)

Getting There – Australians need visas. Sagres is 5h drive from Lisbon. Many charter flights arrive at Faro Airport, 2h east. Buses and trains go to Lagos from Lisbon.

Getting Around – Main roads are well surfaced and less crowded than in central Portugal but getting to most spots involves some off-road driving. Buses take surfboards. Local car rentals: Auto Jardim at $160/w

Lodging and Food – Finding accommodation in Sagres or Lagos is easy. Many locals rent out rooms or whole houses at ± $15/room. There's a surf camp in Lagos – The Surf Experience,

book through Low Pressure Travel Services. A meal can be had for $7. Sagres has its own brand cheap beer.

Weather – Despite its Atlantic position, the Algarve enjoys a Mediterranean climate with cool winter temperatures, it never freezes and 20°C (68°F) at noon is common. Summers are hot, and only 60mm winter rainfall per month puts the Algarve at half the national average. Camping is still an option in winter. The water is warmer by 1-2°C (3-5°F) than central Portugal, and more so from to June-Sept, but cold currents can hit the coast at any time so take a range of rubber.

Nature and Culture – Cape St. Vincent contains a fortress where Prince Henry the Navigator, established his famous school of exploration. This eventually led to Portugal's discovery of the lucrative sea route to India. The nightlife in Sagres and even more so Lagos, is wild and

raucous when summer brings the backpacking hordes. Beware the absinthe! Aljezur near Arrifana has some good ruins to visit.

Hazards and Hassles – Apart from rocks and some localism, there's little to worry about. The undeveloped west coast has few or no locals outside the towns and the Sagres surfers tend to stay at their home breaks. The area is slowly getting more crowded but the vibe remains chilled as there are a lot of waves to choose from. Respect the sharp rocks at the pointbreaks, especially if you have sampled the absinthe!

Handy Hints – There are surf shops in Lagos and Sagres but the range is limited. The Algarve is a well-established tourist destination so English is widely spoken. Reckless driving is the national sport, and the N126 has the highest death toll in Europe!

WEATHER STATISTICS	J/F	M/A	M/J	J/A	S/O	N/D
total rainfall (mm)	60	50	12	1	35	65
consistency (days/mth)	6	6	2	1	3	7
min temp (°C/°F)	9/48	12/54	16/61	20/68	17/62	11/52
max temp (°C/°F)	16/61	19/66	24/75	28/82	24/75	18/64

Cordama

short, tubing left, and some hollow peaks on smaller swells. There are a couple of other spots close to Arrifana that pick up more swell, like the beach peaks of Monte Clérigo, a few kms north. Next town south is Carrapateira with its fickle rivermouth waves and miles of open beachbreaks to the north. A dusty track runs south from Carrapateira to Amado, a consistent spot with a bit of north wind protection. Cordama and Castelejo are adjacent, isolated beaches consisting of a combination of rocky outcrops and sand bars, which offer better potential in the autumn, as winter storms tend to wash the sandbars away. With a moderate sized, clean swell, there are a couple of very good left pointbreaks worth finding in this neighbourhood.

Sagres has three main waves, which can deal with most wind/swell combinations. Beliche faces due south and needs a big N or any S swell to get the powerful, super hollow peaks firing. It is this wave that the infamous Sagres locals have been protecting for years, but the intense aggression has lessened and respectful travellers can score some epic scraps from the legions of bodyboarders that frequent the line-up. Praia de Tonel around the bay from Beliche has a more westerly aspect and will pick up more of the N swells but is a less intense wave. Mareta is a very sheltered break near the town centre and only breaks if there's a huge N swell or a SE wind swell. Big swells wrap around Cape St. Vincent and will hit quality beaches, further along the south coast. Zavial is a great wave which relies on sand to conspire with the rocks and shape up perfect point style righthanders. There's a quality right reef at Praia da Luz called Rocha Negra (Black Rock) which will only handle swells up to headhigh. Lagos has miles of inconsistent beachbreak, which really turn on the goods less than 20 times a year. Short, snappy hollow rides can be had when the 'levant' or south wind blows up a short period, short duration swell.

Consistency is the best word to describe southern Portugal's surf. The same cannot be said for the winds around Cape St Vincent which are notoriously unpredictable and treated with suspicion by the local sailing fraternity. Strange swirling gusts and onshores when the weather map says offshore are known to happen, but on the whole, the Algarve area follows the general summer 'nortada' and winter SW storm winds followed by NE to SE offshores. When the winter offshores do blow, they blow hard and make blind take-offs a regular occurrence. The S wind or 'levant' as it is called in the Mediterranean, is prone to disappear as quickly as it arrived and the swells produced are very fleeting. Average wintertime swells on the west coast are around 8-10ft (2.6-3.3m), with 12-15ft (4-5m) maximums, whilst summer rarely goes flat and regularly gets up to double overhead. The south coast offers perfect shelter with offshore winds and a filtered swell although it is usually flat in summer. The 'nortada' is the dominant wind coming from the N-NW; it usually blows from April to September making a mess of most surf spots at this time. Tides vary from 4-12ft (1.3-4m).

SURF STATISTICS	J F	M A	M J	J A	S O	N D
dominant swell	W-NW	W-NW	SE	SE	W-NW	W-NW
swell size (ft)	5	4-5	2-3	1-2	3-4	4-5
consistency (%)	80	70	50	40	60	70
dominant wind	W-E	W-N	W-N	W-N	W-N	W-E
average force	F4	F4	F4	F3	F3	F4
consistency (%)	70	54	65	67	51	72
water temp (°C/°F)	15/59	16/61	18/64	21/70	19/66	17/62
wetsuit						

Arrifana

11. West Sardinia

Il Medicapo

ALESSANDRO DINI

Summary

+ FAIRLY CONSISTENT SURF
+ SPOTS FACING A VARIETY
  OF DIRECTIONS
+ MELLOW CROWDS
+ HISTORICAL AND CULTURAL SITES

- WINDY CONDITIONS
- SHORT LIVED SWELLS
- COLD WINTER CONDITIONS
- TOUGH ACCESS

Italy is hardly the most popular of surf destinations and it can be hard to believe the locals when they tell you that they see 12ft (4m) swells and can have waves every other day in the winter. These stories shouldn't be disregarded because the dominant NW Mistral wind blows with such regularity and power that Italy, in particular Sardinia, really does get consistent waves. About 200km (125mi) west of Italy and 15km (10mi) south of Corsica, Sardinia is the second largest island in the Med. It's also the most consistent surf location in this tideless sea, as even the east coast of the island picks up easterly swells coming out of the Tyrrhenian Sea, hitting the beaches around Cagliari.

The peninsula of Putzu Idu is regarded as the best surf area in Sardinia, although

Diddo Ciani, Mini Capo

ALESSANDRO DINI

ALESSANDRO DINI

Buggeru in the S has hosted European contests and Alghero in the N has great potential. Putzu Idu is a tiny fishing village set in wild country between cliffs and lagoons. It gets a bit crowded at weekends as waveriders from Oristano and Sardinia's other main cities arrive. There are dozens of potential reefbreaks around the peninsula and plenty of average beachbreaks for

TRAVEL INFORMATION

Local Population:
Sardinia – 1.7M
Coastline: 1,100km (687mi)
Time: GMT+1hr
Contest: National (Sept)

Getting There – Visa: Brazil and South Africa. International entry points are Rome or Firenze (with Alitalia). You can either fly or catch a ferry to Sardinia. Cagliari is a better destination to aim for in Sardinia than Olbia as it is closer to the wave zone. From Cagliari it is a three hour drive to Putzu Idu, or an expensive flight to the nearby town of Oristano.

Getting Around – If you rent a car, get one that can handle dirt roads and expect to pay $200/w. Apart from the main S131 freeway and the city roads, driving is tough going as the Putzu Idu peninsula is wild. Ferries go to/from Corsica, Sicily and Italy.

Lodging and Food – Stay in Oristano for the best hotel choices. Allow $50 for a good double room. There is a basic surfcamp in Is Benas, close to Putzu Idu. Hotel Baia Blue (Mandriola) charges $30/room as does the two star Da Cesare hotel in Putzu Idu. A basic meal is $15-20.

Weather – Despite its location in the middle of the Med, Sardinia experiences a mixed Mediterranean and Oceanic climate with four distinct seasons. Winter is the prime surf time but it's the coldest and windiest time. You could wear T-shirts on the sunniest afternoons but take warm clothing. The good news is rainfall is quite low. Spring and autumn are the best times, especially autumn, with plenty of sunshine and balmy temperatures. Avoid summer for several reasons: heat, droughts, crowds and flat spells! The wind chill factor is high, so even when the water's around 20°C (68°F) you still need a light fullsuit. Bring a 4/3mm for the winter. Take booties.

Nature and Culture – If you have the time then you should stop in Firenze or Rome, remember Italy has 50% of the World Heritage monuments. You'll find lots of culture and history around Oristano. The west coast is beautifully untouched. In winter the only lively bars are in Oristano.

Hazards and Hassles – Surfing only began here in the 80's and numbers are not enough to produce crowds. Weekends and holidays can get busy and then you may have the occasional shouting match, but Italians are generally laid back and good fun to be around. Be careful of rocks when getting in and out.

Handy Hints – Most shops are in Cagliari. Closer is Onda Blu in Alghero, it's better to bring your own boards (maybe a mini gun) Longboarding is big. Try to speak Italian or use your hands like the locals do.

WEATHER STATISTICS	J/F	M/A	M/J	J/A	S/O	N/D
total rainfall (mm)	50	37	19	5	42	67
consistency (days/mth)	8	6	2	1	5	9
min temp (°C/°F)	7/44	10/50	16/61	21/70	17/62	10/50
max temp (°C/°F)	14/47	18/64	25/77	30/86	25/77	18/64

San Giovanni di Sinis

ALESSANDRO DINI

La Laguna
Su Pallo Su
Sa Mesa Longa
Capo Manu
Mini Capo
Funtana Meiga

T.re Scala 'e Sale
Sa Marigosa
Porto Mandriola
Putzu Idu
P.ta de s'Incudina
Cucuru Mannu
Capo sa Sturaggia
P.ta su Bardoni
P.ta is Arutas
Monte Raseddu
Roas sa Murta
Cabras
S. Salvadore
Stagno di Cabras
Le Baracche
Torre Grande
P.ta Maimoni
T.re del Sevo
Sa Sturaggia
Casa Finanza
S. Giovanni di Sinis
Porto di Oristano
Capo s.Marco

beginners. The water quality is great. The focal point is Capo Manu which can really fire on the inside barrel sections. It's a great peak with a shorter, steep left, which eventually closes out, and a longer, hollow right that's rideable from 3-8ft (1-2.6m). It's a forgiving, easy wave to ride, but the rip gets strong, especially in messy, onshore conditions. There are rocks everywhere plus a few urchins, which can make getting in and out tricky, so have your exit spot sussed out before paddling back to shore. Most surfers prefer Mini Capo, especially when the swell is big and stormy. It's a more lined-up wave, and getting in and out from the sheltered beach is easier. The set-up is similar to Capo Manu, with a left and a right - the right has a good hollow section on take-off, whilst the left is shorter and has some small tube sections. If the Capos aren't breaking, check Sa Mesa Longa as it catches the smaller swells. If it's too small, surf at La Laguna (aka la Spiagga), which is an average beachbreak. Another consistent spot is Su Pallo Su, a decent reef that gives good, hollow waves on small, clean swells when the wind is E-SE. If it's flat around the peninsula, head for San Giovanni di Sinis. To the N of the village is a sandy trail that leads to Funtana Meiga, it's offshore with NW winds and favours rights breaking over a flat reef.

The NW Mistral wind is the most consistent wind in the Med. Cold air coming from N Atlantic storms passing over France gets funnelled down the Rhône Valley and increases in speed as it touches the warmer Med. This creates regular 2-10ft (0.5-3.2m) swells on Sardinia's west coast. Most are short period swells, which can rise dramatically within hours. Most of your time will be spent surfing SW facing spots, which are OK in the predominant NW winds. However winds change direction a lot – N and E winds are plentiful. Stay alert and be prepared to drive to find the best wind and swell conditions. There are virtually no tides in the Med.

Jean Sarthou, Capo Manu

CHRISTOPHE DIMULLE

SURF STATISTICS	J F	M A	M J	J A	S O	N D
dominant swell	SW-NW	SW-NW	W-NW	W-NW	SW-NW	SW-NW
swell size (ft)	3	2-3	2	1	2-3	3
consistency (%)	60	60	30	20	50	70
dominant wind	W-N	W-NW	W-NW	N-E	W-NW	W-N
average force	F5	F4	F4	F3	F3-F4	F4
consistency (%)	59	61	59	51	54	56
water temp (°C/°F)	13/55	14/57	19/66	24/75	22/72	16/61
wetsuit						

Capo Manu

CHRISTOPHE DIMULLE

12. Tel Aviv

BEN RAK

Summary

+ Unusual place to surf
+ Good sandbank jetties
+ Historical sites
+ Top quality hotels
+ Israeli culture

− Inconsistent mushy waves
− Crowded line-ups
− Parking hassles
− Fairly expensive
− Civil unrest

Hilton

The Middle East is the only major part of the mid-latitudes where surfing has never taken off. There is certainly surf in Yemen, Oman and Pakistan with their Indian Ocean coastlines open to S swells but for political reasons they are not classed as surf destinations. Israel, on the eastern Meditteranean coast, may seem an odd place to surf, having never been known for its consistency or quality. It is not the place you'd go on a hard-core surf trip: rideable waves are by no means guaranteed, so a blend of patience and luck is a must. However, in this land where western civilisation began, there is certainly no shortage of cultural

PAUL MAARTENS

Lawson

PAUL MAARTENS

TRAVEL INFORMATION

Local Population:
Tel Aviv – 0.8M
Coastline: 278km (175mi)
Time: GMT+2hr
Contest: National

Getting There – No visa (Israeli stamps are a worry if you intend to visit Arab countries afterwards). It's expensive to fly to Tel Aviv as many airlines avoid it for security reasons. East European companies are cheap, but the national airline El Al is the cheapest when it comes to paying for surfboards.

Getting Around – Bus is the best way, since parking and heavy traffic are problems if you use your own transport. To reach Jerusalem by bus takes 45min. Egged, the national bus company, is the 2nd largest in the world. Rental cars cost $30/d. Be sure to arrive at the beach early if you want to find a parking spot.

Lodging and Food – Tel Aviv is costly so if you can't afford the perfectly located Hilton

($200/dble), then reckon on $50-60/dble for a guest house close to Hayarkon's Street (Seaside and Gordon Inn). Eating falafel (chickpea sandwiches) will save you money on food.

Weather – Israel is typically a moderate Mediterranean climate with two extreme seasons. Spring and Autumn would be the nicest time to visit, except that swell expectation is even lower at that time. Winter (Nov-March) can get pretty cold, with temperatures as low as 5°-10°C (41°-50°F) in the morning, but T-shirts are OK on sunny afternoons. It can snow in Jerusalem. Winter rainfall can be quite heavy, but falls on a small number of days, particularly through Dec-Jan. Summers are hot and dry, especially when Sharav desert winds spread a suffocating heat across the country. Overall, Tel Aviv is very sunny, allowing people use solar heating for domestic hot water. For about 2-3 months of the winter, you will need a fullsuit as the water drops to 18°C (64°F), but the summer is perfect for boardshorts.

Nature and Culture – Expect a swarming beach city. Visit Jerusalem, the old walled City which is home to the Dome of the Rock, Western Wall, and the Church of the Holy Sepulchre amongst many other amazing things. There will be plenty of flat days to swim in the Dead Sea or to drive 5 hours to Eilat on the Red Sea.

Hazards and Hassles – Most waveriders are kids on bodyboards, who crowd out the spots after 2pm. Wake up early, especially if you need to park, avoid the beginners' surfboards, and mind the jetties for a worry-free trip. Trouble in the form of terrorist attacks are random in their choice of location, but tend to be concentrated to the Gaza Strip, the West Bank, Jerusalem and along the Lebanese border.

Handy Hints – Since the Paskotwitz/Kancepolsky dynasty launched surfing in the 50's, the surf industry has boomed. Board makers include Ultra-Wave (Herzliah), Inter Surf (Bat Yam), and Woody's on Hayarkon's St. Jewish surfers like harmony and the crowded line-ups are aggression free.

WEATHER STATISTICS	J/F	M/A	M/J	J/A	S/O	N/D
total rainfall (mm)	142	33	2	0	14	140
consistency (days/mth)	9	6	1	0	2	8
min temp (°C/°F)	9/48	12/54	18/64	24/75	21/70	14/57
max temp (°C/°F)	19/66	24/75	28/82	31/88	31/88	23/74

PAUL MAARTENS

diversions to while away the time during flat spells. It's the feeling of surfing somewhere very different that is the reward.

The best wave is located in the centre of Tel Aviv, directly in front of the Hilton, the most prestigious hotel in the city. When it's small, an A-frame peak breaks over a jagged reef between T-shaped jetties, laid parallel to the coast around Tel Aviv. The lefts are longer and more hollow although they can be affected by a powerful backwash. On big days it breaks outside the jetties and the inside becomes mushy. The rocks on the inside can make getting in and out tricky and it gets very crowded with beginners, but a general laid-back attitude means line-up hassles are rare. To the north is the reef at Topsy where fat, mushy sections suit longboarders and are less crowded. Further north is Hazuk Beach, where sloppy little close-outs break during summer at the base of some cliffs, which provide no shelter from the sideshore NW winds. The fact that you pay an entrance fee means crowds are small.

South of the Hilton, in the Mahim district, is a beach next to the old Dolphinarium. The beach itself is nothing special, except that it curves a little bit NE, which is helpful for NW swells or SW winds. Parking here is easy, which is unusual for Tel Aviv! The last beach is Hof Maravi, next to Old Jaffa which offers spectacular views of the old city. Surf beside the jetty poles, but not after heavy rains, due to serious pollution problems. In Bat Yam, have a look at Al Gal and Hagolshim beaches. NW facing Bat Galim in Haifa produces Israel's cleanest waves during SW storms.

Mediterranean waves are almost exclusively generated by localised wind swell. Dominant winds are NW with a more N direction in summer and SW-W in winter. Gusty summer winds will create 1-2ft (0.3-0.6m) chop while the best and most consistent waves are a result of winter SW-W winds. Swells only last a day at a time and lack power and order. There are no sets to speak of, just typical short spaced waves. Winter has some consistency with about 2 rideable days a week in the 1-5ft (0.3-1.6m) range. Although rare, ground swells still develop with nearly 2000km (1250mi) of sea between the east coast of Tunisia and Israel. Lows originating from the North Atlantic storms cross into the Med producing 3-8ft (1-2.6m) W groundswells for Israel. There are virtually no tides in the Med.

SURF STATISTICS	J F	M A	M J	J A	S O	N D
dominant swell	W-NW	W-NW	NW-N	NW-N	NW-N	W-NW
swell size (ft)	2-3	2	0-1	1-2	0-1	2
consistency (%)	50	40	10	30	10	60
dominant wind	SW-NW	W-N	W-N	W-NW	NW-NE	W-N
average force	F4	F3/F4	F3	F3	F3	F3
consistency (%)	55	58	76	77	62	48
water temp (°C/°F)	18/64	19/66	23/74	27/81	25/77	21/70
wetsuit						

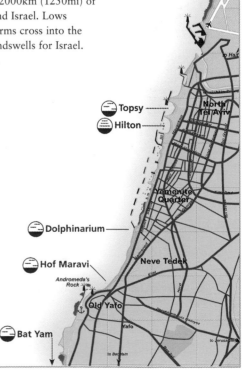

● Hazuk Beach

● Topsy
● Hilton

North Tel Aviv

Yemenite Quarter

● Dolphinarium

● Hof Maravi

Neve Tedek

Andromeda's Rock

Old Yafo

Yafo

● Bat Yam

PAUL MAARTENS

13. São Miguel

Ribeira Grande

ALEX WILLIAMS

Summary
+ VERY CONSISTENT SWELLS
+ UNCROWDED QUALITY WAVES
+ GOOD POINTBREAKS
+ NEARBY ISLANDS FOR FURTHER EXPLORATION

– CONSTANTLY CHANGING CONDITIONS
– SCARY REEFBREAKS
– COOL, WET CLIMATE
– HARD ACCESS TO MANY SPOTS

Populo

PETE ADAMS

When compared to the Indian and Pacific Oceans, the Atlantic contains very few islands. The Mid-Atlantic ridge, an underwater volcanic mountain chain, runs the entire length of the Atlantic Ocean, but only breaks the surface in a few places. The nine islands of the Azores sit 1300km (800mi) west of Lisbon and actually include Portugal's highest peak on the island of Pico. Although they should be easy to spot, sailors referred to The Azores as 'the Disappearing Isles' because of the huge swells that would obscure them from view. It is this kind of reputation that is attracting the seasoned surf traveller to these virgin, wave-drenched shores. These islands are split into 3 groups: occidental (Corvo, Flores), central (Faial, Pico, Terceira, São Jorge, Graciosa) and oriental (Sta Maria, São Miguel) São Miguel is the most populated and most visited island with the only N-facing

ALEX WILLIAMS

beachbreaks in the chain. Surfing was introduced to the islands by Marines from the US army base in Faial in the 60's, however the local waveriding population is still small. As São Miguel is open to most swells and wind patterns, there is almost always a spot that will be working. Being volcanic, the island has steep cliffs which plunge straight into the sea and stretches of coast have the wrong topography for surfing. The 1km (0.6 mi) steep black beach at Ribeira Grande has consistent,

TRAVEL INFORMATION

Local Population:
San Miguel – 130,000
Coastline: 165km (100mi)
Time: GMT-1hr
Contest: local

Getting There – Visa: See Portugal (zones 8-10). Ponta Delgada is the main entry point. Most flights arrive from Lisbon with TAP or SATA ($200rtn). There are also flights from Frankfurt, Boston and San Francisco. Boards free on Portuguese airlines.

Getting Around – Unless you stay in Ribeira Grande and only ride beach peaks, then you really need a car. Basic rental is $220/w. Ferries between islands can be can be cancelled due to rough seas. Inter-island flights don't always have room for boards, expect to pay about $150rtn.

WEATHER STATISTICS	J/F	M/A	M/J	J/A	S/O	N/D
total rainfall (mm)	110	85	50	27	95	110
consistency (days/mth)	14	12	8	6	11	14
min temp (°C/°F)	11/52	11/52	14/57	17/62	16/61	13/55
max temp (°C/°F)	17/62	18/64	21/70	26/79	23/74	19/66

Lodging and Food – The Azores are not a budget destination, Ponta Delgada is the main city and has plenty of hotels ranging from 4-star ($150/dble) to 2-star ($40/dble).) In Rabo de Peixe, there's the Quinta das Areias hotel ($36/dble) or the Residencial Ribeira Grande ($20/dble). Expect to pay about $15 for a meal.

Weather – The Azores high is a bit of a misnomer, as the weather here is anything but settled and stable. It is more accurate to refer to a warm season and a cool season because lows sweep over the Azores constantly - almost every day sees some rain. Summer is mainly sunny and warm, winter is usually cool, windy and wet. Autumn, is the best time with ample swell and reasonable weather. Water temperatures don't drop below 16°C (60°F). You'll need a light fullsuit for most of the year and a springsuit for July-Aug.

Nature and Culture – Most tourists come to trek around the Sete Cidades Caldeira, (volcanic lake), and bathe in the Furnas hot springs, watch whales and enjoy the architecture of the old towns. Ponta Delgada is a laid-back city. Don't expect great nightlife.

Hazards and Hassles – Most reefs are sharp with uneven lava bottoms. Your main concern is going to be timing your trip to correspond with good weather and clean swell. Most of the local surfers are bodyboarders and don't bother getting up for the early.

Handy Hints – Bring at least two boards, including a semi-gun. Local surf shops sell little but wax and leashes. Terceira and São Jorge have good exposed NE shores, which hide some decent waves on bigger swells. Be cool to the locals – they might share their secrets with you.

powerful beachbreak waves where the locals from Ponta Delgada usually surf. There is also a fickle right facing the swimming pool but the set-up is not very stable. When it's small there's a wedgy left at Areias in Ribeira Pequena. The best break around used to be Rabo de Peixe but a harbour development has destroyed this once super hollow, spitting peak. While the offending jetty has created a good left, the quality doesn't match that of the lost wave. East of Ribeira Grande is a long left pointbreak (Sta Iria) that requires a one hour hike but it's seldom surfed despite the quality of the wave. The next spot east is even harder to reach, but worth it, as the left at Baixa de Viola gets good. Four rivers drain out here making the sea bottom much flatter than many other spots on the island. The north coast conceals some other spots, but you'll have to find a track through the fields and explore! On the NW side of the island, at Mosteiros, is a swimming pool with waves breaking along the pool's outer edge, which must be clean to be any good. The south coast needs strong W swells or late summer S swells to provide any decent waves. In Ponta Delgada, Populo is the most famous beach, where hollow peaks, that favour rights, will be as busy as the Azores ever gets. If you head off east you'll pass by some lovely scenery on the way to Ribeira Quente's lefts but the uneven lava rocks may look a bit heavy for most people. As with all the islands in the chain, there is a limited number of surf spots and access is tricky, due to the steep landscape. With few quality beachbreaks, the prevailing reefs are, without exception, shallow and dangerous. Some of the pointbreaks unload in deeper water but snapped boards and kissing the reef are regular occurrences.

PETE ADAMS

Rabo de Peixe

Being located right in the middle of the Atlantic, the Azores are pounded by heaps of lows, bringing with them regular swell. Being so close to the weather systems can mean short duration, disorganised swells, plus the rain that accompanies the fronts. In the wintertime, fishermen turn to farming because the sea becomes too unpredictable. During the summer, lows take a higher track across the Atlantic, meaning better weather and more organised but weaker swells. Winter gets many 4-15ft (1.3-5m) swells from the nearby lows which deepen as they travel towards Europe. The best situation is when the lows sit off Nova Scotia to the north-west. Spring and autumn are the best bet to get medium-sized, clean swells. Conditions change very quickly - stay alert and be prepared to switch to different sides of the island. Wind direction varies greatly, but strong SW is the dominant direction. Winds blow more from the S-SW in winter and N-NW in summer. Tides don't change much, 5ft (1.6m) max.

Jose Gregorio, Ribeira Grande

PETE ADAMS

SURF STATISTICS	J F M	A M J	J A S	O N D		
dominant swell	NW-N	NW-N	NW-N	NW-N	NW-N	NW-N
swell size (ft)	6	5-6	4-5	3	5	6
consistency (%)	70	60	60	50	70	60
dominant wind	S-NW	S-NW	SW-N	W-NE	SW-N	S-NW
average force	F5	F5	F4	F3	F4	F4
consistency (%)	65	63	61	59	56	53
water temp (°C/°F)	16/61	17/62	18/64	22/72	22/72	19/66
wetsuit						

14. Madeira

Punta Pequena and Paul do Mar

PAUL KENNEDY

Summary

+ BIG WAVE SPOTS
+ SPECTACULAR MOUNTAIN SCENERY
+ NO CROWDS
+ SAFE AND QUIET ISLAND VIBE
+ IDYLLIC CLIMATE

− INCONSISTENT
− FEW BEACHES AND SURF SPOTS
− DANGEROUS ENTRY AND EXIT
  POINTS TO THE SURF
− RELATIVELY PRICEY

JOÃO VALENTE

Sitting all alone in the Atlantic, around 550km (345mi) west of the Moroccan city of Casablanca, Madeira stands defiantly in the way of any swell coming out of the North Atlantic. Madeira is the dividing line between the desert islands of the Canaries and the wet Azores. It is an extremely picturesque island, rising sheer out of the ocean, and generations of hard work have moulded its steep cliffs into an amazing system of fertile terraces full of flowering trees. This Portuguese administered island is gaining in popularity with tourists, although there is only one beach on the island, Caniçal, which is only about 20m (70ft) wide. Most of the coastline is made up of plunging cliffs, lava rocks and boulders which don't favour breaking waves until the swell gets big enough to break clear of the rocks. If the swell is less than 4-6ft (1.3-2m), then there is nowhere on the island to surf, but once the surf picks up, it will hold as big as the Atlantic can

Miguel Fortes, Paul do Mar

JOÃO VALENTE

throw at it. It is this ability that has put Madeira firmly on the map as Europe's foremost big wave arena.

Only Faja da Areia on the north coast could be called a small wave spot; it's a left and right peak that breaks best at mid-tide and is powerful but lacks shape. Most of the north coast spots are lefts peeling in close to the shore. To the east is Ponta Delgada which is a shifty, fat wave

TRAVEL INFORMATION

Local Population:
Madeira – 300,000
Coastline: 141km (88mi)
Time: GMT
Contests: Nat (Nov) and
various big wave events

Getting There – As a part of metropolitan Portugal, the same visa rules apply. Madeira used to be expensive and exclusive, but recent years have seen cheaper accommodation and flights. Planes arrive on a runway that overhangs the ocean! Fly TAP via Lisbon, (no board charge) or a charter from London.

Getting Around – Two daily buses from Funchal to Jardim do Mar (4h away), will put you within walking distance of the 3 most famous waves. A basic rental car costs $220/w, bring your own board racks. Travelling from one coast to the other takes at least an hour along a violent, twisting road. A tunnel is being built to link

Paul do Mar and Jardim do Mar, making it a 5min drive instead of a 40min one!

Lodging and Food – Cheap rooms ($15/dble) can be rented in Jardim do Mar from local people who will catch you as you arrive in the town. The main hotel (Estalagem) in town has rooms starting from $40/dble. A good meal costs about $15. Don't miss the Espatada, swordfish, vinho verde and of course Madeira wine.

Weather – Madeira enjoys a subtropical climate but there are some significant differences between the two coasts. While the south gets plenty of sunshine (310 days a year), the north is often veiled in mist and drizzle so you will often need warm, waterproof clothing in the winter, whilst you can get away with a T-shirt year round on the south coast. In the water you will need a light, short arm wetsuit in the winter and a shorty or just boardies in the summer.

Nature and Culture – A peaceful and beautiful island. Hiking trails wind through the terraces, water channels and awesome waterfalls on the north coast. Check the cliffs at Cabo Girao, sunrise at Pico Ruivo, Cangal's whale museum and the toboggan-taxi ride from Monte.

Hazards and Hassles – Getting in and out of the water is a nightmare, as you have to wade in over slippery and sharp boulders whilst avoiding getting slammed by the waves. Bring boots, be patient and remain calm. There are no beaches, exhausting winding roads and frequent landslides. Unless you are ready to tackle some very big waves there is no point in coming here.

Handy Hints – Madeira has only recently been revealed to the surf world, there are only a handful of locals and they are all super cool, give them respect! There is no surf gear available on the island so bring everything you need.

WEATHER STATISTICS	J/F	M/A	M/J	J/A	S/O	N/D
total rainfall (mm)	82	58	12	2	55	95
consistency (days/mth)	6	5	2	1	5	7
min temp (°C/°F)	13/55	13/55	16/61	19/66	18/64	15/59
max temp (°C/°F)	18/64	19/66	21/70	25/77	24/751	21/70

Ponta Pequena

Jardim do Mar

breaking off a headland, which can hold swells of 15ft (5m). The north-east part of the island is rarely surfed due to difficult access and frequent onshores, but Faial and Porto da Cruz may be worth checking out from one of the scenic miradouros (viewpoints). From São Vicente, most people head west to the good left pointbreaks of Contreira (facing a restaurant sign) and Ribeira da Janela. To get them classic, you need a windless day and a clean, moderate sized swell. Although Porto Moniz has a left, it's not reliable, but the spectacular view is. The south coast, and its three fantastic big wave rights, is best accessed by going via Rabaçal. Paul do Mar is hidden behind a huge concrete sea wall that protects the fishing village from a fast, hollow righthand pointbreak. It's a consistent and very challenging wave that breaks quite close to shore. A walk of 15mins to the east will bring you to Ponta Pequena; a more consistent and hollower wave than the other rights which will probably be better on the medium sized days. The main reason people come to Madeira is to surf Jardim do Mar, a serious, world class, big wave spot, which is a 30mins walk to the east of Ponta Pequena. It can hold huge rights and is obviously a dangerous spot. These long workable walls have tube sections for the brave, while most mere mortals are happy to take the survival line. Being caught inside by big sneaker sets at Jardim do Mar is a punishing experience. Another form of punishment is trying to get in and out of the water by clambering over sharp boulders between sets! On the road to Funchal you will pass Ponta do Sol, where there is another Hawai'ian style big wave right. If everywhere is flat, check Machico, where local SE winds can bring mellow onshore waves. It's nothing like Jardim do Mar, but can be a safe and easy option if you're not up to the big stuff!

As with most of the European Atlantic coastline, Madeira is exposed to the NW swells. The SW facing coastline is best on a WNW swell and the standard NE trade winds. Big swells are quite common between Oct-April but Nov-Feb is the heart of the season and is the most consistent time to go. Expect the swells to rise and fall very quickly and be prepared for frequent surprise sets. If you want to be on the best waves then you have to keep a constant eye on the swell on both coasts. Trades are not as strong as in the nearby Canaries; the predominant direction is from the NE for 21% of the time in Jan and 49% of the time in Aug. If a cold front passes by close to the island then the wind will go NW for a time. The best season for offshore E winds and heavy swell action is Nov-Feb. The north coast is onshore much more frequently than the south coast. Tidal range is up to 8ft (2.6m); tide tables are available from Funchal harbour.

SURF STATISTICS	J F	M A	M J	J A	S O	N D
dominant swell	W-N	W-N	N	N	W-N	W-N
swell size (ft)	5-6	5	4	1-2	4-5	5-6
consistency (%)	60	50	30	20	50	40
dominant wind	N-E	NW-NE	NW-NE	N-NE	N-NE	N-E
average force	F4	F4	F4	F4	F4	F4
consistency (%)	50	62	76	77	52	56
water temp (°C/°F)	16/61	17/62	19/66	22/72	21/70	19/66
wetsuit						

Contreira

15. Lanzarote

Morro Negro

CEDRIC BARROS

Summary
+ POWERFUL WAVES
+ LOTS OF SPOTS
+ DRY CLIMATE
+ DRAMATIC SCENERY

− SHARP, SHALLOW LAVA REEFS
− WINDY CONDITIONS
− FIERCE LOCALISM
− THEFTS AND CAR CRIME

The Canary Islands' reputation for being the Hawai'i of the Atlantic is well earned, as these volcanic islands have much in common with their Pacific cousins. NE trade winds fanning heavy reef waves, breaking close to shore in clear blue water, full of fierce locals and under a burning hot sun seems a fair description of both surf zones. The truth is there are many differences, like the climate and water temperature, but when it comes to the waves, the Canaries certainly have powerful, challenging surf reminiscent of the Pacific's surfing Mecca. In terms of wave quality, Lanzarote is the island to head to where the heart of the surf scene is the area between Famara and La Santa.

Famara is a huge arc of sand sitting below spectacular sheer cliffs. You'll find quality sandbar waves that change in height

CEDERIC BARROS

El Quemao

ALEX WILLIAMS

depending on swell direction and which part of the almost 90° curve you surf. This flexibility makes it popular with surf schools and windsurfers. Further north, a ferry from Orzola sails to the island of Graciosa where some heavy reefbreaks litter the circumference of this small desolate island. There are no hotels or private cars and camping conditions are tough on the barren, rocky ground, but it

TRAVEL INFORMATION

Local Population
Lanzarote – 60,000
Coastline: 156km (98mi)
Time: GMT+1hr
Contest: EPSA (Oct)

Getting There – Visa: same as Spain (see 6.Bizkaia). Winter charter flights from most European cities can be very cheap. Spain's Iberia airline is criminal for board taxes. If you are flying to the Canaries from another continent then it is better to fly to Madrid, London or Paris first, and get a connecting flight from there.

Getting Around – Rental cars are the cheapest on earth! (±$110/w). An Opel Corsa will take you everywhere, although the dirt tracks may see it suffering some abuse! Roll-on, roll-off car ferries to/from Spain and the other Canary Islands operate on a regular basis.

Lodging and Food – Most visitors come on package holidays, with accommodation included in the price. This is definitely the cheapest way to do it, but most of the resorts are on the sheltered south-east facing coast. For a surfer-run guesthouse in La Santa village try Pablo Postigo's house or otherwise Pedro Urrestarazu in Caleta. There is also Calimasurf at Famara which can be a good place to go if you are a beginner. Expect to pay around $200/w for accommodation and $10 for a basic meal.

Weather – Being close to the Sahara Desert, (170km/100mi west), Lanzarote enjoys a semi-arid, hot desert climate, that hardly ever sees rain. Its bizarre moon-like landscape has been declared a biosphere reserve by UNESCO. It gets very hot in the summer and sometimes in the autumn, when E winds (Sirocco) blow off the desert. During the winter the same wind can cause wind chill. The cold Canaries Current means that winter seasons will require a 3/2 fullsuit most of the time.

Nature and Culture – Lanzarote is low lying compared to the other Canarian islands; it has a multitude of smooth volcanic cones and large, dramatic, black lava plains. Don't miss the Timanfaya National Park or the lava tubes around Jameos del Agua. The nightlife is hectic around Puerto del Carmen on the east side of the island, as package holidaymakers crowd out the bars and clubs.

Hassles and Hazards – There have been reports of some ugly rip-offs and violence towards travelling surfers. Hardcore locals usually control the big name line-ups, but if you avoid these spots then you shouldn't have much trouble. Beware of the powerful waves, currents, hitting the reef and urchins.

Handy Hints – There are surf shops, but it's better to bring your own gear, strong longer boards, reef boots and a light fullsuit. Lanzarote is a popular winter escape for Europeans in search of sun and parties, but outside the resorts the pace of life slows right down.

WEATHER STATISTICS	J/F	M/A	M/J	J/A	S/O	N/D
total rainfall (mm)	37	22	3	0	18	55
consistency (days/mth)	5	3	1	0	2	6
min temp (°C/°F)	14/57	15/59	18/64	21/70	20/68	16/61
max temp (°C/°F)	21/70	23/74	25/77	29/84	27/81	23/74

Ghost Town

can have some classic days, Punta de Mujeres being the most consistent. With a straight W or SW swell, try El Golfo on the west coast for uncrowded reefs or Playa de Janubio's black sand, beachbreak. Once you've exhausted Lanzarote then there's still the rest of the archipelago to explore!

ROGER SHARP

remains a sanctuary for hardcore surf-trippers. Before making the long hike to Graciosa, check it out with a pair of binoculars from the top of the spectacular mountains on the north of Lanzarote. On a high tide with a N swell, you might surf at the scenic beachbreak Playa de la Canteria before catching the ferry.

Heading west from Famara is San Juan, a picture perfect left and shorter right which has protection from SW/W winds that may blow out the spots around La Santa. If the swell is northerly, try the shallow lefts at Caleta de Cabello which break at high tide or the peaks at Ghost Town. Between here and La Santa is Boca del Abajo, a classic point type left breaking into a small bay on the north side of 'La Isleta' (the headland at La Santa). Deeper water and easy entry/exit points make this a stress free, enjoyable wave to surf, even in large swells. On the south-west point of La Isleta is Morro Negro, a world class right, with long, lined-up walls, a few hollow sections, and a more playful inside. It holds really big surf as well as big crowds and can dish out long hold-downs after the long paddle-outs against the current pushing down the point. Across the channel is La Santa Left (aka The Slab), a fearsome, sucky peak that usually favours lefts. Super consistent once the tide has covered the reef, this is one of the most localised spots, and they may just ask you (politely) to surf elsewhere. The most respected break in La Santa is El Quemao, a short, sucky left that holds 12-15ft (4-5m) offering heavy, humbling barrels and fully deserves its reputation as the 'Pipeline' of the Canaries. It needs some west in the swell and a SE wind but is usually blown out by the dominant NE trades.

If the swell is huge and blown-out on the north and west coasts then head over to the east coast where the swell will be smaller, but cleaner. Jameos del Agua has some classic lefts in front of a car park and it's a popular summertime break. Towards Arrieta are a set of fickle reefbreaks which

With its ideal exposure to N-NW swells, Lanzarote has the most consistent waves in the Canaries. Oct to March sees some major swell activity in the N Atlantic with deep lows sending 4-15ft (1.3-5m) swells onto the exposed reefs. Whilst most swells come from lows heading across the N Atlantic, hurricanes off the east coast of America can send some long distance W swells. Rare S swells can also materialise from lows coming off the west African mainland. Wind strength and direction will govern where you surf more than anything else does. The best conditions occur in late autumn/early winter (Nov-Jan), when the NE trades are at their lightest and have a more ENE aspect. Winds tend to get stronger and more northerly towards the end of winter. In summer the surf is small and erratic. The tidal range (up to 6ft (2m)) is also an important consideration, as most spots are very shallow.

DAN HAYLOCK

Jameos del Agua

CEDRIC BARROS

Tom Curren, San Juan

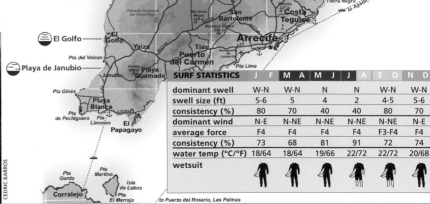

SURF STATISTICS	J F	M A	M J	J A	S O	N D
dominant swell	W-N	W-N	N	N	W-N	W-N
swell size (ft)	5-6	5	4	2	4-5	5-6
consistency (%)	80	70	40	40	80	70
dominant wind	N-E	N-NE	N-NE	N-NE	N-NE	N-E
average force	F4	F4	F4	F4	F3-F4	F4
consistency (%)	73	68	81	91	72	74
water temp (°C/°F)	18/64	18/64	19/66	22/72	22/72	20/68
wetsuit						

FUTURE PROOF SIGNATURE SERIES / **PARKO**

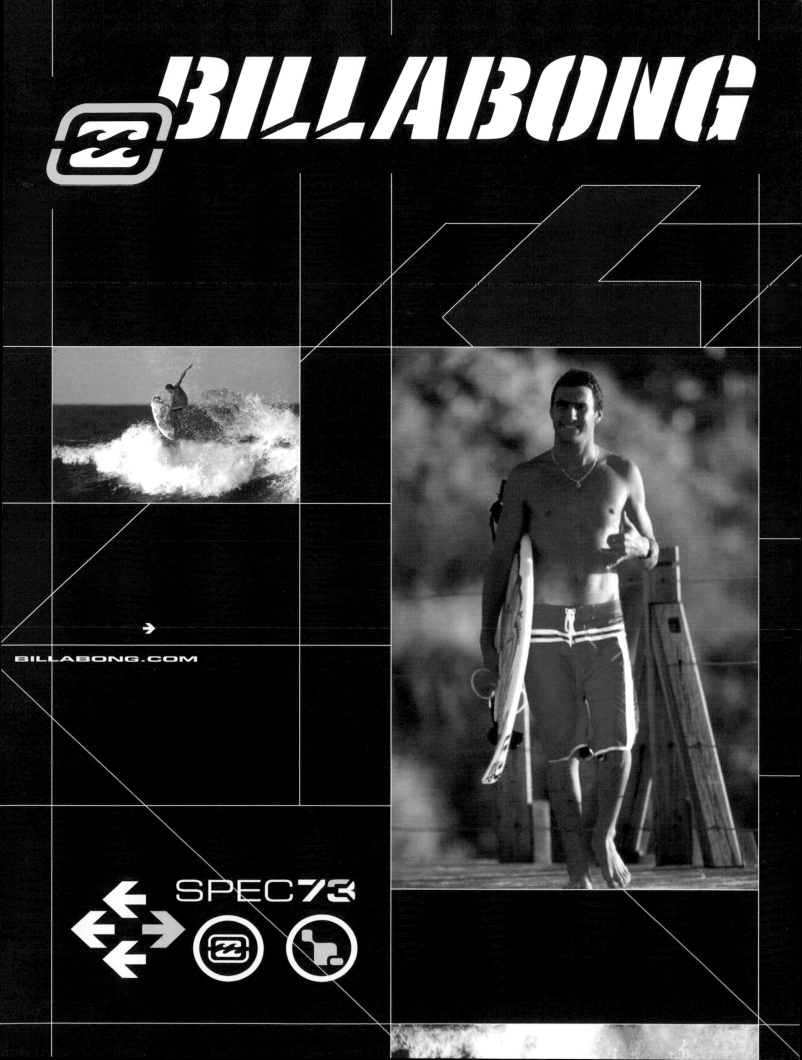

BILLABONG

BILLABONG.COM

SPEC73

Jeffrey's Bay

Africa

Meteorology and Oceanography

Africa's surf zones are far more reliant on the influence of the Atlantic than the Indian Ocean. The north and west African Coast from Morocco to Senegal, receive exactly the same North Atlantic swells that provide Europe's surf. The best location for swell producing low pressures is between Nova Scotia and Iceland especially if they drift south, closer to the Azores. North Africa has an ideal north-west orientation and Morocco in particular picks up plenty of winter swell. The 'Harmattan' NE trade winds blow parallel to the coast, favouring the abundant rights that pepper the coast in Morocco, the Canary Islands and all the way down to Senegal. May-November brings more N winds, which are bad for Morocco and the Canaries but fine for the S-SW facing breaks of Cape Verde and Senegal. These strong summer N-NE winds can whip up surprisingly large wind swell for the east coasts of the Canary Islands but are obviously accompanied by onshore winds, making them very popular with windsurfers. This northern coastline is scoured by the Canaries Current, a consistently cool offshoot from the main North Atlantic, clockwise circulating, surface current which starts its trans-Atlantic journey in the Gulf Stream off Florida, on the same latitude, but loses 8°C (14°F) on the way. This part of west Africa is the only true area of upwelling in the North Atlantic, fitting the global trend of being adjacent to a desert with strong offshore trade winds.

Cape Verde can receive remnants of the strongest South Atlantic swells and some of the backend hurricane swells travelling west to the Caribbean. This is also true of the West African countries south of Senegal's Almadies Peninsular. It is the swell from the constantly raging storms that track between Cape Horn and the Cape of Good Hope that provides the surf for the rest of the African coastline. The South Atlantic doesn't have the contrast in sea and air temps to get a storm spinning enough to become a hurricane, and therefore lacks tropical storm activity. This makes the south and west facing shores of equatorial Africa a little unexciting compared to other areas near the equator. When long range winter S swells do arrive, between April and September, they usually coincide with the SW monsoon bringing light onshores and an intense rainy season to the Gulf of Guinea. These swells are generally small, but very clean and organised, providing fun peeling waves in the Ivory Coast and Ghana. The same N winds blow straight offshore from Dec-April, shaping perfect, small beachbreaks. The water temperatures are no surprise – radiating warmth from the Guinea Current, which flows down to the Benguela Current off Angola.

In Namibia the water temperature drops severely because of the Benguela Current, but the surf gets bigger and more consistent. Often shrouded in dense sea mist and sometimes plagued by SW onshores, Namibia nevertheless holds the promise of challenging waves in a challenging environment. Once again, the cross/offshore winds and large coastal desert combine to provide the world's biggest area of upwelling.

As the name suggests, you can't get closer to the Southern Ocean storms than South Africa. The lows give consistent SW swells combined with SW winds but anything can happen when they pass over the land. Winters get cold and windy but the long coastline conceals plenty of classic surf tucked away in bays, including the planet's best right pointbreak. As the lows march eastwards, the swell and wind directions change, but the SW winter and SE summer pattern is fairly reliable. Benguela's icy grip is loosened across the south coast as the warm Agulhas Current heralds the arrival of the Indian Ocean. Cyclone swell is always a possibility on the east coast, but forecasting one is impossible.

For such a huge continent, there is surprisingly little variation in the tides. Morocco experiences the greatest range in height, but moving south it evens out to a micro-tidal size. The whole continent has a semi-diurnal even tide.

Temperatures, Winds and Currents

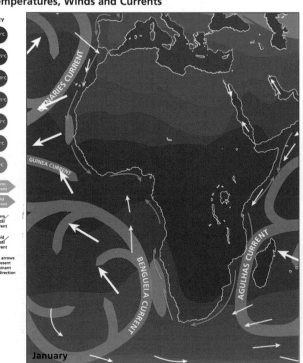

January

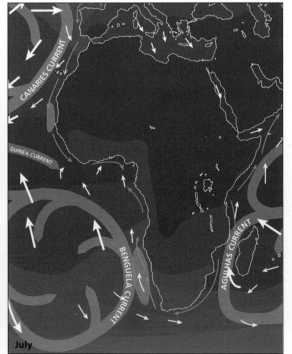

July

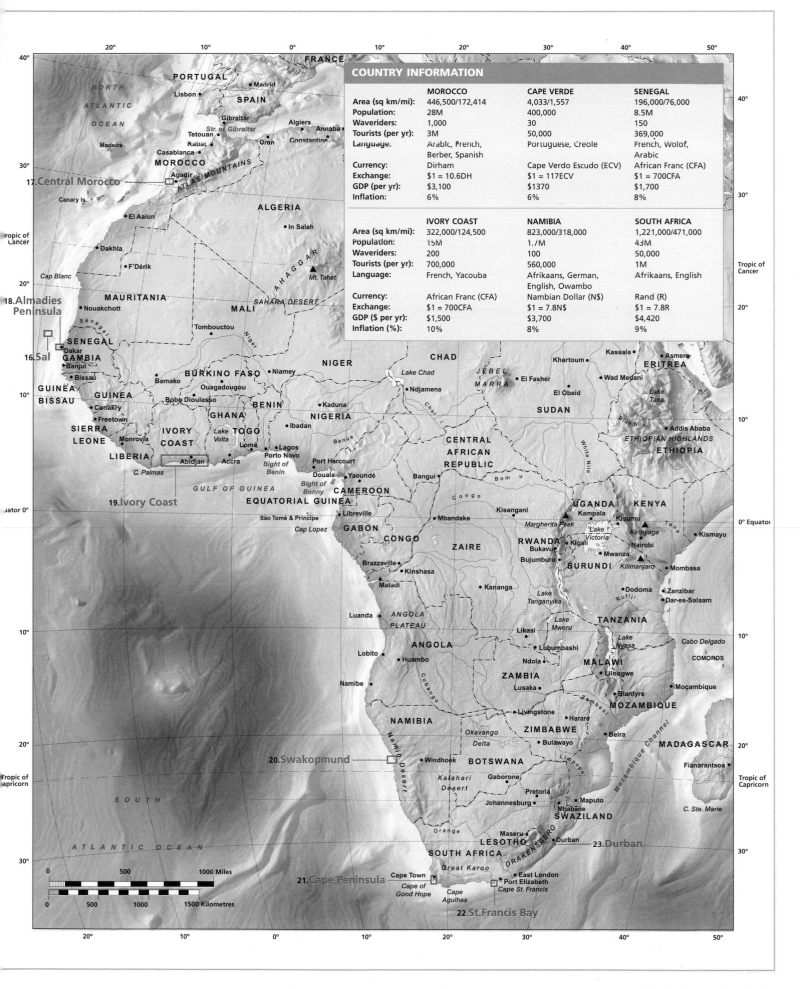

COUNTRY INFORMATION

	MOROCCO	CAPE VERDE	SENEGAL
Area (sq km/mi):	446,500/172,414	4,033/1,557	196,000/76,000
Population:	28M	400,000	8.5M
Waveriders:	1,000	30	150
Tourists (per yr):	3M	50,000	369,000
Language:	Arabic, French, Berber, Spanish	Portuguese, Creole	French, Wolof, Arabic
Currency:	Dirham	Cape Verdo Escudo (ECV)	African Franc (CFA)
Exchange:	$1 = 10.6DH	$1 = 117ECV	$1 = 700CFA
GDP (per yr):	$3,100	$1370	$1,700
Inflation:	6%	6%	8%

	IVORY COAST	NAMIBIA	SOUTH AFRICA
Area (sq km/mi):	322,000/124,500	823,000/318,000	1,221,000/471,000
Population:	15M	1.7M	43M
Waveriders:	200	100	50,000
Tourists (per yr):	700,000	560,000	1M
Language:	French, Yacouba	Afrikaans, German, English, Owambo	Afrikaans, English
Currency:	African Franc (CFA)	Nambian Dollar (N$)	Rand (R)
Exchange:	$1 = 700CFA	$1 = 7.8N$	$1 = 7.8R
GDP ($ per yr):	$1,500	$3,700	$4,420
Inflation (%):	10%	8%	9%

17. Central Morocco
18. Almadies Peninsula
16. Sal
19. Ivory Coast
20. Swakopmund
21. Cape Peninsula
22. St.Francis Bay
23. Durban

CAPE VERDE

SENEGAL

16. Sal

Summary

+ No crowds
+ Shapely reef waves
+ Further exploration possibilities
+ Windsurfing heaven
+ Guaranteed sunshine

− Inconsistent swells
− Open to the wind
− Flat desert landscape
− Fairly expensive

Punta Preta

ALL PHOTOS BY YEP

Cape Verde is the southernmost island group in the boomerang shaped archipelago of Macaronesia. Made up of 10 major islands, Cape Verde was used as a stopping off point for the slave ships heading over to the Americas and descendants of these slaves have mixed with the Portuguese settlers. Previously known as Lhana, Sal is the flattest island and the main tourist entry point because it is home to the world's longest airstrip (4.2km/2.6mi), which is enough tarmac for the Space Shuttle to land on!

Soultripping Expeditions

The surf potential was first discovered in the late 80's, by windsurfers in Santa Maria on Sal. With dominant NE trades and consistent NW swells, the west facing lava reefs hold swells up to 8ft (2.6m).

Apart from Ponta Preta, most spots are fickle, short, hollow reefs. Santa Maria is an 8km (5mi) sandy beach on the southern tip of Sal that catches the all too rare SW swells and summer NE swells. Mainly mellow, small

TRAVEL INFORMATION

Local Population
Sal – 11,000
Coastline: 87km (55mi)
GMT: -1hr
Contest: local

Getting There – All visitors need a visa, and only some nationalities can buy one on arrival. Check with the Cape Verde Embassy first! Major airlines fly from European cities (Lisbon offers the most regular and cheapest flights). You can also fly from Johannesburg, Recife and Boston. Air tickets to Cape Verde are usually expensive.

Getting Around – It's a small island and everything lies within walking distance. You should hire the services of Soultripping (Jérôme Boggio Pasqua) to get to spots on Palmeira. Car rentals (Santana 4WD) are very expensive ($60/d); a quadbike is a good alternative, ($12/d) or a bike. Inter-island flights are with ATR. Boards over 7ft long don't always get on board, so ferries are the alternative.

Lodging and Food – There's a wide variety of international hotels (Morabeza and Belo Horizonte are the best) charging $40/dble/p. Cheap "pensãoes" (Alternativa) start at $18/dble/p. The cheapest meal you will find is cachupa, at about $3, western orientated food costs more like $15 a meal.

Weather – Being the closest islands (620km/387mi) to Africa, Sal and Boa Vista are flat and extremely dry islands due to the strong tradewinds blowing off the desert. This has made the land lightly vegetated, except in the semi-dry riverbeds. Much of the year is reasonably warm (25°C/77°F), although when the dust-loaded E winds (Sirocco) blow from the Sahara, they bring intense heat. July to September is the so-called 'wet' season; at this time it's very warm (30°C/86°F) and humid and you may encounter the occasional SW gale and rain on the coast but it's rare. The cold Canary Current requires a springsuit in the winter to counter the wind chill factor.

Nature and Culture – Most visitors only stay a week in the three windsurfing centres. The diving is some of the best in the West Africa area, such as the Buracona Hole. Visit the former salt fields of Pedra Lume. The villages on Sal are quiet, but there are a couple of discos at the weekend in the main town.

Hazards and Hassles – Sharp lava rocks and urchins are a common danger. Most visiting surfers are actually windsurfers, while the locals tend to ride bodyboards and some have reached a high standard. There's little localism to worry about but show respect. The flying windsurfers at Punta Preta can be dangerous. On dry land there is little to worry about, except the sun's intensity.

Handy Hints – There are no surf shops and the only boards you can rent are windsurf boards. Waves don't get big and heavy enough to need a gun, although the wind can keep you trapped in the lip of the wave, so a slightly bigger board may be useful.

WEATHER STATISTICS	J/F	M/A	M/J	J/A	S/O	N/D
total rainfall (mm)	3	0	0	10	30	16
consistency (days/mth)	2	0	0	2	3	2
min temp (°C/°F)	19/66	19/66	20/68	22/72	23/74	21/70
max temp (°C/°F)	23/74	24/75	25/77	27/81	26/79	25/77

Punta Palmeira

Cape Verde is the only archipelago in the Atlantic that catches due S and N swells. The positioning of the islands means they interfere with each other for any given swell direction, and only the biggest ground swells will travel this far. This means that Cape Verde is a relatively inconsistent island destination. Sal is blocked by Boa Vista island from the S-SE swells, and is only able to pick up NW swells and the NE wind swells. The best swell generators are the lows that come off Nova Scotia and track over the Azores, between November and February. Early season is the better time as there are more E winds blowing offshore. NE winds blowing from the Sahara Desert are the standard, year round trades. The later in the winter you visit, the more N-NE winds you can expect, which are inconvenient for most surf spots. During the summer, you may encounter a rare SW gale. NE trades can create mushy wind swell

beachbreaks, there is also one of the few lefts breaking on a reef close to a hotel. It's used as an indicator to the west coast swell size. Towards the west is Ponta do Sino, a mixture of sand and reef that's usually bigger than Santa Maria but often blown-out. The best wave, 30 minutes walk from Santa Maria, is Ponta Preta, which has long rights peeling over black boulders. It's best with a decent NW swell, low tide and when the usual sideshore wind is light. The point picks up any good swell and breaks quite a distance away from the rocks, although the end of the ride suffers from backwash. There's also an awesome left, but it's exposed to the wind and breaks hard onto rocks: experts only. Rife is a wavesailing spot that offers poor surfing conditions. Monte Leão can produce perfect, long rights and has the advantage of being quite sheltered from the wind, although it needs a big NW swell or a moderate W-SW to begin breaking. The most consistent section, even when small, is right below the Sleeping Lion Mountain. Alibaba, on the other side is usually bigger but frequently blown-out. Curral Joul is supposedly a wave-magnet breaking offshore but it rarely does its thing and getting in and out is a nightmare. Fontana is a pretty place, located in a small bay that produces a mysto right when the swell is big. The best small swell option is probably Palmeira; a left where a clear channel makes its way to a small hollow peak, usually there's only time for one manoeuvre before it closes out on the rocks. If you're lucky, and the persistent NE trade winds stop blowing, then the regulation 1-5ft (0.3-1.6m) NE wind swell might clean up, meaning a check for rare long lefts at the far end of Santa Maria or Fragata beaches. There may be some good discoveries on the east coast in such conditions, but it's sharky. Don't forget about the other islands!

on the east coast, which can get up to a decent size. Tidal ranges are minimal (<3ft/<1m), but they still effect the shallow reefs, causing most waves to break too close to the rocks at high tide.

SURF STATISTICS	J F	M A	M J	J A	S O	N D
dominant swell	W-NE	W-NE	S-SW	S-SW	W-NE	W-NE
swell size (ft)	4	3	2	0-1	2-3	4
consistency (%)	50	40	20	10	40	50
dominant wind	NE	NE	N-NE	N-NE	N-NE	NE
average force	F4	F4	F4	F4	F4	F4
consistency (%)	65	61	94	79	82	67
water temp (°C/°F)	21/70	21/70	24/75	26/79	27/81	25/77
wetsuit						

Neighbouring island jewel

17. Central Morocco

MOROCCO

Anchor Point

ALEX WILLIAMS

Summary
+ SWELL CONSISTENCY
+ LOTS OF UNCROWDED SPOTS
+ LONG RIGHTHANDERS
+ ISLAMIC CULTURE

− FREQUENTLY MESSY LINE-UPS
− THIEVES AND TOUTS
− NORTH WINDS

MARC FENIES

Boilers

MARC FENIES

Despite its North African location, Morocco is very much a part of the European surf trail. Located between 20° and 35° latitude with a NW facing coastline, Morocco has all the key elements for an outstanding surf destination. The Taghazoute area in the south nestles behind a big cape, which funnels the predominant north winds into an offshore direction. The spots are all easily accessible by road with the waves generally breaking right over flat rock and sand. With balmy winter land temperatures, cheap living and a fascinating cultural diversity, Morocco is a must for the European surf traveller.

The most northerly spot of this zone, is the scenic beach of Immesouane where mellow rights are protected from the wind. Tamri is a wind exposed rivermouth/beachbreak picking up plenty of swell on small days. On the southern tip of Cape Ghir is another small swell option called Boilers. This right sucks off a submerged ship boiler and rattles off fast, very close to the urchin infested rocks. The wind can be

TRAVEL INFORMATION

Local Population:
Agadir – 850,000
Coastline: 3,446km
(2,150mi)
Time: GMT
Contest: local

Getting There – 90 day tourist visas are issued on arrival. Taghazoute is 30km (20mi) from Agadir airport, $13 by taxi. Ferries from Algeciras (Spain) to Ceuta or Tangiers. The national airline is Royal Air Maroc.

Getting Around – The driving is best described as interesting! Be prepared for erratic local drivers, French/Arabic road signs, unmarked junctions, narrow, unsurfaced roads, few street lights and random police check points. Morocco is heaven for free camping in vans and motorhomes, which is the best way to see and surf this vast country. Fuel is slightly more expensive in Morocco than Spain at around $0.85/l. A basic hire car costs $190/wk.

Lodging and Food – Big resorts are to be found in Agadir. Clean, deluxe bungalows close to Anchor Point ($40/dble) or at the

Auberge Imourane Surf School in Tamghart (B&B ±$500/w). Houses can be rented cheaply in Taghazoute ($10/dble) or basic cell-like rooms (from $2/dble). The food is excellent, like seafood and vegetable tagines. Alcohol is only available at tourist locations, but sweet mint tea is everywhere. A good meal shouldn't cost more than $8.

Weather – Morocco's central surf zone is a semi-tropical venue. The winter climate gives warm days, chilly nights and some rainfall. In Agadir, you may see 40mm of rain a month in mid-winter, making the rivermouth breaks very dirty. Summer gets extremely hot with virtually no rain. With minimum water temps at 16°C (60°F), a 2mm short-sleeve fullsuit is ideal or a spring suit either side of winter.

Nature and Culture – Morocco is a sensory feast full of amazing natural and cultural beauty. Unforgettable sights close to Agadir include the edge of the incomparable Sahara Desert, best seen around the small Oasis of Tata or to the east of Goulmine. Check the snow capped mountains of the High Atlas (ski resorts), or the Anti Atlas around Tafaroute. A

trip around the ancient medina city of Marrakesh, with its colourful souks, is a must.

Hazards and Hassles – In the water the only dangers to worry about are urchins and rocks. On land, guard your possessions; there are a lot of thieves around. Smoking hash is illegal, and police regularly check tourist's luggage or cars for it and dish out heavy fines and stiff prison sentences. Huge black scorpions live under stones and bits of wood. Touts and scamming opportunists are everywhere; beware the carpet shop scam! On the whole Moroccan people are very friendly.

Handy Hints – Respect the Muslim culture, which is tolerant and far from Islamic fundamentalism. Women should avoid wearing skimpy clothing in the old medina cities and small traditional villages. The month long Ramadan festival can see a lot of shops closed and a reduced public transport service. Only use your right hand to eat. Surf gear is available in Casablanca, Rabat and there are small shops in Taghazoute. There are also rental boards at Tamghart.

WEATHER STATISTICS	J/F	M/A	M/J	J/A	S/O	N/D
total rainfall (mm)	40	20	3	1	13	35
consistency (days/mth)	5	4	2	1	2	5
min temp (°C/°F)	9/48	11/52	15/59	18/64	16/61	10/50
max temp (°C/°F)	21/70	22/72	24/75	27/81	26/79	21/70

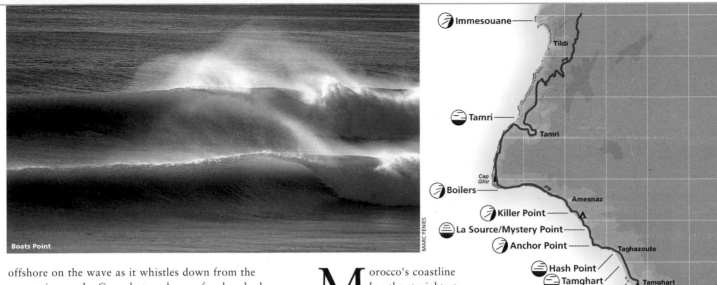

Boats Point

MARC FENIES

(Map labels)
- Immesouane
- Tildi
- Tamri
- Tamri
- Cap Ghir
- Boilers
- Amesnaz
- Killer Point
- La Source/Mystery Point
- Anchor Point
- Taghazoute
- Hash Point
- Tamghart
- Tamghart
- Devil's Rock
- Banana Beach
- Agadir
- Agadir
- Inezgane
- Sidi Tonar
- Boats Point
- Tifnite
- Inchaden
- Douirane
- Ifriane

offshore on the wave as it whistles down from the mountains on the Cape, but onshore a few hundred meters out to sea! There are some well protected reefs and a few marginal beachbreaks on the drive south to Killer Point, named after the Killer Whales sometimes seen here. It's a long righthand point that holds surf up to 15ft (5m) but be careful of the rocks and caves in front of the take-off zone. A freshwater spring in the rocks marks La Source, a good left and right, which shuts down when the swell picks up. Mysteries is a fickle, high tide righthander which relies on the sand combining with the reef. Next is Anchor Point, a world famous right pointbreak, which holds massive swell and can break for up to 1km (0.6mi), all the way to the town of Taghazoute (spelt Tarhazoute at one end of town). Anchor's needs a sizeable swell to produce long sectiony lines, with occasional barrels. In Taghazoute, there's a reef and sand point, Hash Point, which is very protected from the swell. On the nearby Tamghart beach, you will find fun waves, more suited to beginners. Banana Beach is much the same, but picks up more swell. Next to this is Devil's Rock, another good wave breaking both left and right that offers steep barrelling sections on the right day.

Don't expect to get much surf in Agadir itself. For a change of scenery, drive down to Tifnite, less than an hour south of Agadir, where Boats Point offers really good uncrowded waves. To the south unfolds the vast Sahara Desert, which in Moroccan/Western Sahara territory stretches 2000km (1250mi) down the coast to Mauritania. To surf down here requires serious planning and a 4WD equipped to cope with the harshest of environments... however, you could well be rewarded by some epic, totally virgin spots.

Morocco's coastline has the straightest swell exposure in the North Atlantic. The NW exposed beachbreaks can suffer from a swell excess, but that's when the pointbreaks

SURF STATISTICS	J F	M A	M J J	A S	O N	D
dominant swell	NW-N	NW-N	NW-N	NW-N	NW-N	NW-N
swell size (ft)	5	4-5	3-4	1-2	4	5
consistency (%)	80	60	30	30	60	70
dominant wind	N-NE	NW-NE	NW-NE	E-SW	NW-NE	N-NE
average force	F3	F3	F3	F3	F3	F3
consistency (%)	35	56	70	82	63	36
water temp (°C/°F)	16/61	17/62	19/66	22/72	21/70	18/64
wetsuit						

and sheltered spots are surfed. In winter, tradewinds from the NE will make light to moderate cross-shores at most spots, whilst SW facing spots like Taghazoute will be offshore. Mid-April is the start of the strong NW 'Chergui', a wind that blows-out most spots until mid-September. During this period, straight N winds blow for 40% of the time, with the relative lack of swell, this is the worst period to surf in Morocco. However, if you're into wave sailing, check out Essaouira. Tides vary from 2-6ft (0.6-2m).

Immesouane

MARC FENIES

Boilers

18. Almadies Peninsula

N'gor Rights

Summary
+ SPOT QUALITY AND QUANTITY
+ EASY ACCESS
+ NO CROWDS
+ BUDGET TRIP
+ AFRICAN LIFESTYLE

– URCHINS
– ONSHORE WIND ON EXPOSED SHORE
– LOCAL HUSTLERS
– QUITE INCONSISTENT

Most surfers who visit Senegal head straight to the prime surf area on the Almadies Peninsula, just outside Dakar. This westernmost tip of Africa juts out into the ocean and the peninsula has one of the largest swell windows in the world. Swells can appear from the SE all the way around to the N, which is about 260°! Another great thing about this zone is that most of the spots lie within easy walking distance of each other.

N'gor beach is always flat as it's sheltered by an island, but there is great surf peeling off both ends of the island.

The righthander here is the most consistent reefbreak around, and was one of the destinations in "Endless Summer". The light blue line-up is easily accessed by jumping out of the dug-out canoes that regularly cross the half-mile channel. Anytime the cross-shore

Pilule, Ouakam

NE trade winds blow, head to the south side of the peninsula but only if the swell is above 4-6ft (1.3-2m) at N'gor Island. It's a short ten to fifteen minute walk or a cheap taxi ride from N'gor village to the SW facing reefs. Around here, out of the wind, you'll find clean, offshore conditions, as the swells will have wrapped 180° around Almadies Point. The amazing contrast from the blown-

TRAVEL INFORMATION

Local Population:
Dakar – 1M
Coastline: 700km (440mi)
Time: GMT-1hr
Contest: Local bodyboard

Getting There – No visas are needed for stays of fewer than 90 days. Yoff airport is 5mins from N'gor and there are many charter flights from Paris. Driving from Morocco is a hardcore adventure requiring thorough planning and at least 10 days of desert driving, plus an army escort through the war zone north of Mauritania. Fly!

Getting Around – Most of the spots are within walking distance or a short taxi ride. For a trip to Dakar, take a Cars Rapides (15c) or a taxi ($4). Renting a car from private owners costs ±$30/d and much more from an official rental car company.

Lodging and Food – N'gor Island is quiet, (Carla's is a good place to stay), but being stuck there can be a hassle. N'gor offers everything from basic rooms ($15/dble) to the Club Med and other deluxe hotels. The best deals are the Warung surf camp or Brazzérade. Local food is cheap and monotonous.

Weather – Senegal marks the border between the Sahara Desert and tropical West Africa, which begins in Casamance to the south of Dakar. It's dry most of the time, except from July to September. The water temp drops below 18°C (65°F) in the heart of the winter, thanks to the cold Canary Current passing along the edge of this coastline. Combined with the wind chill, an occasional 2mm fullsuit may be needed in the winter and a springsuit throughout the rest of the year. The 'Harmattan' wind brings a choking dust from the Sahara.

Nature and Culture – Dakar is a big city with markets, shops and nightlife. Take the boat ride

to the former slave island of Goré, nowadays a beautiful spot with only an old fort to remind you of its dark past. The surfers hangout is "The Spot", below the Diarama hotel.

Hazards and Hassles – With only about 150 local waveriders it's rare to find more than 15 people at any spot. Sharks are rumoured to patrol the coastline, but fish are plentiful so you are unlikely to re-enter the food chain! Your main enemies are the sea urchins. Malaria and Yellow Fever are not major threats in the N'gor area, but precautions should be taken anyway. Your biggest hassle will be street hustlers, eager to sell you things.

Handy Hints – Senegal is a very French destination. It's easy to phone and fax from télécentres. The Tribal Surf Shop at 'Le Virage' has a good range of SAF boards and various bodyboards. They also have a good board repair service. Locals use the south end of N'gor beach as a toilet.

WEATHER STATISTICS	J/F	M/A	M/J	J/A	S/O	N/D
total rainfall (mm)	1	0	5	135	105	2
consistency (days/mth)	1	0	1	10	7	1
min temp (°C/°F)	17/62	18/64	21/70	24/75	24/75	22/72
max temp (°C/°F)	25/77	24/75	28/82	30/86	30/86	26/79

Ouakam

PHILIPPE CHVODIAN

A lthough N'gor's latitude is low (14°), which usually means inconsistent surf, it still receives frequent swell, mostly from the N/NW in the 2-10ft (0.6-3.3m) range. The best low pressures are those that develop between Nova Scotia and Iceland. The waves can be powerful, reaching 8-10ft (2.6-3.2m), so a semi-gun will help. From Aug to Oct, Senegal also receives 3-6ft (1-2m) S/SW swells, courtesy of the hurricanes that are born off the coast of west Africa.

out, north side of the peninsula to the straight offshore south side, is aided by the seemingly much lighter winds. From Club Med to Vivier, the reefs produce quality rights and lefts that are generally short on length, but not on power. These spots require careful judgement because any wipeout gives you a fair chance of hitting the bottom, which is covered in zillions of urchins. Just south of Les Mamelles lighthouse, Ouakam stands out as Senegal's world class spot. The wave breaks only about 20-30 times a year, but when it does, make sure you are on it as the left and right peak guarantees a barrel either way. The wave is fast, crisp and relatively easy to get into, but unforgiving down the line and even just a few people can create crowd pressures on the tight take-off zone. Towards Dakar, more spots are to be found on the Corniche Ouest. These reefs have excellent shape and break consistently, yet people rarely surf these spots due to heavy pollution from the city, carrying rumours of disease and sharks. If there's not enough swell to wrap around the Almadies Cape then there are spots to the north of N'gor. Between N'gor and Yoff Island are a couple of reef and sand points which are rarely surfed, apart from Le Virage. The last option is Yoff beachbreak, which consistently picks up most swells and is a mellow, less challenging wave.

There is also a narrow window for long distance southern hemisphere swells to sneak in some 1-4ft (0.3-1.3m) waves. The 'Harmattan' (N-NE) trade winds blow from Nov to April becoming more NW from March to June. Sometimes the wind starts blowing before dawn and then calms down around noon. The short wet season typically has W-SW winds. Tidal range is never over 6ft (2m) but it can affect shallow spots.

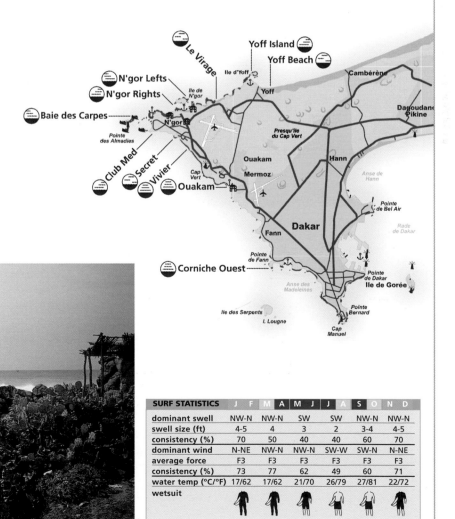

Secret Spot

YEP

SURF STATISTICS	J F	M A M J	J A	S O	N D	
dominant swell	NW-N	NW-N	SW	SW	NW-N	NW-N
swell size (ft)	4-5	4	3	2	3-4	4-5
consistency (%)	70	50	40	40	60	70
dominant wind	N-NE	NW-N	NW-N	SW-W	SW-N	N-NE
average force	F3	F3	F3	F3	F3	F3
consistency (%)	73	77	62	49	60	71
water temp (°C/°F)	17/62	17/62	21/70	26/79	27/81	22/72
wetsuit						

19. Ivory Coast

Grand Drewin
MARC FENIES

SENEGAL
GUINEA BISSAU
GUINEA
SIERRA LEONE
LIBERIA
IVORY COAST

Summary

+ EMPTY LINE-UPS
+ AFRICAN LIFESTYLE
+ COOL BEACHBREAKS, EASY POINTS
+ LIGHT WIND PATTERNS
+ JUNGLE SCENERY AND ANIMALS

– INCONSISTENT SWELL
– LACK OF BIG WAVES
– MALARIA AND HYGIENE THREATS
– FAIRLY EXPENSIVE
– CIVIL UNREST

Located on the Gulf of Guinea, the Ivory Coast (Côte d'Ivoire) contains 515km (320mi) of exposed, southerly facing shoreline. This equatorial country picks up the South Atlantic swells, which break on a variety of beaches and reefs, backed by swaying coconut trees and endless lagoons.

Going from east to west, the first spot is Assinie, close to the Ghanaian border. It's the most popular surf destination in the country with easy beachbreak conditions and a French run surf camp. The wave at Assinie breaks fast and hollow and always picks up any available swell, until it closes out over 5ft (1.6m). Winter conditions are usually 1-2ft (0.3-0.6m) and clean, which makes it an ideal place to learn to surf. Assinie

MARC FENIES

Francis Vilasco
MARC FENIES

beachbreak peels off quickly and needs the regular offshores to stop it being a straight-hander. When the swell gets over 4-6ft (1.3-2m), and Assinie is maxed out, then it's necessary to head west, towards the pointbreaks. From Assinie westward to Mafia, there's a 20km (12.5mi)

TRAVEL INFORMATION

Local Population:
Abidjan – 2,500,000
Coastline: 515km (320mi)
Time: GMT
Contest: local

Getting There – Like most African countries you need a visa before departure (±$35). There are lots of charter flights from Paris and scheduled flights from most European capitals and New York. It takes 2 hours by taxi to get to Assinie from Abidjan, about 100km (60mi) away.

Getting Around – Assinie beachbreak is right in front of the surf camp. You can arrange a trip to the rivermouth breaks towards Ghana by motorised dugout from the surf camp. When there's a bigger swell, surf camp operators can take you to the rights west of Abidjan. The road network is one of the best in Africa. It will take 4-5h to reach Niega.

Lodging and Food – In Assinie you can rent a hut for $4/dble but it's rough. You can also

book into the nearby Club Med hotel but it's not cheap. Assinie surf camp bungalows are traditionally styled and well equipped. They're also close to the beach to catch the cooling sea breezes and avoid the worst of the mosquitoes. It costs $35/dble/fullboard. Local food is cheap.

Weather – The climate is hot and humid and rain is the keyword for the weather. There is a short rainy season corresponding with the SW monsoon during Oct-Nov and again from mid-May to July. From Dec to mid-April and Aug to Sept, it's usually dry. Highest temps are around 35°-37°C (95°-99°F), occurring from March to June and with humidity levels at 100%, it can become a little unbearable. The coolest months are Aug, Sept and Jan. The water temp never drops below 23°C (74°F) and often hits 28°C (82°F). Wetsuits are not necessary, but a rash vest is needed for sun protection.

Nature and Culture – This is a totally rural, African beachlife trip with little to do at night. When it's flat, Abidjan (2 hours away) is the

best city trip to take. Jungle trips involve money and at least 2-3 days. Canoe trips around the lagoon, 10 minutes away from Assinie, will reveal crocodiles, birds and other exotic fauna.

Hazards and Hassles – You need to have yellow fever injections and anti-malaria medication is a must. Line-ups are always empty because spots are plentiful, except on weekends when expatriates from Abidjan hit the surf. Locals hardly ever surf as most West Africans have a healthy distrust for the ocean and can't swim. Beware of the sun as it burns, even when overcast. Beaches are supposedly full of stingrays and small sharks, especially at rivermouths but they pose little threat.

Handy Hints – The Ivory Coast, or is a very French destination. There are 2 surf shops in Abidjan. The surf camp manager is a shaper who fixes and rents boards (±$14/d). The heat sometimes gets unbearable so it's best to get a room with A/C unless you're staying right on the beach.

WEATHER STATISTICS	J/F	M/A	M/J	J/A	S/O	N/D
total rainfall (mm)	33	145	487	117	140	150
consistency (days/mth)	4	8	18	8	10	10
min temp (°C/°F)	23/74	24/75	24/75	23/74	23/74	23/74
max temp (°C/°F)	32/92	32/92	30/90	28/82	28/82	31/88

November to April is the best time to catch the clean beachbreaks like Assinie, which only work on small ground or wind swells anyway. The pointbreaks work more frequently in the northern hemisphere summertime, because the groundswell is coming from the southern hemisphere wintertime. These swells, born in the Roaring Forties have to travel 10,000km (6,250mi) and consequently, a lot of decay takes place. Whilst they can be well lined-up, the swells never exceed 8ft (2.6m) and the typical range is from 3-6ft (1-2m). The best swell season is April to September but it is also the rainy season when malaria is an issue. The Harmattan is a cool and dry N wind that blows offshore from December to May (10-20%), although around lunch time a gentle onshore sea breeze picks up and ruins the waves. From June to September, the SW monsoon blows a mild onshore most of the time, but on the whole, wind strengths are fairly light. At this equatorial latitude, tidal ranges are very low at about 3ft (1m) max, and only affect some shallow spots.

stretch of empty beachbreaks. Further west, is the beach town of Grand Bassam, whose heavy shorebreak waves are hardly ever worth surfing, but nearby La Passe has some magic days. There is a deep water trench just offshore from Abidjan, which creates a long close out wave with horrendous rips for about 10km (6mi) either side of the capital and is referred to locally as 'La Barre'. The beaches on either side of this trench have a more gently sloping bottom and don't suffer from the rip as much. West of Abidjan is Grand-Lahou, a tourist zone with a 'passe' where a sandbank holds a decent right and a left, best on an incoming tide. Next is Dagbego, in front of the 'Hotel Best of Africa'(sic), where there is a very nice beach with a right breaking from the tip of a rocky point. It needs a big swell to give long, workable walls, which won't be hollow. Sassandra main beach is dirty but the rights off the pink granite reef can produce rides of up to 100m. There are some other good right pointbreaks around that are worth searching for. The coast from San Pedro to Tabou consists of rocky headlands and small beaches such as Grand Drewin, where a fat righthander breaks in a small cove facing a fishing village. There's also a shipwreck break nearby but this area swarms with mosquitoes during the rainy months. Victory Beach and Monogaga are two mellow waves ideal for longboarders. San Pedro is a black lava reef where waves break in crystalline waters surrounded by lush jungle. It also has a consistent low tide shorebreak. From here towards the Liberian border access becomes difficult and the surf spots are located in very remote areas.

SURF STATISTICS	J F	M A	M J	J A	S O	N D
dominant swell	S	S-SW	S-SW	S-SW	S	S
swell size (ft)	2	2-3	3-4	4	3	2-3
consistency (%)	60	60	70	50	60	60
dominant wind	S-W	S-W	S-W	S-W	S-W	S-W
average force	F2	F3	F3	F3	F3	F3
consistency (%)	65	73	75	82	74	72
water temp (°C/°F)	27/81	28/82	27/81	25/77	24/75	26/79
wetsuit						

MARC FENIES

Assinie

STEPHANE MIRA

20. Swakopmund

ANGOLA
NAMIBIA
SOUTH AFRICA

Cape Cross
ROD BRABY

Summary
+ Uncrowded, consistent swells
+ Amazing scenery and wildlife
+ Undiscovered possibilities

− Cold water
− Extreme temperatures
− Onshore winds
− Constant fog
− Difficult access

Namibia is not your standard surf trip destination. A harsh environment, heavy waves and the cold Benguela Current makes it a place suitable only for the most hardcore of riders. It's an 1800km (1125mi) drive from Cape Town to Swakopmund, the best place to start your trip.

The main surf spot is a powerful reefbreak called Guns which is about 20km (12.5mi) to the south of Swakopmund, back towards Walvisbaai. Look for the Dolphin Park Chalets. You can't miss it. This left pointbreak produces classic long walls on a moderate W or a big SW swell. It's best from low to mid tide and can hold surf of up to 10-12ft (3.3-4m). A few hundred metres south is another reefbreak called

ROD BRABY

ROD BRABY

Mussels, which only works in the biggest of swells. The next spot, Last Toilet is found about 2km (1.25mi) beyond the railway restaurant on the Langstrand section. It's a small wave spot, working at low tide. There's also a sectiony left reef called Paradise that winds off a rocky point in a bay, a few km's south of Swakopmund. On the

TRAVEL INFORMATION

Local Population
Swakopmund – 25,000
Coastline: 1,250km(780mi)
Time: GMT+2hr
Contests: National

Getting There – Most nationalities don't need a visa, but all need to travel via South Africa. SAA operates daily flights from Johannesburg to Windhoek, with a connection to Swakopmund. The daily Cape Town to Walvisbaai flight is expensive. You can drive from Cape Town along a 1,800km (1,125mi) tarred road or on the alternative gravel track which is spectacular.

Getting Around – Swakopmund is Namibia's top resort town. 4WD rental cars are expensive ($100/d). Unless you drive up from South Africa, your best bet is to surf in town and hire a car to get down to Guns when necessary. It's a good idea to go to the Cape Cross region with a specialist tour agency, like Charlie's Desert Tours.

Lodging and Food – Founded by the Germans in 1892, Swakopmund is a blend of colonial town and modern architecture with a variety of good hotels, pensions and coffee shops selling German cakes and pastries. Budget for between $25-$50 for daily living costs.

Weather – Namibia has a dry climate typical of a semi-desert country - droughts are a regular occurrence. Days are mostly warm to very hot 20°-35°C, (68°F-95°F), while nights are generally cold 0°-10°C (32°F-50°F)). Temps in the interior are lower because of the altitude, while along the coast, the cold Benguela Current reduces rainfall and causes an everlasting fog (340 days per year!). On a few days a month, often in winter, when the Berg wind blows offshore, the temps can soar. Humidity comes more from the fog (50mm/yr) than rain (20mm/yr). You will need a 3/2 fullsuit from Dec-April and a thicker fullsuit from May-Nov.

Nature and Culture – Although Swakopmund offers entertainment like a casino, aquarium

and waterslides, you haven't come all this way to pretend you're at home. Don't miss the Skeleton Coast, which is the oldest desert in the world. Amongst its amazing sand dunes are spooky shipwrecks and unique wildlife. Further afield are a couple of sites that may turn out to be the highlight of your trip, the most renowned being the Etosha National Park and the Kalahari Desert.

Hazards and Hassles – The cold water and numerous seals bring the feared Great White Shark. However, it's actually much safer than people believe. In reality you're more likely to be attacked by a seal during the breeding season (Oct-Nov). There have been two reported bites by seals on surfers. A bigger danger is hitting shallow reefs. Sandstorms can make driving near impossible.

Handy Hints – Bring all the surf equipment you need with you, nothing is available here. There is plenty of scope for exploration; Namibia's best waves may be as yet unridden. Drive on the left.

WEATHER STATISTICS	J/F	M/A	M/J	J/A	S/O	N/D
total rainfall (mm)	3	6	1	1	0	0
consistency (days/mth)	1	2	1	2	1	1
min temp (°C/°F)	15/59	14/57	10/50	8/46	10/50	13/55
max temp (°C/°F)	23/74	23/74	23/74	20/68	19/66	22/72

ROD BRABY

edge of town is Tiger Reef, which breaks in front of a rivermouth. In town is the infamous Lockjoint, found halfway between the Pier and the Mole breakwaters. It's a super hollow reefbreak that unfortunately is very fickle. Beyond the main swimming beach is Thicklip, a bowly left reef, breaking just south of a rock groyne on Strand Street. It works best on a pushing tide with a moderate swell. A few kilometres north is Vineta Point, a small swell left in front of a rock groyne that works best at high tide. The shallow reef gives the wave a bowly take-off. Just to the north, at the end of town, is a reefbreak known as Fiji, which is a much easier wave to surf than the previous spots. It's a long, 130km (80mi) drive along salt roads to the Fur Seal Reserve at Cape Cross where the next decent spots can be found. Portuguese explorer Diego Cão, the first European to reach Namibia, erected a 6ft (2m) high cross here to commemorate his land fall. This is a remote area to surf. The dauntingly named Skeleton Coast starts at the Ugab rivermouth, just 75km (45mi), to the north. There are two long left pointbreaks here, which are offshore in the dominant S wind. Main Break, the furthest out along the point, is the most consistent wave, with long, fun lines. The take-off area is at the end of the wall dividing the main car park from 100,000 seals, which lend a unique aroma to the surf! Further down the point is a fast, rocky, hollow section called Graveyards. The final section is Factory Point, in front of a slaughterhouse. It's not as good as the other two waves and smells worse than the seals! Surfing used to be banned up here and the rule was enforced by an old German man who used to shoot at surfers with a shotgun! Play by the rules and pay the fee

of $1.50 per person and $1.50 per car. The park officials don't like surfers much and if there are any problems they could ban it again at any time. The nearest campsite (which is very basic) is about 40km (25mi) to the south, at the 'mile 72' marker post. There's a small restaurant at the seal factory.

From May to Sept, you can expect consistent 6-10ft (2-3.3m) SW swells. Most spots are fickle reefs, hidden away behind miles of sand dunes. All of the reefs require patience, except for the Cape Cross points which pick up lots of swell and are consistently offshore in the S winds. The dominance of the S winds varies from 56% of the time in Oct to 45% in June, S-SE being the year round prevailing direction. The tidal range can reach 6ft (2m). Try to get a tide table in Swakopmund.

SURF STATISTICS	J F	M A	M J	J A	S O	N D
dominant swell	W-SW	W-SW	W-SW	W-SW	W-SW	W-SW
swell size (ft)	2-3	4	5	5-6	4-5	3
consistency (%)	50	60	70	70	60	60
dominant wind	SE-S	SE-S	SE-S	SE-S	SE-S	SE-S
average force	F4	F4	F4	F4	F4	F4
consistency (%)	75	81	76	73	77	77
water temp (°C/°F)	20/68	18/64	15/59	13/55	14/57	16/61
wetsuit						

Factory Point

CHUCK GRAHAM

NAMIBIA

SOUTH AFRICA

21. Cape Peninsula

Dunes

GARTH ROBINSON

Summary
+ CONSISTENT
+ MULTI-ASPECT SPOTS
+ WIDE SWELL WINDOW
+ RELATIVE LACK OF CROWDS
+ MOUNTAIN AND SEA LANDSCAPES
+ CHEAP URBAN ENTERTAINMENT

− COLD WATER YEAR ROUND
− UNSTABLE WINDY WEATHER
− CITY ENVIRONMENT
− KELP STRESS

The coastline of South Africa is the oldest shoreline on earth, and aeons of erosion have created an underwater topography ideal for creating good waves. This has made South Africa home to some of the best mid-latitude surf you'll find anywhere in the world. The irregular shoreline of the Cape Peninsula, along with its 180° swell window, allows it to offer the best density of varied spots in the whole country.

Justin Strong, Outer Kom

PAUL KENNEDY

Hout Bay

PAUL KENNEDY

Milnerton Lighthouse in the north of this zone is an average beachbreak, whilst nearby The Wedge is the place to go if you fancy polluted barrels. Cape Town itself has several good spots –

Thermopylae is a rarely breaking, long, left point off a sunken ship but it needs a huge swell and pollution is bad. Can be surfed in SW winds. Localised Glen Beach, close to Sea Point, is a good beachbreak favouring rights. Llandudno is much the same and has the advantage of being well sheltered from SE gales, the Gat section here throws out spitting tubes. The Hoek, below spectacular Chapman's Peak Drive, is considered a world class, tubey

TRAVEL INFORMATION

Local Population:
Cape Town – 3M
Coastline: 2,800km
(1,750mi)
Time: GMT+2hr
Contest: National (July)

Getting There – Only Brazilians need visas. South Africa is not an international travel hub so flying there is not very cheap, except from London, which can have some bargain priced tickets. Most of the 50+ airlines fly to Johannesburg. Straight flights to Cape Town are easy to come by but more expensive. South African Airways board tax is $90!

Getting Around – The road network is excellent and a rental car can be a smart move: expect to pay $150/w, gas is cheap (50c/l). Consider buying a car if you spend more than a couple of months travelling around the country. J-Bay is an 8 hour drive. Traffic keeps to the left.

Lodging and Food – There are youth hostels in Camps Bay and Muizenberg. You can stay in backpackers in town for $5 (Cloudbreak Lodge) or in Kommetjie (Fendt Guesthouse or Tabankulu) for $20. Expect to spend $8 for a good meal. Local wine and lobster are both excellent and cheap.

Weather – Weather patterns are very unstable, but rainfall is low. Winters (May-Sept) bring many cold fronts and low pressures over the peninsula. As the coastal lows pass over, wind and clouds move in from the NW, rain starts falling and the ocean gets rough. As the cold front passes over, SE winds blow from False Bay to Table Bay, creating the famous misty tablecloth on Table Mountain. Summers are usually warm and dry, but very windy in the afternoon. Due to the cold Benguela Current, the water hardly ever gets over 15°C (59°F) and sometimes gets colder in summer (down to 9°C/48°F) than in winter on W facing areas.

Nature and Culture – Apart from being a great blend of mountain and sea, the Cape Peninsula offers the ethnic variety of three million diverse people. There are plenty of cultural sites and some great bars and nightclubs, where girls outnumber men seven to one! Take the classic cablecar ride up Table Mountain.

Hazards and Hassles – The shark factor here is not as much of a problem as in other areas of South Africa. The main worry is the thick kelp at some spots and the oceans' power. For such a big city, crowd pressure is low. The city is South Africa's safest, but you still need to be careful.

Handy Hints – Because of the Rand's devaluation, living costs in South Africa are really low, making this well developed country excellent value. Stock up on surf gear here from the numerous well-supplied surf shops.

WEATHER STATISTICS	J/F	M/A	M/J	J/A	S/O	N/D
total rainfall (mm)	10	30	82	77	37	14
consistency (days/mth)	2	4	9	10	11	2
min temp (°C/°F)	16/61	13/55	9/48	7/44	10/50	14/57
max temp (°C/°F)	26/77	24/75	19/66	18/64	20/68	24/75

Misty Cliffs

PAUL KENNEDY

Muizenberg

PAUL KENNEDY

A-frame but you have to be patient and wait for the right conditions: low tide and a medium swell. More consistent is Noordhoek Beach, which holds fun surf of variable quality. About two thirds of the way down Noordhoek Beach is Dunes, which can produce epic barrels, ridden only by those hardcore enough to walk in! On big days, many big wave bomboras start to work on outer reefs, but ask the locals for advice first. One of these spots is Dungeons where the first 'Big Wave Africa' contest was held in June 2000. Close to here is Kommetjie, which is in

Antarctica's S-SW swells are consistent and powerful from March to September, providing lots of 6-10ft (2-3.2m) swells, so there's nearly always a rideable wave somewhere on the peninsula. The first swells in this period (March-April) tend to be the cleanest, before the major winter cold fronts sweep across the peninsula from May to September. Throughout winter are many rainy days accompanied by NW winds and plenty of swell activity, meaning the S-facing spots are the go. The summer starts in October and lasts until March bringing with it the strong SE winds known as 'The Cape Doctor.' On days when a high pressure protects the country, winds and swell diminish, warm 'Berg' winds are offshore and SW-exposed spots will have small and perfect conditions. Tidal range can reach 10ft (3.2m); most surf shops have tide tables.

the heart of the surf action. Long Beach is the first popular spot; it is crowded but produces clean, short lefts, perfect for big moves. The Kom is next along; Inner Kom has fun lefts which break over kelp beds, while Outer Kom offers powerful shifting peaks that can easily catch you in the impact zone. Next is 365's, another bombora, so named because the wedging barrel is so round that it's supposedly more than 360°! Crayfish Factory is a ferocious right and is Cape Town's scariest wave when a huge groundswell hits.... several near-death experiences have occurred here. There are some good spots in the Cape Point Nature Reserve, like the rocky rights of Olifantsbos which attract occasional crowds despite the $1.5 fee. Spots facing E in False Bay need a huge swell to work, check Black Rocks or Kalk Bay, although these are localised spots. A better option may be Muizenberg, which has fun sloppy waves with enough peaks for everyone and is offshore in NW winds.

SURF STATISTICS	J F	M A	M J	J A	S O	N D
dominant swell	SE-SW	SE-SW	SE-W	SE-W	SE-W	SE-SW
swell size (ft)	3	5	6-7	7-8	5-6	3-4
consistency (%)	60	70	90	80	70	70
dominant wind	SE-S	SE-S	SE-NW	SE-NW	SE-SW	SE-S
average force	F4	F4	F4	F4	F4	F4
consistency (%)	61	55	75	78	66	60
water temp (°C/°F)	16/61	16/61	15/59	14/57	15/59	16/61
wetsuit						

Crayfish Factory

PAUL KENNEDY

SOUTH AFRICA

NAMIBIA

22. St. Francis Bay

Summary
+ J-BAY'S WORLD CLASS RIGHTS
+ WORLD CLASS WAVES
+ CONSISTENT SWELLS
+ FREQUENT OFFSHORE WINDS
+ CHEAP
+ SCENERY OF THE DRAKENSBERG MOUNTAINS

− SHARKS
− COOL WATER AND WIND CHILL
− SHARP MUSSEL COVERED ROCKS
− UNCERTAIN SECURITY AND POLITICAL SITUATION

Supers – Jeffrey's Bay

ALL PHOTOS CHRIS VAN LENNEP

Halfway between Durban and Cape Town is South Africa's best and most consistent surf zone. The frequent winter SW swells and the occasional E swells that hit this SE facing coastline, turn on dozens of classic pointbreaks that are hidden away inside crescent shaped coves. Jeffrey's Bay (J-Bay) is obviously the most renowned wave and is considered one of the best righthanders in the world. SW facing spots are exposed to plenty of Roaring Forties swell but are often onshore in the best swell season. Oyster Bay, to the west of J-Bay, is one of these places, only really worth surfing during the predominant summer E winds. The first well-

Tom Curren, Jeffrey's Bay

On the surf rich Garden Route to the west of J-Bay

regarded wave in this zone is Seal Point, but bear in mind that this has been the site of a few shark attacks. You will also find a good beachbreak here. Nearby Shelley Beach also has small, fun waves. Thanks to the Endless Summer films, we all know about the perfect rights of Cape St. Francis (or Bruce's Beauties). The wave, though not as good now as in the past, is still a classic barrelling

TRAVEL INFORMATION

Local Population:
J-Bay – 30,000
Coastline: 2,800km
(1,750 mi)
Time: GMT+2hr
Contests: WCT (July1)

Getting There – Brazilians require visas. Europe has plenty of flights to South Africa, and London in particular can be excellent value. Flights from elsewhere are common but not especially cheap. Most airlines only fly to Johannesburg and a connection to J-Bay's closest airport, Port Elizabeth, is around $180/rtn. Driving from Johannesburg to J-Bay takes 13hrs.

Getting Around – The excellent road network and cheap costs mean that car rentals ($150/w) are an excellent way to get about. Fuel is cheap at 50c/l. Consider buying a car if you going to spend a few months in the country. Drive on

the left and be prepared for the unpredictable whilst driving! Local transport is not advised.

Lodging and Food – During summer all accommodation may be full. In winter the crowds die down and prices drop and beds can be had in surfer's hostels for as little as $2.50/d. Better quality options are the Cape St-Francis Holiday resort, J-Bay Beach Hotel, Rick's Place or the Savoy. A good meal costs $8. The fish is excellent.

Weather – The J-Bay area has an unstable climate but one that is generally dry. Summers are warm and you could even surf in a shorty. For the remainder of the year you will need a good fullsuit. Temps can vary widely from day to day. The hot Berg winds can bring high temps and great weather off the mountains, followed a day later by a cold front coming off the sea, bringing a sudden drop in temperatures.

Nature and Culture – There's very little to do here other than surf. Surfers hangout in the Breakaway Tavern or Ricks, which occasionally have groups playing. The Drakensberg Mountains are a long but worthwhile trip.

Hazards and Hassles – Sharks are everyone's big fear down here. The chances of getting bitten however, are very remote, even though May-June '98 was a bad time. Use common sense and avoid surfing during the sardine runs. During heavy rains and at dawn or dusk are also dangerous times. More realistic threats are the razor sharp mussels that line the rocks where you get in and out of the water, and the crowds that perfect J-Bay attracts.

Handy Hints – With the Rand's devaluation, living costs in South Africa have become very cheap. Surf gear bought from the J-Bay surf shops can be a very good deal.

WEATHER STATISTICS	J/F	M/A	M/J	J/A	S/O	N/D
total rainfall (mm)	35	47	62	57	62	50
consistency (days/mth)	5	6	5	6	8	9
min temp (°C/°F)	16/61	14/57	9/48	7/44	11/52	14/57
max temp (°C/°F)	25/77	24/75	21/70	20/68	21/70	23/74

St. Francis Beach

righthander but one that takes a big E swell to kick it into life. Leftovers is an underrated wave which can offer long rides when the swell comes up from the south. Hullet's Reef in St. Francis Bay is the ideal place for beginners as it has mellow lefts on small swells. The rare but quality left of Clapton's Coils near to the Aston Bay Road is also worth a look. J-Bay is made up of seven different sections, the three really good parts of this world class right being Boneyards, Supertubes and Tubes. When it's really big the different sections connect up giving leg-achingly long rides! These three sections of the wave are always the busiest. If you want a more mellow session then surf Kitchen Windows, Magna Tubes or Albatross. Getting in and out of the water at all these spots can be a painful experience thanks to the razor sharp mussels. Whichever section of the wave you choose to surf you will be rewarded with hollow, fast and long waves. To make any of the barrels involves taking a high and tight line.

Van Staden's Mouth, on the way to Port Elizabeth, is a nice place, but the beachbreak is of poor quality. Sea Vista has an inconsistent left reef that might be the site of your first or last surf in this zone if you are using Port Elizabeth airport as an entry/exit point. Noordhoek is a very consistent wave, although the predominant SW winds are onshore. Summerstrand is a beachbreak, which handles the wind reasonably well. The mushy rights of Millers or the reefbreaks found at The Fence on Cape Recife road near the Humewood suburb are all worth checking out.

Antarctica's Roaring Forties provides plenty of 6-15ft (2-5m) S-SW swell from March to Sept. If you're lucky there will be weeks of back to back swells. Occasionally strong E winds or tropical cyclones occurring from Jan-March can provide short lived E swells. All lows tend to travel past South Africa quickly and can often push strong SW winds in over the bottom half of the country. This makes SE facing spots like J-Bay a much better bet for good wind directions. From Nov to March the wind changes direction and blows primarily from the E, not good for the majority of spots. From April to Oct light NW winds blow straight offshore in the morning, turning SW (cross-shore) in the afternoon. Tidal range can be significant so get a tide table from the J-Bay surf shops.

SURF STATISTICS	J F	M A	M J	J A	S O	N D
dominant swell	E-SW	SE-SW	SE-SW	SE-SW	SE-SW	E-SW
swell size (ft)	2-3	4-5	5	5-6	4-5	3
consistency (%)	50	60	80	70	70	60
dominant wind	E-W	E-W	SW-W	SW-NW	SW-NW	E-W
average force	F4	F4	F4	F4	F4	F4
consistency (%)	88	61	70	73	67	86
water temp (°C/°F)	21/70	19/66	17/62	15/59	16/61	19/66
wetsuit						

Seal Point

23. Durban

SOUTH AFRICA
NAMIBIA

Durban overview

ALL PHOTOS CHRIS VAN LENNEP

Summary
+ CONSISTENT
+ QUALITY BEACHBREAKS
+ URBAN ENTERTAINMENT
+ CHEAP

− LOTS OF ONSHORE DAYS
− CROWDS
− STREET VIOLENCE
− SHARKS AT UNNETTED BEACHES

South Africa is one of the world's best surf destinations with 2,800km (1,900mi) of coastline split between the Atlantic and Indian Oceans. Despite better waves elsewhere in South Africa, Durban has become the country's surf centre because of a high population density of surfers and a great year round climate. South swells wrap around the Bluff Peninsula, and focus on the long piers and groynes that punctuate the coastline. When the conditions are right, then powerful, hollow beachbreaks are the result. There are a few reefs to consider including the world class tubes of Cave Rock. Most Natal spots are best on low to mid tides with light offshore winds, which unfortunately, are rare. Many foreign surfers coming to South Africa have sharks at the top of their mind, however Durban has not had a single attack since shark nets were put in place in 1962.

The waves in Durban get crowded but drive a mere 15

Bay of Plenty

mins out of town and empty peaks start appearing. Umhlanga Rocks resort to the north is one such example where several good peaks have the advantage of being netted against sharks. Cabana Beach is a surf focal point with some good reefs.

After you've crossed the Umgeni rivermouth you'll find African Beach in front of the Golf Course and if the wind

Riverside
Umgeni River
Umgeni road
Morningside
African Beach
Overport
Greyville
Snake Park
Bay of Plenty
North Beach
Dairy Beach
The Wedge
Addington
Vetch's Reef
The Point
Cave Rock
Natal Bay
Congella
The Bluff
Island view
Kings view
Anstey's
Wentworth
Brighton Beach

Clinton 'Gigs Cellier', Vetch's Reef

is calm, there can be a good shorebreak. Onwards there is a long stretch of semi-crowded breaks before you get to Snake Park where the locals live up to the name of their spot! The popular city beaches of the Bay of Plenty are home to South Africa's most intense surf scene. Consistent and hollow waves break on both S and E swells, typically breaking about 100m offshore between several rock jetties. Surfboards are prohibited in the patrolled swimming zones from 9am to 5pm, so areas like North Beach are only surfed by bodyboarders. The designated surfing area is Dairy Beach, which can be surfed any time of day. The Wedge is a quality wave, breaking down the side of a damaged pier just south of the Bay of Plenty spots. Towards Addington, the waves have less power and size making it a good place to go during heavy S swells. Next to the Natal Bay harbour entrance is Vetch's Reef, a rare right pointbreak over a shallow reef. The south side of this harbour, in a well to do neighbourhood, Anstey's gets good lefts and rights breaking a long way offshore, which really fire on a small E swell. When the swell gets overhead, Cave Rock is the place to be when world class, Hawai'ian style, righthand barrels, explode across the shallow reef. These gaping, spitting tubes are suitable for experienced surfers only, and there is never any shortage of them in the line-up. Your final option is Brighton Beach, a swell magnet that has good waves but is easily blown out.

The Wedge

Between April and Sept, swells arrive with regularity, from the lows in the Roaring Forties zone. These low pressure systems move in an easterly direction, away from the Natal coastline - this means less swell exposure than the Cape Provinces. The lows have to travel pretty close to the coastline and this happens enough in winter (May-Oct) to provide regular 3-10ft (1-3m) S-SE swells on the Durban beaches. In summer (Nov-April) flat spells are common and long, although high pressure generated NE winds can produce head high, choppy, onshore waves. Occasional 4-8ft (1-2.5m) E swells come from tropical cyclones between Jan-March but don't rely on them. The coast to the north of Durban is best under 6ft (2m) whereas the south coast can hold 10ft (3m) surf. The NE wind messing up the waves is one of the worst aspects of Durban surfing. Best conditions occur through the winter with plenty of S swells and offshore SW winds, even though this time of year can see strong SE (onshore) winds blowing out the surf by lunch time, so get up for the dawn patrol. Most Natal spots are best from low to mid tide.

Cave Rock

SURF STATISTICS	J F	M A	M J	J A	S O	N D
dominant swell	N-E	SE-S	SE-S	SE-S	SE-S	N-E
swell size (ft)	2	4	4-5	5	4	2-3
consistency (%)	50	60	80	80	70	60
dominant wind	NE-S	NE-S	NE-SW	NE-SW	NE-SW	NE-S
average force	F4	F4	F4	F4	F4	F4
consistency (%)	77	69	71	72	70	75
water temp (°C/°F)	25/77	25/77	23/74	20/68	22/72	23/74
wetsuit						

TRAVEL INFORMATION

Getting There – (See 21.Cape Peninsula). Internal flights from Jo'Burg to Durban are ±$110/rtn. Driving from Jo'Burg takes 5-6h.

Getting Around – Local transport is reliable and the road network is excellent. Rental cars are cheap and ensure you'll get more waves. Expect to pay $150/w - fuel is cheap (50c/l).

Lodging and Food – Downtown Durban offers the full range of accommodation options. Around the Bay of Plenty are lots of surfer friendly guesthouses such as Gillespie Street (±$15/d). More upmarket options include Blue Waters Hotel ($35/d). Umhlangha Rocks is a good place to be based if you don't want the hassles of the city. A good meal costs about $8.

Weather – The Natal coast is subtropical and has 230 days of sunshine a year. Summers (Oct -

Feb) see temps between 20°-30°C (68°-86°F) with big afternoon thunderstorms. During the winter temps never drop below 10°C (50°F) and often rise above 20°C (68°F). Breezy mornings are the only time it'll feel cold. The NW Berg winds preceding a cold front can warm things up for a day, followed by a dramatic drop in temps as the front passes. Cyclones occasionally hit the coast to the north of Durban. Thanks to the Agulhas Current, the water hardly ever drops below 20°C (68°F). A fullsuit would be needed only on the chilliest of mornings.

Nature and Culture – In Durban, Seaworld and the Natal Sharks Board are good afternoon fillers. The Indian district has plenty of shops to sample different curries. The nightlife in Durban is good. Longer but extremely worthwhile trips include going on safari in the Kruger and Kalahari Gemsbok national parks.

Hazards and Hassles – All the beaches mentioned in this text have efficient shark nets. The unnetted Natal beaches claim 75% of South Africa's shark attacks – Amanzimtoti has the worst attack record in the world. More likely threat is beach violence and theft. There can be some localism problems at certain spots. Blue Bottle jellyfish in summer.

Handy Hints – With the devaluation of the Rand, living costs have become very low in recent years. Surf gear is the cheapest in the world.

Local Population: Durban – 1,000,000
Coastline: 2,800 km (1,750mi)
Time: GMT+2hr
Contests: WQS (Jun, Jul)

WEATHER STATISTICS	J/F	M/A	M/J	J/A	S/O	N/D
total rainfall (mm)	125	102	47	32	75	122
consistency (days/mth)	10	8	4	3	8	11
min temp (°C/°F)	20/68	19/66	11/52	11/52	16/61	18/64
max temp (°C/°F)	28/82	27/81	23/74	22/72	23/74	26/79

THE SURFER'S PATH

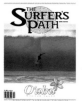

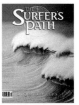

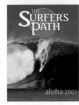

This watery planet seems to be getting smaller doesn't it? Satellite this, cyber that, cheaper flights to further fields etc. - they might or might not affect most people. But to surfers, it makes a world of a difference.

Surfers are dreamers. We ride waves through the day, then re-ride them in our sleep and mind-surf in our daydreams. These little flashbacks can keep us going through the flat spells and dry times, which we inevitably encounter, in Real Life.

Fuelling these dreams are visions of perfection. Perfect waves are what we all want - and what most of us just don't get enough of.

So we travel. Monthly, twice a year, annually or whenever we can afford it - one thing is for sure - to 99.9% of wave riders, a regular surf mission is essential.

Like the original explorer heroes of yesteryear, who found secluded perfection in places like J Bay, Garajagan et al, we can still go for the crusty pioneer approach, hacking bush and bedding down with the snakes and spiders at night. Or we can jump in a van and jam down the coast to poach our neighbour's waves. And don't forget the luxury option, like the all-inclusive surf-Nirvanas at G-land, Tavarua etc - guaranteed perfection, with X amount of extras. However we do it, we're doing what so many people just can't in their lives. We're making daydreams happen, we're hunting for a perfection, which we sometimes actually find.

Six times a year The Surfer's Path brings you clean, hot pictures from around the world nestling neatly among a wealth of information for the travelling surfer. Every two months we feature a region, an area or a break that we think is worth a trip, giving you as much info as we can about the waves, getting there, staying there, who lives there, what's going on there and much, much more.

The Surfer's Path keeps you updated on changes that affect the surf traveller - anything from super air-fare deals to new ways of opening a tin of beans, from insurance to insurrections, from visas to venereal diseases - so if you're planning a trip, you know the score.

Who knows what it means to be a surfer. There's something extra, something that makes our lives wildly different from those of the uninitiated, but none of us really know what that is. One thing is for sure - we know exactly what we want. And to get it, like the pilgrim or the holy man, we follow our own roads to our own perfection. Call it what you want, but we call it The Surfer's Path.

Surf, Travel, Live Good.

THE SURFER'S PATH

aloha 2001

HAWAII~ISLAND CREATIONS   SEVERSON'S ART OF LIVING   INDO WISDOM   FREEWHEELING

Subscribe online to The Surfer's Path
at
network26.com

St-Leu

Indian Ocean Islands

Meteorology and Oceanography

The Indian Ocean sits primarily in the southern Hemisphere, so most of the swells are generated between the Roaring Forties and the Howling Fifties. These low pressure systems make the journey from the Cape of Good Hope to the SW tip of Australia with year round regularity. They spin through the expanse of the cold Southern Ocean spraying out swell, the bulk of which heads towards Indonesia and Western Australia. These predominant SW swells are considered the most reliable and consistent source of quality surf on the planet and, Indonesia in particular, is perfectly placed to receive them. While both these zones are in different chapters of this Guide, their swell, wind and tide features are completely dictated by the Indian Ocean. The eastern side of this vast ocean is exposed to the SW swells for a shorter duration so wave size deteriorates as the swells propagate towards the Maldives and Sri Lanka. Madagascar, Réunion, and Mauritius are much closer to the Roaring Forties lows and maintain some sizeable waves, but the SE to S trade winds can spoil the party in winter. Once the NE trades take over in November, it's time to watch out for cyclones forming in the 15°-25°S latitudes and travelling west towards the Mascarene Islands and Madagascar. These swell producers are a real plus, providing sizeable swell for the east coasts of all the islands when the southern low pressures are at their weakest. Unfortunately, they are few and far between as well as being accompanied by the NE to SE trades of the region. The SE trades reach maximum intensity from June to October, which is especially true in the 15°-25°S range whereas the equatorial latitudes of the Maldives and Sri Lanka are influenced by monsoonal periods (Dec-March: NE and June-Oct: SW). Major tropical storms also affect the Arabian Sea and the Bay of Bengal (May-June and Oct-Nov) meaning there are some waves going unridden in frontier surfing destinations such as Yemen, Oman, Pakistan, India, Bangladesh and Myanmar.

Western Australia picks up the lion's share of the SW swell, bending it onto some famous righthand reefs down south, and long lefthand points up north. The south-west coast holds the big swells with aplomb, but the relentless onshores blight the afternoon surf. The north-west coast suffers from the strong winds, but if they are S enough, the lefts will fire.

Indonesia is the modern surf traveller's Mecca because the Indian Ocean serves up virtually constant, long distance lines of organised swell to equatorial latitudes where the trade winds are reliably offshore. These SE winds groom the lefts on the western coasts from April to Oct, and the NW wet season winds leave south and east facing coasts clean from Dec to March. A bit of vagueness during switchover and some non-committal directions in the northern regions barely detract from the glorious combinations of wind and tide that bless the Indonesian archipelago.

Currents are most notable in the North Indian Ocean because unlike the Pacific and Atlantic, a seasonal current reversal takes place. This coincides with the monsoon, flowing NE towards Africa in winter (Nov-Mar) and then in the opposite direction toward India in the summer months (June-Oct). Called the Somali Current, it follows the wind but changes little in temperature. Further south, the anticlockwise rotation of the Agulhas Current keeps Madagascar and the Mascarenes fed with warm water, before heading east along with the Roaring Forties storms until it swings up past the western Australian coast. Here, off the north-west Australian reefs that fringe the Great Sandy Desert the telltale signs of upwelling surface. This massive eddy finishes its circuit as the South Equatorial Current which flows westward back to Africa and the Agulhas. The Indian Ocean also feeds the warmest sea (the Persian Gulf) and the saltiest sea (the Red Sea).

Tides in the region are predominantly semi-diurnal although West Australia is mixed. Ranges are generally small apart from some areas like the Mozambique Channel and the far reaches of NW Australia, which goes close to the top of the height chart.

Temperatures, Winds and Currents

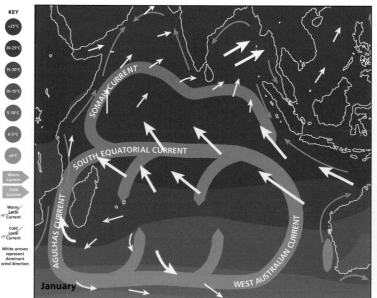

KEY
>25°C
20-25°C
15-20°C
10-15°C
5-10°C
0-5°C
<0°C
Warm Current
Cold Current
Warm Local Current
Cold Local Current
White arrows represent dominant wind direction

January

July

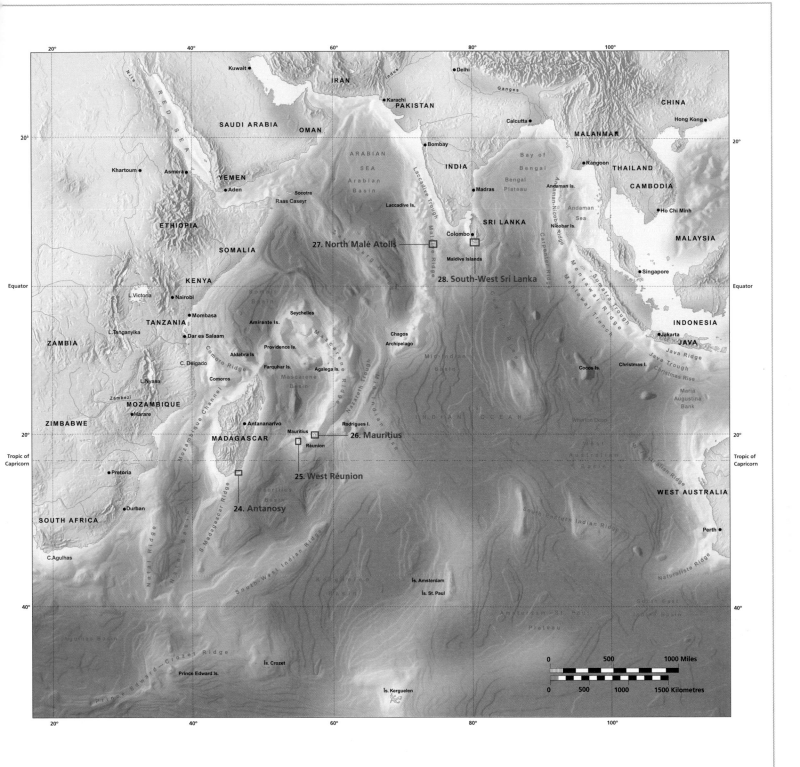

27. North Malé Atolls

28. South-West Sri Lanka

26. Mauritius

25. West Réunion

24. Antanosy

COUNTRY INFORMATION

	MADAGASCAR	RÉUNION	MAURITIUS	MALDIVES	SRI LANKA
Area (sq km/mi):	587,000/110,322	2,510/970	2,000/772	298/115	65,000/25,096
Population:	15M	675,000	1.2M	300,000	19M
Waveriders:	50	1,000	500	50	500
Tourists (per yr):	138,000	250,000	300,000	400,000	500,000
Language:	Malagasy, French	French, Creole	French, English, Hindi	Sinhalese, Divehi, English	Sinhalese, Tamil, English
Currency:	Malagasy Franc	French Franc	Mauritian Rupiah	Rufiyaa	Rupee
Exchange:	$1=6300 FMG	1$=7FF	$1=28Rs	$1=12Rf	$1=85Rs
GDP ($ per yr):	700	8,000	3,200	2,200	500
Inflation (%):	35	2	6	3	18

MADAGASCAR
MAURITIUS
RÉUNION

24. Antanosy

Monseigneur right

ALL PHOTOS BY YEP

Summary

+ UNCROWDED SPOTS
+ BEACH AND REEFBREAKS
+ CONSISTENT SWELLS
+ DIRT CHEAP LOCAL COSTS

− SHARKS
− BASIC HOTELS
− WINDY DAYS
− EXPENSIVE FLIGHTS AND VISAS
− NO ROADS

Ambinanibe dunes

Despite Madagascar being one of the most uncrowded and potentially epic surf zones on the planet, it has been kept off the surfing map mainly because of a reputation for shark infested waters. Recently, intrepid travellers have started to explore the 800km (500mi) strip between Fort-Dauphin and Tulear and discovered that it actually isn't that sharky. This coastline faces into the SW swells and is blessed with predominant offshore conditions. Surf charter boats have started cruising the coast between Anakao and Morombe, and it's likely that the awesome potential of this area will be tapped soon. It seems that Ifaty, one hour north of Tulear, will be the west coast surf hub of the future. On the south coast, it's a tough trip to the Antandroy area, where a left pointbreak peels in a desert environment.

Fort-Dauphin is home to a wide range of wave types. The NE winds are funnelled offshore on the SW facing beaches and sharks are rare. There's a good right pointbreak in front of the Monseigneur

Bay Hotel, provided there's a bit of swell and that the E-NE isn't blowing. It is inconsistent, but rides are long and safe whilst the handful of stoked locals are totally unaware of localism. On the other side, Libanona Beach has some potential reefs. Baie des Singes further down the beach has 3km (2mi) of average waves breaking over sparse rock reefs. It's often sideshore here, and favours high tide. The much better option is to walk 30 minutes to Ambinanibe and its powerful, tubing rights. It's by far

TRAVEL INFORMATION

Local Population:
Fort-Dauphin – 25,000
Coastline: 4,828km
(3,017mi)
Time: GMT+3hr
Contest: no

Getting There – Visa: All visitors need visas, obtained upon arrival. Antananarivo is one of the most difficult and expensive capitals to fly to. Easiest done from Europe, Mauritius, Réunion or South Africa. Air Madagascar is reliable and doesn't charge much for boards. Flights to Fort-Dauphin from Antananarivo, are about $150/rtn. Dep. tax: $15

Getting Around – Book early and unless you have ample time, fly as much as possible as the road system in the south is non-existent. Zebu cow carts are the local rudimentary form of transport. Taxi-Brousse (Buses) travel at about 15km/h (10mph). It's hard to rent motorised dugouts; most are sailing pirogues. A 4WD with driver is good but expensive ($100/d).

Lodging and Food – Madagascan costs are ridiculously cheap. However, SHTM run hotels have a fixed rate of $50/dble (Dauphin, Galion, Miramar). The Petit Bonheur facing Monseigneur offers good rooms for $10/dble. A kite-surf camp has opened in Ambinanibe. Food is dirt cheap at $5 for a full seafood feast.

Weather - The SE tip of Madagascar enjoys a moderate tropical climate with two seasons; Nov to Feb is the official rainy season with stifling temps and frequent thunderstorms. The actual rainfall west of Fort-Dauphin drops drastically, and the SW region is technically a desert. Winters are dry and warm with moderate cool spells, especially when the S winds pick up. Although the east coast can be struck by cyclones, the risks in Fort-Dauphin are low. Fort-Dauphin is only 20km (12.5mi) away from 2000m high peaks at the bottom of the eastern mountain range. This gives it a microclimate with NE winds, whilst the rest of the south coast has SE winds. The surf season

has lukewarm water temps with occasional cool upwellings and wind-chill. Bring a shorty.

Nature and Culture – Pic St-Louis and the surrounding high mountains offer great scenery. Fort-Dauphin is a peaceful town with a few bars, restaurants and a market. It provides the base for trips to the Andohahela lemurs, Anony lake birds and whale watching.

Hazards and Hassles – Remember that Fort-Dauphin is shark-free, it's only further up the east and west coasts that you need to worry. Monseigneur has a channel and the reef is smooth. There are few hassles on land and in the water. This area has no malaria.

Handy Hints – No equipment is available. You don't need a big wave gun. People build major tombstones then sacrifice Zebu cows for funerals, respect their beliefs. Malagasy names can be difficult. Lavasoa agency for expeditions in Fort-Dauphin can be recommended.

WEATHER STATISTICS	J/F	M/A	M/J	J/A	S/O	N/D
total rainfall (mm)	242	130	10	10	30	200
consistency (days/mth)	16	9	2	2	7	15
min temp (°C/°F)	23/74	21/70	18/64	17/62	17/62	21/70
max temp (°C/°F)	30/86	29/84	24/75	25/77	27/81	30/86

Baie des Singes

Madagascar's surf comes from the same swells that hit nearby Réunion and the rest of the Indian Ocean all the way to Indonesia. Lows in the Roaring Forties zone send SW-S swells to the S facing shoreline of Madagascar. From May to Sept, expect regular swells producing 4-12ft (1-4m) swell on the SW exposed shores. Most breaks don't face directly into the swells, so their average wave heights are smaller, (Evatra, Monseigneur) at around 2-8ft (0.6-2.6m).

the best and most consistent beachbreak in Fort-Dauphin. If you're into windsurfing, the Baie des Galions further west is a perfectly shaped cove. The Fort-Dauphin beach rarely breaks properly but there are amazing shipwrecks, of which 7 are exposed and many more submerged. There are further potential beachbreaks in the east but you need a 4WD or a boat to get you there. The best spot around is Evatra, which is a very good rivermouth left, breaking on a SW facing reef and sheltered from the worst of the cross-shore winds. Whilst you're in the area check Lokaro Island. It's a 3hr drive to Manafiafy (Ste-Luce) but the SW facing reefs are worth a look and if you're unlucky with the swell, the beach is a true gem. Further afield there are many spots to discover but the 'big fish' threat is real. The east coast, where the mountain range meets the Indian Ocean, records an average of 13 bites a year around Tamatave. The west coast around the Mozambique Channel is the home of the notorious Zambezi Shark (also known as the Bull Shark or Bronze Whaler) which likes to swim up rivers to forage. The west coast also has 700km (437mi) of offshore coral barriers, which has great surf potential.

December to March sees some cyclone swells on the E facing spots. The prevailing NE wind provides a great set up for offshore conditions. From Nov to March the wind shifts between SE and NE, while the surf season is much blessed by E-NE winds. However, these "offshore trades", magnified by the mountains, are strong and sometimes shift onshore, as low pressures approach the coast in winter. Sept to Oct is considered the windiest time. The tidal range is minimal (less than 2ft (0.6m)) on this side, whilst it becomes more significant towards the Mozambique Channel.

SURF STATS	J F	M A	M J	J A	S O	N D
dominant swell	N-E	SE-SW	SE-SW	SE-SW	SE-SW	N-E
swell size (ft)	4	5	6	6-7	5-6	3
consistency (%)	50	60	80	70	70	50
dominant wind	NE-SE	NE-SE	NE-SE	NE-S	NE-S	NE-SE
average force	F4	F4	F4	F4	F4-F5	F4
consistency (%)	75	69	57	53	52	65
water temp (°C/°F)	26/79	25/77	24/75	22/72	23/74	25/77
wetsuit						

Antandroy area

25. West Réunion

MOZAMBIQUE
MADAGASCAR
RÉUNION
MAURITIUS

Chemin surprise, St. Leu

MARC FENIES

Summary

+ CONSISTENT YEAR ROUND
+ SPOT DIVERSITY
+ SCENIC COUNTRYSIDE
+ SAFE TOURISM

– EXPENSIVE
– CROWD PRESSURE
– SHARK THREATS
– BUSY ROAD TRAFFIC

French governed Réunion Island is located on a perfect latitude to receive consistent swells and great tropical weather. It's a volcanic island with 3000m peaks, an active volcano (latest eruption 19/10/2000) and black sand beaches. This mountainous countryside has a big influence on weather patterns with a rain shadow cast on the leeward west coast. As a consequence of lower rainfall, coral reefs have developed here. Rain has shaped ravines that funnel water into the sea and then through coral passes. Most of the thirty reported spots on the west coast, break on fragmented barrier reefs, quite a distance from the beach. There's also normal rock bottoms but they are less numerous and usually have murky water... a good home for sharks. There are also a few average black sand beachbreaks, along with the popular white sand, sunbathing beaches of Roches Noires or Boucan

Cirque de Salazie

MARC FENIES

Tarzan, St. Leu

MARC FENIES

The surf zone starts in the north at the unsightly Possession Harbour. The first spot here is a big wave break called Le Port. Rarely ridden and hard to find, it has a nasty shark factor. St-Gilles is the area's main centre with bars, shops, hotels, good nightlife and at least 17 breaks scattered around 12km (7.5mi) of coastline. The

TRAVEL INFORMATION

Local Population:
St-Denis – 125,000
Coastline: 207km (129mi)
Time: GMT+4hr
Contests: WQS (June4)

Getting There – Aussies and South Africans need visas. Réunion airport only has direct flights from Mauritius, Madagascar, South Africa and France. To get cheap flights from France you must avoid the July-August holiday period.

Getting Around – The mountainous interior means driving mainly on the N1 coastal road, which is busy at rush hours. Being based in St-Leu will save too much driving around. The "Cars Jaunes" bus service is reliable (you clap your hands to stop the bus). A rental car costs from $215/w.

Lodging and Food – St-Leu's Apolonia is perfect but the double room costs $85/dble. VVF is $35/$60. St-Leu campsite is only open in

August. For cheaper deals, stay in guesthouses ($20-$30/dble) slightly out of town or go to St-Pierre or St-Gilles. There is also a reasonably priced VVF at St-Leu. Spicy Creole cuisine or imported French food is the standard, costing around $15 or even less from "camion bars"

Weather – The tropical climate is very much influenced by the high mountains. The windward coast is extremely wet with humidity levels amongst the highest in the world, while the west coast is rather dry. The mountains are often overcast, while the coast enjoys clear skies swept by the trade winds. The cyclone season lasts from December to March with major destructive cyclones hitting the island every 3 years or so. This period is the warmest and wettest, whilst mid winter can feel cool. May-June and Sept-Oct are usually the best weather months. Springsuits are the most rubber needed.

Nature and Culture – The interior of the island is beautiful. Maïdo is a 2000m peak that has a

breathtaking view over the west coast. Cirque's like Mafate, Cilaos and Salazie are great places for trekking and admiring the view. Piton de la Fournaise, on the east side is the second most active volcano in the world.

Hazards and Hassles – Réunion has a bad record for shark attacks on surfers with at least one a year, although they are rarely fatal. Don't surf in murky water, on your own, before dark or after heavy rains and you should be fine. Fire coral, sea urchins and shallow reefs are the real threats. With only about 30 spots and many surfers, the line-ups are competitive. St-Leu is localised, and there have been sporadic incidences of violence here.

Handy Hints – It's a French island with white 'Zoreils', (the name of people from mainland France), raising the standards of living. Mixed race locals speak Creole. The bars are lively and play local Sega and Maloya music. There are good surf shops, but gear is very expensive.

WEATHER STATISTICS	J/F	M/A	M/J	J/A	S/O	N/D
total rainfall (mm)	240	225	77	60	45	247
consistency (days/mth)	12	11	11	11	7	10
min temp (°C/°F)	23/74	22/72	16/61	17/62	18/64	21/70
max temp (°C/°F)	30/86	29/84	27/81	25/77	26/79	28/82

Pointe au Sel

Le Port
La Possession
Saint-Denis
Pointe des Galets
Saint-Paul
Cap Requin
Boucan
Boucan Canot
Aigrettes
Roches-Noires
L'Hermitage
Saint-Gilles-les-Bains
Passe de l'Hermita
Pointe des Trois-Bassins
Pointe des Trois-Bassins
La Caffrine
Saint-Leu
Saint-Leu
Pointe au Sel
Cirque de Salaz
3070m Piton des Neiges
Cirque de Cilaos
Etang-Salé
L'Etang-salé les bains
Saint-Louis
Pointe de l'Etang-Salé
Saint Pierre
Pic du Diable
Pic du Diable
La Jetée

MARC FENIES

first very good set up is Boucan, with rights and lefts, while Roches Noires has many good spots, ideal for beginners. Further down the coast, divers relish the fabulous natural lagoon reserve at L'Hermitage Pass. Surfers here have the choice between an epic left and a barrelling right. Both are sharky, work on small swells and need rare N winds. The Trois-Bassins area is a swell magnet, having waves when everywhere else is flat and has

Trois-Bassins

SYLVAIN CEZENAVE

played host to WCT and WQS contests since the early 90's. In the bend of a lagoon, the famous lefts of St-Leu provide a true world class wave with an easy paddle-out. It starts with a long and easy wall, ideal for turns, before a bowly, hollow section throws out a shallow tube, which finishes close to shore. L'Etang-Salé is the windsurfer's equivalent of St-Leu, due to a high SE wind exposure. The

south coast around St-Pierre is very consistent, with the majority of waves being rights, such as the scary Pic du Diable and La Jetée big wave spot. There are good right pointbreaks on the S and E coasts, but it is sharky. There have been attacks here, and surfing is not advised.

The main swell is generated by the Roaring Forties around South Africa. During the southern hemisphere winter there are frequent SW swells varying in size from 3-15ft (1-5m). Although these swells can occur year round, the summer season is characterised more by NE tropical storms, but with only about 10 depressions in 6 months, it can hardly be called consistent. SE trade winds blow constantly with a more E-NE direction during the summer (Nov-Mar) and more S-SE during winter (May-Sept). The wind can also produce 2-6ft (0.6-2m) onshore wind swell on the windward coast and cross/off-shore on the SW coast. Tides are only significant at shallow spots. Tide tables are not easy to get.

SURF STATISTICS	J F	M A M	J J	A S	O N	D
dominant swell	N-E	S-SW	S-SW	S-SW	S-SW	N-E
swell size (ft)	4-5	5-6	6-7	7-8	6	3-4
consistency (%)	70	80	90	90	80	60
dominant wind	E-SE	E-SE	SE-E	SE-E	E-SE	E-SE
average force	F4	F4	F4	F5	F4	F3
consistency (%)	65	64	60	76	69	58
water temp (°C/°F)	28/82	27/81	26/79	24/75	25/77	26/79
wetsuit						

St. Gilles and La Digue

MARC FENIES

MOZAMBIQUE
MADAGASCAR   RÉUNION
MAURITIUS

26. Mauritius

Tamarin Bay

ROB GILLEY

Summary
+ Tamarin's world class left
+ Quality reefbreaks
+ Exotic conditions
+ Moderate prices

– Heavy localism
– Lack of SW exposure
– High population density
– Expensive flights

Mauritius has gained an exotic image in the heart of surfers thanks to the 1974 surf film, "Forgotten Island of Santosha". It focused largely on Tamarin Bay, a perfect wave that became a symbol of escapism. The spot had been surfed since the early 60's, but the epic 8-10ft (2.6-3.2m) swell featured in the film, captured the attention of the surfing world. Unfortunately, Tamarin turned out to be inconsistent, leaving many travelling surfers disappointed. Since then the focus has shifted to the more consistent, neighbouring island of Réunion. Mauritius has a lack of optimum south-west facing shores, while the south facing coast is frequently blown out by SE trade winds. The local surfing tradition goes back years, but it has developed in a sad way, leading to a terrible reputation for localism. Throughout the 90's,

MARC FENIES

White Short local at Tamarin Bay

MARC FENIES

white Mauritians dubbed the 'White Shorts', have controlled Tamarin's waves with a violent iron fist, and any visiting surfer can expect intimidation or worse.

South-westerly swells have to wrap heavily to break along the reef at Tamarin, so a biggish swell is needed for it to even start breaking. This long, barrelling left becomes very shallow at low tide, although an inside reform keeps

TRAVEL INFORMATION

Local Population:
Mauritius – 1.2M
Port-Louis – 150,000
Coastline: 177km (110mi)
Time: GMT+4hr
Contests: Local

Getting There – Visa: None required. Flying there is expensive; most flights come from European capitals (Paris and London), Réunion, Madagascar and South Africa. Air Mauritius charges for boards. Dep tax is $10. It's 1h30min from Mahébourg (the capital) to Tamarin.

Getting Around – Tamarin is the northern limit of the surf zone and so you'll need a rental car to roam the south-west. A basic reef Cub (small open top 'car') is $28/d. Hiring a taxi costs around $30/half-day. Le Morne to both Passe lefts involves a boat ride, costing around $20/h. Local buses are usually packed.

Lodging and Food – Tamarin is fairly cheap. Chez Jacques (Lagan) is $10-$15/dble. Tamarin hotel costs $35/dble. Le Morne has 3 deluxe resorts (Paradis, Berjaya, Pavilions) facing the Passe, the cheapest is Pavilions at $160/dble/half-board, the best deals are packages. Food is cheap and spicy ($5 meal).

Weather – Mauritius differs from the classic monsoon pattern, and its year round moderate rains generally fall at the end of the day. It's usually hotter and wetter but with less cyclonic risk during the summer (Dec-April). Winter begins in May, but temperatures remain warm enough for most visitors, and this period is considered the most pleasant time. The east coast is drier than the west coast. The water can get a little chilly in winter, requiring a springsuit as opposed to the regulation boardies and rashy.

Nature and Culture – Unlike Réunion, Mauritius is hilly rather than mountainous, and only the

Trou aux Cerfs crater testifies to the ancient volcanic activity. The beaches are some of the most beautiful in the world. Port-Louis spice markets, Pamplemousse Gardens and Moka Town are all worth a visit. Shellorama Museum next to Tamarin is interesting.

Hazards and Hassles – The "White Shorts" are a threat to non-Tamarin locals, but other spots are cool and usually uncrowded. Coral heads are a worry at low tide Tamarin. Most coral reefs are dangerous and involve long paddles from the shore. The island is safe and disease free. There are always sharks about.

Handy Hints – There are good shapers in Tamarin, and having a locally made board can make you feel safer in the Tamarin line-up! Bring travellers cheques, as you will get the best exchange rate for them. Mauritius is a peaceful blend of Catholics, Protestants, Hindus and Muslims.

WEATHER STATISTICS	J/F	M/A	M/J	J/A	S/O	N/D
total rainfall (mm)	205	174	81	61	38	82
consistency (days/mth)	11	10	7	6	4	6
min temp (°C/°F)	23/74	21/70	17/62	17/62	17/62	19/66
max temp (°C/°F)	30/86	29/84	26/79	24/75	26/79	29/84

Blue Bay

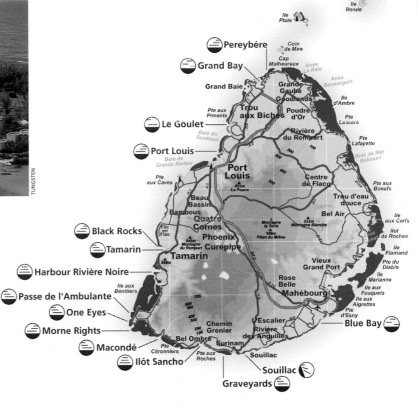

the local kids happy. It is the best wave on the island, and therefore it's also the most crowded. There's a decent right on the other side of the bay called Black Rocks and the harbour in Rivière Noire can also have a peak. As Tamarin only works for 5-6 days a month in the winter season, it's a good idea to stay on the more consistent Le Morne Peninsula. Opposite the Paradis Hotel, Passe de l'Ambulante is a very consistent, long left that wraps around the reef offering fun waves, but they are a paying boat ride away. The next pass, One Eyes, has better shaped waves, especially when it's small. It used to involve a long hike but now there's a road to the Berjaya Resort, which looks out onto the break. The channel takes 15 minutes to paddle across so save some energy for the return leg. On a big swell, a rare but wild break called Morne Rights can be ridden out on the south-west tip of the island. Macondé is a short, hollow left that can handle any size, but requires some N or E in the wind and a ten minute paddle. All the spots further east only work in the morning or with summer NE winds. One of the best on the south coast is Ilôt Sancho, which gets weird rights and lefts on the edge of the reef. Graveyards is another left, facing a cemetery; it's rarely good but usually rideable. The best pointbreak is probably the left in Souillac, which breaks on a small swell and a N wind. The rest of the island is inconsistent. The Blue Bay resorts have potentially good reefs but generally straight onshore winds. North of Tamarin, Port Louis has a right, Le Goulet can be an excellent left and the Grand Bay tourist hub has a north facing, white sand beachbreak that's nothing special. Pereybére can hold a half decent right on a NE swell, but Mauritius surf revolves around the SW swell generated by the Roaring Forties below South Africa.

During the southern hemisphere winter there are frequent SW swells varying in size from 2-10ft (0.5-3.3m). Although these SW swells can appear year round, the summer season is characterised by NE tropical storms, but with only about 10 depressions in 6 months, it's hardly consistent. Of these, one or two will be strong cyclones that can be dangerous and destructive. Winter S-SE trades blow constantly and with a greater strength and frequency from July-September. Summer winds veer more E-NE, which can also bring 2-6ft (0.6-2m) onshore wind swell to the windward coast and cross to offshore conditions on the surf-blessed SW corner. Tides are only significant at shallow spots. Tide tables aren't easy to get.

Souillac

One Eyes

SURF STATISTICS	J F	M A	M J	J A	S O	N D
dominant swell	N-E	S-SW	S-SW	S-SW	S-SW	N-E
swell size (ft)	4	5	6	6-7	5-6	4
consistency (%)	50	70	8	80	70	50
dominant wind	NE-SE	E-SE	E-SE	E-SE	E-SE	NE-SE
average force	F4	F4	F4	F4	F4	F3-F4
consistency (%)	82	64	61	76	69	77
water temp (°C/°F)	27/81	26/79	24/75	22/72	23/74	25/77
wetsuit						

27. North Malé Atolls

LACCADIVE ISL.
INDIA
SRI LANKA
MALDIVES
CHAGOS
ARCHIPELAGO

Summary
+ ATOLL PERFECTION
+ WORLD CLASS RIGHTS AND LEFTS
+ CALM WINDS
+ NO HASSLE
+ LUXURY RESORTS

− CONSISTENTLY SMALL
− CROWDED
− BOAT ACCESS RESTRICTIONS
− TOP PRICES
− NO BUDGET LAND TRIPS

Pasta Point, home to Atoll Adventures

JOHN CALLAHAN

The Maldives are part of a submarine plateau sitting 20-30m below the surface of the ocean. The islands didn't exist until coral formations built up on top of each other, eventually creating an archipelago of tiny islands scattered over a huge area. There are 26 different low-lying atolls, comprising of 1,200 islands spread along an 800km (500mi) long, vertical line. The ridge extending from the Lakshadweep to Chagos Islands is 2000km (1250mi) long. The result is a vast area of shallow seas dotted by islands creating a perfect surfing paradise.

Most of the islands get no surf, but the S/SE facing coastline gets waves on reef passes that break close to the shore. Unless you are staying in the Tari surf resort, then you will usually have to rely on the irregular 'dhonys', (local boats), to reach many of the waves. From the air, what

appears to be some classic set-ups are a bit misleading, as there are not that many spots in North Malé unless the swell is big. South Malé Atoll has quite a few spots and while the atolls to the south get more swell, these can only be reached on a chartered boat.

Malé itself has a break which used to produce excellent peaks but because of development work, it now

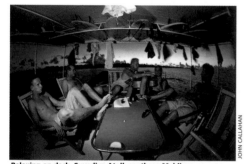
Relaxing on deck, Suvadiva Atoll, southern Maldives
JOHN CALLAHAN

Damien Hobgood
JOHN CALLAHAN

TRAVEL INFORMATION

Local Population:
Malé – 100,000
Coastline: 644km (402mi)
Time: GMT+5hr
Contest: Local

Getting There – No visa. Malé is reasonably priced from Europe, Sri Lanka and SE Asia. It's a well-organised tourist destination with boats picking you up on arrival and taking you to your resort. Tari is a breathtaking 1h30 boat ride away. Dep tax is $10.

Getting Around – Forget cars and roads, use dhonys, speedboats or even hydroplanes depending on your budget. Tari constantly operates dhonys from 6am to 6pm to nearby spots, while other resorts work business hours (9h-12h, 14h-17h) and may charge extra.

Lodging and Food – Either stay on a charter boat or book a resort. A basic hotel in Malé is $30/dble and a dhony $80/rtn to the northern breaks. It's not a budget trip. Yacht trips are ±$150/d. Package resort deals cost between $100-$500/dble. Tari is the best option ($150/dble). Imported goods make the price of almost everything very high; beer - $3, water - $4.

Weather – Typical tropical, monsoon climate with plenty of rainfall. The NE monsoon (Iruvai) is the driest period with lighter winds from the E to N. During this time (Dec-Mar) temps soar and sunshine is plentiful. From May-Oct the monsoon comes from the SW (Hulhangu), bringing a few storms, gusty winds and regular rainfall to the atolls. July-Aug features many rainy, stormy days and the water is somewhat cooler at this time, requiring a shorty. Most of the year averages around 27°C (80°F).

Nature and Culture – Besides fantastic diving and dreamy beaches, there is little else to do. Lohi and Kani resorts are ideal for families. The trip to Malé is worth a visit. Alternatively check out some of the 80 other resort islands but be prepared to cough up some big money.

Hazards and Hassles – Despite loads of marine life, it's safe. Be careful of shallow reefs (most of the coral is dead), tidal rips and sunburn. This area gets crowded with surf trippers during the peak season. You can avoid crowds by heading into the deep south on a charter boat but it doesn't come cheap.

Handy Hints – There's a surf shop in Malé but it's better to bring everything with you. Guns are not necessary. Originally the islands had nothing but fish, but now all the resorts are small factories producing fresh water, electricity and importing veggies, meat and alcohol.

WEATHER STATISTICS	J/F	M/A	M/J	J/A	S/O	N/D
total rainfall (mm)	32	40	240	212	172	113
consistency (days/mth)	2	2	13	13	10	6
min temp (°C/°F)	23/74	25/77	25/77	24/75	24/75	23/74
max temp (°C/°F)	29/84	31/88	31/88	29/84	29/84	29/84

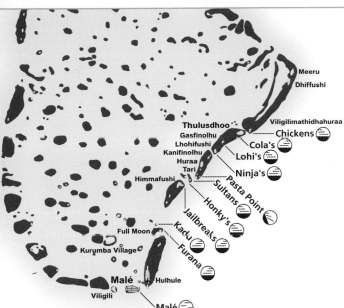

STÉPHANE MIRA

The Maldives is made up of hundreds of coral islands called atolls

COURTESY ATOLL ADVENTURES

Honkys and Sultans

only works properly at low tide and is packed with locals in the afternoons. Close to Malé is Furana, an excellent long right, that needs just the right swell and winds to get it going. A consistent spot is Himmafushi, also named Jailbreaks, as the island off which it's located is the national jail. Surfing here used to be banned, but now it's possible to ride the fantastic right, which has several sections. Not suprisingly, you're not allowed to set foot on the island and you need a permit to surf there. Very close to the Tari surf camp is an island where a couple of very good waves can be found - Honky's is the left and Sultans the right. Sultans is the most consistent wave, breaking with two different sections that get a little out of control over 8ft (2.6m). Honky's is a good spot to check in the typical NE winter winds. This weird but excellent left bends around the reef so much that the second section, the Ledge, is bigger than the take-off zone. When it's on, it's a truly world class wave. Tari surf camp guests have exclusive rights over Pasta Point (the island used to be an Italian resort), another killer long left sweeping around the edge of the island. The next two spots can be found on resort islands popular with both surfers and divers, however both the waves lack power and consistency. Ninja's in Kanifinolhu is a mellow right, so named because of its popularity with the Japanese and where longboarders and beginners congregate. Lohi's is a good left, but it only breaks on a strong swell and is very sensitive to the dominant SW winds. This wind sensitivity

also applies to Cola's rights but they are much more consistent and pick up all the available swell. Cola's will become a perfect, intense barrel on a NW wind. Furthest north is Chickens, another long left pointbreak, usually ridden either side of the SW monsoon.

The same swells hitting Indonesia deliver the goods to the Maldives except that the latitude is higher and the SE exposure is less convenient. March to Oct is the most consistent swell season with usual 2-6ft (0.6-2m) waves on the most exposed breaks. Several stormy 6-10ft (2-3.3m) swells will occur through winter (Dec–Mar) but are usually messy and windy. May-Aug favours rights because the SW monsoon blows out the lefts. The lefts get good again when the winds shift to W-NW in Sept-Oct. The best period is March-April with many glassy days and NE winds, ideal for the lefts. Waves typically break from 2-5ft (0.6-1.6m) and although not big, they can be perfect. Nov-Feb suffers from many flat days and is favoured by divers who have priority on dhonys at some mixed resorts. Tides are unpredictable but create intense rips between islands, making it impossible to paddle across channels. Depending on swell, wind and tide, you have either incoming or outgoing currents, so check with the dhony captain. High tides are safer at most spots.

SURF STATISTICS	J F	M A	M J	J A	S O	N D
dominant swell	S-SE	S-SE	S-SE	S-SE	S-SE	S-SE
swell size (ft)	2	3-4	4-5	5-6	4	2
consistency (%)	40	60	80	80	60	40
dominant wind	N-E	SW-NE	SW-W	SW-W	SW-NW	SW-N
average force	F3	F2-F3	F3	F3	F3	F3
consistency (%)	74	71	70	53	83	73
water temp (°C/°F)	27/81	28/82	27/81	26/79	27/81	27/81
wetsuit	🩳	🩳	🩳	🩳	🩳	🩳

PHILIPE CHEVODIAN

Pasta Point

28. South-West Sri Lanka

Midigama

TARA MOLLER

Summary

+ QUALITY MELLOW WAVES
+ OFFSHORE NE MONSOON
+ BUDDHIST MECCA
+ CHEAP

− CONFLICTING WIND AND SWELL PATTERNS
− SMALL WAVES
− NO WORLD CLASS SPOTS
− SEWAGE AND LOCALISM
− CIVIL UNREST

S ri Lanka, a teardrop-shaped island below India, is the highest latitude, reliable surf destination in the Indian Ocean. The south coast is open to the same regular, long distance SW swells, that pepper Indonesia. Arugam Bay, on Sri Lanka's east coast, was a very popular port of call for surfers travelling across Asia in the 70's, but trips here came to a halt in 1983 with the outbreak of civil war between the Tamil Tigers and the Sri Lankan government. Surfers forced to look elsewhere for waves didn't take long to discover the Hikkaduwa reefs.

Victor

G.J.DE KONING

G.J.DE KONING

Over the years, the south-west has become a popular spot to hang out and surf, being cheap, safe and full of local colour. The variety of mellow reefs at Hikkaduwa tend to favour lefts which perfectly groom the small, clean swells. The most consistent spot is Main Reef which has fun lefts and rights on a flat coral reef facing the Surfing Beach Guest House but expect crowds and some over the top localism. North is Benny's, an outside reef that is reached after a five minute paddle and offers a pretty radical and fairly consistent left that can hold big swells.

TRAVEL INFORMATION

Local Population:
Hikkaduwa – 100,000
Coastline: 1,340km (837mi)
Time: GMT+5hr30
Contest: Local

Getting There – No visa for stays of up to one month. It's fairly cheap to fly to Colombo with Air Lanka. There's no charge for boards and you can get a free stopover in the Maldives. There are no domestic flights due to the civil war. Hikkaduwa is 3h from the airport. Dep tax is $10

Getting Around – There's no need to rent a car. A taxi to the airport is ±$40/o-w and if you're on a budget trip then take a train for $1. Renting a 125cc motorbike costs $5/d but be careful. Drive on the left.

Lodging and Food – Sri Lanka can be done on a real shoestring budget. Staying in Hikkaduwa can cost less than $5/dble for a

reasonable room (Surfing Beach Guest House), or $20 for a deluxe hotel (Casalanka). Apart from rice and curry, there's plenty of cheap and healthy food. Expect to pay $3 for a meal.

Weather – It's a typical tropical monsoon climate with 2 definite seasons. Maha means NE monsoon (Nov - Mar) and this is the driest and sunniest period for the SW. The transition periods have very hot temperatures but relief can be found in the mountains. The rainy monsoon lasts from April to Oct and the 'Yala' winds blow strong SW, onshore, bringing lots of rain. This rainy period lasts until Nov, which is the coolest, most pleasant time to travel. Most of the year the water temperature remains a perfect 27°C (81°F), so you can ride rubberless.

Nature and Culture – The island where Jonah was spat out of the whale and Adam and Eve walked in paradise has much more to offer than average surf or snorkelling on the coral reefs. Visit colonial Gallé, climb Adam's Peak

for the spectacular sunrise and see the Buddhist temples in Kandy. Wildlife (elephants and monkeys) is plentiful. Hikkaduwa has surprisingly good nightlife.

Hazards and Hassles – There have been some serious cases of violent localism towards visiting waveriders from the local Hikkaduwa surfers. Bring a good attitude, be mellow in the line-up and instead of aggression, you'll be treated well. Sewage pollution and coral cuts mix badly. As a big tourist resort, many local people make their money by scamming gullible tourists.

Handy Hints – The A-Frame surf shop is the base for Mambo Surf Tours, who can arrange trips to waves in other areas of the country. Boards can be rented for $1/h. A gun is not needed. This area is trouble-free regarding the civil war. Learn a few words of Sinhala and you'll be greeted with smiles.

WEATHER STATISTICS	J/F	M/A	M/J	J/A	S/O	N/D
total rainfall (mm)	92	190	282	132	255	250
consistency (days/mth)	8	15	22	15	19	15
min temp (°C/°F)	22/72	23/74	25/77	25/77	24/75	22/72
max temp (°C/°F)	31/88	31/88	31/88	29/84	29/84	30/86

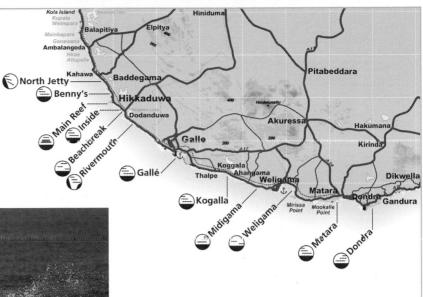

Another spot to check out on a big swell is North Jetty, which has long lefts. South of Main Reef is Inside Reef, which is another left peak that deals out some power. Beyond here is a long stretch of beachbreak, which varies from a fat wave, ideal for beginners, to a fun, wedgy shorebreak, good for bodyboarders. If it ever gets big, the rivermouth will have a rideable wave, although the water can be very dirty.

Gallé is southeast from Hikkaduwa and is the most interesting colonial town in the area. A good left breaks near the jetty just outside of town, but it doesn't work very often. A bit further east is Kogalla, where two

SURF STATISTICS	J F	M A	M J	J A	S O	N D
dominant swell	S-SW	S-SW	S-SW	S-SW	S-SW	S-SW
swell size (ft)	3	3-4	5	6	4-5	3
consistency (%)	50	50	30	30	40	50
dominant wind	N-E	NE-SW	SW-W	SW-W	SW-NW	N-E
average force	F3-F4	F3	F4	F4	F4	F3
consistency (%)	85	59	89	89	80	60
water temp (°C/°F)	27/81	28/82	28/82	28/82	27/81	27/81
wetsuit						

TARA MOLLER

expensive hotels are located. The reefs here don't pick up much swell, but when it's on, the left is excellent. Midigama is a small village further east, which is less consistent than Hikkaduwa and more exposed to S winds. There are two spots: a long, fat left and a short, powerful right breaking over a shallow reef. Conditions here are far more primitive than Hikkaduwa but far less crowded. The beachbreak in Weligama can be surfed even when small and the rest of the south coast is blown-out. Matara is rumoured to have a decent left, while there's an equally fickle right at Dondra, but they both need some north in the wind and this is rare. Much further east are the legendary rights of Arugam Bay but guerrilla activity is a very real problem in that area, and surfers are advised to be cautious in this area.

The same swells that turn Indonesia on, deliver the goods to Sri Lanka, although the higher latitude causes some swell decay. The main problem is that the most consistent SW swell season (April - Oct) will be accompanied by frequent SW onshores. It's still possible to surf in the morning

but expect rain, dirty water and strong winds with the 3-8ft (1-2.6m) swells. If it were safe, this is the ideal time to travel to the south-easterly coast around Arugam Bay. The best time for the south coast is at the start and end of the dry season (November to April), when NE winds are most likely to coincide with the bigger SW groundswells. During the dry season, waves are typically 2-6ft (0.6-2m) and clean, so it's rare to see it totally flat in Hikkaduwa at any time of year. Even during the NE monsoon, the afternoons tend to go onshore. The S wind affects the spots east of Gallé far more than the Hikkaduwa breaks. Tidal ranges are minimal, and the A-Frame surf shop in Hikkaduwa provides tide tables. Most shallow reefs will change significantly with the tides.

G.J.DE KONING

Unawatuna

QUIZ
SPOTS AND LOCALS ARE ALL MIXED UP. MATCH THE FACES WITH

Celestino

Shonan

Sunset Beach

Heidi

* Win a week stay in G-Land !

Liliana

Puerto Escondido

Carcavelos

Luis

www.surftrip.net
The most complete worldwide surftrip atlas online !

NEWS / ARCHIVES
Keep in touch with surftravel and eco-logical issues

SURFCAMS
Check the latest conditions throughout the world

E-SHOP
Order among a vast choice of guidebooks & maps

SURFERS "Я" US
Subscribe to our free mailing list and let us know your feedback

www.surftrip.net — around the world in 80 wavezones

THE STORMRIDER EUROPE

surfing indonesia

THE LINEUP SHOTS. SUBMIT YOUR ANSWERS ON www.surftrip.net

Roca Bruja

● Tsukasa

Chasity

Wilderness

Gunns

Andrew

Andrea

Easkey

around the world in 80 wavezones
Check the Stormrider Guide zones with updates and more stuff !

STATS
Unique database for climate, wind and swell

PIX
16 killer pictures per zone with captions

MAPS
Zoomable spot maps with bathymetry

COMMENTS
International english infos about spots, swells, winds and tides

TRAVEL
Updated key facts & factors and travel guide essentials

© Credits : Braby, Chevodian, Fitzpatrick, Lolopipe, Tsuchiya, Van Lennep, Williams, Yep.

East Asia

Meteorology and Oceanography

Asia is sandwiched between the hyperactive SW groundswells of the Indian Ocean and the fickle NE Pacific typhoons. Whilst these two oceans provide Asia with most of its waves, the China Sea (which is the largest sea in the world) and the Japan Sea also influence the surf. The quality year round swells from the Indian Ocean (described in Indian Ocean chapter) combine with occasional cyclone swell from storms at each end of the Indonesian archipelago; The Bay of Bengal above Sumatra and the Timor Sea, below Nusa Tenggara.

Asia's Pacific side is definitely not as generous, relying on typhoons and monsoon swells. The primary season for surf in the Philippines and Japan is June-November, when an estimated 25 typhoons or tropical storms roll west towards the China Sea. The western Pacific experiences the strongest cyclonic activity in the world but nevertheless, typhoons are less reliable sources of waves than groundswells. However, August-September is a fairly consistent time to score these magic swells. Typhoon swells differ from groundswells, with 8-10 waves per set, sometimes as many as 12-15, compared to the more normal 4-6 that groundswells produce.

The track of these typhoons, as with all tropical storms, is hard to predict. Most commonly, they will form in the open ocean over Melanesia and head due west towards the Philippines, before starting to arc northwards in the direction of Japan. It is this arc that produces NE swell for the Philippine spots and SE swells for Japan. The Philippines benefit from a deep ocean trench that is 10km (6mi) deep and does a great job of attracting and amplifying marginal swells for Siargao and the SE region. Japan is less fortunate and the southern areas rely entirely on typhoon generated swell, because otherwise the surf is knee to waist-high wind chop. The situation isn't improved by onshore SE winds during the typhoon season, until the freezing winter northerlies kick in towards November. The winter months will see some NE groundswell being sent down off the back of the big lows that spin across the North Pacific, but most of the size is heading in the opposite direction. When these short-lived swells do occur they mainly affect Honshu in Japan and the more NE exposed parts of the Philippines. The NE monsoon from mid-December to March can be responsible for a bit of windswell in the South China Sea, producing rideable waves in Vietnam, Taiwan and West Luzon. From May to mid-September the SW monsoon over the Indian Ocean side of Asia mostly affects Thailand in the Andaman Sea.

New Ireland province of Papua New Guinea relies on windswell kicked up by the NW monsoon between Nov and April. Offshore mornings followed by the onshore trades and generally smaller swells are the main menu in this diverse Melanesian outpost.

Winds in the Philippines are dictated by the monsoons, which blow from the south-west June to Nov and from the north-east Dec to April. The transition periods (May) will be south-easterly. For Japan, the winds are more SE in summer and a cold N in winter.

The Kuroshio Current is part of the big North Pacific circulation pattern, warming the Philippines before the Kamchatka Current brings icy water down from the Aleutians for Japan. Papua New Guinea receives warm water from the Equatorial Counter Current and is the birthplace of El Niño.

The tidal range is minimal (mostly under 6ft/2m) except in the Nusa Tenggara (eastern islands) of Indonesia where larger tides occur. Most tides in the surf areas occur twice daily with irregular ranges from one tide to another, except for Papua New Guinea where mixed tides have a big affect on the waves.

Temperatures, Winds and Currents

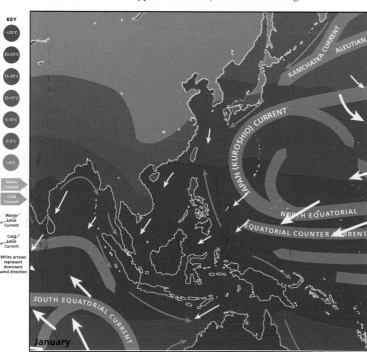

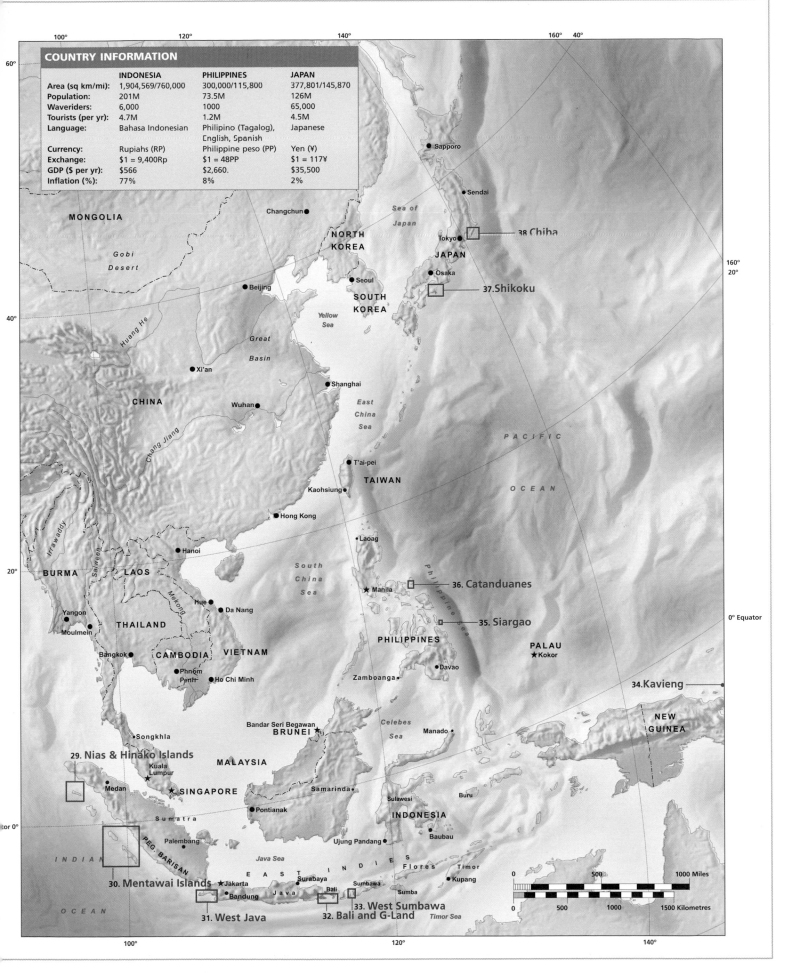

COUNTRY INFORMATION

	INDONESIA	PHILIPPINES	JAPAN
Area (sq km/mi):	1,904,569/760,000	300,000/115,800	377,801/145,870
Population:	201M	73.5M	126M
Waveriders:	6,000	1000	65,000
Tourists (per yr):	4.7M	1.2M	4.5M
Language:	Bahasa Indonesian	Philipino (Tagalog), English, Spanish	Japanese
Currency:	Rupiahs (RP)	Philippine peso (PP)	Yen (¥)
Exchange:	$1 = 9,400Rp	$1 = 48PP	$1 = 117¥
GDP ($ per yr):	$566	$2,660.	$35,500
Inflation (%):	77%	8%	2%

MONGOLIA

Gobi Desert

NORTH KOREA

Sea of Japan

• Sapporo

• Sendai

Changchun •

JAPAN

Tokyo •

38. Chiba

• Beijing

Seoul •

SOUTH KOREA

Osaka •

37. Shikoku

Yellow Sea

Great Basin

Xi'an •

CHINA

• Shanghai

East China Sea

Wuhan •

PACIFIC

Chang Jiang

• T'ai-pei

OCEAN

Kaohsiung •

TAIWAN

Hong Kong •

• Laoag

Hanoi •

BURMA

LAOS

South China Sea

Philippine Sea

36. Catanduanes

★ Manila

Yangon •

Hue •

• Da Nang

35. Siargao

Moulmein •

THAILAND

PHILIPPINES

PALAU

0° Equator

CAMBODIA

VIETNAM

★ Kokor

Bangkok •

Phnom Penh •

• Ho Chi Minh

• Davao

34. Kavieng

Zamboanga •

Bandar Seri Begawan

Celebes Sea

NEW GUINEA

• Songkhla

BRUNEI ★

Manado •

29. Nias & Hinako Islands

MALAYSIA

Kuala Lumpur ★

Samarinda •

Buru

Medan •

★ SINGAPORE

• Pontianak

Sulawesi

INDONESIA

tor 0°

Sumatra

Palembang •

Buru

Baubau •

INDIAN

PEG. BARISAN

Ujung Pandang •

Flores

Timor

30. Mentawai Islands

★ Jakarta

Surabaya •

Sumbawa •

Sumba

• Kupang

• Bandung

Java

Bali

33. West Sumbawa

OCEAN

31. West Java

32. Bali and G-Land

Timor Sea

0		500		1000 Miles

0	500	1000	1500 Kilometres

29. Nias and Hinako Islands

Lagundri Bay lineup

MARC FENIES

Summary

+ WORLD CLASS RIGHTS
+ CALM WINDS
+ OFF THE BEATEN TRACK FEEL
+ DIRT CHEAP COSTS

− LONG, HARD ACCESS
− MALARIA
− CROWDS
− SUFFOCATING HEAT AND HEAVY RAIN

The perfect righthander at Lagundri Bay on the island of Nias was the first world class wave discovered in the Sumatra region. Nias was first surfed in 1975 by Australian surf pioneers Peter Troy, Kevin Lovett and John Giesel. They put up with swarms of malarial mosquitoes and the most primitive of living conditions to ride absolute perfection in the jungle. More recently discoveries have been made on a group of little islands called the Hinako's including two excellent, big wave spots which are super consistent

MARC FENIES

Philippe Mombet, Nias

PHILIPPE CHEVODIAN

and have reduced the crowd pressure in Lagundri. These days, it's much easier to get to Nias Island, but it still retains a feeling of being at the edge of the world.

TRAVEL INFORMATION

Local Population:
Nias & Hinako's – 600,000
Coastline: 380km (236mi)
Time: GMT+8hr
Contest: WQS (Early June)

Getting There – Visas are needed by Portuguese and South African nationals. There are flights and ferries from Jakarta and Penang (Malaysia) to Medan. SMAC have closed down. Garuda (surfer friendly airline) do 3 internal flights for $100. Weekly flights leave from Padang to Gunung Sitoli ($32), book early. The bus and ferry route through Sibolga to Gunung Sitoli/Teluk Dalam is long, tiring, but very cheap! It takes about 2 hours from Gunung Sitoli on a new road to Lagundri by minibus.

Getting Around – Once in Lagundri everything lies within walking distance. Teluk Dalam is a short 'Bemo' ride away. Most roads are poorly surfaced. Renting a motorbike is easier than using trucks and bemos.

Lodging and Food – The 3-star Sorake Beach Resort, facing the Indicators reef is the best

hotel on the island. It has A/C rooms charging around $80/dble. There are losmen built on stilts overlooking the point, which have free or dirt-cheap accommodation, although you are supposed to eat in them. There are surfcamps at Asu and Bawa. The food gets boring with fish and rice for most meals but it's cheap.

Weather – Nias has a typical equatorial climate with very high temperatures and humidity, which vary little year round. Western Indo dry season is from May-Sept, but frequent 1-2 hour showers can still be expected, usually at night. The rainy season is from October-April. The water is some of the warmest in the surf world. The lack of wind is good for glassy surf, but makes it feel really hot. It takes time to adapt.

Nature and Culture – Bawomataluo village has an impressive temple, shown on the 1000Rp note; it is located less than 1 hour from Lagundri. Obstacle jumping and war dances take place throughout southern Nias.

Hazards and Hassles – Lagundri used to be malaria-infested. The disease has taken out

several surfers but recently lots of swamps have been dried out, so reducing the threat. In the Hinako Islands malaria is a serious health risk. The mosquitoes are chloroquine-resistant! Lagundri is a deep water spot but most reefs around here are shallow so be prepared to hit the bottom. Lagundri is no longer the chilled out place it once was. For many years, visiting surfers have left behind their old gear for the local groms, who now think all surfers must do the same. Be warned that one or two locals have been known to get violent if you refuse. It's a complicated situation and one with no easy answers. Stay with a recommended family. The further away from the main restaurant you stay, the more relaxed the vibe.

Handy Hints – The Nias Surf Club can be helpful for suggestions of local visits, and with advice on where to buy, rent or fix boards. Bring your own equipment with you. Take boots, helmet and 7-8ft guns for the Hinako's. There is a small clinic and a police station in Lagundri. Best money exchange rate is back on the Sumatran mainland or in Gunung Sitoli. There are now internet facilities in Teluk Dalam.

WEATHER STATISTICS	J/F	M/A	M/J	J/A	S/O	N/D
total rainfall (mm)	115	117	150	160	235	237
consistency (days/mth)	7	8	9	9	14	15
min temp (°C/°F)	22/72	22/72	23/74	23/74	22/72	22/72
max temp (°C/°F)	30/86	32/90	32/90	32/90	31/88	29/84

The Machine

DAVID PU'U

The main Lagundri wave is the point, facing the Sorake Beach tower. If the swell is over 4ft (1.3m), it wraps perfectly down the side of the reef giving possible 4-7 second barrels before emerging onto a fading wall. It breaks in deep water over a weed-covered bottom with a handy channel. A channel in the reef called 'The Keyhole' gives easy access from the losmans direct to the take-off zone. Local kids and beginners surf a reform wave on the inside named Kiddieland. Further outside of the main point is the Indicators reef, so named as it's a useful barometer for approaching sets. If it weren't for its treacherous end section it would be one of the most perfect waves around. For brave and skilled surfers only. On the other side of the bay is a left called The Machine that pumps when the swell is massive. There are also a variety of other waves in the neighbourhood, within walking distance to the west or back towards Teluk Dalam harbour. This harbour is also the place to negotiate the best deal on a boat to the Hinako Islands. It takes 4-5 hours ride to reach the island of Bawa where another right breaks, although that is where the similarities with Lagundri end. It is a shifty peak breaking far out, with a filthy end bowl section. Bawa requires a N wind. If the wind is from the S then motorboat 15km (10mi) north to Asu, where despite the malaria risks, hard-core surfers hang out and ride the big,

perfect lefts that make Asu fully deserving of its world class title. Beware the gnarly, dry-reef end section of the wave, dubbed the 'Nuclear Zone.'

Normally, equatorial shores have a lack of exposure to swells, but the South Indian Ocean is the most efficient swell machine on the planet. Expect numerous 6-10ft (2-3.3m) SW swells from April-Oct, some occasional 3-6ft (1-2m) swells during the off-season and various 2-6ft (0.6-2m) cyclone swells. Due to the latitude, wind patterns are pretty calm giving glassy conditions for 15% of the time. There are no real dominant winds. January to May has many NW days, June to Sept is SE and Oct to Dec is from the NE. Tidal ranges are only 2-3ft (0.6-1m) but it has an effect on the super shallow reefbreaks.

SURF STATISTICS	J F	M A	M J	J A	S O	N D
dominant swell	S-SW	S-SW	S-SW	S-SW	S-SW	S-SWI
swell size (ft)	3-4	4-5	5	6	5-6	4
consistency (%)	60	70	80	90	70	60
dominant wind	SW-NE	SE-N	E-SW	E-SW	SW-N	SW-N
average force	F2	F2	F2	F2	F3	F3
consistency (%)	55	56	47	56	63	59
water temp (°C/°F)	29/84	28/82	28/82	27/81	27/81	28/82
wetsuit						

Asu, Hinako Islands

PHILIPPE CHEVODIAN

30. Mentawai Islands

ALL PHOTOS SEAN DAVEY

Summary

+ TOP SWELL CONSISTENCY
+ MANY WORLD CLASS SPOTS
+ CLEAR WATER
+ EXOTIC ISLANDS
+ UNIQUE CULTURE

− BROKEN BOARDS
− DANGEROUS NAVIGATION
− MALARIA INFESTED
− VERY EXPENSIVE BOAT TOURS
− SOME CROWDED LINE-UPS

Despite their ideal location for getting the most out of the SW swells that consistently pour through the Sunoa Trench, the Mentawais have only been surfed since the early 90's. This is because these islands, lying about 90km (55mi) off the Sumatran mainland, are one of the wildest places on earth. Many of the tribal inhabitants of the more remote islands have had, until recently, little contact with the modern world, preferring instead to live their own age-old lifestyle. Add the fact that malaria is endemic and the untouched rainforest is almost impenetrable, then it's little wonder that the Indonesian

Lance's Right

government deterred surfers or tourists from visiting the Mentawais. These days, yacht charters take groups into this extremely fragile environment where even the waves

TRAVEL INFORMATION

Local Population:
Mentawais – 30,000
Coastline: 960km (597mi)
Time: GMT+8hr
Contest: No

Getting There – Visa: Portuguese and South Africans need visas. Most flights go to Jakarta or Bali from where you can get a connection to Padang. Otherwise Merpati, Sempati and Silk Air all have international flights to and from Singapore to Padang. It's a 5-6 hour ride by speedboat to Siberut Island or a much longer and uncertain ferry ride.

Getting Around – Most surfers are likely to be aboard one of 25 or so boats operating in the Mentawais. It is possible to charter independently, but there is pressure to join one of the charters. If you do charter independently, be aware that seas are rough, navigation tricky and underwater obstacles a threat. Make sure you have plenty of safety tools and spares onboard.

Lodging and Food – Living aboard a boat is a unique experience. The major and reliable

operators are STC, GBI, and Good Sumateran. Trips are for 10-12 days and cost $100-$300/day depending on the luxury of your boat. If sleeping afloat doesn't appeal then try Losmen Wavepark at E-Bay ($70/d) or Lance's Left ($40/d). Harder, but maybe more rewarding is staying with the villagers – be generous in return.

Weather – The Mentawais have a typical equatorial climate with very high temperatures and humidity. Temperature variations are minimal year round. Equatorial Indo "dry" season is Jan-Aug, but frequent 1-2 hour showers can be expected, usually falling at night. Rainy season is Sept-Dec, which requires an umbrella or poncho as it rains frequently (Sumatra means storms!). The water is some of the warmest to be found in any surf region, sometimes feeling too hot! The lack of wind is good for glassy surf but it makes it feel really hot. The heat takes time to adapt to.

Nature and Culture – The virgin forest, rugged topography, unique flora and fauna and a tribal society, which until recently was unpolluted by outside thought, all add up to make the Mentawais an ideal spot, not just for an exotic surf trip, but also for trekking.

Unfortunately the eco-friendly tours offered by various surf and trekking companies have done little to benefit the local populations, with many visitors and tour operators treating the native Mentawai people as little more than a Disney attraction. Remember that you are in the lucky position of witnessing life in these remote and wonderful islands, try not to enforce western values on the people you meet and remain as culturally sensitive as possible.

Hazards and Hassles – The surf is intense. Be prepared for long hold-downs and nasty reef cuts. Boat operators can provide first-aid assistance, but any major injury this far from expert medical attention can be fatal. Staph infections are commonplace. Strong rips are a hassle. Rampant and very dangerous strains of malaria are a serious threat, whilst snakes and intense heat are further problems.

Handy Hints – Bring lots of spare surf equipment with, it will be needed! In the prime season, bigger boards are needed, as there are some big waves. Try to come with a group of surfers all at the same level, as your boat captain will then take you to spots suitable for your abilities.

WEATHER STATISTICS	J/F	M/A	M/J	J/A	S/O	N/D
total rainfall (mm)	112	117	155	155	235	238
consistency (days/mth)	9	9	10	11	16	16
min temp (°C/°F)	22/72	22/72	22/72	22/72	22/72	22/72
max temp (°C/°F)	30/86	32/90	32/90	32/90	30/86	30/86

Lance's Rights

Muarasigep
Tg Siopa
Tabekat Bay
Padang
Kagologolo
Silogui
Silogui Bay
PULAU SIBERUT
Muarasaibi
Saribua Bay
Sakubo
Siberut Ba
Tg Simasuket

Note: Due to an initial dispute between boat operators many of the spots have two names We are using Great Breaks International (GBI) spot names.

E-Bay
Nyang Nyang
Mainu
Nipussi
Pananggalan
Karangmajet
Four Bobs
Simakaka
Pototogat
Telescopes
Pitoyat
Ciburu Bay
Scarecrows
PULAU SIPORA
Sigici
Semelo i Bay
Siduamata
Katiet
Lance's Rights
Lance's Left
Tg Sumlayu
Simaganjo
Bommie Peak
Tg Simatobe
Sikasap strait
Silabulabu
Pasangan
PULAU PAGAI UTARA
Sikakap
Seai
Macaronis
Simakalo
Gilligan's
Mapooepooe
Rags Left
PULAU PAGAI SELATAN
Bitojat
Rags Right
Sibigau
Thunders
Tiop
P. Sibaruburu

are very sensitive to winds and tides. There is always a perfect, crystal clear wave reeling off somewhere, close to the tree-lined shore of coral encrusted lava. Just hope that not too many other boatloads of wave-hungry surfers are on to it.

The main island is Siberut with a great concentration of reefs at the southern end of the island. The Nyang-Nyang area has several spots like E-Bay, which needs a W swell, and Nipussi Rights, which are average but consistent. Pit Stops is a fun righthand wall ending on a sandy beach while the shallow rights of Bankvaults are for experts. The straight edged Karangmajet Island holds a few breaks including Four Bobs which peels into a lagoon but it's Sipora that may be the best island in the archipelago. Telescopes in the north is a consistent left, ideal for anyone and works on a typical SW swell, SE wind combo. Off Pitoyat harbour is Scarecrows; a short, wedgy left, which is usually best on a dropping high tide. In the south of Sipora Island are the mythical Lance's Left and Lance's Right. Lance's Left is a forgiving mixture of workable walls and barrel sections, while Lance's Right is dangerous, fairly fickle and usually crowded with boats. South are the twin islands of Pagai Utara and Pagai Selatan, the northern-most of which is home to another famous Mentawai jewel, Macaronis. This is a machine like left, which produces an intense barrel on the first section before backing off into a slashable inside wall. Bommie Peak is for only the bravest of big wave riders. Nearby, Gilligan's provides waves suitable for anyone's ability. On Sibigau, Thunders can turn bigger swells into challenging left pits that shift around a lot.

The super consistent South Indian Ocean swells produce numerous 6-12ft (2-4m) SW swells from March-Nov and less consistent 3-6ft (1-2m) swells during the off-season. There's also a chance of some 2-6ft (0.6-2m) cyclone swells. The off-season is less crowded and the waves are not as heavy

as prime season. Swells can bend and wrap around the islands, making any wind direction an offshore possibility. Wind patterns are pretty calm, glassy 20% of the time, although there can be sudden squalls with strong, variable winds. Dominant winds run parallel to the islands, so the most consistent spots are offshore either on a NW or a SE wind. Unlike most of Indo, SE trades are not so reliable. Tidal ranges are only 2-3ft (0.6-1m) but this will affect shallow spots where coral reefs lurk just below the surface.

SURF STATISTICS	J F	M A M	J J	A S	O N	D
dominant swell	S-SW	S-SW	S-SW	S-SW	S-SW	S-SW
swell size (ft)	5	6	7	8	6-7	5
consistency (%)	70	85	90	90	90	70
dominant wind	W-NW	W-NW	NW-W	NW-W	W-NW	W-NW
average force	F3	F3	F3	F3	F3	F3
consistency (%)	42	37	41	53	60	46
water temp (°C/°F)	29/84	28/82	28/82	27/81	27/81	28/82
wetsuit						

Adam Leslie, Trev's Alley

31. West Java

Ombak Tujuh

Summary
+ GOOD CONSISTENCY
+ WORLD CLASS PANAITAN ISLAND
+ VARIETY OF WAVES
+ CHEAP

− CROWDED CIMAJA
− SEA URCHINS
− HARD ACCESS TO SOME SPOTS
− POLLUTION, DISEASE AND MALARIA

ALL PHOTOS SEAN DAVEY

Aside from a few notable exceptions, it seems that most of the Sumatran and Javan mainland coastline is devoid of the world class spots found on their small offshore islands. These coastlines are open to the same SW swells, but much of the Sumatran mainland is sheltered by offshore islands, while Java consists principally of a dangerous, black sand shorebreak, where few reefs have managed to form. However, the western end of Java does have excellent mainland surf, even though the area's world class waves are to be found on Panaitan Island.

On the south-westerly tip of the Ujung Genteng National Park, is the Ujung Genteng harbour where huge, intimidating

Turtles

rights and lefts break. A short distance north is Mama's losmen, which offers cheap accommodation and food, in front of a high tide left. Further north, opposite a prawn farm, are the fun lefts of Turtles. The wave comes out of

TRAVEL INFORMATION

Local Population:
Jakarta – 10M
Coastline: 2,885km
(1,793mi)
Time: GMT+8hr
Contest: Local

Getting There – Visa: (see 29.Nias). Cheap flights to Jakarta, which is also Garuda's hub for domestic flights. It takes 2 hours to get to Cimaja overland, 5 hours to Ujung Genteng. Airline Dep tax is $10. There are numerous ferries from/to Sumatra.

Getting Around – Rental cars from $20d. Drive on the left and give way to bigger vehicles. Renting a bemo (small minibus) with a driver may be a better option. Public transport is plentiful around Pelabuhan Ratu. To reach Panaitan Island go to Merak and try to rent a boat for the journey (it's a 7-8 hour boat ride). Many small local boats get into difficulty out here so the safer option is a yacht charter.

Lodging and Food – The 15km (10mi) beach from Pelabuhan Ratu to Cisolok has plenty of hotels. The 'Samudra' is $60/dble. In Cimaja rooms can be rented cheaply from the 'Penginapan' and "Mustika Rat" losmans. Mama's losmen in Unjung Genteng is dirt cheap. There's no lodging on Panaitan Island, sleep on your boat. Food costs are minimal.

Weather – This is a wet, tropical climate and the dry season, (May-Oct) is the best time to visit. SE trades blow offshore on most spots and the weather is good, with only occasional evening thunderstorms. The rainy season, (Nov-April) on the coast can see morning drizzle, whereas afternoons have intense rains. At this time, it can rain all day, but you may get lucky and have plenty of sunshine. Humidity levels are high in the rainy season and it brings out the insects. As for water temperatures, a pair of booties will be the only neoprene you will need year round.

Nature and Culture – The Prahus (boats) in Pelabuhan Ratu harbour are worth seeing. The

national parks are home to some great and very rare wildlife such as rhinos, snakes and tigers. There's rafting on the Citarik River or bathing in the Cisolok hot springs. You can visit a tea plantation or accept a cheap, relaxing massage from one of many local practitioners.

Hazards and Hassles – The surf around Cimaja is mellower than the Indo standard, but sea urchins and local crowds are not. The inside close-out at Turtle's can catch you out. Avoid rivermouths after rains, as hepatitis is common. Panaitan reefbreaks are treacherous. Malaria is common – take precautions.

Handy Hints – Unlike Bali, there are no real surf shops, so take spares. A gun is only needed for the heavier waves. In the Panaitan area, take everything you may need for survival. Finally, don't wear green boardshorts or rash vests in the water, Nyai Loro Kidul, the Goddess of the Sea, was born in Pelabuhan Ratu (Queen's harbour) and every year she likes to take the life of young men in the sea, who are always it seems, wearing green!

WEATHER STATISTICS	J/F	M/A	M/J	J/A	S/O	N/D
total rainfall (mm)	300	117	105	55	77	172
consistency (days/mth)	18	13	8	5	7	13
min temp (°C/°F)	23/74	23/74	23/74	23/74	23/74	23/74
max temp (°C/°F)	29/84	31/88	31/88	31/88	30/86	30/86

Panaitan Rights
Inside
One Palm Point

Sunda Strait

Unjug Kulon
National park
320m Raksa

Citeureup
Camara

Kadupandak

Gunungkencana

Sareweh
Citorek

Mount Halimun
1929m
Halimun
Reserve

Tg Alangalang

Sumur

JAVA

Panaitan Strait

P. Peucang
Tg Tancangpare

Paraja Bay

Mahendra

Tg Gede

Ujung Kulon
National park
457m Payung

Situpotong

Cilangkalian

Cikotok

Cikawung

623m Honje

Muarabinuangeun

Tg Panto

One Palm Point

Tg Tereleng

Tg Sodong

Bayah

Cisolok

Cimaja

361m

Baya Beach

P. Tinjil

Baya Reef

Tg Layar

Karang Haji
Indicators
Samudra
Loji

C'da dap

P. Deli

Cimaja & Indicators

Ciemas
481m Astana

Cikadal

Ujang Genteng
National Park

Ombak Tujuh
Turtles
Mama's
Ujung Genteng Harbour

Cibeber

deep water and peels nicely down the line, before closing out onto dry reef and rusty water pipes. Turtles sometimes gets classic but the real class spot is Ombak Tujuh just around the corner, but only accessible by boat or a marathon drive. Ombak Tujuh translates as Seven Waves and is definitely the big wave spot, capable of holding swells up to 15ft (5m). The coral ledge protrudes into deep water forcing the waves to jack up suddenly, making for elevator drops, right by the cliffs.

It's a 3 hour journey north to Pelabuhan Ratu; a popular resort for Jakarta's well off. Breaking in front of the famous Samudra Hotel is a poor quality beachbreak in small swells. A big swell turns Samudra into a nasty close-out with strong rips, but should be perfect for Loji, just a short trip south. This long, shapely rivermouth left is not a challenging wave, but the fun rides are tempered by river pollution after rains, and urchins. Most surfers head 8km (5mi) north to Cimaja Beach. It's a forgiving performance wave popular with the Jakarta locals who like to practice big manoeuvres and is a rare right in the land of lefts. However, the short ride makes it the most disputed spot around. Impatient experts can paddle over to the alluring Indicators wave, but take a gun, a helmet and extra care. Batu Karang is a dangerous right suitable for experts only. Karang Haji is a mellow longboard type right, breaking between 2 exposed rocks in smaller swells. West of the Cimaja area is the town of Baya, an empty version of Kuta Beach on Bali, with punchy beachbreaks and a good, rocky left to the east. Options are limited between Baya and the horseshoe shaped island of Panaitan in the Ujung Kulon National Park. The major show here is the world renowned One Palm Point; a left holding some of the longest barrels on earth before

wrapping into a more workable inside section. It is super shallow, very dangerous and hard to get to. In the same bay is Inside, another much mellower left. With the NW winds of the wet season, a bunch of reliable rights break in 3 different spots inside this bay

Roaring Forties lows send plenty of 6-12ft (2-4m) swells from April-Oct. The SSW direction is perfect for this SW facing area. Even the off-season is rarely flat, because of the Southern Ocean's constant swells in the 2-6ft (0.6-2m) range. The offshore trade wind starts in April when gentle E-SE winds blow until Oct. November is a transitional month with oscillating winds predominately from the south. Through the wet season (Dec-Mar), it shifts to W-NW with W first and then NW. Tides are mixed so get a tide table. There's a big tide and a small tide every day that affect most breaks.

SURF STATISTICS	J F	M A M	J J	A S	O N	D
dominant swell	S-SW	S-SW	S-W	S-W	S-SW	S-SW
swell size (ft)	4	5	6	7	6	4-5
consistency (%)	60	80	90	90	80	70
dominant wind	W-NW	W-NW	E-SE	E-SE	E-SE	SE-NW
average force	F3	F3	F4	F4	F4	F3
consistency (%)	55	62	62	73	66	76
water temp (°C/°F)	29/84	28/82	28/82	27/81	27/81	28/82
wetsuit						

Former Rip Curl Search ad

Cimaja Rights

32. Bali and G-Land

G-Land

GEOFF RAGATZ

Summary
+ MANY WORLD CLASS SPOTS
+ PERFECT LEFT SET-UPS
+ INTERESTING CULTURE
+ TOURIST HEAVEN
+ CHEAP

– CROWDED WAVES
– BUSY AND NOISY STREETS
– TOUTS AND HUSTLERS

Bali is "The Island of 1000 Temples" which the locals believe is blessed by the gods. The gods certainly have blessed the local surfers, because they live in a perfect tropical surf paradise. Although 30 years of tourism has drastically transformed the landscape and the line-ups, Bali remains an essential surfing experience. There is no denying the quality and quantity of its surf, particularly if you include the legendary long lefts of Grajagan, a short boat ride away on the eastern tip of Java. SW swells wrapping consistent lines around the Bukit Peninsula into straight offshore winds create a list of world class lefts, including Uluwatu, Padang Padang, Bingin and Kuta Reef. Add to these the quality beachbreaks of Kuta and Legian, plus the east side rights of Nusa Dua, Sanur and Shipwrecks on Nusa Lembongan, then it becomes obvious that Bali is a feast for travelling surfers.

Nusa Lembongan

GEOFF RAGATZ

Uluwatu

GEOFF RAGATZ

Uluwatu is one of Bali's most consistent waves. Broken into three sections, Inside Corner breaks in front of the cave in small and medium swells. This leads into the Racetrack section which needs mid tide or higher. The low tide Outside Corner needs well overhead swells to start breaking and is a difficult section to stay in position for. Ulu's is generally sectiony when its small, but it links up for long rides with good barrels in the middle and down through Racetracks when the waves get bigger.

TRAVEL INFORMATION

Local Population:
Bali – 3M
Coastline: 437km (271mi)
Time: GMT+8hr
Contest: Grommet (July)
WCT (June)

Getting There – Denpasar Airport (Kuta) is a major international flight hub. Boats to Nusa Lembongan leave from Sanur/Benoa and take 1h30 ($7). G-Land is reached by speedboat or sailing yacht from Benoa harbour.

Getting Around – Motorbike rentals from $5/d. Board shoulder straps are essential. Driving conditions are sketchy! Crazy Bemo (taxi) drivers are everywhere. 4WD Suzuki rental is $25/d. New bitumen roads have made break access simple.

Lodging and Food – Cheaper and better value accommodation can be found in Legian. Losmen cost from $5-$25/d or exclusive resorts for $20-$100/dble. Nusa Dua only has deluxe resorts. At Ulu's, you can crash in the 'warungs' above the break for $5/d or the Bali Cliffs Resort, $110/dble.

Weather – The dry season from May-Oct is very warm, with gentle sea breezes and some overnight rains. Average temp is 28°C (82°F). Nov-April is hotter, wetter, and more humid. Jan-Feb suffers from heavy afternoon rains and stifling humidity. The mountains can be quite cold. Water temps are a steaming 28°C (82°F).

Nature and Culture – Unusually for Indonesia, the Balinese are Hindus and nurture a fascinating culture on the island. Favourite tourist haunts include the artist village of Ubud, sunrise over Lake Batur and the lofty, volcanic peak of Agung mountain, which dominates the landscape. There are also temples, shops and great restaurants serving international and local Indonesian meals. Kuta nightlife is a hedonistic melting pot.

Hazards and Hassles – Malaria is prevalent at G-Land, but not on Bali. Be careful of thieves, scammers and shallow reefs! Dugongs (sea cows) may pop up in the line-up, but they're harmless. There's a 15ft (5m) Tiger Shark and heaps of Black Tip Reef Sharks that live around the G-Land reef, but the fishing is good and no surfer has ever been touched.

Handy Hints – There are about 20 major, well-stocked surf shops, but it's still better to bring your own gear. Learn some basic Indonesian, which is easy to pick up. Beware the prostitutes, who aren't always what they seem!

WEATHER STATISTICS	J/F	M/A	M/J	J/A	S/O	N/D
total rainfall (mm)	300	177	105	55	77	172
consistency (days/mth)	18	13	8	5	7	13
min temp (°C/°F)	23/74	23/74	23/74	23/74	23/74	23/74
max temp (°C/°F)	29/84	31/88	31/88	31/88	30/86	30/86

Muncar
Medewi
Bali Strait
Penggragoan
Penebel
Batukau
Antosari
Bangli
Amlapura
Candi Dasa
Tabanan
Ubud
Gianyar
Klungkung
Padangbai
Kusamba
Tanjung Kucur
Tg Kucur
Mengwi
Sukawati
Cucukan
Alas Purwo National Park
Plengkung
Tanah Lot
Batubulan
Denpasar
Lembongan
Nusa Lembongan
Toya Pakeh
Canggu
Seminjak Sanur
NUSA PENIDA
Tg Purwo
Legian & Kuta
Legian
Sanur
G-Land
Kuta Reef
Kuta
jimbaan bay
Tg Bantenan
Balangan
Dreamland
Bukit Badung
Impossibles/Bingin
Uluwatu/
Padang Padang
Uluwatu
Nusa Dua
Badung Strait
Nyang Nyang
Nusa Dua
Green Ball

The wave is usually zooed out, but it does spread the crowd by allowing take-offs almost anywhere along the line. Descending the cliff ladder into the cave and paddling back into it on a sizeable day at high tide are both difficult but quintessential parts of the Uluwatu experience.

Just to the north is the rarely breaking Padang Padang, Bali's most feared and desired barrel. It's always crowded and a small take off-zone exacerbates the dangers of the reef below. Impossibles, as the name suggests, has 3 very fast sections, which are rarely crowded, but rarely makeable! Bingin is best described as short, sharp and shallow. It's a tight take-off zone and dry reef shutdown at the end of this consistent left known as 'the tube garden'. Dreamland peaks off a beautiful white beach in deep water and has the least challenging waves on the Bukit Peninsula. Balangan is an average consistency spot with two different peaks that can link up and fire when the swell is bigger. The Kuta-Legian tourist strip holds quality beachbreaks which are well attended, particularly by the local surfing community who demand respect. It's a long stretch of beach so hassles can always be avoided by choosing another peak. The chaos of the Kuta traffic, souvenir vendors, piles of rubbish and dubious water quality are the downsides of surfing this area. Kuta and Airport Reefs are good quality waves, always crowded, and reached by local canoe or a long paddle. To the north are a couple of spots that are blown out by lunchtime like the peaks at Canggu. Medewi is an easy pointbreak, ideal for beginners or longboarders. During the wet season (Nov-Apr), the other side of the Bukit holds super consistent, chunky righthanders at Nusa Dua and Sanur's localised, but fantastically hollow rights.

The nearby island of Lembongan hosts 3 good spots; Playgrounds, an easy to ride peak, the treacherous rights of Lacerations and Shipwrecks fun, high tide rights. Otherwise, a trip to 'the best wave in the world', the legendary Grajagan, or G-Land, is easy to arrange from Bali. The long, super consistent wave is made up of 4 sections; Kong's, Money Trees, Launching Pad and Speedies. It will test the abilities of even the best surfers, as leg-achingly long walls transform into cavernous pits or tight, high envelopes depending on its mood. The bigger the better for G-Land as the sections link up and the tubes stay open. Both surf camps (Jungle and Jo-Jo's) cling to the edge of dense jungle, home to panthers, monkeys and snakes that visit the camps for a late night snack. Other spots like Tiger Tracks or Tanjung Kucur are a long jungle hike.

SW swells from 3-12ft (1-4m) are constant from April to Nov, and frequent in the 'off' or wet season, when 2-6ft (0.6-2m) swells and the occasional 8-10ft (2.6-3.3m) tropical cyclone can hit. Swells are focused onto the Bukit Peninsula because of the deep water channels on either side of Bali, graphically illustrated by overhead Nusa Dua when everywhere else seems too small. The SE trade season is usually April to Oct but transition months can have oscillating winds blowing mainly from the south. Winds then shift W-NW for the wet season. Tide tables are posted in surf shop windows. There is a big and a small tide each day, and some spots only work at certain stages of the tide.

SURF STATISTICS	J F	M A	M J	J A	S O	N D
dominant swell	S-SW	S-SW	S-W	S-W	S-SW	S-SW
swell size (ft)	4-5	5-6	6-7	7-8	6	4-5
consistency (%)	60	80	90	90	80	70
dominant wind	W-NW	E-NW	E-SE	E-SE	E-S	SE-NW
average force	F3	F2	F3	F3	F3	F3
consistency (%)	65	88	74	80	79	72
water temp (°C/°F)	29/84	28/82	28/82	27/81	27/81	28/82
wetsuit						

Padang Padang

33. West Sumbawa

Scar Reef

SYLVAIN CAZENAVE

Summary
+ CONSISTENT SWELLS
+ WORLD CLASS WAVES
+ SEMI-CROWDED AT THE WORST
+ EXPLORE OTHER ISLANDS

– SE TRADE WIND RESTRICTS CHOICE
– SLOW OVERLAND ACCESS
– LACK OF ALTERNATIVE ACTIVITIES
– LACK OF CULTURAL SITES

The deep water trench on the eastern side of Bali heralds the beginning of the Nusa Tenggara Islands, which sprawl all the way to Papua New Guinea and the Pacific. Sir Alfred Wallace noted the flora and fauna were from a totally different world, more akin to Australia than Asia. Nusa Tenggara's, (The Eastern Islands) climate is far drier; supporting a brown landscape of scrub and bush, unlike the lush jungles to the west. Fortunately, the one thing Nusa Tenggara has in common with the rest of Indo is plenty of epic waves. For a decade and a half, charter boats have been plying the coasts of Lombok, Sumbawa, Sumba, Savu and Roti. Surf camps have sprung up on the east and south coasts of Lombok and the Lakey area of Sumbawa, drawing ever greater numbers to these fascinating surf shores.

Although many lucky surfers have described Desert Point, Lombok as the best wave on earth, it is the western half of Sumbawa that has a higher concentration of consistent, quality

Tamboro Volcano

BILL MORRIS

Tony

MARC FENIES

waves. The erratic nature of two waves in Sekongkang Bay gives them the collective name Yo-Yo's. The area is a swell magnet, where waves bounce off the cliffs, forming steep, fast drops into a short, punchy right called The Wedge. Mid bay is another right called The Hook. These spots do not handle SE trades or major swells. There are other spots on the south coast around Sejorong, but again, they can't handle wind or bigger swells. In such circumstances it is better to carry on north up the east

TRAVEL INFORMATION

Local Population:
Sumbawa – 400,000
Coastline: 1,309km (814mi)
Time: GMT+8hr
Contest: No

Getting There – Visa: (see 29. Nias). Merpati flies several times daily from Bali to Sumbawa Besar ($50/o-w). From Bali the overland route is long and arduous, involving a 5hr ferry ride, then an 8hr bus ride followed by another 2hr ferry ride.

Getting Around – The main road across the island follows the northern coastal route. The road down the west coast is not much fun. From Sumbawa's westerly entry points of Poto Tano (ferry) or Sumbawa Besar (flight), it's a further 3hr journey to Taliwang/Jereweh and the waves. Most people charter boats from

Benoa Harbour in Bali. Make sure that it has full safety gear before you agree to a price.

Lodging and Food – Chartered boats around the spots will cost about, - STC $1500/7d, Island Express - $695/6d, Sri Noa Noa - $980/11d, these prices are all-inclusive. All boats will have a chef on board who will cook tasty and healthy food. There's usually free beer and good fishing. Land based losmen accommodation will be spartan.

Weather – Warm, but rarely overly hot temps, gentle sea breezes and some overnight rains temper the dry season from May-Oct. The average temp is 28°C (82°F). Nov-April is wetter, cloudier and hotter. Jan-Feb suffers from heavy rains and stifling hot temperatures. Warm clothing is needed for forays into the mountains. West Sumbawa is drier than the eastern end of the island and

nearby Bali. Water temps are 28°C (82°F) year round. Boardies and rashy or a shorty for protection against reef rash.

Nature and Culture – Flat day options include fishing and snorkelling, otherwise take a long book. Sumbawa is not as culturally rich as Bali. There are some great buffalo races in the rice paddies, but most of the more interesting sites are a long way from the waves.

Hazards and Hassles – Hitting the reef is going to be your major worry. Malaria is also a problem and, if you're travelling overland then communication and access will be frustrating.

Handy Hints – Take everything you need with you from Bali. You will need a gun, maybe two, for those frequent 8ft (2.6m)+ conditions. This trip is usually linked in with one to Lombok. Be very careful of cheap offers in Bali, scams happen!

WEATHER STATISTICS	J/F	M/A	M/J	J/A	S/O	N/D
total rainfall (mm)	300	177	105	55	77	172
consistency (days/mth)	18	13	8	5	7	13
min temp (°C/°F)	23/74	23/74	23/74	23/74	23/74	23/74
max temp (°C/°F)	29/84	31/88	31/88	31/88	30/86	30/86

Gary Elkerton, The Hook – Yo-Yo's

SYLVAIN CAZENAVE

coast of Sumbawa to Malok Bay, home of Super Suck. Nestled under a big headland on the south side of the bay, this world class left only works on bigger SW swells, but it will stay offshore all day in the SE trades. The name says it all, especially at low tide, when take-offs are critical and very long barrels are unavoidable. There is a resort here and some cheap losmen accommodation but remember this wave is fickle. A little further north is Scar Reef, another walled-up left with constant backdoor sections that demand high speed to stay clear of the aptly named reef. Its personality changes constantly through the tide with perfect bowls giving way to super fast walls. Opposite Scar Reef is another break, Downtowns. It's a nice right and left peak with fun surf at high tide. On the south side of Jellingah is Benete, another classic left. This one is top to bottom from the peak to the final section where it closes-out. It's also less consistent because the trade winds blow it out easily and it's only safely surfed

at high tide. Labuhan Lahat is a fishing town beside a beautiful bay where you can stay and on a big swell surf the right. The wave is called Fly, probably because of the sun-dried fish, which attract zillions of flies. The most northerly spot is called, appropriately enough, Northern Rights, a treacherous spot that needs a rare N wind.

MARC FENIES

Lakey Peak, Central Sumbawa

Those Roaring Forties lows are responsible for 6-12ft (2-4m) swell from April-Oct. The traditional Indo off season (Nov-March) is rarely flat because of the southern latitude's constant swells in the 2-6ft (0.6-2m) range and the occasional 8-10ft (2.5-3m) tropical cyclone. The SE trade wind season starts in April and lasts until Oct. Towards the end of the season more S winds blow. During the off season the wind shifts to a W-NW direction, starting with W predominance and moving around to a NW direction towards the end of March. This is a good time to check the south coast or head to Lakey Peak in central Sumbawa. Whenever you visit, you will find that mornings are frequently offshore. Try to get a tide table because Sumbawa is diurnal meaning there is a big tide and a small tide every day. Tide effects most breaks.

Periscopes, Central Sumbawa

BILL MORRIS

SURF STATISTICS	J F	M A	M J	J A	S O	N D
dominant swell	S-SW	S-SW	S-W	S-W	S-SW	S-SW
swell size (ft)	4	5	6	7	5-6	4
consistency (%)	60	80	905	90	90	70
dominant wind	W-NW	E-NW	E-SE	E-SE	E-S	SE-NW
average force	F3	F2	F3	F3	F3	F3
consistency (%)	65	88	74	80	79	72
water temp (°C/°F)	29/84	28/82	28/82	27/81	27/81	28/82
wetsuit						

PAPAU NEW GUINEA

New Ireland

INDONESIA

New England

AUSTRALIA

34. Kavieng

Summary

+ CONSISTENT, SEASONAL SWELLS
+ CLEAN, TROPICAL WAVES
+ UNCROWDED, PERFECT SURF
+ SHORT IDYLLIC BOAT RIDES
+ MELANESIAN AND PAPUAN CULTURE

− LACK OF POWER AND SIZE
− VERY RAINY SURF SEASON
− DIFFICULT AND EXPENSIVE ACCESS
− HIGH MALARIA RISKS
− CIVIL UNREST IN CERTAIN AREAS

Tarangau

ALL PHOTOS JOHN CALLAHAN

Papua New Guinea is a fascinating kaleidoscope of different peoples, cultures and landscapes. The fact that there are more than 750 different languages and that it has been wrestled over by the Germans, English, Australians and Indonesians only gives a hint to the diversity of this country's cultures. Each different area of this country hosts a different racial group, Papuans in the south, New Guineans in the north, Highlanders in the mountains and on the eastern Islands, Melanesians, who bring a distinct South Pacific influence to the country. It is these islands, bearing unlikely names such as New Britain, New Ireland and New Hanover that hold the best surf.

The Bismarck Archipelago of Melanesia faces NE into the Pacific and the New Ireland

Chris Malloy

Felix the Anchorboy

atolls are best situated to pick up any available NW to NE swells. On the Papua New Guinea mainland, the south coast around Port Moresby is drier, flatter and exposed to the erratic cyclone swells coming up from the south - Hula is probably the most consistent place to surf these swells. The north coast of the mainland is a better bet. Places like Wewak, Aitape and Vanimo are known to produce consistent waves during the NW monsoon. It

TRAVEL INFORMATION

Local Population:
Kavieng – 5,000
Coastline: 5,152km
(3,220mi)
Time: GMT+10hr
Contest: No

Getting There - Visa: 60 day tourist cards issued on entry. Most flights are to Port Moresby where you can get an internal flight to Kavieng with Air Niugini. Australia has the most flight connections with PNG. From Indonesia you can fly directly from Irian Jaya (the Indonesian half of New Guinea island), to Kavieng with Garuda. Dep tax is $6.

Getting Around - To get around on dry land use the PMV's, (public motor vehicles) but you'll need a boat to access most of the different spots. Boat transport will be included if you come here on a package, for which you will pay around $1,265 from Sydney, including flights.

Lodging and Food - There are few hotels and resorts in this area and they're all expensive. A basic hotel costs about $50/dble but most surfers stay at the Nusa Island Retreat on Nusa Lik, which will take no more than 12 people at a time. The fresh seafood is excellent.

Weather – Dry season is a bit of a misnomer as it's always very wet with a yearly average of 10ft (3.2m)/year. Also, with a surf season that corresponds with the NW monsoon you can be sure of a good soaking. It also gets very hot and is constantly sticky. Port Moresby is much drier, whilst the west of New Britain island has up to 20ft (6.4m) of rain a year! Cyclones actually hitting this area are a rare occurrence.

Nature and Culture - The diving is world class. On land you can play volleyball and snooker, visit the crocodile farm or the W.W.II relics. A totally unique experience is the "shark calling"

– local people using coconut shell rattles and their voices to attract the sharks. Pidgin is a strange mix of local and English vocabulary, which can be hard to interpret.

Hazards and Hassles - Papua New Guinea has a bad reputation as a violent and unstable country. This is true in certain areas such as the neighbouring island of Bougainville, but the Kavieng area is pretty safe. Even petty theft is quite rare, but remain vigilant. Reefs are super shallow and full of sharks, Stonefish and sea snakes. A much greater health risk is malaria and infection from reef cuts.

Handy Hints - There is no surf gear available anywhere. Bring your standard shortboard and some reef boots. It would be very rare to find even the smallest of crowds in the water. There is reasonable hospital care in Kavieng. Contact Worldsurfaris for package trips to Nusa Lik.

WEATHER STATISTICS	J/F	M/A	M/J	J/A	S/O	N/D
total rainfall (mm)	434	368	169	154	178	283
consistency (days/mth)	22	21	8	6	7	14
min temp (°C/°F)	24/75	23/74	23/74	22/72	23/74	24/77
max temp (°C/°F)	30/86	31/88	31/88	30/86	30/86	31/88

was this coastline that suffered the recent, catastrophic tsunami.

Since the discovery of the right at Piccinniny, Kavieng Harbour and the surrounding atolls have become the centre of surf attention in Papua New Guinea. Open to any N or NW swell and well removed from the threats of violence that can plague other areas of Papua New Guinea, Kavieng is a relatively safe and very exotic place to hunt for waves. On the downside, the surf spots are very sensitive to tide, wind and swell size, while long distances between spots make a boat pretty much essential. Piccinniny is an impressive right that reels off the main wharf in Kavieng for up to 200m (700ft). It's a heavy, barrelling wave that has been ridden at 8-10ft (2.6-3.2m), where boots are indispensable to negotiate the sharp reef whose depth is measured in inches! On the north-eastern tip of Nusa Island is a reliable, pitching, left barrel, but it should only be attempted when conditions are perfect, as it's very shallow. Whenever the swell is over 6ft (2m), long rights, called The Long-Long, break off a perfect bend in the barrier reef at the southern tip of Nusa Lik. The water here is deeper than most surrounding spots and it handles winds from the north. A more consistent, north facing spot can be found on nearby Nago Island, where a well shaped, powerful left, breaks on the outside reef and is best ridden at low tide. The further west you head, the bigger and more consistent the waves become.

Ross Williams, Tarangau Island

The bulk of Papua New Guinea's waves come from NW wind swells which provide regular 3-6ft (1-2m) waves from Nov-April. Don't visit during El Niño years, as the waves are very inconsistent. Nearby islands like Tarangau always seem to have some sort of rideable wave during the surf season. Due to the contorted nature of the reefs and the way the swells wrap around onto them, there should always be somewhere offshore. The more exposed spots will only be surfed early in the morning, as the offshore mornings turn onshore most afternoons. November is the month with the lightest winds. While the supposed dry season (May-Oct) sees offshore SE winds, there is far less swell. The tidal range can reach 12ft (4m) and most spots favour mid to low tide. It's not too hard to get a tide table from Kavieng Harbour or the numerous diving resorts.

SURF STATISTICS	J F	M A	M J	J A	S O	N D
dominant swell	NW	NW	–	–	–	NW
swell size (ft)	4-5	3-4	1-2	0-1	1-2	3-4
consistency (%)	80	70	30	10	30	70
dominant wind	W-N	NW-E	E-S	E-S	SE-SW	
average force	F3	F2-F3	F3	F3	F3	F3
consistency (%)	60	58	62	75	63	57
water temp (°C/°F)	28/82	28/82	28/82	27/81	28/82	28/82
wetsuit						

Tarangau Island

Edmago is a small island to the south-west of Nago, which has a left and a right at different stages of the tide - the better bet is the mid tide right. A final option is on uninhabited Tarangau where a super consistent right breaks off a beautiful, white sand beach. There's also rumoured to be a spot to the east of Kavieng that is accessible by road and worth checking in W winds and good N swells.

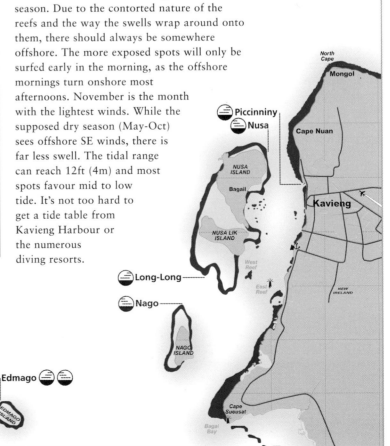

PHILIPPINES

INDONESIA

35. Siargao

Summary
+ WORLD CLASS REEFS
+ PLENTY OF UNCROWDED SPOTS
+ TROPICAL CONDITIONS
+ CHEAP LIVING COSTS

– GENERALLY SMALL SURF
– LONG FLAT SPELLS
– LONG TRANSFER JOURNEY
– POLITICAL INSTABILITY

Cloud Nine

JOHN CALLAHAN

The 7,107 islands of the Philippines in many ways form a parallel to Indonesia. The quality of the reefs is similar, the climate much the same and the beaches as beautiful. It differs only in swell consistency. The Philippines lie at the west end of the Pacific and relies on E swells, which are generated by typhoons travelling along the East Asian coastline from July to Nov. A deep water trench and a better swell exposure make the south-eastern area of the Philippines the prime wave theatre. Discovered in the early 80's, it's a remote place surrounded by many unexplored islands and feels a lot like Bali in the 70's. There

JOHN CALLAHAN

Taylor Knox, Pilar Point

JOHN CALLAHAN

are many world class reefs on the 27km (17mi) of coastline exposed to swell on Siargao. A few of the spots are outside reefs that can only be accessed by boat. General Luna is a good place to be based during the SW monsoon and Pilar is better during the NE trades.

TRAVEL INFORMATION

Local Population:
General Luna – 15,000
Coastline: Siargao –
122km (76mi)
Time: GMT+8hr
Contests: Local (Sept)

Getting There – Most nationalities get a three week visa on arrival for free; 59 day visas cost $35 and must be obtained before your arrival in the country. Most visitors arrive in Manila. Cebu is the closest airport to the waves. Siargao Island is a mission to reach. The usual way is on the overnight ferry or on a 4hr catamaran ride to Surigao City (flights are not reliable with boards), then a 3hr boat ride to Dapa and a thirty minute bus ride to General Luna. Dep tax is $20

Getting Around – 'Jeepneys', (local buses), are reliable and frequent for the hop between General Luna and Pilar as well as almost all 'Barrios' (villages). It's easy to walk between the different spots or if you are staying at one of the surf camps then a guide will drive you around. Keep some spare money on you for

boat (banka) rides, they're cheap, and there are loads of them.

Lodging and Food – The Philippines is a very cheap destination with plenty of accommodation options. There are a couple of surf camps on Siargao Island, such as the Green Room surf camp (Cloud Nine, $35/dble), General Luna Maite Surf Express resort ($25/dble) or the Tuason Cottages ($35/dble). In Pilar there's Junior's Resort ($25/dble), and Pacifico should have a surf camp very soon. Food is very cheap and revolves around fish and rice; $5 a meal.

Weather – The Philippines are hot and humid year round. The Pacific side of the Philippines is subject to two monsoon patterns, the NE monsoon (Amihan) from Nov to April not only brings onshores and small wind swell, but also huge amounts of rainfall. In July the SW monsoon (Habigat) starts blowing, this brings less rain and better winds patterns. Typhoons rarely make landfall this far south, but if they are going to, then July-Nov is the risk period. The water is warm year round, so you'll only need boardshorts and a rash vest.

Nature and Culture – The diving and fishing are both excellent. There is plenty of potential for discovering unknown surf spots on the remaining Philippine islands. Siargao Island has some natural hot springs near Lake Mainit, giant caves on Hikdop Island or whirlpools in the Surigao straits. For night-time entertainment go to Los Ninos Locos in General Luna.

Hazards and Hassles – The Philippines go through periods of political instability. At the time of going to print there was a serious problem with foreigners being kidnapped in the south of the country making it unsafe to visit - check out the latest before you leave. Siargao is hard to get to. There is a small band of competitive local surfers and quite a lot of foreign surfers but everyone is spread out over plenty of different spots. Rain, intense heat and malarial mosquitoes are present.

Handy Hints – Bring all your own surf gear, including a semi-gun. A guy called Neil Berte does a fine job fixing boards. Filipinos are usually very friendly, but there is the occasional bit of localism at Cloud Nine.

WEATHER STATISTICS	J/F	M/A	M/J	J/A	S/O	N/D
total rainfall (mm)	460	380	141	154	220	524
consistency (days/mth)	21	20	11	12	15	22
min temp (°C/°F)	23/74	23/74	24/75	24/75	24/75	23/74
max temp (°C/°F)	29/84	31/88	31/88	31/88	31/88	29/84

Tuesday Rock

JOHN CALLAHAN

Cloud Nine is the most consistent wave, being a world class barrelling right and a shorter left. It's a real swell magnet on a small to moderate swell. It takes about an hour to walk from General Luna to Cloud Nine and on the way there are several other good spots. Tuason Point is one of these waves, a seriously heavy left. On big swells there is a rarely ridden outside wave as well. Horseshoe is another spot on the way to Cloud Nine, it's a wedgy peak that is highly rated. General Luna itself is hardly ever rideable but it serves as a good indicator to swell size at the other spots. Daco Island is only 4km (2.5mi) south of General Luna, home to a long, fun right called Barrio. Rent a boat to get there. From General Luna it is close to the islands of East Bucas, Casulian, Lajanosa, Mamon and Antokon. These waves aren't really suited to beginners but they're not especially critical. The place to be based during the NE trades is Pilar, a one and a half hour boat ride from General Luna. Pilar has two offshore reefs that have outstanding waves. Pancit Reef breaks beyond a couple of big rocks. A long, consistent, soft-breaking right that holds double overhead waves and is best at low tide. Nearby is Stimpys, a ferocious left that wraps around the reef into very shallow water and is only suitable for experts. The Pilar area is generally not as crowded as the General Luna region, yet the bay holds many good lefts that are better surfed during NE storms. On SW winds drive north to Caridad which, with a good swell and full tide, reveals a perfect left. Further north, near San Isidro is Pacifico, a long, hollow and consistent left. Up toward the northern cape, the Rizal area is a good hunting ground.

The Philippines don't have great swell exposure because the only real swell generator is from typhoons travelling W-NW towards Japan. They may form at any time but July-Dec is the prime time, peaking through Sept-Oct. There is an estimated 15-20 swells in each season, that provide several days of E-NE swells between 3-8ft (1-2.6m) with occasional 12ft (4m) days. The best time is during the SW monsoon from July-Nov when the wind is predominantly offshore. After this the wind switches around to the NE. The NE monsoon only brings small onshore wind swells. The May-June transition period sees winds blowing from a S to an E direction, though it's usually calm. The tidal range is minimal but most shallow reefs are better surfed from mid-high tide.

Pacifico

PHILIPPE CHEVODIAN

Gabe Davies, Stimpys

PHILIPPE CHEVODIAN

SURF STATISTICS	J F	M A	M J	J A	S O	N D
dominant swell	–	–	–	N-E	N-E	N-E
swell size (ft)	1-2	1-2	2	3-4	4-5	4
consistency (%)	20	20	40	70	60	60
dominant wind	NE-E	NE-E	E-S	S-W	SW-NE	NE-E
average force	F4	F4	F3	F3-F4	F3-F4	F4
consistency (%)	85	80	67	59	56	65
water temp (°C/°F)	23/74	23/74	24/75	25/77	24/75	23/74
wetsuit						

36. Catanduanes

PHILIPPINES

INDONESIA

ALL PHOTOS JOHN CALLAHAN

Summary
+ WORLD CLASS RIGHTHANDER
+ EMPTY WAVES
+ EXOTIC, TROPICAL PARADISE
+ CHEAP AND MELLOW TRIP

– LONG FLAT SPELLS
– LACK OF QUALITY SPOTS
– UNSUITABLE FOR BEGINNERS
– WET CLIMATE
– DIFFICULT ACCESS

A glance at a map of the 7,107 islands of the Philippines could leave you feeling dizzy over the apparent surf possibilities this country offers. Located just off the Bicol region of South Luzon (the main island), Catanduanes Island juts out into the Pacific and appears to be an ideal swell magnet for the NE typhoon swells. The first Philippine surf explorers arrived in the mid 80's, followed in 1988 by Surfer magazine, who published the story of a trip to Catanduanes. The idyllic photos of a palm fringed, white sand beach with a barrelling righthander just offshore, put the Philippines under the surf world's spotlight. Majestics seemed the perfect name, however the pictures were deceiving, not showing how quickly the wave breaks or how inconsistent it is. Many surfers have been drawn to Catanduanes by the pictures

and ended up spending weeks waiting around for Majestics to do its thing. However, when it does show its potential, it is undoubtedly a class act.

The reason Catanduanes Island is not as consistent as you would expect could be due to the fact that it lies just a little outside the influence of the offshore deep water trench and maybe needs a more direct E swell, which is rarer than the standard N/NE swells. Other factors that

TRAVEL INFORMATION

Local Population: Catanduanes – 210,000
Coastline: Catanduanes – 210km (131mi)
Time: GMT+8hr
Contest: no

Getting There – Visas required for stays longer than 21 days (see 35.Siargao). Most international flights go to Manila, then a connection to Legaspi and finally a ferry to Virac, the main town on Catanduanes. There are direct flights to Virac with 'Asian Spirit' but surfboards can present problems. From Virac a jeepney, (local bus), takes about 2hrs to Puraran (Majestics). Dep tax is $20

Getting Around – This is pretty much a one spot zone and you may find little reason to move around. Much of the coastline is accessible only by foot, down muddy trails.

WEATHER STATISTICS	J/F	M/A	M/J	J/A	S/O	N/D
total rainfall (mm)	460	380	141	154	220	524
consistency (days/mth)	21	20	11	12	15	22
min temp (°C/°F)	23/74	23/74	24/75	24/75	24/75	23/74
max temp (°C/°F)	29/84	31/88	31/88	31/88	31/88	29/84

Hire a boat to scout out the hidden reefs; much of the east coast is uncharted. Jeepneys are the local form of transport

Lodging and Food – You can stay in one of several huts on stilts facing the surf. Puting-Baybay up to the north and Majestic Resort are sometimes referred to as surf camps. $5 should get you a bed for the night. Food is also cheap at $2-$3 for a basic meal.

Weather – The Philippines are hot and humid year round. The Pacific side of the island is open to two different monsoons. The NE monsoon (Amihan) lasts from Nov-April and not only brings onshores and small wind swells, but also huge amounts of rainfall. After the May-June transition period, the SW monsoon (Habigat) starts blowing, bringing drier weather and offshore winds. Even though the

swell comes from typhoons they rarely make landfall in the Philippines, although there is always the risk between July-Nov. If they do hit be prepared for devastation.

Nature and Culture – Don't miss the 2,500m (8,200ft) Mayon Volcano near Legaspi. The beaches here are some of the best in the world and the crystal clear water makes for excellent snorkelling and diving conditions. Climb up to the Puraran Pass for some amazing views.

Hazards and Hassles – Reef cuts and malaria are your biggest enemies. Be prepared for flat days. Crowded line-ups are rare. There is the risk of civil unrest, especially in the cities.

Handy Hints – Don't expect to find any surf gear available. The local surfers, who are friendly and dedicated, always appreciate new gear.

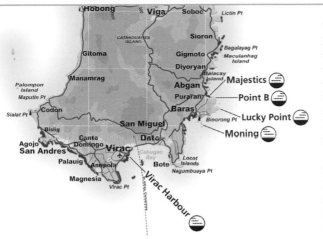

Puraran

will conjure up a fun left inside Virac harbour, which has plenty of opportunities to bust out some big moves. None of the spots ever get very busy, as there are only a handful of local and visiting foreign surfers. Typhoon swells are different to groundswells in that sets have around 8-10 waves in them, sometimes 12-15, as compared to the more normal 4-6 that groundswells produce. The island is big and certainly hides more spots. Hire a boat in Virac and go and explore.

Catanduanes' inconsistency has led surfers to explore other islands, most notably Samar, Camarines, Siargao and the main island of Luzon, which has the highest number of known surf spots. On Luzon, Charlie's Point in Aurora Province is the most well known wave, being the location for the surfing clip in the film 'Apocalypse Now'. Potentially, the best Luzon spots are found on the west coast around La Union close to San Fernando, where the South China Sea produces reliable wind swells during the NE monsoon from Nov to April.

Swell exposure is not great, coming only from typhoons travelling in a W-NW direction towards Japan. They can form at any time but the majority occur between July and Nov and the peak months seem to be Aug-Oct. There's an estimated 15-20 typhoons a year, each one providing 2-4 days of swell between 3-8ft (1-2.6m), with peak swells hitting 12ft (4m). The best time is from July to Oct when the swells are cleaned up by an offshore, SW wind. By November the wind is shifting round to an onshore, NE direction, although this transition period sees quite a lot of swell activity. The NE monsoon only brings small, onshore wind swells. The May-June transition period will bring E-S winds, which fluctuate in strength and direction all the time, but generally it's quite calm. The tidal range is large and most of the shallow reefs are only rideable from mid to high tide.

may prevent you from surfing Majestics are onshore winds and low tides making the reef dangerously shallow. To be surfed safely you must have at least a 2-3ft (0.6-1m) swell with offshore winds. Remember that this is one of the hollowest and fastest righthand barrels around. It only works from mid to high tide and is best on the push. If conditions are too sketchy at Majestics, try Point B further to the south but beware of the exposed rocks. It can be a brilliant righthander, but it's not suitable for beginners. When Majestics and Point B are onshore, the lefts of Moning, should be working at high tide. By renting a boat you can reach Lucky Point, in between Point B and Moning. It's another fine right, which picks up all available swell. Big stormy days on the south coast

SURF STATISTICS	J	F	M	A	M	J	J	A	S	O	N	D
dominant swell	–		–		–		N-E		N-E		N-E	
swell size (ft)	1		1		1-2		3		3-4		3-4	
consistency (%)	10		10		20		50		60		40	
dominant wind	N-E		N-E		E-SW		S-W		SW-NE		N-E	
average force	F4		F3		F3		F3-F4		F3		F3-F4	
consistency (%)	79		70		57		63		76		75	
water temp (°C/°F)	24/75		24/75		25/77		26/79		25/77		24/75	
wetsuit												

Hans Hagen

37. Shikoku

CHRIS VAN LENNEP

Summary
+ WORLD CLASS RIVERMOUTH WAVES
+ WARM WATER IN THE SURF SEASON
+ LAID BACK AMBIENCE
+ AMAZING CULTURAL EXPERIENCE

– INCONSISTENT TYPHOON SWELLS
– FLAT WINTERS
– RELATIVELY WET CLIMATE
– VERY HIGH LIVING COSTS

The islands of Japan are strung out across the north-western corner of the wave rich Pacific, yet very few surfers will ever visit these interesting shores. The cost factor is enough to put most people off, but add in heavy crowds, intense industrialisation, an utterly alien culture and inconsistent waves, then it's hardly surprising that few foreign surfers ever make the effort. For those who have enough money and can handle the flat spells, then Japan can be a rewarding surf destination. Amongst the best places in the country to head for is Shikoku, Japan's fourth largest island. Shikoku is made up of four provinces and is quintessentially Japanese; water gardens full of temples, traditional fishing harbours and crystal clear rivers meandering through open countryside. The exposed SE facing coastline

JOHN CALLAHAN

Inouda Rivermouth

CHRIS VAN LENNEP

crosses the Kochi and Tokushima provinces, where abundant rainfall feeds numerous rivers. When these rivers spill into the sea, they help to form decent sandbanks for the typhoon generated swells to break on, resulting in some grinding righthand rivermouth breaks.

Kaifu, in Tokushima, is probably the best place to score the quality rivermouth waves. It's about 45mins

TRAVEL INFORMATION

Local Population:
Shikoku – 4,300,000
Coastline: 1,951km
(1,220mi) (Shikoku)
Time: GMT+9hr
Contest: National (Aug)

Getting There – Visas are needed by South Africans. The quickest but not necessarily the cheapest way of getting to Kaifu is by flying to Osaka and getting the ferry from Nanko to Kannoura, an uncomfortable 7hr journey. The national airline is JAL.

Getting Around – Trains run along the coast but are frequently packed. A rental car costs about $250/w and fuel is around $1.20/l. If you can't read Japanese then driving yourself around will be a nightmare. You usually have to pay to park at the beach.

Lodging and Food – Japan is the most

expensive destination in the world. If money is a concern keep out of Osaka and the big cities. Youth hostels are about the cheapest accommodation options, but they will still set you back $30 a night for a dorm bed! Minshukus are family guesthouses, and are a much better option, although more expensive at ±$50/dble. The local food is delicious and very healthy, sushi and rice will cost about $8-10 a meal.

Weather – Shikoku has an extreme climate with cold, continental winters and hot, sticky summers. It is however, not as extreme as the Chiba area further north. Spring and summer on the south coast are extremely wet; autumn sees a much drier weather pattern. Good news, as this is also the prime swell season. The water never gets very cold and during the surf season it is at its warmest, never requiring more than a springsuit. Bear in mind that some typhoons hit the islands in the south of Japan.

Nature and Culture – There are spectacular views from the Seto-Ohashi Bridge outside of Osaka. There is a road in this area used by Buddhist pilgrims, along which are 88 temples. The Yosakoi Festival in Kochi in mid-Aug is unmissable.

Hazards and Hassles – Seismic activity is the highest in the world, but it's not really something that you need to worry about. The largest typhoon swells can get a bit intimidating. Local surfers are supercool to foreigners (Gaijin) but despite this it's worth avoiding the popular spots and ridiculous crowds on Sundays.

Handy Hints – A growing surf industry is forming in this area and there are plenty of surf shops and shapers. However gear is very expensive - a new board will set you back $1200! Somewhat amazingly, you can't always rely on your credit card being accepted, so carry some cash.

WEATHER STATISTICS	J/F	M/A	M/J	J/A	S/O	N/D
total rainfall (mm)	95	190	352	282	267	85
consistency (days/mth)	10	13	15	12	9	7
min temp (°C/°F)	3/37	8/46	16/61	23/74	18/64	6/43
max temp (°C/°F)	12/54	18/64	25/77	30/86	26/79	16/61

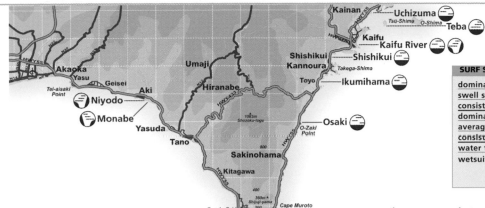

SURF STATISTICS	J F	M A	M J	J A	S O	N D
dominant swell	–	–	–	SE-S	SE-S	SE-S
swell size (ft)	1-2	1-2	2	3-4	4	4
consistency (%)	10	10	20	60	70	50
dominant wind	W-NE	W-NE	E-SW	E-SW	N-E	W-NE
average force	F4	F4	F3-F4	F3	F4	F4
consistency (%)	80	61	57	62	56	76
water temp (°C/°F)	17/62	16/61	22/72	27/81	25/77	20/68
wetsuit						

from Cape
Muroto and is in the
heart of the scenic Ana
Quasi national coastal park.
When it turns on it has heavy
tubing rights in both the rivermouth
and the neighbouring beach. When it's
on, it's guaranteed busy, but especially so on Sundays. It
can hold a decent sized swell and has been ridden up to 10-12ft
(3.3-4m). South of Kaifu is a beachbreak in Shishikui, which is a
real swell magnet. Ikumihama Beach is very popular with surfers
from Osaka, who use the overnight ferry from Nanko to surf the
mellow waves. If a S swell hits, Osaki will have consistent peaky
lines breaking over sand and boulders. On the western side of
Cape Muroto, there's more quality rivermouth waves, but they
need perfect conditions to produce the goods. Monabe is one
such spot, as is the excellent Niyodo, which can have world class
lefts and rights. Luck is needed to get a strong SE-S swell and the
wind with some N or E in it. To the north of Kaifu there are
smaller waves like Uchizuma, a little beach that closes-out over
4ft (1.3m). It is a useful indicator to what may be happening on
the nearby islands. Renting a boat is the only option but it may
be worth it as Teba is rumoured to have a long right.

Like many east facing locations, the exposure to swell is hardly
perfect. Unlike the Chiba area to the north, swells only come
from typhoons, of which there's an average of 20 swells per
season (July-Nov). The swells are unpredictable, lasting from
several hours to several days depending on the track and speed of
the typhoon. Expect SE swells of 2-8ft, (0.6-2.6m), that usually last
for 2-3 days. The chances of experiencing a lot of flat days are very
high and on a short trip, during a bad season you may not get to
surf anything above 1-2ft (0.3-0.6m) wind chop. Winds blow from
the N in the winter, which gives dry, cold and offshore conditions.
In the summer
the wind shifts
to the SE and
brings heavy
rain. It rarely
gets very windy,
except when a
passing low
pressure system
or a typhoon
hits land. Tidal
range doesn't
exceed 6ft (2m).

JOHN CALLAHAN

CHRIS VAN LENNEP

38. Chiba Prefecture

Summary

+ GREAT RIVERMOUTH BREAKS
+ WARM SUMMER CONDITIONS
+ UNIQUE CULTURAL DESTINATION

− INCONSISTENT
− FREQUENTLY SMALL AND MUSHY
− CROWDS AND POLLUTION
− VERY EXPENSIVE

HISAYUKI TSUCHIYA

The Land of the Rising Sun is made up of four major islands (Hokkaido, Honshu, Shikoku and Kyushu) and a thousand lesser islands, split between the influence of the warm Kuroshio and the cold Oyashio currents. Although the main island of Honshu gets occasional surf from NW wind swells coming off the Sea of Japan, most of the more consistent spots are those exposed to the late summer typhoon swells, or short lived NE groundswells. The long tradition of fishing has had a negative influence on surfing, with harbours and tetrapods built in many of the areas that catch the best swells. Surfing is now a well-established sport that has been growing in popularity since World War II. Kanagawa, Ibaraki and

HISAYUKI TSUCHIYA

Niijima Island – Hot Springs

CHRIS VAN LENNUP

Shizuoka areas all have some good spots but the most popular surf zone for Tokyo-based surfers is the Chiba Peninsula, a mere 30min drive from the city.

Most of the spots are mediocre beachbreaks. At the north end of the peninsula is Choshi, a large fishing town with plenty of south facing beachbreaks that work on

TRAVEL INFORMATION

Local Population:
Tokyo area – 24M
Coastline: 29,751km
(18,590mi)
Time: GMT+9hr
Contests: WQS (Aug)
National

Getting There – Visas are needed by nationals of South Africa. There are direct flights to Tokyo from all over the world but they are not necessarily cheap. The national airline is JAL. Narita Airport is conveniently located west of Tokyo not far from Choshi. It's only a 30 min train ride to the coast from Tokyo.

Getting Around – The best way to get to the beach is by train. They are fast and frequent but expensive. Rental cars cost about $250/w, fuel's about $1.20/l. Traffic, especially on the main roads, is intense and if you don't speak or read Japanese then forget about driving on your own as you'll get hopelessly lost. There are fees for parking at the beach and at certain popular spots.

Lodging and Food – Japan and Tokyo in particular, is the most expensive destination in the world. The Minshukus, (family run, basic lodging) around Katsuura are the cheapest places to stay - full board costs about ±$70/dble. Local cuisine is tasty and healthy, sushi and rice cost about $15/meal.

Weather – Japan is a land of extreme temps with sticky summers and bitterly cold winters with the air coming straight from Siberia. Despite being dry, winter (Nov-March) should be avoided at all costs, as the freezing temps and strong, gusty winds are certain to keep you out of the water. Spring (April-May) is the best time because of clear, skies, pleasant temps and celebrations. Summer is typhoon season, hot and wet, but it's a good time for surf in Japan, especially late summer. Most rainfall comes in the form of brief, heavy showers. The autumn gets cold very quickly. Despite freezing winter temps the water doesn't get all that cold. Oct-May requires up to a 4/3 steamer and June-Sept a springsuit.

Nature and Culture – Tokyo is a city buzzing with life. Visit the central Ginza area for its shopping, Shinkuju for night-time entertainment or Akihabara for electronic goods. The perfect volcanic cone of Mt. Fuji is well worth a visit and if it stays flat for a long time then the Wild Blue Wave Pool in Yokohama with its 2ft (0.6m) waves may quench the thirst.

Hazards and Hassles – Locals are cool towards 'Gaijin' (foreigners). Avoid surfing on Sundays the beaches get engulfed by waveriders. Pollution can be severe.

Handy Hints – There are plenty of surf shops, but at $1200 a board, they are way overpriced. Crime rates are low, mutual respect is something that extends to all parts of daily life, including in the waves - there can be a hundred people on each peak but no aggressive localism or jockeying for waves. Longboarding is becoming very popular.

WEATHER STATISTICS	J/F	M/A	M/J	J/A	S/O	N/D
total rainfall (mm)	67	117	155	145	215	80
consistency (days/mth)	7	11	12	11	13	6
min temp (°C/°F)	-2/28	5/41	15/59	21/70	16/61	3/37
max temp (°C/°F)	9/48	15/59	23/74	29/84	24/75	14/57

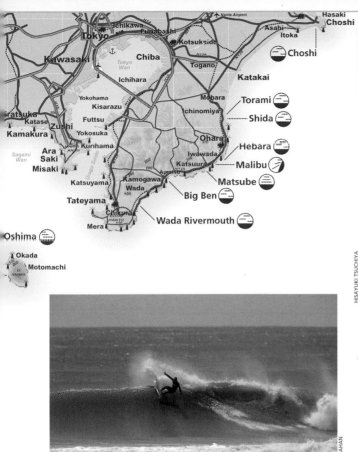

HISAYUKI TSUCHIYA

JOHN CALLAHAN

Kelly Slater, Torami Beach

Japan suffers from East Coast Syndrome so the best swells have to originate either from typhoons or from lows to the NE. The typhoon belt produces an average of 20 swells per season (June-Nov). Typhoon swells are unpredictable and can last from either several hours to many days, depending on the track they take across the Pacific. They can send 2-8ft (0.6-2.6m) SE swells, which last two or three days. There are many flat days and if you're unlucky, you may end up surfing no more than 1-2ft (0.3-0.6m) mush. Wintertime, NE groundswells are somewhat more frequent but are usually less than 4ft (1.3m) and the water can be fiercely cold at this time. Winds blow from a N direction in winter giving cold and dry conditions whilst in the summer the wind shifts to the SE which brings rainfall. In the late summer the offshore kicks back in and the typhoons continue to pump in the swells. Tidal range doesn't exceed 6ft (2m) but effects some spots.

typhoon swells. This is one of the few spots that can be crowd free, especially towards Shida. There are only a few access points to this powerful beachbreak that on W winds, high tide and a clean, moderate swell, can produce perfect barrels. These waves however can't be described as 'clean' as this area is let down by the brown coloured water and industrial waste that frequently pollutes the beach. Hebara is a consistent beachbreak, and has thus been chosen as a WCT contest site. North of Katsuura, towards Shingoan is a set of reefbreaks that produce fast, barrelling waves, whilst the area up towards Onjuku is a good place to look for empty peaks. South of Katsuura is a right pointbreak called Malibu that's best at high tide. Matsube is a treacherous reefbreak known for its righthand tubes. Kamogawa has plenty of peaks; one of the prime spots being a longboard wave called Big Ben. A submarine canyon just off Kamogawa funnels the swell into this spot. Wada is a rivermouth break that can be excellent and it's one of the few places that breaks well on N/NE swells. Tokyo Bay itself is very sheltered and only works on the heaviest of typhoon swells. To escape the crowds, take the ferry over to Oshima or Niijima, which are quiet, mellow islands. Niijima was once a WCT contest site and has a consistent beachbreak as well as a few reliable reefbreaks.

SURF STATISTICS	J F	M A	M J	J A	S O	N D
dominant swell	NE	NE	–	SE-S	SE-S	NE
swell size (ft)	3-4	2-3	2	3-4	4	4
consistency (%)	40	50	50	70	80	60
dominant wind	W-N	W-NE	NE-SW	E-SW	N-E	NW-NE
average force	F4-F5	F4-F5	F4	F3-F4	F4	F4
consistency (%)	73	66	71	67	54	63
water temp (°C/°F)	13/55	15/59	18/64	21/70	19/66	17/62
wetsuit						

JOHN CALLAHAN

Shane Beschen, Torami Beach

THE TRADITION ENDURES

BEAU YOUNG

"ONE FAMILY WITH 2 WORLD CHAMPIONS.
HISTORY WAS MADE TODAY—DON'T FORGET IT."

JOEL TUDOR

SUNDAY OCTOBER 8, 2000

PRAIA DO ROSA, SANTA CATARINA

OXBOW WORLD LONGBOARD CHAMPIONSHIPS

TOES ON THE NOSE | CLASSIC SURFWEAR | WORLDWIDE

WWW.TOESONTHENOSE.COM

0044 1205 722745

Bell's Beach

Australia

Meteorology and Oceanography

Australia is the only island continent on the planet, and within those two descriptive words are clues to this prolific surfing location. As an island it is surrounded by no less than 3 oceans and 4 major seas, while as a continent it represents a surfable coastline of epic proportions. Australia offers an unrivalled diversity and quantity of swells, in a range of environments from tropical to trembling cold. Unlike any other continent, Australia has a long southern coastline which faces the Southern Ocean and its mountainous seas. The storms that circulate around the 40°S latitude form a belt of the most efficient swell producers around, spraying the Indian Ocean's eastern shores, including Western Australia (see Indian Ocean chapter). Once these Roaring Forties low pressure systems enter the Great Australian Bight, they lose little intensity and continue to bombard the southern coastline with SW swell. Cliffs ring the coastline of the Bight, which is largely inaccessible until the SW facing shore of South Australia greets the swell head-on in one of the most inhospitable desert environments. Powerful waves abound as the coastline unfolds to the east where peninsulas and islands jut out into the swell providing sanctuary from the strong SW-W winds, but not the most feared sea creature in a surfer's psyche. The surf just keeps getting bigger into the state of Victoria and mountainous bomboras beckon the brave on the coast down to Cape Otway. The SE facing coast of The Great Ocean Road is resplendent with righthand points and protection from the SW gales that bring big waves to the first 'Surfing Reserve' in the world. These spinning storms continue on their easterly course, blasting south or over the top of Tasmania, which is gaining a reputation for tow-in size waves, and into the Tasman Sea. It is in this famously rough body of water that the low pressure can share its swell with more than just Australia. Not only will SE-S swell pump up the east coast of the continent, but a larger amount of SW swell will flow out to New Zealand, most of the Polynesian

Islands in the South Pacific, and on rare occasions make it all the way to Hawai'i. Reality returns on the east coast where swells are usually heading away from it but proximity is the key and New South Wales scores enough SE-S swells from April-Nov to keep the world's densest surfing population in the water. During these winter months the winds can be a cold SW from the mountains of the Great Dividing Range but as the land heats up, the summer NE wind takes over and is responsible for providing some small choppy windswells, while east coast surfers wait for the summer saviour – the cyclone swell. Trying to predict a cyclone's path is near impossible, but they are generally considered to form in the Coral Sea off north-east Australia and either head south towards Queensland, or run parallel to the coast and out towards New Zealand or further east towards Polynesia, almost always taking a southerly path. This means that cyclone swell is exclusively from the NE for most of the eastern seaboard and sometimes due E for Queensland. Outside of the cyclone season (Jan-April) the north-eastern coast picks up S-SE swells from the Tasman Sea and any locally generated wind swells from the NE-SE. The Great Barrier Reef remains an interesting surfing enigma, as there is definitely surf along its outer frontier. The northern coast or top end of Australia is fairly devoid of surf apart from some seasonal activity in Darwin, or cyclone swells for the NW facing coast, leading back around to the Indian Ocean swells south of the North West Cape.

The West Wind Drift directly affects the southern shores and Tasmania, bringing full rubber year round conditions, even in blazing desert heat. The East Australia Current keeps the southern half of the east coast cool in winter while Queensland receives warmth directly from the South Equatorial Current.

Apart from the extreme NW coast, Australia tides are quite mellow, the rule being a semi-diurnal type with mid-range mostly under 2m (6ft).

Temperatures, Winds and Currents

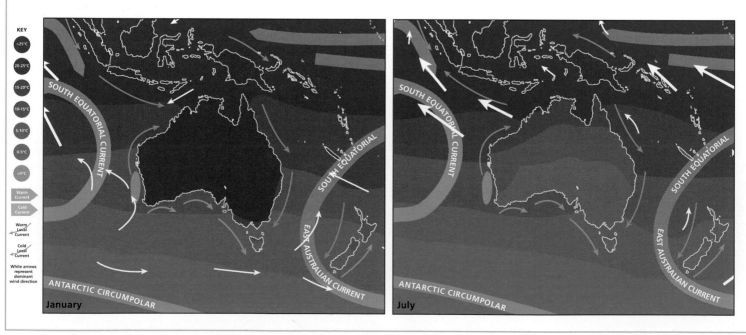

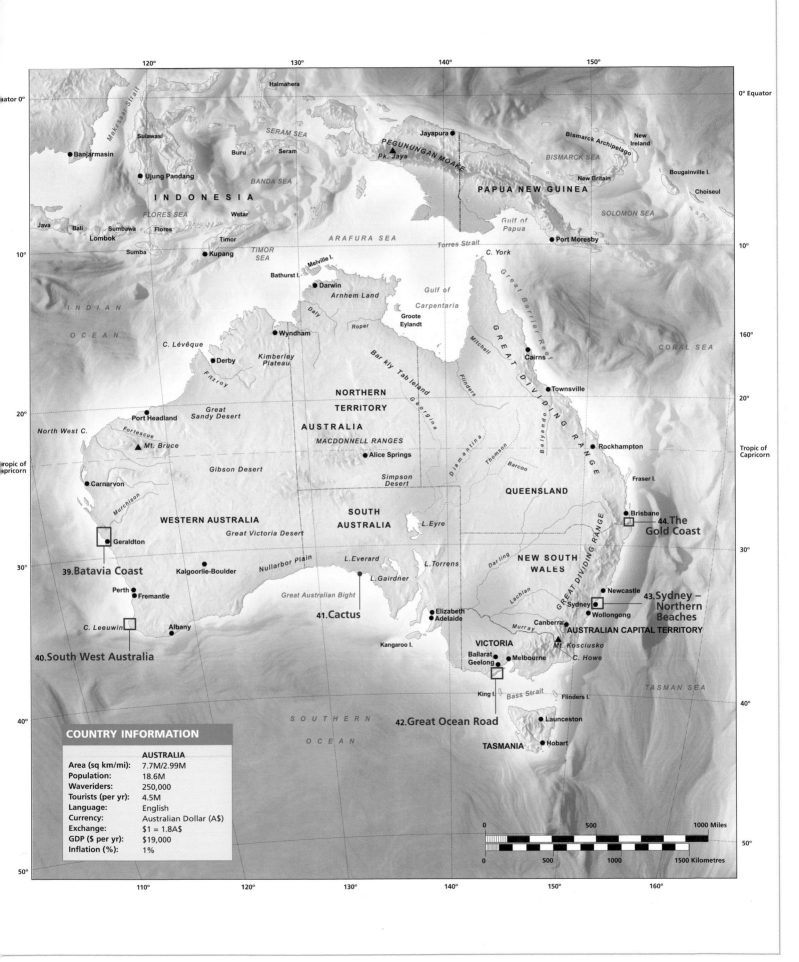

0° Equator

SERAM SEA

Halmahera

Sulawasi

Banjarmasin

Buru   Seram

Ujung Pandang

BANDA SEA

INDONESIA

FLORES SEA   Wetar

Java   Bali   Sumbawa   Flores

Lombok

Sumba

Kupang

TIMOR SEA

Timor

Jayapura

Pk. Jaya

PEGUNUNGAN MOAKE

Bismarck Archipelago

New Ireland

BISMARCK SEA

New Britain

PAPUA NEW GUINEA

Bougainville I.

Choiseul

SOLOMON SEA

Gulf of Papua

Port Moresby

Torres Strait

C. York

ARAFURA SEA

Melville I.

Bathurst I.

Darwin

Arnhem Land

Gulf of Carpentaria

Groote Eylandt

Daly

Roper

Wyndham

INDIAN OCEAN

C. Lévêque

Derby

Kimberley Plateau

Fitzroy

Barkly Tableland

Mitchell

Flinders

GREAT BARRIER REEF

CORAL SEA

Cairns

GREAT DIVIDING RANGE

Townsville

Port Headland

North West C.

Fortescue

Mt. Bruce

Great Sandy Desert

NORTHERN TERRITORY

AUSTRALIA

MACDONNELL RANGES

Alice Springs

Georgina

Diamantina

Burdekin

Thomson

Barcoo

Rockhampton

Tropic of Capricorn

Fraser I.

Carnarvon

Murchison

Gibson Desert

Simpson Desert

QUEENSLAND

WESTERN AUSTRALIA

Great Victoria Desert

SOUTH AUSTRALIA

L. Eyre

Geraldton

39. Batavia Coast

Kalgoorlie-Boulder

Nullarbor Plain

L. Everard

L. Gairdner

L. Torrens

Darling

NEW SOUTH WALES

Brisbane

44. The Gold Coast

Perth

Fremantle

C. Leeuwin

Albany

40. South West Australia

Great Australian Bight

41. Cactus

Elizabeth

Adelaide

Lachlan

Murray

Newcastle

Sydney

Wollongong

43. Sydney – Northern Beaches

Canberra

AUSTRALIAN CAPITAL TERRITORY

GREAT DIVIDING RANGE

Kangaroo I.

VICTORIA

Mt. Kosciusko

C. Howe

Ballarat

Geelong

Melbourne

42. Great Ocean Road

King I.

Bass Strait

Flinders I.

TASMAN SEA

SOUTHERN OCEAN

Launceston

TASMANIA

Hobart

COUNTRY INFORMATION

AUSTRALIA	
Area (sq km/mi):	7.7M/2.99M
Population:	18.6M
Waveriders:	250,000
Tourists (per yr):	4.5M
Language:	English
Currency:	Australian Dollar (A$)
Exchange:	$1 = 1.8A$
GDP ($ per yr):	$19,000
Inflation (%):	1%

0   500   1000 Miles

0   500   1000   1500 Kilometres

39. Batavia Coast

WESTERN
AUSTRALIA

Houtman
Albrolhos
Islands

Jakes

TUNGSTEN

Summary

+ CONSISTENT POWERFUL SWELLS
+ WORLD CLASS SPOTS
+ BREAK VARIETY
+ UNCROWDED

– HOWLING SUMMER WINDS
– LONG PADDLES TO OFFSHORE REEFS
– 4WD AND ALL SUPPLIES REQUIRED
– DESERT DANGERS

Luke Hitchings, Albrolhos Islands

BILL MORRIS

BILL MORRIS

North of Perth is one of the harshest environments Australia can dish up. The Gibson Desert and The Great Sandy Desert conspire with a rugged, dangerous coastline to remind travellers of their human frailties. The same booming surf that claimed many 17th century Dutch ships, aiming for Batavia (Jakarta), now attracts surfers who aren't afraid of a challenge. Geraldton and Kalbarri form twin outposts of civilisation 500km (300mi) from the capital, where a hardy crew of locals ride epic offshore reefs, which can be quite sensitive to the constant swell and strong winds. Knowing where and when is half the battle. Knowing your limitations is the other.

The zone starts well south of Geraldton with Dongara's long lefts at Port Denison and the mixture of rock and sand peaks at Headbutts and Flat Rocks. Geraldton is known as the crayfish capital of the world and relies on fishing for its existence. Many of these fishermen are surfers who must have plenty of paddling power to access the reefs sitting 20 minutes offshore. Hell's Gate is an all tides, powerful and shallow righthander, breaking 1km

TRAVEL INFORMATION

Local Population:
Kalbarri – 2,000
Coastline: 25,760km
(16,100mi)
Time: GMT+10hr
Contest: Local

Getting There – Visa: All nationalities need a visa, usually issued on arrival, except for New Zealanders. From Perth there are 2 Western Airlines flights per week to Kalbarri: $90/o-w. Geraldton has more flights. Drive 6h or take Westrail buses ($35/o-w) direct or though Ajana. Dep tax: $18.

Getting Around – Main scenic road and secondary "sealed" roads are good but many spots require heavy duty 4WD and full supplies. To surf remote peaks over the sand dunes and rocks, be ultra prepared. Driving speed is slow and beware of animals.

Lodging and Food – Kalbarri is a popular resort and gets filled quickly during vacations. It offers

anything from resorts ($55/dble), B&B (Seafront Villas: $35/dble), motel (Motor Hotel: $25) and dorms (Backpackers: $8). A meal is $6. The crayfish are fantastic and cheap.

Weather – The midwest is semi-arid, between the cyclonic monsoon rains in the north and the cold fronts around Margaret River in the south. Being primarily in the short scrub desert, the day and night temperature range can be as extreme as 30°C (86°F). Take warm clothing for dawn patrols and take extra care to keep hydrated. These conditions are normal in summer, which is definitely not the best surfing season. In winter, what little rainfall there is falls at night. Most days will be sunny and not too hot or windy. The water is very stable, varying a few degrees from 18°-21°C (65-70°F), requiring a light steamer (short sleeves or short legs are common) at the most and boardies or a shorty on summer days.

Nature and Culture – In Kalbarri, Murchison River inland gorges and the Rainbow Jungle are good visits. To swim with dolphins, go to Monkey Mia, 4hr north. In Geraldton, don't miss the museum (shipwreck stuff). Because of a mutiny aboard the Batavia in 1629, 2 sailors were dumped ashore, the first white men in Australia!

Hazards and Hassles – Despite abundant sea life (Tiger, Bronze Whaler and Mako sharks), reef cuts and powerful waves are the real aquatic threats. Be fully prepared for desert survival... the wrong decision could jeopardise your life! Insects and snakes are plentiful. Population is low but many are hardcore surfers, so remain humble. If the locals aren't surfing the main spots, then something is probably wrong.

Handy Hints – You need a gun for winter. There are 3 shops in Geraldton and 1 in Kalbarri. Those unprepared for the wilderness should consider guided surfing tours with experts like Surfing Safaris (Rockingham, Perth).

WEATHER STATISTICS	J/F	M/A	M/J	J/A	S/O	N/D
total rainfall (mm)	7	18	72	65	20	5
consistency (days/mth)	1	3	9	10	6	2
min temp (°C/°F)	20/68	17/62	12/54	10/50	11/52	16/51
max temp (°C/°F)	33/91	31/88	24/75	22/72	25/77	29/84

Red Bluff

BILL MORRIS

Blue Holes — Kalbarri

Jakes

Bluff Point

Port Gregory

PORT GREGORY ROAD

Horrocks Northampton

Bowes River

Coronation

Drummonds

Sunset Beach

Hell's Gate Geraldton

Tarcoola

(0.6mi) out in front of the Point Moore lighthouse. A smaller, sluggish, left reefbreaks directly in front of the lighthouse. Whenever conditions don't suit the reefs the locals usually surf the stretch from Back Beach down to Tarcoola. There are good breaks north of the peninsula like Sunset Beach, next to the Suncity Tourist Park. The Chapman River spot is rarely crowded despite quality lefts maybe because locals prefer the hollower walls at Drummonds, especially at high tide and on big swells. Further north and 5km (3mi) off the North-West Coastal Highway, Coronation has fun, reliable, beachbreak peaks, popular with windsurfers. A guided 4WD tour around here will undoubtedly uncover some other good spots, off the sealed road. Bowes River near Northampton is a great spot to camp for a few days. It's consistent and the mixed sand and reefbreaks are not too heavy. Kalbarri at the mouth of the Murchinson River has become a popular holiday resort. Only 3km (1.8mi) south of town is a pure gem of Indian Ocean power called Jakes, holding up to 15ft (5m) lefts breaking for 200m plus. If you can handle the elevator drop and the locals' pressure, barrels will be plentiful. On smaller swells and occasional NE winds, Blue Holes will produce nice rights on a ledge nearby.

Further north, past the wilderness of Dirk Hartog Island above Shark Bay (400km/250mi) the Gascoyne Region holds more epic waves. These awesome wild spots like Red Bluff, Turtles or Gnaraloo are located between Carnavon and Exmouth. North of Exmouth starts the Coral Coast, which faces away from the SW swells and is subject to extreme tides. The more adventurous can try and hire a crayfish boat to get to the dangerous waters of the Houtman Abrolhos Islands, some 40km (25mi) off Geraldton, home of Supertubes and more virgin spots.

The WSW facing shores of the Batavia Coast are well exposed to the Antarctica Roaring Forties, serving up the same SW swells as Indonesia. Although this is their is only swell source, expect many 4-10ft (1.3-3.3m) swells. The best surfing season is the heart of winter when the biggest swells wrap in the NW-facing coves where S-SW winds would be cross/offshore. It's rarely flat on the exposed spots but wind

BILL MORRIS

Abrolhos Islands

will be the key factor. Southerly winds are dominant varying from 64% (Jan) to 14% (June). Most of the summer (Oct-Mar) features gusty winds blowing ceaseless for weeks: a great spot for sailboarders! During winter, the wind compass pattern is wider and weaker with some perfect offshore E-NE winds. Tidal ranges are average, with spring tides never exceeding 6ft (2m) but it gets more dramatic as you travel up north.

Gnaraloo

TUNGSTEN

SURF STATISTICS	J F	M A	M J	J A	S O	N D
dominant swell	S-SW	S-W	S-W	S-W	S-W	S-SW
swell size (ft)	4-5	5-6	6-7	7-8	6	4-5
consistency (%)	50	70	90	90	80	50
dominant wind	S-SE	S-SE	E-SW	E-SW	SE-SW	SE-SW
average force	F5	F4	F4	F4	F4	F4-F5
consistency (%)	83	70	66	68	76	88
water temp (°C/°F)	21/70	21/70	20/68	19/66	18/64	19/66
wetsuit						

40. South-West Australia

WESTERN
AUSTRALIA

Houtman
Albrolhos
Islands

Summary
+ MASSIVE SWELL EXPOSURE
+ WORLD CLASS REEFS
+ LOTS OF POWER
+ DRAMATIC COASTLINE

− COLD AND WET WINTERS
− ISOLATED, DANGEROUS REEFS
− WINDY
− 4WD ACCESS

Three Bears

BILL MORRIS

Margo, North Point

BILL MORRIS

Surfing has become synonymous with Australia, especially on the east coast where the large surfing population is exposed to numerous contests held in generally small surf and constantly canvassed by the industry and mainstream media. This is not the case in Western Australia, where a few contests are held in generally huge surf, and the media circus rarely shows its face. The Margaret River area of W.A. is perceived as Australia's most consistent and challenging big wave forum, where pretensions and pretenders are quickly washed away. Whilst the north-west conceals Indo-like lefts, the area south of Cape Naturaliste is littered with rocky ledges and pointbreaks that get battered by giant Roaring Forties swells. The scenic Caves Road skirts the coastline, meandering through forests, gentle hills and around vineyards that overlook the sea where dozens of world class spots are ridden by a truly hardcore crew.

Love Hodel, The Box

BILL MORRIS

Travelling south of the capital Perth and around the small wave zone of Geographie Bay leads to the protected reefs of Cape Naturaliste. If a huge swell is running and the SW winds are blowing, then the NE facing breaks found here will be offshore and pumping. The laid-back lefts at Rocky Point are the most popular, especially with surfskis

TRAVEL INFORMATION

Local Population:
Margaret River – 3,000
Coastline: 25,760km (16,100mi)
Time: GMT+10hr
Contests: WQS (April) National (Nov)

Getting There – Visa: see Geraldton/Kalbarri. Perth has a quieter airport than Sydney. You can fly from Sydney to Perth for $350/o-w, or take the 65 hour 'Indian Pacific' train ride for $220/o-w. Otherwise there's the long, tedious Greyhound bus ride (the Red Eye) for $200/o-w. Margaret River is a further 230km (145mi) from Perth.

Getting Around – Hiring a car in Perth is near essential if you want to be on the best spots - expect to pay $30/d. The coastline is rugged, with many high cliffs and long dirt tracks, a 4WD is the only way to reach some spots, especially after heavy rains. However many great spots have nice, surfaced roads leading to them. The traffic is slow, the kangaroos are not.

Lodging and Food – Western Australia is full of campsites and caravan parks and the towns have plenty of cheap hotels. Recommended ones are in Gnarabup (Surf Point Lodge: $25/dble), Prevelly Point (Town Backpackers: $20); Gracetown Chalets ($200/w) and Yallingup (Smith's Villa: $330/w). A decent meal costs about $6.

Weather – The seasons are distinct with summer (Dec-Feb) enjoying hot temps and very little rain. Autumn is a great time but from May-Aug it gets pretty wet and cold with storms often hitting the coast accompanied by gusty SW-W winds. Sept marks the start of spring and some rainy days, but generally it's fine. A light steamer is the suit of choice year round, although on windless summer days a springy will be fine.

Nature and Culture – The Margaret River area produces great wine, so a vineyard tour is a

good way to kill a day on the unlikely chance of it ever going flat. The Mammoth Cave is a good visit. Take a boat to Flinders Island to see the Bottlenose dolphins and the Fur seal colonies. Perth, and its urban distractions, is not too far away.

Hazards and Hassles – The waves can be big and powerful, more suited to experienced surfers. Getting caught inside can be really heavy and many reefs are super shallow! The bush is full of spiders and snakes; watch out for the deadly Tiger snake. Locals are hardcore and don't like bad wave manners amongst visitors but the waves are plentiful, so there's rarely a problem.

Handy Hints – You will need a gun or two. Cheap, quality boards from Performance Surfboards (Injidup) or Maurice Cole. There are surf shops in Dunsborough, Yallingup and Margaret River.

WEATHER STATISTICS	J/F	M/A	M/J	J/A	S/O	N/D
total rainfall (mm)	21	52	200	195	95	32
consistency (days/mth)	3	8	18	21	14	7
min temp (°C/°F)	14/57	12/54	10/50	8/46	9/48	12/54
max temp (°C/°F)	24/75	23/74	18/64	16/61	18/64	22/72

ROB GILLEY **North Point**

and bathers from Dunsborough. There are some more beginner orientated beachbreaks and reefs before rounding Cape Naturaliste onto the west facing coast. The peak at Windmills works on small swells and has tubey sections in an offshore east. The next spot south is accessed by a 4WD track. Three Bears, a Yallingup waveriders favourite, is a set of three lefts varying in difficulty from Baby Bears to Mama Bears to Papa Bears: a steep, hollow wave, with hungry rocks. With a population of 500, Yallingup is a major surf community, and the unchallenging peaks facing the car park can work on all tides and swells. From here south to Injidup the coast is dotted with reefs like Supertubes and Pea Break, both busy, critical, pitching rights on small swells. The point at Injidup needs size before the lumbering lefts get going. Gracetown and Cowaramup Bay is the next easily accessible area where the long, barrelling, bowls of North Point's rights, face the equally long workable walls of South Point's lefts across a large bay. Big Rock, another shallow, sucky right, gets intimidating over 5ft (1.6m) but still attracts plenty of natural footers to this crowded stretch of coast. Between here and Margaret River are many small swell options that spread out the crowds. 10km (6mi) west of the town of Margaret River, its main break Margaret River (aka The Point) can be found, grinding down the reef. It is a peak in swells up to 6ft (2m) but Margarets is all about size and the lefts will handle plenty of that. Heartstopping drops, lumpy bowls and cutback walls are all part of the waves' personality. Dense crowds, windsurfers, drop-ins, hold-downs and localism are all part of the experience. The Box, opposite Margarets, is in a world of its own, when a big swell and higher tides produce square, righthand barrels that hopefully have at least a couple of inches of water to cover the dry reef. Beyond scary! To the south, Redgate breaks mainly over sand, creating hollow, punchy peaks in smaller swells. This whole area swarms with serious surfers riding serious breaks and there are at least half a dozen top quality spots with board snapping power to burn.

Injidup TUNGSTEN

The area from Cape Naturaliste to Cape Freycinet is fully exposed to the furious SW swells produced by the Roaring Forties. Western Australia receives the same swells as Indonesia but they can be much larger, although not as clean and orderly. In the winter especially, there can be days of huge, onshore mush. Expect numerous 6-20ft (2-6.4m) swells in the winter but usually only the sheltered spots will be rideable. Changeover seasons are the best bet as there are plenty of 4-12ft (1.3-4m) days at the most exposed spots. Even summertime is rarely flat, when plenty of 2-8ft (0.6-2.6m) swells can occur. The wind factor is the most significant factor because WA is plagued by strong S-SW. During the late summer/autumn there can be days with SE-S winds, but don't bet on it. When a high pressure sits over SW Australia, the mornings will typically be offshore, before an afternoon sea breeze (the Fremantle Doctor) blows out the surf. Tidal ranges are minimal and there is only one tide a day.

SURF STATISTICS	J F	M A	M J	J A	S O	N D
dominant swell	S-W	S-W	S-NW	S-NW	S-W	S-W
swell size (ft)	5	6	7	8	6-7	5
consistency (%)	55	70	90	90	80	50
dominant wind	SE-S	SE-S	SW-NW	SW-NW	S-W	SE-S
average force	F4	F4	F4-F5	F5	F4-5	F4
consistency (%)	67	52	49	61	66	54
water temp (°C/°F)	19/66	21/70	19/66	17/62	16/61	18/64
wetsuit						

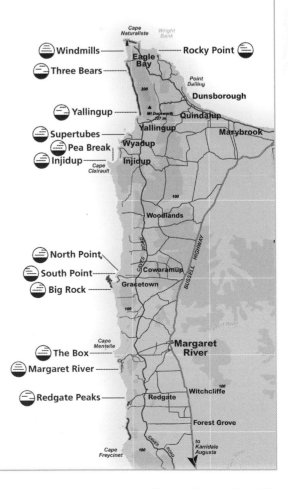

- Windmills
- Three Bears
- Yallingup
- Supertubes
- Pea Break
- Injidup
- North Point
- South Point
- Big Rock
- The Box
- Margaret River
- Redgate Peaks

Rocky Point

Cape Naturaliste / Wright Bank
Eagle Bay
Point Dalling
Dunsborough
Mt Duckworth 207 m
Yallingup
Quindalup
Marytook / Marybrook
Wyadup
Injidup
Cape Clairault
Woodlands
Cowaramup
Gracetown
BUSSELL HIGHWAY
CAVES ROAD
Cape Mentelle
Margaret River
Redgate
Witchcliffe
Forest Grove
Cape Freycinet
to Karridale Augusta

SOUTHERN
AUSTRALIA

WESTERN AUSTRALIA

VICTORIA

41. Cactus

Blackfellows – off the map but in the area

MARC FENIES

Summary
+ CONSISTENT SWELLS
+ QUALITY REEFBREAKS
+ POWERFUL LEFTS AND RIGHTS
+ CHEAP LIVING
+ HARDCORE TRIP

– GREAT WHITE SHARKS
– COLD WATER
– DEADLY SNAKES
– FLIES
– FIERCE LOCALS
– DESERT CONDITIONS

MARC FENIES

Australia's interior consists mainly of desert while the coastline, which is more exposed to wet oceanic influences, is a lot greener. Two exceptions are the NW coast of Western Australia and the Great Australian Bight coast of South Australia, where the great waves of Cactus can be found. This zone sits beneath the Great Victoria Desert between the Eyre Peninsula and the endless dusty, red Nullarbor Plain.

Nullarbor means 'no trees' which is the vista that greets travellers on the Trans-Australia 'Indian Pacific' train. Despite the desolation, this is a real Mecca for the hardcore Australian surf traveller. Point Sinclair is the real name of the private land formerly owned by surf movie-maker Paul Witzig, who, during the sixties, was one of the

BILL MORRIS

first to pioneer the outstanding waves of Cactus.

Most waveriders from the Adelaide area can't resist the call of the desert, but rarely go further than the Eyre Peninsula. Those that make the journey as far as Penong

TRAVEL INFORMATION

Local Population:
Cactus – 3000
(campers per year)
Coastline: 25,760km
(16,100mi)
Time: GMT+9hr30
Contest: No

Getting There – Visa: Everyone except New Zealanders. Sydney to Adelaide is a ±2h flight from ($220/o-w), while a coach costs ($80) and a train would cost $60 with speedlink. It's an 800km (500mi) drive from Adelaide to Cactus, passing through Ceduna and Penong. From Penong there is no public transport to Cactus.

Getting Around – Although you can make it to Cactus without a 4WD, make sure you're fully equipped with spare parts, fuel and extra tyres. Desert breakdowns can be serious... always stay with your vehicle. Spots are all within walking distance of each other but watch where you step.

Lodging and Food – Camping only. The land is private property (Foreshore Park) where you

can camp for $3/d. There's no electricity and no luxuries other than the small shop selling basics. Take everything you need with you, including water.

Weather – This is a harsh desert climate! It's always hot in the afternoons, summers are suffocating and mornings are chilly, especially in the winter when you will need warm clothing at night. Coastal upwelling and a cold offshore current means that the water temperature hardly ever gets above 14°C (57°F), which is a bizarre contrast when the summer land temps reach 40°C (105°F). The wind-chill factor can be pretty bad. Take a 4/3 steamer and booties, year round.

Nature and Culture – There's very little around this area except dust, shimmering salt pans and flies, from whom there is no escape (except when surfing). It's a wild and untamed area which many people would consider hell.

Hazards and Hassles – The shark factor has

always been high and White Pointers have taken bites out of a few people, although there hadn't been a fatality since 1975. However in late September 2000, a honeymooning Kiwi surfer, Cameron Bayes (25) was tragically taken by a White, during an early surf at Cactus lefts. The next day, another surfer (Jevan Wright, 17) was taken 250km (150mi) SE of Cactus, near Elliston, and in both cases, no bodies were recovered. Due to the ferocity of the attacks the line-ups have been empty and the campsite deserted. Even the territorial locals are leaving it to the true lords of the line-up. The surfers will inevitably return but the threat is undeniably real. On land, the flies can be mind numbingly annoying, but they're not as bad as the King Brown snakes, which have lethal bites.

Handy Hints – Cactus is not a place for the faint-hearted, so be prepared for a serious desert experience. Bring several boards (guns for the bigger days) and a winter suit. Gravelle is a good local shaper.

WEATHER STATISTICS	J/F	M/A	M/J	J/A	S/O	N/D
total rainfall (mm)	11	17	48	40	21	13
consistency (days/mth)	3	4	10	10	7	3
min temp (°C/°F)	17/62	15/59	9/48	7/44	11/52	15/59
max temp (°C/°F)	25/77	23/74	19/66	18/64	21/70	24/75

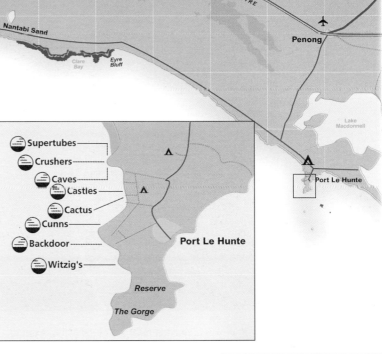

'The Rock Hole', head another 21km (13mi) south down a white lime, dirt road to Point Sinclair. The most southern spot is an outside break called Witzig's, which is a powerful left with dredging take-offs. In the northern corner of this bay is a hectic right, unimaginatively named Backdoors, simply because it shares the same barrelling ferocity of its Hawai'ian namesake. The peak is difficult to read which may explain its lower popularity with the locals, making this a good choice for the traveller. Cactus Bay has 4 major spots beginning with Cunns, a fairly inconsistent, mid tide left that's a good place to go if Cactus gets too crowded. Strangely enough, Cactus itself is the least intimidating wave in the area as the lefts usually offer an easy entry with a nice little barrelling section. Once again, the locals will probably be surfing another break, unless it is having a good day on a headhigh swell at low to mid tides. In the middle of the bay is Castles, where it's a case of inside zippery reforms on small days and outside grinding barrels on big days. Outside Castles is serious in terms of power and shark threats. The adjacent deep channel is the breeding ground for hundreds of Bronze Whalers and is easy access to the coast for the mother of all Noahs, the Great White Shark. It is Outside Castles where most bites have occurred, including the attacks on a notorious but now deceased local nicknamed 'Shark Bait' because he had been knocked off his board and mauled several times! Just on the other side of this spooky channel is Caves, a phenomenal right which is the locals' favourite and regarded as the best spot in the Cactus area. With morning offshores and a decent swell, it can become a reeling, world class, voluminous barrel breaking over a shallow ledge. Caves holds a good size, prefers lower

tides and must be offshore NE. There's also a localism factor to take into account, as guys have settled down here purely to surf this spot and they enforce strict laws about wave priority. On the other side of the small peninsula are two other board-breaking, shallow reefs, which are seldom ridden. Crushers is the left and Supertubes the right.

STEVE RYAN

Low pressure systems generally pass below South Australia, although in winter they will sometimes strike the coast in the east of the state. The winter swell exposure is massive with constant 6-12ft (2-4m) swells, but they are frequently messed up by onshore SW winds. Summers are still very consistent for swell, but the wind patterns aren't stable. Mornings are often offshore (NE), whilst afternoons suffer from onshore sea breezes. Early winter is a better bet for offshores than late winter. The winds can get pretty strong, making good wave sailing conditions but poor surf. Tides vary a lot and affect the quality of the waves.

MARC FENIES
Cactus

SURF STATISTICS	J F	M A	M J	J A	S O	N D
dominant swell	S-SW	SE-SW	SE-SW	SE-SW	SE-SW	S-SW
swell size (ft)	4	4-5	5-6	6-7	5-6	4
consistency (%)	40	60	80	80	70	40
dominant wind	SE-S	E-SW	N-E	S-W	S-W	S-W
average force	F3-F4	F3	F4-F5	F4-F5	F4-F5	F4
consistency (%)	55	78	48	60	69	62
water temp (°C/°F)	13/55	14/57	13/55	12/54	12/54	13/55
wetsuit						

42. Great Ocean Road

STEVE RYAN

Summary

+ CONSISTENT SWELL
+ DOMINANT OFFSHORE WINDS
+ BIG-WAVE RIGHT POINTBREAKS
+ SPECTACULAR SCENERY

− UNPREDICTABLE WEATHER
− COOL WATER YEAR ROUND
− SUMMER FLAT SPELLS
− CROWDED BREAKS

Victoria is the southern extent of the Australian mainland, hemmed in by the angry waters of Bass Strait and the Tasman Sea, but perfectly situated to receive the mountainous swells from the Southern Ocean. The Great Ocean Road twists torturously atop cliffs overlooking an eroded coast of limestone cliffs, sea stacks and caves, where a plethora of beach, reef and pointbreaks unload in a pristine and uncrowded environment. Since the early 60's, Torquay and Bell's Beach have become a surfing epicentre, being home to leading surfwear manufacturers, Quiksilver and Rip Curl, plus the site of the longest running contest and the only Surfing Recreation Reserve on the planet. Victoria has many other quality surfing locations like Wilson's Promontory, Philip Island and the Mornington Peninsula, but it is the Great Ocean Road that is the focus of attention. This 340km (210mi) scenic drive west of Melbourne, is a

Danny Wills, Bell's Beach

STEVE RYAN

Torquay

VINCENT BIARD

surfer's dream as it passes the many right pointbreaks that line both sides of Cape Otway.

The western side of Cape Otway picks up all the available swell so if it's small then the powerful beachbreaks of Johanna will be working. Crowded in summer with the Torquay crew, it can be a punishing paddle-out and has a habit of dramatically increasing in size without warning. Further west are the legendary big waves of Easter Reef in Port Campbell where 20ft+ (6.6m+) slabs of ocean are ridden by only the finest

TRAVEL INFORMATION

Local Poulation:
Torquay – 5,000
Coastline: 25,760km
(16,100mi)
Time: GMT+9hr30
Contest: WCT (April)

Getting There – Visa: All nationalities except New Zealanders. Melbourne (3M pop) is ±1hr flight from Sydney ($160/o-w), or a 900km (560mi) drive - a coach costs $35. From Melbourne it's 120km (75mi) to Torquay, passing through Geelong (125,000 pop).

Getting Around – The Great Ocean Road is a spectacular drive, as it winds its way though the limestone sculptures around Port Campbell. Renting a car costs $25/d.

Lodging and Food – Plenty of cheap backpacker accommodation at around $10/dble/p, good options are Nomad's at Bells Beach ($10/dble/p) or Anglesea Backpackers. Motels start from $25/p; the Surfcoast Retreat is recommended. Food is pretty cheap; a good meal can be had for $10.

Weather – South Victoria has the coolest weather in mainland Australia, but not the wettest, with only 680mm. The weather is very changeable. Avoid June-Aug, if you're not into a cold trip. The changeover seasons can be pleasant, even though you still have to be prepared for cooler spells and gusty winds. Summers, (Dec to Feb), are fairly dry and warm, averaging 22°C (72°F). Summer water temps rarely get over 20°C (68°F) and winters

dip down to 13°C (55°F). A 4/3 mm steamer for winter and a 3/2mm or springy for summer.

Nature and Culture – Visit the Twelve Apostles and the Cape Otway National Park. Surfworld, in Torquay, is the best surf museum in Oz. Go hiking around Point Addis or visit the Kangaroo reserve. The pub is a way of life in Oz, and Victoria is home to the country's favourite beers.

Hazards and Hassles – Aside from reef rubs, riptides and crowds, there is nothing to worry about. The shark factor is low. Drownings are common in the big waves on the western side.

Handy Hints – Strapper shop in Torquay or Surf & Fish in Apollo Bay issue good surf reports and have short boards from $230, or $290 for a gun.

WEATHER STATISTICS	J/F	M/A	M/J	J/A	S/O	N/D
total rainfall (mm)	37	66	74	92	86	60
consistency (days/mth)	8	12	16	20	16	13
min temp (°C/°F)	14/57	13/55	9/48	8/46	9/48	12/54
max temp (°C/°F)	24/75	21/70	16/61	14/57	16/61	21/70

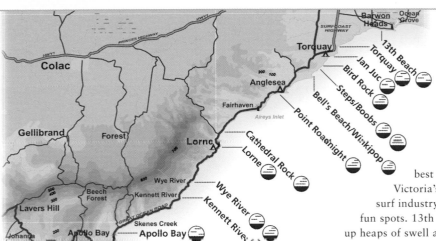

SURF STATISTICS	J	F	M	A	M	J	J	A	S	O	N	D
dominant swell	SW-S		SW-S		SW-S		SW-S		SW-S		SW-S	
swell size (ft)	4		4-5		5-6		6-7		5-6		4	
consistency (%)	50		70		80		80		70		50	
dominant wind	S-W		S-W		W-N		W-N		SW-NW		S-W	
average force	F4		F4		F4		F4-F5		F4-F5		F4	
consistency (%)	53		49		49		57		56		55	
water temp (°C/°F)	18/64		19/66		16/61		13/55		14/57		16/61	
wetsuit												

best avoided at high tide. Torquay is Victoria's surfing capital, with a thriving surf industry, surf museum and some good, fun spots. 13th Beach is full of peaks that pick up heaps of swell and it gets hollow on NE winds with an incoming tide. A quieter alternative to 13th Beach is Point Lonsdale, an all round beachbreak.

Easter Reef

watermen. On the east side of Cape Otway through a beautiful National Park is Apollo Bay, where there is a right off the harbour and some average beachies. Kennett and Wye Rivers both have fun rivermouth breaks and an option of a righthand point wave in smaller swells. Crowds become a problem closer to Lorne, which is a popular holiday resort, especially in the summer. On a major SE swell with SW winds, super long rights will section down Lorne Point, but it is inconsistent. Cathedral Rock is also inconsistent because it needs a big swell to kick-start the awesome rights that the locals are always on to. Anglesea is a typical coastal town that has some decent beachbreaks for the hordes of groms and fun rights at Point Roadnight for the mellow mal-riding Dads. Next stop north is Victoria's most famous surf spot, Bell's Beach: a classic and consistent right point that breaks on almost any tide, any wind and any decent swell. It's a long wave broken into 3 sections (which link up in huge swells) starting at Rincon, into Bell's Bowl and finishing in the shorebreak. Next door is Winkipop, a long, fast and hollow pointbreak that can handle solid swells over the shallow reef. Higher tides, 6-8ft (2-2.6m) and NW winds will create warp speed walls that are never short of talented takers. Boobs has a rare left off the peak and Steps has walled up rights which are both quality small swell reefbreaks. Bird Rock is a short, sucky, right reef, revered by the dedicated locals that dominate the tiny take-off zone. Closer to the busy town of Torquay is Jan Juc, a decent but permanently crowded beachbreak, that's

The south-west facing coast can get huge, with W-S swells up to 15ft-20ft (4.8-6.4m) possible, which then wrap around Cape Otway to the SE facing coastline, where the swells become much cleaner and orderly. While they lose some size, places like Bell's will still regularly get triple overhead and bigger. Dominant W-SW winds will be cross/offshore on this side blowing into plenty of 2-15ft (0.6-4.8m) swells. Tasmania blocks Victoria from SE swells. Due S swells tend to be better for a lot of the SE facing spots. Westerly winds dominate, tending more SW in summer and NW in winter. Tidal range can be 8-10ft (2.6-3.2m), so get a tide table. The pushing tide can increase the wave size and quality.

Winki Pop

43. Sydney, Northern Beaches

QUEENSLAND

NEW
SOUTH
WALES

VICTORIA

Summary
+ WIDE SWELL WINDOW
+ VARIETY OF BEACH AND
  REEF WAVES
+ URBAN ENTERTAINMENT
+ EASY ACCESS

− RARELY CLASSIC
− THICK CITY CROWDS
− RATHER EXPENSIVE

Dee Why Point

ALL PHOTOS SEAN DAVEY

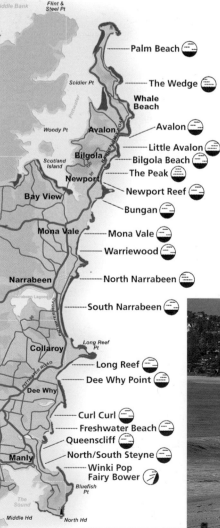

Flint &
Steel Pt
Middle Bank

Palm Beach

Soldier Pt
The Wedge
Whale
Beach
Woody Pt
Avalon — Avalon
Scotland
Island
Bilgola — Little Avalon
Bilgola Beach
Newport — The Peak
Bay View — Newport Reef
— Bungan
Mona Vale — Mona Vale
— Warriewood
Narrabeen — North Narrabeen
— South Narrabeen
Collaroy
Long Reef Pt
— Long Reef
— Dee Why Point
Dee Why
— Curl Curl
— Freshwater Beach
— Queenscliff
Manly — North/South Steyne
— Winki Pop
   Fairy Bower
Bluefish Pt
The Sound
Middle Hd   North Hd

Noodle, Little Avalon

I n 1914, when Duke Kahanamoku arrived in Australia
to show off his swimming prowess, he also gave a
surfing demonstration at Freshwater Beach. It was a
momentous occasion that was to
change the image of Australia across
the world - surfing had arrived! Since
that time, surfing has grown intensely
in popularity right around Australia's
25,260km (16,000mi) coastline. Since
the World Championships in 1964,
Sydney has produced a string of
talented surfers, unequalled by any
other world surf location. This large
city population takes pride in its
beach culture, and has in many ways
ruled the Aussie surf scene.

Sydney's broken, jagged coastline is
broken into 3 main regions divided
by two large estuaries. Cronulla on
the southerly outskirts, is separated
from the city beaches by Botany Bay.
Here there are consistent beachbreaks
on a long crescent of sand, plus the
quality righthander, Cronulla Point

and some good reefs including the awesomely square
barrels of the famous Shark Island. The city beaches
from Bondi to Maroubra are flanked to the north by
Sydney Harbour (which has some breaks in huge swells),
and have less variety of waves with lots of surfers
competing for the predominantly sand bottom breaks.
The Northern Beaches can provide great waves,
especially in the rarer E-NE groundswells and most days
have some sort of rideable waves. Protection from all
wind directions except SE is possible, and the variety of
spots caters to all surfing abilities. The first beach north
of Sydney Harbour is Manly,
which is split into 4 different
areas. Manly is the southern
corner, well protected from
the bigger southerly swells
and always crowded with
swimmers and tourists. South
Steyne produces classic lefts
on a NE swell, whilst North
Steyne is a good beachbreak
even on the usual S wind/S
swell combination. At the
north end, a rivermouth can
groom some good banks for
Queenscliff but it is always

Narrabeen

North Narrabeen

crowded, with hot locals from Queensland Boardriders Club who have, over the years made their impression on the WCT circuit. Manly's southern headland is home to Winki Pop and Fairy Bower, consistent quality righthand pointbreaks that handle big swells from most directions. Pollution problems have eased, unlike the crowds, since the outfall pipe at the point was extended out to sea. Freshwater or Harbord Beach is a small protected cove that can have a good righthander at the southern end but crowds out quickly with overprotective locals. Curl Curl is an exposed beach, picking up the most swell on the northern beaches and works reasonably well in most conditions, although it's rarely perfect. The challenge of Dee Why Point has been attracting surfers for years, and the ledgy, sucking right gets classic with the frequent winter S swell, S wind combo. It's a very technical wave ruled by the hardcore locals that patrol a small take-off zone in front of a swimming pool built on the rock ledge. From Dee Why beach up to Long Reef there are dependable beachbreaks plus 9 different bombora reefs that handle swells up to as big as it gets. 'Longie Bombie' will focus S swell and be dead offshore in the common NE wind.

Long Reef headland hides some reefbreaks before the shelter of Collaroy affords beginners a perfect training area in all but the largest of swells. The long crescent of South Narrabeen usually has uncrowded waves that are hollow and very fast. These near close-outs become perfect long lefts and shorter rights at North Narrabeen, because a lagoon flows into the sea, constantly moulding good sandbars. The line-up here gets ultra crowded and competitive including many a famous surfer from the local area. Warriewood is sheltered from S winds while Mona Vale is a less crowded bet on a NE swell. Bungan is a small beach and a long walk down the cliffs but has punchy waves in smaller swells. Newport Beach has a couple of different spots including Newport Reef and Newport Peak, which is Tom Carroll's favoured training ground. Bilgola Beach has mellow waves for beginners and semi tropical scenery. Avalon is well exposed to both SE and NE swells and is a hotbed for talented surfers. Little Avalon has a beast of a righthander at the bottom of the cliffs. The tip of the peninsula is a luxury residential area with a few spots worth checking, like The Wedge at Whale Beach and the beachbreaks at the south end of Palm Beach.

An east facing coastline is usually a bad omen in a world of W ground swells, however, Sydney is pretty consistent but rarely epic. S to SE groundswells are the most reliable swell providers from April-September, but many of the Northern Beaches favour the NE swells. NE wind swells in summer may include the rare cyclone generated swells in Feb/March. The surf is usually waist to headhigh on the beachbreaks, although it can easily exceed double overhead on the best swells when spots like Fairy Bower, Dee Why Point and Narrabeen turn on the goods. Prevailing winds are better in the winter (SW), while summers are typically offshore (NW) in the mornings, before the NE sea breeze picks up. Most beachbreaks and reefs work best on the incoming tide, even though tidal range is minimal.

SURF STATISTICS	J F	M A	M J	J A	S O	N D
dominant swell	NE	NE-SE	SE	SE	SE	NE
swell size (ft)	2-3	3-4	4	4-5	3-4	2
consistency (%)	60	70	60	60	50	60
dominant wind	N-S	N-S	S-W	S-W	N-NE+S	N-NE
average force	F4	F3-F4	F4	F4	F4	F4
consistency (%)	84	73	56	57	51	54
water temp (°C/°F)	21/70	20/68	18/64	15/597	16/61	19/66
wetsuit						

TRAVEL INFORMATION

Getting There – Visa: All nationalities except New Zealanders. Most visitors arrive at Kingsford Smith Airport in Sydney. Dep tax is $20

Getting Around – Getting around the 30km (19mi) is slow by bus. A rental car makes life easier ($30/d). Ferries from Sydney Circular Quay go to Manly. Drive on the left.

Lodging and Food – Lots of Youth Hostels and Backpackers at about $12/d. Recommendations include Manly Paradise Motel ($50/dble), Narrabeen Sands Hotel ($40/dble), Avalon B&B ($45/dble). Food is cheap, especially from the take-aways and coffee shops. Meals from $6.

Weather – Sydney has a subtropical climate, which makes the best time to visit the changeover seasons of spring (Mar-Apr) and autumn (Oct-Nov), when temperatures of around 24°C (75°F) are normal. Winters are never very cold, with afternoon temperatures frequently hitting 20°C (68°F). Mid summer is not a great time to be in Sydney as it's hotter, wetter and less consistent. You will need a 3/2 steamer for the May-September period, springsuit or boardies for the remainder of the year.

Nature and Culture – Sydney is a cosmopolitan city with plenty of nightlife. The Northern Beaches have large areas of parkland and natural Australian bushland. Oceanworld in Manly is worth a visit to see the local marine creatures you will be swimming with.

Hazards and Hassles – Shark worries are minimal as the beaches are all netted. The locals are very competitive but aggressive localism is fairly rare. Surf clubs organise lots of weekend contests. All the Northern Beaches suffer from pollution depending on the wind direction. During the summer, NE winds bring jellyfish including the stinging 'Bluebottles'.

Handy Hints – There are many surf shops where you can find cheap gear. Boards from $230.

Local Population: Sydney – 3,800,000
Coastline: 25,760km (16,100mi)
GMT: +10hr
Contests: WQS (April) local (year round)

WEATHER STATISTICS	J/F	M/A	M/J	J/A	S/O	N/D
total rainfall (mm)	103	125	129	92	75	84
consistency (days/mth)	11	12	11	10	10	10
min temp (°C/°F)	18/64	15/59	10/50	8/46	12/54	16/61
max temp (°C/°F)	26/79	23/74	19/66	18/64	22/72	25/77

QUEENSLAND

NEW SOUTH WALES

44. Gold Coast

Kirra

SEAN DAVEY

Summary
+ WORLD CLASS RIGHT POINTS
+ NEAR-PERFECT TROPICAL CLIMATE
+ FLAT DAY ENTERTAINMENT
+ INEXPENSIVE

– SUPER CROWDED SURF ARENA
– FEW LEFTS
– GENERALLY SMALL WAVES

Hope Island   Coomera Island

South Stradbroke Island

Nerang Head

The Spit

Narrowneck

Southport

Main Beach

Surfer's Paradise

Broadbeach

Mermaid Beach

Nobby Beach

Miami

Burleigh Head

Burleigh Heads

Palm Beach

Currumbin Point

Tugun

Bilinga

Kirra

Coolangatta Airport

Greenmount

Kirra

Coolangatta

Snapper Rocks

Tweed Heads

Duranbah (D-Bah)

Queensland's Gold Coast is one of the most intense surf zones in the world, combining 40km (25mi) of legendary spots with a huge, hungry surf population. It's the most visited stretch of coastline in Australia, but don't be misled by the name 'Surfer's Paradise', as the heart of this zone is dominated by skyscrapers, not palm trees and the hordes of tourists rule out anything approaching deserted. However, year round warm temperatures, a raging nightlife and endlessly long, right pointbreaks tempt southerners and foreigners alike to try their luck in Australia's most competitive line-ups.

From Sea World you can take a look at The Spit, which receives plenty of swell. It isn't quite as developed as the rest of this coast and has tons of empty peaks stretching as far as Main Beach. Narrowneck used to be off the surfer's radar until an artificial reef was built to create a perfect sandbar for lefts on NE swells. Surfer's Paradise itself is more dedicated to swimmers, so don't surf between the flags as the lifeguards don't have a sense of humour. Heading south towards Burleigh Heads, there

Kirra

JOLI

are miles of fun beachbreaks, which range from straight-handers to long workable walls. Broadbeach and Miami are two of the best spots, but this whole stretch will close-out when the swell is over 6-8ft (2-2.6m), which is when all the pointbreaks will be working.

In front of the magnificent Pandanus Trees National Park are the equally magnificent rights of Burleigh Heads. These thick barrels breaking over sand in front of a basalt boulder shoreline can be awesome when the swell has south in it and the wind is offshore. After a long, leg-aching ride to the shorey close-out, it's a jog

Greenmount

SYLVAIN CAZENAVE

back up the point and over the slippery boulders before dashing for the outside against the rip which drags you back down the point. It's not as long as Kirra and not as crowded, but unfortunately it's more localised. The next classic, right pointbreak is The Alley at Currumbin, which has very long rights, well sheltered from the strongest SE winds. Rarely a barrel, it lazily peels for hundreds of metres, just asking to be ripped to pieces. It is such an accommodating wave that all types of surfcraft tackle it, making the crowds a bit daunting.

The next break south is the Gold Coast nugget called Kirra, the longest small wave barrel in the world. Air drop into various tube sections, which suck out below sea level, adding sand to the already ridiculously powerful and thick lips. Super long, slabby sections need breakneck speed to negotiate while praying the inevitable drop-in won't happen on the deepest tube of your life. After the First Groyne was built in the early 70's, Kirra went into coma for a couple of years before re-awakening better than ever when the sand returned. Second Groyne was built in 1980 and gets just as dredgy as big brother. Kirra holds major swells plus crowds that all other crowds can be measured by!

Coolangatta is another urban area with the best waves found at Greenmount Point, which are long easy rights, protected from the dreaded E winds. Just around the point is the popular Snapper Rocks, with long rights which can break into Rainbow Bay. Cruisey, performance walls frequented by not so cruisey, longboarding locals. Duranbah or D-Bah sits on the north side of the Tweed River, which marks the border with New South Wales. The rivermouth jetties have helped form powerful, wedging peaks that provide ample tube time at one of the world's finest beachbreaks. D-Bah soaks up the swell and people, making it one of the 'Goldies' main surfing focal points.

The main 2-8ft (0.6-2.6m) NE-E swells occur from December-March, which is the tropical cyclone season in the Coral Sea. At this time one can expect about 2-3 swells per month lasting between 3-7 days. However, they're not as predictable and consistent as Antarctic lows and if the cyclone is too close, the surf will be choppy and erratic. Winter produces 2-8ft (0.6-2.6m) SE swells on the E-SE exposed breaks. The best winds (SW-SE) often blow from May to August, which is

Kirra

not the cyclone season. Between January and April, winds are usually light with a dominant S-E direction. The most unfavourable period starts in September when lots of N winds mess up the E-NE facing coastline. It starts to improve again in December. As a general rule the beaches are better at high tides and pointbreaks at low. Tidal range can reach 6ft (2m), so get a tide table.

SURF STATISTICS	J F	M A	M J	J A	S O	N D
dominant swell	NE	NE	SE	SE	SE	NE
swell size (ft)	4-5	4-5	2-3	2	2-3	3
consistency (%)	70	60	40	30	40	50
dominant wind	E-S	E-S	SE-SW	SE-SW	N-SE	N-SE
average force	F4	F4	F4	F4	F4	F4
consistency (%)	62	63	59	49	61	73
water temp (°C/°F)	25/77	24/75	21/70	19/66	20/68	23/74
wetsuit						

Snapper Rocks

TRAVEL INFORMATION

Getting There – Visa: all nationalities except New Zealanders. International flights to Brisbane then internal flights to Coolangatta (1hr30 away by car). Both are $350/rtn from Sydney. The bus from Sydney takes 20hrs and costs $80/rtn.

Getting Around – Rental cars are reasonable ($30/d but as low as $20/d with a local company). Fuel is (80c/l). Bikes or the Surf Side buses can be good, cheap ways of getting around.

Lodging and Food – Accommodation is plentiful, Coolangatta being the best place to stay. Budget hotels cost around $25/dble, youth hostel dorms from $12/d and a sea view room in a motel would be $35-45/dble. Varied international menus from $5-7 for a big meal.

Weather – There is little to fault about the Gold Coast's subtropical weather. November to April is the 'wet' season with some rainy days

and warm temperatures. Cyclones usually only affect northern Queensland. It stays pleasant throughout the dry season (May-October) but nights can get a little bit chilly. For 6 months of the year, you can surf in boardshorts and rash vests, or a shorty for the early mornings. In the dry season you may need a 2mm steamer in the early morning. A springsuit would be the all round winter wetsuit.

Nature and Culture – This is a great place for organised entertainment with Sea World, Wet 'n' Wild, Cableski Movie World, Dreamworld, Currumbin Sanctuary and Fleays all keen to occupy you on the flat days. Also more than happy to separate you from your money is Jupiters Casino. There is some mega nightlife action on Orchid Avenue.

Hazards and Hassles – The most likely problems are drop-ins and collisions at zooed

out spots. You stand more chances being attacked by an aggro local, than a shark! NE winds bring in the nasty Bluebottle jellyfish. The skin cancer rate is very high. Use more than just sunscreen.

Handy Hints – There are more than 50 surf shops stocking all the gear at bargain prices. The Aussie beer culture leads to some serious nights out but it's still crowded for the dawn patrol. Cheap food and drink at RSL Clubs. Queensland has a reputation as the 'Police State', with harsh drink driving penalties and draconian cannabis laws. Avoid them where possible!

Local Population:
Gold Coast – 275,000
Coastline: 40km
Time: GMT+10hr
Contests: Junior (Jan)
WCT (Mar)

WEATHER STATISTICS	J/F	M/A	M/J	J/A	S/O	N/D
total rainfall (mm)	185	170	114	66	72	118
consistency (days/mth)	13	13	9	7	8	10
min temp (°C/°F)	20/68	18/64	12/54	9/48	14/57	18/64
max temp (°C/°F)	28/82	27/81	22/72	21/70	24/75	28/82

Pacific Ocean Islands

Meteorology and Oceanography

Everything about the Pacific Ocean is big! Dwarfing the Atlantic with a surface area twice the size, the Pacific covers a third of the globe and is by far the Earth's biggest single feature. It is also the deepest ocean, holds the tallest mountains and the largest coral reef, but even more importantly, it is home to the planet's biggest surf!

Whichever corner of this vast surfing playground you care to scrutinise, there is always some wave action to talk about. The main stage is the line of volcanic islands that extend from New Zealand to Hawai'i – at the centre of the 'Ring of Fire', which encircles the Pacific.

With no less than five swell producing sources, islands like Hawai'i, Tahiti or Samoa are fortunately exposed to both hemispheres' storms, plus there's always a chance of cyclones, hurricanes and typhoons.

South Pacific lows are the source of most groundswells, which travel from Australia towards South America, at latitudes between 35° and 60°S. Statistics show a slightly less intense pattern than the Indian Ocean Roaring Forties or the North Pacific, but it is still a major swell producer. Polynesia gets sprayed from April to September and the SW swells only fade slightly in the southern hemisphere summer. New Zealand is directly in the path of the southern band of low pressure systems and parts of

Temperatures, Winds and Currents

the South Island register an average wave height of 10ft (3.5m), but swells can come from the Tasman Sea to the west, cyclones to the north, or depressions to the east. This four sided attack makes for consistent waves but the wind statistics are less rosy. Strong SW to W winds dominate the scene, meaning the convoluted coastline plays an important part in wind protection. Wind becomes less of a problem as you head north towards the South Pacific islands. None of these islands has a clean window to the southern swells and New Caledonia, Fiji, Tonga and Samoa, all suffer from the swell shadow cast by New Zealand. This shadow doesn't stop all the SW swell and once the lows move further east, the S and SE swells will hit these Polynesian shores. The strongest North Pacific storms in the Aleutians will bring smaller, clean lines to the north coasts of the islands, particularly Tahiti. The Pacific cyclone activity off the east coast of Australia is the least predictable of the world's tropical storm zones so swell forecasting is more luck than good planning. Generally, cyclones form between 10° and 20°S, just off the end of New Guinea or Queensland, and then head south in an arc towards New Zealand. If the storm stays far enough away from any of these islands extremely good surf conditions will probably result. If they don't stay far enough away, extreme devastation will definitely result!

One phenomenon that is quite predictable across Polynesia is the E trade winds, which veer more S in the winter N in the summer. Variations are rare, and that means west facing spots are ideal for most South Pacific islands.

The North Pacific storms are more seasonal and more extreme than their southern counterparts. In winter, the ocean comes alive from October to March, pounding the northerly coasts of Hawai'i with the world's biggest waves. The Aleutian low pressures usually start winding up in the Russian Kuril and blast across the North Pacific to Alaska. It is these winter swells that fire up the legendary North Shore of Oahu, but in summer it's the smaller S swells that keep the locals happy or the year round, east coast wind swell. And as if that wasn't enough swell, the hurricanes (Chubascos or Cordonazos) forming off Mexico send summer swells to Hawai'ian east coasts from July to October. The trade winds are reliably NE because Hawai'i sits in the northern hemisphere, and the equatorial trades are deflected by the rotation of the earth. The rare Kona S wind can appear irregularly, but usually in late summer.

The two main circulations of Pacific currents are made up of a few sub-currents. The South Pacific sends cold

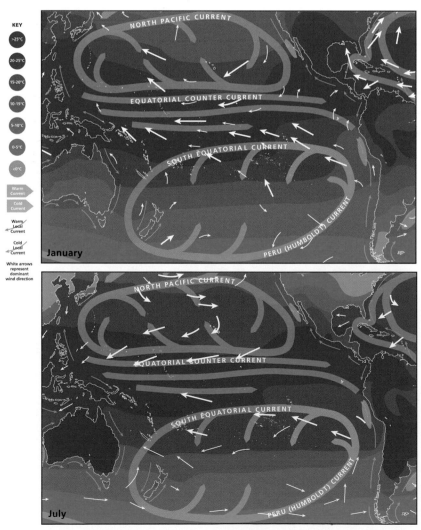

KEY
>25°C
20-25°C
15-20°C
10-15°C
5-10°C
0-5°C
<0°C

Warm Current
Cold Current
Warm Local Current
Cold Local Current
White arrows represent dominant wind direction

NORTH PACIFIC CURRENT
EQUATORIAL COUNTER CURRENT
SOUTH EQUATORIAL CURRENT
PERU (HUMBOLDT) CURRENT
January

NORTH PACIFIC CURRENT
EQUATORIAL COUNTER CURRENT
SOUTH EQUATORIAL CURRENT
PERU (HUMBOLDT) CURRENT
July

Shanghai
Tropic of Cancer
Hong Kong
South China Sea
Manila
Equator
Kuching
Tropic of Capricorn
Perth

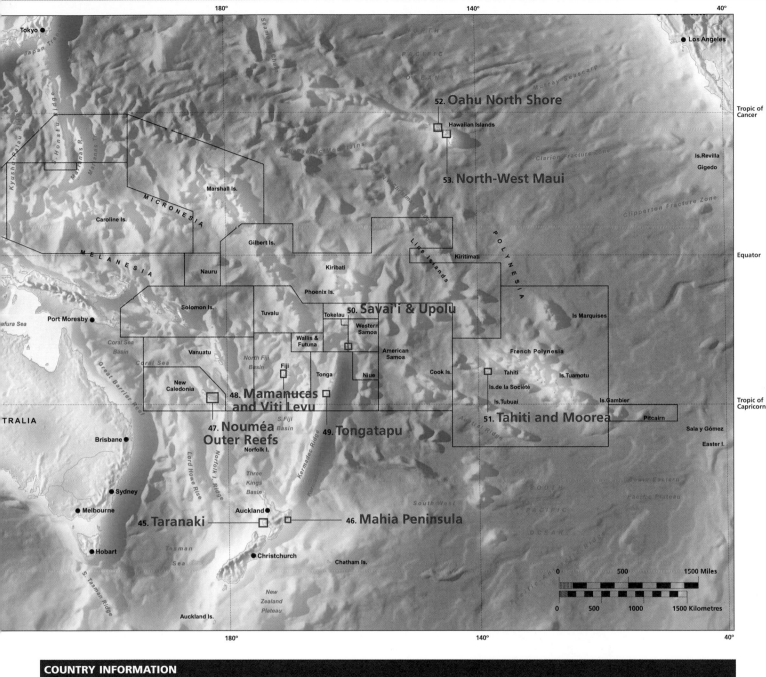

COUNTRY INFORMATION							
	NEW ZEALAND	NEW CALEDONIA	FIJI	TONGA	SAMOA	FRENCH POLYNESIA	HAWAI'I
Area (sq km/mi):	270,534/104,454	19,000/7,170	18,270/7,054	747/288	2,831/1,093	4,200/1,544	16,640/6,425
Population:	3.7M	200,000	800,000	110,000	170,000	250,000	1.2M
Waveriders:	15,000	100	1,000	30	30	3,000	75,000
Tourists (per yr):	1.7M	90,000	350,000	30,000	85,000	211,000	6.5M
Language:	English, Maori	French, Melanesian	English, Fijian dialects	Tongan, English	Samoan, English	French, Tahitian	English, Pidgin
Currency:	NZ Dollars (NZ$)	Franc Pacifique (FCP)	Fijian Dollar (F$)	Pa'anga (T$)	Samoan Tala (S$)	Franc Pacifique (FCP)	US Dollar ($)
Exchange:	$1 = 2.2NZ$	$1 = 130FCP	$1 = 2.1F$	$1 = 1.9T$	$1 = 3.2S$	$1 = 130FCP	$1 = $1
GDP ($ per yr):	17,000	10,000	5,700	2,200	1,900	14,500	27,500
Inflation (%):	2	2	1	2	1	2	2

water from the West Wind Drift into the Peru (or Humboldt) current then up into the western flow of the South Equatorial Current. The North Pacific gyre spins in the opposite direction whereby the North Equatorial Current, sweeps past Japan (Kuroshio Current) and into the North Pacific Current and finally into the California Current. There is an Alaskan and Aleutian offshoot plus a weird Equatorial Counter Current, which flows at odds to the other two Pacific Equatorial Currents. The weirdest current by far is the powerful El Niño, which will cross the Pacific from Papua New Guinea to Ecuador then down to Peru, carrying warmer than normal water. This current can affect world weather patterns and happens every 3-8 years.

Tidal ranges are small <6ft (<2m) but they usually matter on shallow reefbreaks. Semi-diurnal types are most common except in the Solomon's (diurnal) and Micronesia (mixed).

NEW ZEALAND

North Island

South Island

45. Taranaki

One of many secrets in the area

CORY SCOTT

Summary
+ VARIETY OF CONDITIONS
+ CONSISTENT BIG SWELLS
+ QUALITY, UNCROWDED SPOTS
+ SNOWY, VOLCANIC SCENERY

− COLD AND WET CLIMATE
− WINDY CONDITIONS
− COLD WATER

New Zealand plunges far into the Southern Ocean and feels the full force of the Roaring Forties swells that march out of the deep. The North Island of the country is an easy place to visit, receives some classic waves and yet it is still relatively untapped by travelling surfers. Closer to the capital Auckland, is New Zealand's most famous wave, the super long, perfect left point of Raglan. Another 5 hours south is the Taranaki area and the host of waves that fan around the base of Mt Taranaki from Waitara in the north to Hawera in the south. This area gets the most swell and has the greatest concentration of quality spots on the North Island. There are a few surfers around who like to protect their secret spots, but there are a lot of breaks and plenty of scope for exploration.

Chris Blain, Fitzroy

CORY SCOTT

Mount Taranaki

CORY SCOTT

If the wind is calm (unusual for this region), check Waitara Bar rivermouth. On high tides and major swells, the reefs and sandbars of the Waiwakaiho rivermouth can be ideal for longboarders. In the town of New Plymouth, Fitzroy Beach requires a fairly big swell to become a classic beachbreak that has low tide barrels. In winter (May to Oct) the best option is to be in the New Plymouth to Oakura area. There are many good reefs in

TRAVEL INFORMATION

Local Population:
New Plymouth – 50,000
Coastline: North Island – 3,450km (2,155mi)
Time: GMT+12hr
Contests: Nat (Jan)
National (March)
Pro-am (June)

Getting There – No visa is necessary for most nationalities. Most visitors fly into Auckland. Air New Zealand charges for boards. To drive from Auckland to New Plymouth takes 5hr; it is a little shorter from Wellington. To fly costs $100/o-w or a bus costs $35. Departure tax on international flights is $10.

Getting Around – The public transport in New Zealand is not efficient, you will appreciate having a hire car to cruise around the 'surf highway'. Hitch-hiking is more common in the mountains than on the coast.

Lodging and Food – New Zealand is a cheap place to travel through. There are plenty of backpackers' hostels and beach camps, all of which are cheap. The Wavehaven in Oakura is a nice villa that can host up to 24 people with prices ranging from $5 for a dorm to $8/dble. The Opunake backpackers cost $18. New Plymouth is more upmarket. It shouldn't cost more than $6 for a basic meal.

Weather – Sitting so low down in the southern hemisphere, New Zealand's North Island has a moderate wet climate influenced by SW-W winds sweeping over the country year round. The weather changes quickly and anything can happen. Rainfall is quite heavy from May-Aug with cold temps and plenty of snow on Mt. Taranaki (Mt. Egmont). Winter is the best time for bigger, consistent swells and good skiing/snowboarding conditions. Summer can hardly be called tropical. Keep some warm clothing

with you. It's the same story in the water - a good 4/3mm fullsuit in the winter and a 3/2mm fullsuit for the summer will suffice.

Nature and Culture – Aotearoa or The Land of the Long White Cloud, is a heaven for outdoors sports enthusiasts. You can ski, climb, bungee, paraglide, hike, swim and everything else in between. Snow capped Mt. Egmont dominates the skyline around Taranaki. Stratford is a nearby, interesting town.

Hazards and Hassles – There is nothing to get overly worried about. Be prepared for the cold, wind and rain. Most local surfers are cool and friendly to visiting surfers.

Handy Hints – There is cheap gear at the Del Free 'n' Easy or Seasons in New Plymouth. New Zealand has a slow and easy pace of life, but a highly developed infrastructure.

WEATHER STATISTICS	J/F	M/A	M/J	J/A	S/O	N/D
total rainfall (mm)	80	87	225	125	97	97
consistency (days/mth)	7	9	11	13	9	8
min temp (°C/°F)	13/55	11/52	7/44	6/43	8/46	11/52
max temp (°C/°F)	21/70	18/64	14/57	12/54	15/59	18/64

Raglan

SEAN DAVEY

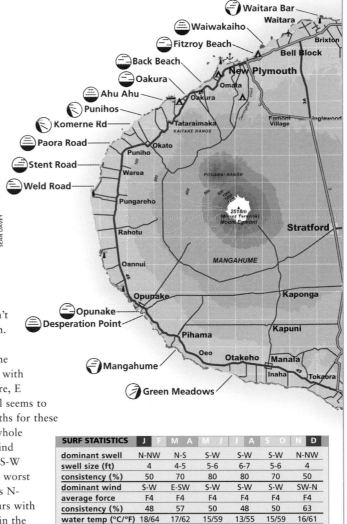

New Plymouth, but for a mellower surfing environment, it is recommended to drive down to Oakura. This is where most New Plymouth based surfers head for shelter when the strong SW winds blow and the consistent waves of Back Beach regularly turn on the quality. In Oakura proper, there is a high tide beachbreak, suitable for beginners and some reefs to the south that are worth investigating. Ahu Ahu has poorly shaped lefts and occasional sucky rights. The area swarms with decent reefs: Punihos, Paora Road and Stent Road are the best known. Stent Road is the most consistent spot around with two reeling, barrelling rights.

When the winds turn to the N/NE in the spring/summer, head for Opunake, a town of 1,600 people that hosts a good beachbreak and several nearby killer spots. These waves are very consistent and uncrowded but exposed to SW winds. Low tide is better. Desperation Point is a big wave spot that holds 15ft (5m) surf. On a good swell with clean conditions, Mangahume has lefts and rights breaking into a rivermouth. Finally, Green Meadows in Pihama is one of Taranaki's gems, a pointbreak that has long, excellent rights. All around here are small tracks leading through farms to the ocean and waves. Always ask permission before crossing someone's property and close all farm gates.

New Zealand is exposed to swell from all sides of the compass, but it is the west coast that picks up the lion's share of SW-W ground swells coming out of the Roaring Forties zone. Taranaki receives regular 4-12ft (1.3-4m) surf year round, but the prime time is between April and Oct. There's a slight possibility of NW swells or cyclones in summer (Dec-March), but don't hold your breath. The best winds occur through the summer months with plenty of offshore, E winds. Feb-April seems to be the best months for these winds. On the whole the dominant wind comes from the S-W year round. The worst wind direction is N-NW, which occurs with most regularity in the spring. It's a six hour drive to the east coast, a good option when big storms turn the west coast onshore. Tidal range is significant and effects most spots, especially rivermouths. Tide tables are easily available.

SURF STATISTICS	J F	M A	M J	J A	S O	N D
dominant swell	N-NW	N-S	S-W	S-W	S-W	N-NW
swell size (ft)	4	4-5	5-6	6-7	5-6	4
consistency (%)	50	70	80	80	70	50
dominant wind	S-W	E-SW	S-W	S-W	S-W	SW-N
average force	F4	F4	F4	F4	F4	F4
consistency (%)	48	57	50	48	50	63
water temp (°C/°F)	18/64	17/62	15/59	13/55	15/59	16/61
wetsuit	🏄	🏄	🏄	🏄	🏄	🏄

Motu Mataa, Stent Road

CORY SCOTT

JOHN CALLAHAN

NEW ZEALAND

North Island

South Island

46. Mahia Peninsula

ALL PHOTOS CORY SCOTT

Summary
+ VARIETY OF ASPECTS
+ DOMINANT OFFSHORE WINDS
+ CONSISTENT, QUALITY SPOTS
+ BEAUTIFUL, WILD AREA

− COLD AND WET CLIMATE
− WINDY
− COLD WATER

The Mahia Peninsula is located on the east coast of the North Island, between the cities of Gisborne and Napier. The peninsula is a beautiful, hilly promontory, with isolated, golden sand beaches and wonderfully clear water. It has a flexible array of reefs, points and beaches, which between them will catch any swell direction going. The predominant SW winds are perfect for many of the exposed spots plus somewhere will always be offshore, no matter what the wind direction. It attracts people from all over the country to take part in the numerous outdoor sports that this area is suited to, yet there are no hotels, resorts or amusement parks and everything remains truly wild. The laid-back, country feel is somewhat tempered by localism, so a low profile attitude is needed.

This zone is packed full of decent spots with at least 4 reefbreaks, 6 pointbreaks and a powerful beachbreak. The black sandy beach accounts for the name of the closest reef to Nuhaka. Black's Beach is a good quality peak, with a nice barrel section. To reach the next spot east involves getting permission

Daniel Kereopa

to cross private property. A gravel track leads down to a spot called Rolling Stones, so named because of the boulders littering the shorebreak. On a good quality swell, this morphs into a world class, righthand pointbreak and on the other side of the bay, a left. Further towards Blue Bay is Railways, another good righthand point that requires a massive swell from the south. Opoutama itself has a 6km (4mi) long, average beachbreak that rarely goes flat. Right by the cliffs, is Mahia Reef, which offers mellow lefts regardless of the tide, but again it only breaks on major swells. Diners

TRAVEL INFORMATION

Local Population: Opoutama – 1,500
Coastline: North Island – 3,450km (2,155mi)
Time: GMT+12hr
Contest: Gisborne/Napier

Getting There – (See 45.Taranaki). It will take 7-8h to drive from Auckland to Mahia. The nearest airports to Mahia are Gisborne and Napier ($110o/w). The nearest sizeable town is Wairoa.

Getting Around – (See 45.Taranaki). You can hitch from Opoutama to the more accessible spots, but it's likely to involve long waits.

Lodging and Food – Accommodation in and around Mahia is quite basic. You can camp or there are some good value rooms available from the Mahia Beach or Blue Bay Motor Camps (±$32/dble). For much better quality hotels you need to stay in Gisborne. Expect to pay around $6/meal. Fish & chips are cheap ($3).

Weather – The east coast remains drier than the west coast because of the rain and wind shadow provided by the mountainous interior. Winter is the time to go for the biggest swells and the possibility of snowboarding. Summers are pleasant but not overly warm. Same wetsuit requirements as Taranaki.

Nature and Culture – The peninsula is a wild area that is a paradise for divers, fishermen, windsurfers, bird watchers and horse riders. It is a mellow place, and not the place to go searching for rowdy nightlife. Napier is an interesting Art Deco city and Gisborne is one of the surf cities of New Zealand.

Hazards and Hassles – (See 45.Taranaki). Despite its peacefulness, there can be the occasional localism problem. Give the large local Maori population plenty of respect.

Handy Hints – Surf gear can be bought in the Gisborne or Napier surf shops.

WEATHER STATISTICS	J/F	M/A	M/J	J/A	S/O	N/D
total rainfall (mm)	75	75	87	93	56	60
consistency (days/mth)	8	8	11	12	10	8
min temp (°C/°F)	14/57	11/52	6/43	5/41	8/46	12/54
max temp (°C/°F)	24/75	21/70	16/61	14/57	18/64	22/72

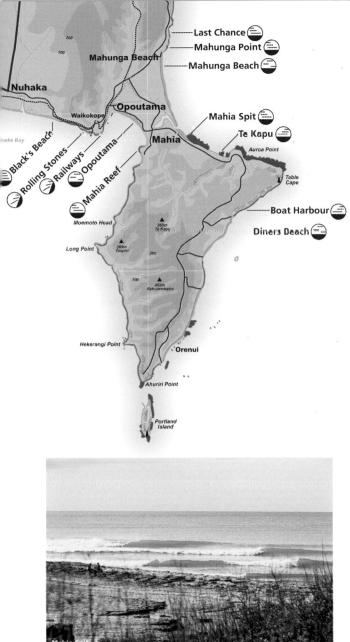

Last Chance
Mahunga Point
Mahunga Beach
Mahunga Beach
Nuhaka
Opoutama
Waikokope
Mahia Spit
Te Kapu
Mahia
Auroa Point
Black's Beach
Rolling Stones
Railways
Opoutama
Mahia Reef
Table Cape
Moemoto Head
365m Te Kapu
Boat Harbour
Diners Beach
Long Point
369m Taupui
200
402m Rahuimokairo
Hekerangi Point
Orenui
100
Ahuriri Point
Portland Island

New Zealand has great exposure to swells from every direction, and this is the sort of surf trip that will involve lots of driving around, checking various spots and keeping a constant eye on the changing weather conditions. The west coast is the most consistent side of the island, as the majority of swells roll in from the W-SW. The east coast receives fewer swells, but enjoys a dominant offshore wind. It is however only around six hours driving time between east and west coasts. With more than 180° of swell direction options and 360° of wind direction options, the Mahia Peninsula is one of the most versatile New

SURF STATISTICS	J	F	M	A	M	J	J	A	S	O	N	D
dominant swell	SW-S		SW-SE		SW-SE		SW-SE		SW-SE		SW-S	
swell size (ft)	2-3		3-4		4-5		5		5		3	
consistency (%)	40		60		70		70		60		40	
dominant wind	S-N		NE-SW		S-W		S-W		SW-NW		SW-N	
average force	F4		F4		F4		F4		F4		F4	
consistency (%)	63		63		50		52		51		64	
water temp (°C/°F)	18/64		16/61		13/55		12/54		12/54		15/59	
wetsuit												

Zealand surf locations. Between April and Oct, Mahia receives ample 3-10ft (1-3.3m) swells from the SW-NE and even through the summer months there will be plenty of good days. Summer (Jan-March) is also the time for the unreliable cyclone swells, but the NE window is relatively narrow, and the Bay of Plenty to the north will make more out of them. The dominant SW winds blow offshore and are lighter than on the exposed west coast. Winds often blow from the N in summer and S in winter. The tidal range is large, up to 12ft (4m) and can greatly affect the quality of the waves.

Mahia Spit

Beach, the only consistent spot on the actual peninsula, is an average, empty beachbreak. The righthander at Boat Harbour breaks very rarely. Te Kapu is a pair of quality reefbreaks called First and Second Reef, which are both fun rights with plenty of opportunities for high performance turns. If the reefs are suffering a little from wind and are messy then the beachbreak may be worth a look. Mahia Spit is dominated by a curiously shaped headland. It favours lefts, which can be excellent, and will hold major swells. The outside section is suited more to experienced surfers as it is super shallow and fast. The inside is a much easier wave but it gets crowded at weekends. Mahunga Beach is a perfect, high tide, longboard wave with fun lefts at the north end of the beach. If nowhere else in this area is working properly, then there is a good chance of finding something worthwhile at the appropriately named Last Chance. It is best on a N-E swell and mid tide, but getting down to the waves can be tricky.

Danny Carse

VANUATU

Loyalty Isl.

New
Caledonia

NEW CALEDONIA

47. Nouméa Outer Reefs

ALL PHOTOS PHILLIPE CHEVODIAN

Summary

+ VIRGIN SPOTS
+ VARIETY OF BARRIER REEF BREAKS
+ EXOTIC YACHT TRIP

− MOST SPOTS ONLY ACCESSIBLE
  BY BOAT
− EASILY BLOWN-OUT
− VERY EXPENSIVE
− INCONSISTENT

Nouméa sits on the edge of the largest lagoon in the world and has traditionally been a big windsurfing destination. It's only in the last couple of years that New Caledonia has begun to reveal its potential for outer reef barrels to a waiting surf world. Though the waves that have been found here are the equal of anywhere else in the South Pacific, it is unlikely that New Caledonia is ever likely to become as popular as some of its neighbouring island states. The reason being that the waves break on reef passes between 5-20km (3-12mi) offshore, and stretched along a 700km (400mi) fringing barrier reef, which is too far for even the most hardcore

Gabe Davies

of paddlers! This means that unless you can afford to be on an expensive charter yacht, then you aren't going to do a lot of surfing.

There is only one consistent spot on the island near Bourail, which breaks close to the shore. According to locals, the peak at Roche Percée used to be as impressive as the surrounding scenery, but in recent years,

TRAVEL INFORMATION

Local Population:
Nouméa – 65,000
Coastline: 2,254km
(1,408mi)
Time: GMT+11hr
Contest: local

Getting There – Visas are needed by citizens of Australia, South Africa and Brazil. New Caledonia is expensive to get to with major airlines including Qantas, Air New Zealand and some charter flights from France. Local carriers are Air Vanuatu and Air Calin. The airport is 45km (30mi) from Nouméa.

Getting Around – Transport on the island is superfluous, as all the action takes place offshore. Boats to get out to the waves are expensive. You can rent a Zodiac from Nouméa for morning hops out to the surf for about $70. For more surf time but a bigger dent to your wallet, stay on a charter boat out by the

waves. You have a choice of either the Raid Ngatahi ($150/d) or La Violante ($1800/10d June-July) with STC.

Lodging and Food – If you have the right frame of mind for it, then life on board these full luxury class charter boats is relaxed though somewhat cramped. Food on board will have huge helpings of the freshest seafood available and as much beer as you can drink. About the only drawback is that nights at sea can be noisy and rough. On land most of the hotels are also good, but not especially cheap. Le Lagon costs ±$40/dble. Imported food is pricey.

Weather – The warm, sticky, wet season lasts from December to April and the chances of torrential rain and cyclones are always present. The best surf occurs during the dry season (May-Oct), while the best all round months to visit are Sept-Nov. Deep winter (July-Aug) may feel a little colder than you

would expect of a tropical destination. In deep winter, a light shorty for early or windy sessions is recommended, otherwise boardshorts and a rash vest.

Nature and Culture – If you're not surfing then onboard activities are limited to sunbathing, fishing or scuba diving (about another $40). On land there is trekking, horse riding and exploring the many caves.

Hazards and Hassles – It's a very safe island, so the only worries are the standard tropical surfing hazards of reef cuts, sun stroke and marine life. There is some political rivalry between the local Canaques and white Caldoche, but it doesn't effect tourism.

Handy Hints – The French influence in New Caledonia is very strong and the standard of living is high. There are no surf shops so bring all your own equipment.

WEATHER STATISTICS	J/F	M/A	M/J	J/A	S/O	N/D
total rainfall (mm)	110	135	95	83	47	60
consistency (days/mth)	10	11	11	9	6	6
min temp (°C/°F)	23/74	22/72	19/66	17/62	18/64	21/70
max temp (°C/°F)	29/84	27/81	24/75	23/74	25/77	28/82

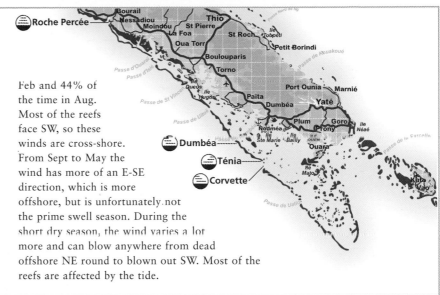

sandbanks have clogged up the reef pass through which the swells squeeze, decreasing the size and quality of the waves. Despite very few local surfers, this wave still gets quite busy at weekends. There are rumoured to be some other good waves in the vicinity only accessible by boat.

Getting to the outside reef passes is time consuming and expensive, however many people choose to stay in the capital, Nouméa and catch a boat out to the waves each morning. It's a two hour return journey to the best known waves of Dumbéa, Ténia and Corvette. This leaves precious little surfing time, as the wind tends to pick up and blow out many of the spots by 10 or 11am.

By far the best option is to book a place on a yacht and cruise around the south facing reefs. Doing this is expensive and not as easy to organise as in the Mentawais or Maldives. STC have been operating a yacht here since June 2000. If you are on your own boat, take care on these passes as New Caledonia has the highest rate of shipwrecks in the South Pacific! Offshore reef passes are everywhere, just waiting for a Roaring Forties S swell or E cyclone swell to wake up the waves. Most of the spots have not yet been named and those that have are mainly lefts. Waterworld can be found close to a shipwreck, Twister is so named because of the storms that occurred when it was first surfed and Mirage because of the clarity of the water and views down to the reef. This is an extreme place to go surfing, there is no one else for miles around, except your surfing partners and lots of sealife! Many of the boats for rent are actually used by diving operators, so you should get some good opportunities to check out the underwater life. Living out at sea on a boat is an amazing experience, but tensions can and do mount between all the passengers. Claustrophobics need not apply.

Feb and 44% of the time in Aug. Most of the reefs face SW, so these winds are cross-shore. From Sept to May the wind has more of an E-SE direction, which is more offshore, but is unfortunately not the prime swell season. During the short dry season, the wind varies a lot more and can blow anywhere from dead offshore NE round to blown out SW. Most of the reefs are affected by the tide.

Didier Pitier

S well comes primarily from the Roaring Forties and is funnelled through the Tasman Sea and onto the SW facing coast of New Caledonia. May to Sept is the prime time with consistent S-SE swells producing 2-10ft (0.6-3.3m) waves. The swell shadow cast by New Zealand makes for shorter swell duration. The cyclone season also produces occasional E swells but they're fickle and the spots that break on these swells, like Île des Pins, are hard to reach. Year round the wind blows primarily from the SE: around 71% of the time in Jan-

SURF STATISTICS	J F	M A	M J	J A	S O	N D
dominant swell	E-NE	E-NE	S-SW	S-SW	S-SW	E-NE
swell size (ft)	2	3-4	4-5	5-6	4	1-2
consistency (%)	20	50	70	70	60	20
dominant wind	E-SE	E-SE	NE-SW	NE-SW	E-SE	E-SE
average force	F4	F4	F3	F3	F3	F4
consistency (%)	71	65	78	79	60	63
water temp (°C/°F)	26/79	25/77	23/74	21/72	22/70	24/75
wetsuit						

48. Mamanucas and Viti Levu

TUVALU
WESTERN SAMOA
WALLIS & FUTUNA
Vanua Levu
Viti Levu
FIJI
TONGA

Summary

+ Super consistent
+ Variety of world class reefs
+ Choice of resorts
+ Easy access

− Resort owned waves
− Dangerous reefs
− Very expensive
− Civil unrest

Swimming Pools – Namotu

ALEX WILLIAMS

The 322 islands of Fiji form the epitome of the surf travel dream. A magical archipelago of white sand beaches and tropical vegetation ringed by shallow coral reefs, which get bombed by heavy, hollow lefthanders that set the standard for wave quality around the world. Most of the waves break on barrier reefs in the Mamanuca group of islands to the west of Fiji's main island, Viti Levu. The only wave that isn't to be found out on the barrier reefs is the rare beachbreak of Sigatoka Dunes. Most of the reef waves in Fiji are lefts, with a few classic rights. Surf camps and boat access to the waves around the Mamanucas make Fiji, or more to the point, Tavarua, an expensive but essential surf experience.

Tavarua is the place to go for the ultimate 21st century surf trip. Its luxury accommodation, exclusive access to the

JOLI

Michael Burling

JOLI

lefts of Restaurants and monopoly over Cloudbreak's incredible lefts make it the focus of one of the surf world's most pressing debates - can someone legally charge you money to surf a wave? According to Fijian tribal laws, the reefs surrounding an island belong to the

TRAVEL INFORMATION

Local Population:
Viti Levu – 450,000
Coastline: 1,129km
(705mi)
Time: GMT+12hr
Contest: WCT (June)

Getting There - Automatic 30 day visa. Centrally located in the South Pacific, Fiji is a main stop off point for trans-Pacific flights. Nadi airport is closer to the Mamanucas than Suva. Departure tax is a huge $40! If you intend to stay at the Tavarua surf camp during the peak season, then book well in advance.

Getting Around – Most people stay in one of the resorts, which provide airport transfers. Most of the outer reefs are reached by boat for only $50rtn/pp! This is waived if you have booked an all-inclusive holiday (good idea). Local bus transport is cheap and reliable. Car rental is $300/w and not really necessary.

Lodging and Food – Expensive! Surfing in Fiji has become something of an impossible dream for the everyday surfer. In total it's going to cost you a minimum of $150/day. Namotu resort will set you back $135/day. Plantation and Natadola on Viti Levu are both upmarket, expensive places. Budget options, which don't include the boat rides out to the reefs, (see above), work out only a little cheaper. Try either the Seashell Cove at $35/day or Club Masa at $40/day. The food is good, revolving around fish, taro, rice and fruit. Try some kava, the local brew.

Weather – Fiji has a tropical climate that sees stable temps and ample rainfall, although compared to neighbouring island groups, it is somewhat drier. The rainy season extends from Nov-April, peaking through Dec-March, when temperatures are at their warmest (30°C/86°F). Humidity levels can reach an uncomfortable 100%. Cyclones are an occasional occurrence. When the SE trades increase in strength in May, the weather becomes much drier. It becomes cooler at this time as well but it rarely falls

below 15°C (59°F), so being cold is never an issue. Year round board shorts and a rash vest, maybe a shorty for the coldest days in July-Aug.

Nature and Culture – Fiji is a tropical beach paradise. Diving, fishing and sailing are all excellent. On the main islands you can visit temples, sand dunes and beautiful mountains.

Hazards and Hassles – Most surf spots are shallow so be careful of hitting the reef. Cover up from the sun and mosquitoes (no malaria). Fijian people are very friendly, few of them surf and those that do are cool. There are fairly regular rumours working their way around the world surf community about Cloudbreak being open to all comers - don't put much faith in this. Drink only bottled water.

Handy Hints – Bring your own surf gear. There is a good surf shop near Ed's Bar in the Martintar area of Viti Nadi, called "Viti Surf Legends". Fijians have an enviable lifestyle and culture that should be respected.

WEATHER STATISTICS	J/F	M/A	M/J	J/A	S/O	N/D
total rainfall (mm)	300	320	105	60	72	170
consistency (days/mth)	16	17	10	7	8	11
min temp (°C/°F)	23/74	23/74	21/70	20/70	21/68	22/72
max temp (°C/°F)	30/86	30/86	28/82	26/79	28/82	30/86

Jon Roseman, Cloudbreak
ALEX WILLIAMS

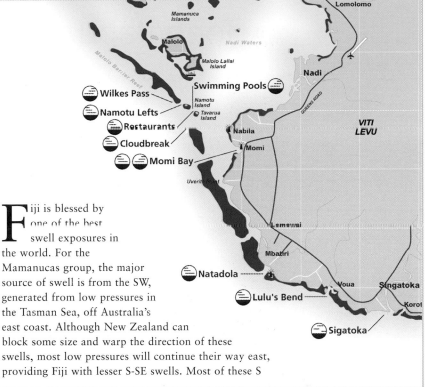

headman of that island, as does everything on and around that reef - this includes the waves. On Tavarua the rights to the waves at Restaurants were bought up in exchange for development projects on the island. This has allowed the surf camp to claim exclusive rights to Restaurants and more controversially, Cloudbreak, which though not owned by the camp, is impossible for non-guests to surf due to heavy enforcement (except on Saturdays). Restaurants is the ultimate in perfect lefts with long, hollow walls, but is inconsistent. Cloudbreak is the outside bombora that vies for the title of 'world's best left' with G-Land. It's consistent and holds big swells. For expert surfers when over 6ft (2m).

To the north of Namotu is Wilkes Pass, named after a group of pirates who escaped from the authorities through the reef pass here. It's a high tide right with long, fast, barrelling waves finishing with a bowly inside section. Like most of Fiji's rights, it is sensitive to SE trade winds. Glassy, rainy days are the best time to surf it, which is also true for Swimming Pools, a much mellower right further south. The most serious Namotu waves are the heavy barrels found at Namotu Lefts, especially when the swell reaches 8ft (2.6m). However, they are always more forgiving than Tavarua. Another peak called Desperate is worth a check when everything else is flat.

When the swell is big, a wave breaks in Momi Bay, in front of Seashell Cove. The right by the lighthouse is usually offshore plus there is a less reliable left. Natadola is a beautiful resort beach with a shorebreak that's good for bodysurfing. Outside of this at high tide, waves break on both sides of the reef pass – the lefts are more consistent but rarely get classic. If you stay in Natadola then Lulu's Bend is another high tide barrel worth investigating. The Sigatoka sand dunes offer 5km (3mi) of beachbreaks in wonderful scenery without crowds. In the future, new waves will be discovered on the reefs to the east of Suva.

Fiji is blessed by one of the best swell exposures in the world. For the Mamanucas group, the major source of swell is from the SW, generated from low pressures in the Tasman Sea, off Australia's east coast. Although New Zealand can block some size and warp the direction of these swells, most low pressures will continue their way east, providing Fiji with lesser S-SE swells. Most of these S

Cloudbreak
JOLI

swells range in size from 3-15ft (1-5m), March-Nov being the best time. Despite year round swell activity, the summer rainy season (Dec-Feb) has smaller, less consistent N-NE swells in the 2-6ft (0.6-2m) range. These are generated from remote NW Pacific lows which will hit the archipelago's north shores (Yasawa, Vanua Levu). Through summer (Nov-March), the winds are generally lighter and from a SE-NE direction - NE is bang offshore in the Mamanucas. Trade winds increase slightly in strength from May to Nov, and blow from the SE. Most spots will be cross/offshore year round. Despite minor tidal ranges, most spots are very shallow and will be affected by low tide.

Namotu Lefts
ALEX WILLIAMS

SURF STATISTICS	J F	M A	M J	J A	S O	N D
dominant swell	NW-N	SW-S	SE-SW	SW-SE	SW-S	NW-N
swell size (ft)	4-5	5	6-7	7	6	5
consistency (%)	70	85	90	90	80	70
dominant wind	NE-SE	NE-SE	E-SE	E-SE	E-SE	E-SE
average force	F4	F3-F4	F4	F4	F4	F4
consistency (%)	63	72	64	62	73	67
water temp (°C/°F)	28/82	27/81	26/79	25/77	25/77	26/79
wetsuit	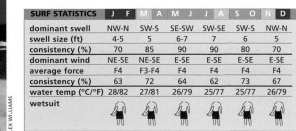					

49. Tongatapu

ALL PHOTOS SEAN DAVEY

Summary

+ UNCROWDED SPOTS
+ PERFECT REEFS
+ GREAT CLIMATE

– LIVE CORAL REEF DANGERS
– COOLER WINTER WATERS
– LACK OF VARIETY IN ORIENTATION
– EXPENSIVE LOCATION

The Tonga archipelago includes 170 islands divided into 4 separate groups. Starting with Niuas in the north, working south through Vava'u, Ha'apai and finally, at the southern end of the archipelago, Tongatapu. Lying about 3,000km (1,875mi) to the east of Australia, Tongatapu is Tonga's main island, including the capital Nuku'alofa. Tongatapu is made up of a raised coral platform, where constant wave action has cut a shelf into the cliffs of the south coast, but to the north there are some low lying reefs with many offshore islets. Most surf spots are all squeezed onto a remarkable reef bend on the west side of the island, where trade winds blow straight offshore. SW swells

Ha'atafu Beach Resort

Joe Curren

produce grinding lefts through the southern hemisphere winter (April-Oct), whilst less consistent N swells favour the shorter, shallow rights from Nov-March.

The most southerly spot is The Pass, a hollow left which is the most consistent small swell wave on the island but it closes out over 6ft (2m). On the other side of The Pass is a right (sometimes called The Alley), that

TRAVEL INFORMATION

Local Population:
Tongatapu – 110,000
Nuku'alofa – 25,000
Coastline: Tonga –
136km (85mi)
Time: GMT+12hr
Contest: Local

Getting There – No visa is necessary. You can fly direct to Tonga from Australia, Hawai'i, California, Samoa, New Zealand and Fiji. It's expensive and a bit of a hassle to get to Tonga but is well worth the effort. The departure tax on international flights is $25.

Getting Around – Most of the breaks lie within 10 minutes walk of each other and are rarely more than a 100m paddle from the shore. A boat trip to the reefs in the north of the island shouldn't cost more than $10 per person. Rental cars, ($50/d), are not worth bothering with. Charter boat companies go to Tonga. To reach Eua Iki Island you can either fly or go by boat.

Lodging and Food – Aussie expat Steve Burling and his Tongan wife Sesika have excellent rooms available at the Ha'atafu Beach Resort. The facilities and food are good and they only take up to 15 people. Otherwise try the Paradise Shores Resort. Like much of the South Pacific, it is not cheap at $100/d.

Weather – Tonga's low latitude means subtropical conditions of less rain but cooler temps. The difference between the wet and dry seasons is not as significant as on neighbouring islands. The rainy season begins in Dec and runs through to April. Temps are high at this time and there's lots of rain, especially in March and April. Tonga lies within the cyclone belt. There is on average a major cyclone strike every 20 years, moderate ones every three years and small ones twice a year. The dry season has cooler temps, around the low 20°C's (68°F) and occasionally a strong S wind bringing cold, wet spells. A shorty is needed through colder periods from June-Oct.

Nature and Culture – Life in Tonga revolves around the beach and the sea; there are excellent opportunities for snorkelling and diving, fishing, and whale watching. On land there are some old stone tombs and possibilities for caving. Eua Iki Island has some good hiking. Ha'atafu in the north of the island is a 15km (10mi) Protected Beach Reserve. The clubs and bars in Ha'atafu and Nuku'alofa can be pretty lively.

Hazards and Hassles – Most of the reefs are live coral, for which you will need boots - be careful of reef cuts as they can be easily infected. Medical help is rudimentary. There are only a few locals and the atmosphere is cool.

Handy Hints – Bring everything that you need with you, including spare boards. 'The Friendly Islands' are the last kingdom left in Polynesia. Respect local religious beliefs and try to adapt to the slow pace of life.

WEATHER STATISTICS	J/F	M/A	M/J	J/A	S/O	N/D
total rainfall (mm)	210	287	102	107	112	120
consistency (days/mth)	11	13	11	8	9	9
min temp (°C/°F)	22/72	22/72	19/64	18/66	18/64	21/70
max temp (°C/°F)	29/84	29/84	26/79	26/79	26/79	28/82

Motels

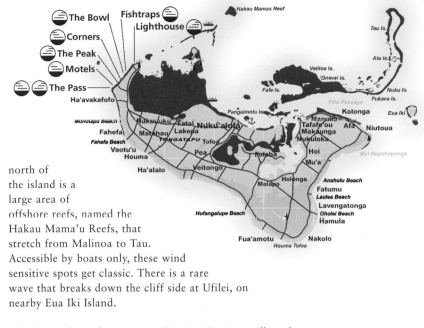

north of the island is a large area of offshore reefs, named the Hakau Mama'u Reefs, that stretch from Malinoa to Tau. Accessible by boats only, these wind sensitive spots get classic. There is a rare wave that breaks down the cliff side at Ufilei, on nearby Eua Iki Island.

breaks in the summer season. It's quite a treacherous, sectiony wave. The consistent lefts at Motels are long and hollow with fast walls no matter how small the swell. Next wave north is The Peak, a small swell right that becomes dangerous over 4ft (1.3m). Corners is a long, workable left wall that's deeper and safer than many of the other spots. Moving further NE around the island, it becomes less consistent, but it's home to the island's most challenging wave. The Bowl doesn't break very often but when it does it's an exceptional ride, holding almost any swell size and bending around the reef with a heavy bowl section, similar to Ala Moana in Hawai'i. Fishtraps, another rifling left, is a case of the bigger the swell, the better and longer the wave. Close to its namesake, Lighthouse is a dangerous, barrelling right suitable for experienced surfers only. Get friendly with the locals and many more spots will reveal themselves. Spots with names like E.T's, Loonies, Sharkie's and Razors. In the

With good exposure to Roaring Forties swells and the deep water Tonga Trench just to the east, Tonga should be much more consistent than it actually is. However, for the swell to hit the NW facing breaks, it has to wrap in from the SW and loses size, whilst E swells don't register at all. New Zealand has a blocking effect so the best swells are those produced by rare lows forming to the north of New Zealand's North Island. Only the strongest NW Pacific lows will register on the NW-N coast. Trade winds blow from the E-SE, year round, from 48% of the time in Aug to 68% in Jan. There is more of a S angle in the dry season and N in the wet season. Occasionally Tonga will be hit by gale force W-NW winds but they never last long. The tidal range is minimal, but low tide is still too shallow for many spots.

SURF STATISTICS	J F	M A	M J	J A	S O	N D
dominant swell	NW-N	S-SW	SE-SW	SE-SW	S-SW	NW-N
swell size (ft)	4-5	5	6-7	7	6	5
consistency (%)	60	80	90	90	80	60
dominant wind	E-SE	E-SE	E-SE	E-S	E-S	E-SE
average force	F4	F4	F4	F4	F4	F4
consistency (%)	65	65	55	64	73	68
water temp (°C/°F)	26/79	26/791	24/75	22/72	23/74	24/75
wetsuit						

Heath Walker

50. Savai'i and Upolu

ALL PHOTOS ANDREW CHRISTIE

Jeremy Walters, Boulders

Summary

+ YEAR ROUND CONSISTENT SWELL
+ WARM AND UNCROWDED
+ SAMOAN CULTURE
+ EXPLORATION POSSIBILITIES

− MANY BLOWN OUT-DAYS
− REMOTE, DIFFICULT ACCESS
− WET CLIMATE
− SHARKY
− NO SURFING ON SUNDAYS

The main islands of Western Samoa are actually a couple of ancient volcanic cones rising up from the ocean bed. They are amongst the largest of the South Pacific islands, with a dramatic and mountainous terrain that ample rainfall keeps lush and green. The two islands called Upolu and Savai'i, are well situated to receive numerous swells from both the N and the S.

Upolu is the more developed of the two islands with the majority of the resorts and decent surf spots. The western island, Savai'i is much wilder with fewer known breaks, but potential for discovery. Generally, the waves are very hollow and powerful, breaking over shallow barrier or lava reefs usually within 500m of the shore. In a few spots, big gaps in the barrier reefs allow the surf to break on lava reefs fringing the shore. The southern facing coasts hold the best quality waves, which are uniformly shallow and more suited to expert surfers. The north coast has fewer spots and receives less swell, making it more suitable for intermediate level surfers.

Koby Aberton

Jeremy Walters

On the north coast there are average waves in Apia but it is Lauli'i where the best wave can be found - a right that breaks very close to the shore and has plenty of tube sections. Lautaunu'u is an average right that actually breaks on all tides, which is a rare bonus in Samoa. There are also various good quality breaks in Ti'avea Bay near the power plant.

On the south coast, the reefs off A'ufaga Village attract plenty of lefts and rights but the highlight is a world class

TRAVEL INFORMATION

Local Population:
Savai'i – 50,000
Upolu – 120,000
Coastline: Upolu – 188km (117mi)
Time: GMT-11hr
Contest: Local

Getting There – A 30 day visa is granted on proof of return air ticket and booked accommodation. There are direct flights from New Zealand, Australia, Hawai'i and Fiji with Polynesian, Air NZ, Air Pacific and Samoan Air. Most resorts do pick-ups from the airport. Dep tax is $20.

Getting Around – The reliable bus service reaches most of the mainland spots. For the spots that break a long distance offshore a boat is needed, costing around $10/rtn. The ferry service to Savai'i from Upolu leaves from Mulifanau and takes 1hr30min. Renting a car is expensive at $250/w and is hardly necessary.

Lodging and Food – Western Samoa is one of the cheapest countries in the South Pacific. If you're willing to rough it then there is accommodation for $20 a night for a 'falé' (thatched hut). During the N swell season, a good place to stay in Apia is the Outrigger Hotel. There are two surf camps on the south coast; Salani Surf Resort and the Samo'ana.

Weather – Western Samoa has a wet tropical climate with the rainy season occurring during the summer (Nov-April). The remainder of the year is dry with occasional showers. The south side of the island is wetter than the north, which is protected by the mountains. Samoa sits on the edge of the cyclone path, so they are a rare possibility. Coastal temps are idyllic at around 29°C (84°F) year round, water temps also never drop below 27°C (80°F), which is slightly above the South Pacific average. Even the trade winds

are lighter than in many other South Pacific islands. Obviously it's year round boardshorts.

Nature and Culture – The Samoan's have a fascinating culture, and there are a few rules which are crucial to respect including a ban on Sunday surfing! Diving and deep-sea fishing are both excellent. There's very little to do at night.

Hazards and Hassles – Most of the reefs are super shallow and dangerous and hospital care is fairly rudimentary. Infections from reef cuts are a problem. There are lots of Tiger Sharks but no recorded bites. Plenty of mosquitoes but no malaria. Drink only bottled water.

Handy Hints – Bring all your surf gear with you including at least one spare boards, reef boots, rash vests and antiseptic for reef cuts. See the wilds of Savai'i with Savai'i Surfaris. Bring $US.

WEATHER STATISTICS	J/F	M/A	M/J	J/A	S/O	N/D
total rainfall (mm)	397	300	152	100	162	315
consistency (days/mth)	20	16	10	9	12	9
min temp (°C/°F)	24/75	23/74	23/74	23/74	23/74	23/74
max temp (°C/°F)	30/86	30/86	29/84	29/84	29/84	30/86

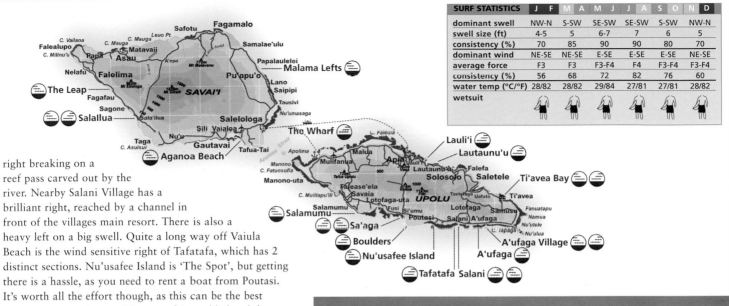

SURF STATISTICS	J F	M A	M J	J A	S O	N D
dominant swell	NW-N	S-SW	SE-SW	SE-SW	S-SW	NW-N
swell size (ft)	4-5	5	6-7	7	6	5
consistency (%)	70	85	90	90	80	70
dominant wind	NE-SE	NE-SE	E-SE	E-SE	E-SE	NE-SE
average force	F3	F3	F3-F4	F4	F3-F4	F3-F4
consistency (%)	56	68	72	82	76	60
water temp (°C/°F)	28/82	28/82	29/84	27/81	27/81	28/82
wetsuit						

right breaking on a reef pass carved out by the river. Nearby Salani Village has a brilliant right, reached by a channel in front of the villages main resort. There is also a heavy left on a big swell. Quite a long way off Vaiula Beach is the wind sensitive right of Tafatafa, which has 2 distinct sections. Nu'usafee Island is 'The Spot', but getting there is a hassle, as you need to rent a boat from Poutasi. It's worth all the effort though, as this can be the best wave in Western Samoa. It's a set of 3 world class lefts that can connect up when the swell is over 8ft (2.6m) and offer epic rides. The SE trade winds blow offshore and it can hold waves of up to 15ft (5m) but it's too shallow and dangerous at low tide. Boulders is a good, big wave left with long rides and deeper water, sheltered from the wind. Sa'aga is a reverse version of Salani with some fun lefts and a heavy treacherous right. To the west is Salamumu, another heavy, hollow, high tide left.

Jeremy Walters, Boulders

Over on Savai'i Island, Malama Lefts are easy to ride with simple access off the point. Good waves can also be found on the SE coast down by Salelologa, The Wharf has clean rights on a moderate swell and Aganoa gets a really bowly inside section. The Leap is the Samoan version of Pipe...big, round and dangerous. Access is by boat and like Nu'usafee Island, it is well worth the effort. Salailua has a deep channel and manageable walls breaking both ways.

doesn't suffer from flat spells. The primary source of swell is from April to October when S-SE swells coming off Antarctica lows generate regular 3-12ft (1-4m) waves. From Nov to March, Samoa receives N-NE swells generated by major northern hemisphere storms, which are the same winter swells that rock the North Shore of Oahu. The islands are also open to occasional cyclone swells coming from the NW-NE. The bad news is that the E-SE trade winds blow out spots half the time in the dry season (Aug). The wet season (Feb) is generally accompanied by glassy conditions. The tidal range never exceeds 5ft (1.6m) but even small changes effect the shallow reefs.

Centrally located in the South Pacific, Western Samoa is an excellent swell magnet, picking up swells from any direction with little loss in size or power. SW-NW swells can be slightly blocked by neighbouring Tonga, Fiji, Tuvalu and the remote Gilbert Islands, but generally, Samoa

Blake Johnston, Coconuts

51. Tahiti & Moorea

KIRIBATI

Marquesas Islands

Tuamotu Archipelago

Society Islands

Tubuai Islands FRENCH POLYNESIA

Teahupoo

LAURENT MASUREL

Summary

+ POWERFUL, CONSISTENT WAVES YEAR ROUND
+ BARRELS!
+ BEAUTIFUL LANDSCAPES
+ CHILLED OUT ISLAND LIFESTYLE

– VERY EXPENSIVE
– DIFFICULT ACCESS
– LOCALISM AT SOME SPOTS

Tahiti sits at the centre of French Polynesia and now, thanks to the relatively recent discovery and media glut coverage of a scary reef-pass wave, it sits firmly at the centre of the surfing universe. Comprising of about 118 small islands spread out over five archipelago's, (Société Islands including Tahiti, Marquesas, Tuamotu, Gambier and Tubuai), and covering an area of ocean the size of Europe, the scope for perfect waves is unlimited. There are dozens of islands in this chain that receive classic waves, which more often than not go unridden. On the whole, the quality of the spots is exceptional and the waves are varied.

When the winter N swells roll in, Moorea

LAURENT MASUREL

ROB GILLEY

Island is worth the effort for the pair of quality waves at Hauru Point (Club Med) and Irihonu (the Bay of Cook). Take a dugout to these spots from the Bali Hai Hotel. Moorea also gets plenty of decent waves through the S swell season, and if it's big, then head to the east side near the airport and the long, carvable rights of Temae.

TRAVEL INFORMATION

Local Population: Tahiti and Moorea – 150,000
Coastline: 2,525km (1,578mi)
Time: GMT-10hr
Contest: WCT (May)

Getting There – Visa: everyone except the French and Americans (who get a 30 day permit on arrival) need visas. Everyone needs a return air ticket to be granted entry. Tahiti has good air connections with Australia, Europe and US.

Getting Around – Local trucks provide good, cheap transport around the island. Getting from the shore to the waves usually involves paddling for 30-45 min across the lagoon or more sensibly renting a dugout for $10/rtn. A rental car costs about $50/d. The ferry to Moorea Island costs $12/rtn.

Lodging and Food – Like much of the South Pacific, Tahiti is not a cheap place to visit. At the

bottom of the accommodation range are the dorm beds at the Papeete Hotel, which charges at least $15/p. A decent hotel will cost around $100-150/dble, (Meridien). Half-board with the use of a dugout at the Moana surfcamp is around $100/day. A local 'falé' in Teahupoo costs $45/day. Eat at the 'roulottes' where local food will cost from $8 but more frequently you'll spend around $20-30 on a meal.

Weather – During the wet season from Nov to April, there will be a heavy downpour every other day. El Niño years are very wet. Cyclones hit the country on occasions. In the dry season, the high mountains effect the weather patterns and cause the south coast to see some rain. The temps are near perfect at 23°-30°C (74°-86°F) year round. The water hovers around 25-27°C (77°-80°F).

Nature and Culture – If you need a break from getting barrelled, then head up into the beautiful mountains, visit some of the caves, go diving and snorkelling or just chill out

amongst the lush landscape. Occasional dugout races are worth watching.

Hazards and Hassles – Respect the locals' deep feeling of pride. The waves are super heavy and the reefs are shallow and full of fire coral. Currents at the mouth of reef passes can be very strong. Teahupoo is one of the most dangerous waves in the world and should only be tackled by the most advanced of surfers. It has already seen one surf-related death. Sharks although common, pose no real threat. Don't eat poorly cooked fish, as there is a chance of catching Ciguatera. There are lots of mosquitoes but no malaria.

Handy Hints – Bring all your own surf gear, as equipment here is very expensive. Bring at least two boards, including a gun made especially for local conditions (heavy barrels!). Other essentials include reef boots, sun cream and a helmet. Tahiti is a French speaking destination, but French people may find themselves the object of some bitterness.

WEATHER STATISTICS	J/F	M/A	M/J	J/A	S/O	N/D
total rainfall (mm)	300	170	95	67	75	195
consistency (days/mth)	14	11	7	6	7	13
min temp (°C/°F)	23/74	23/74	21/70	20/68	21/70	23/74
max temp (°C/°F)	30/86	30/86	29/84	28/82	29/84	30/86

There can be problems when surfing Temae because the locals covet this inconsistent right, so tread lightly. On the other side of the island, Haapiti has nice lefts and doesn't need so much swell.

A one hour ferry ride to the north coast of Tahiti, will see the same winter swells crank up a succession of good reefs like Matavai, Point Come and Motuau. Further east, the less challenging beachbreaks at the rivermouth of Papenoo, can provide a fun, hollow session. All these spots are really just a warm up for the barrels on the SW coast of Tahiti. Close to Papeete is Taapuna, the first of the world class spots, being a hollow, dredging and technically testing lefthander. An easier alternative can be found in Sapinus, opposite the Tahiti Museum, or the fickle Maraa, which holds up even when the trades aren't blowing. Beginners can head for a good beachbreak in Papara, which is a nice rest from the intensity of the surrounding reefs. The next classic spot is on the Iti Peninsula where the flawless lefts of Vairao offer epic barrels. Every once in a while a new spot bursts into the surf world's psyche and totally redefines the word heavy. Teahupoo is the barely rideable left reef pass that has made every other spot pale in comparison and now that Laird Hamilton has begun towing-in on unbelievably heavy waves here, our fascination with this freak of nature seems set to continue. Only the bravest (or barmiest) need apply.

Teahupoo

LAURENT MASUREL

At a southern latitude of 17°, Tahiti is perfectly exposed to the super consistent S-SW swells which hammer the south coast year round, but peak between April and Oct. Expect the surf to range from 4-15ft (1.3-5m) in season and 2-5ft (0.6-1.6m) in the off-season.

Exposure to the summer N/NW swells between Nov and March is less generous. Tahiti receives about half the swell of Hawai'i. Even so, this time of year will still see plenty of 3ft-8ft (1-2.6m) swells. Dominant trade winds come from the east and blow from 40-60kph (25-40mph).

During the May to Oct dry season, (Maraamu), the wind has more of a SE-E angle, whilst the wet season, (Toerau), sees the wind coming more from the N-NE. Even with these strong winds mornings will usually be glassy. Tidal range is very small.

SURF STATISTICS	J F	M A M	J J	A S	O N	D
dominant swell	N-NW	S-SW	SE-SW	SE-SW	S-SW	N-NW
swell size (ft)	5	5-6	7	7-8	6-7	5-6
consistency (%)	70	85	90	90	80	70
dominant wind	NE-SE	NE-SE	E-SE	E-SE	E-SE	NE-SE
average force	F4	F4	F4	F4	F4	F4
consistency (%)	75	78	60	62	70	72
water temp (°C/°F)	27/81	27/81	26/79	25/77	26/79	27/81
wetsuit						

ROB GILLEY

52. Oahu North Shore

Kauai
Oahu
Molokai
Lanai   Maui
Kahoolawe
HAWAI'I
Hawai'i

Summary
+ THE PROVING GROUND
+ BIGGEST, HEAVIEST WAVES
  IN THE WORLD
+ MYTHICAL SURF CULTURE
+ GREAT SPECTATOR ARENA

− DANGEROUS SURFING CONDITIONS
− AMAZING CROWD PRESSURES
− LACK OF HOTELS AND NIGHTLIFE
− NOT SUITABLE FOR BEGINNERS
− EXPENSIVE

Pipeline

GRANT MYRDAL

Shane Dorian, Waimea Bay

JOHN CALLAHAN

There is no denying that the North Shore of Oahu is surfing's Mecca. Its undisputed attractions challenge every surfer on the planet to find out if they have got what it takes. Conquering the fear of dropping into a bomb at Pipe, or paddling over the edge of a Waimea cliff represent the zenith of the surfing experience. Thousands make the pilgrimage every year to the Hawai'ian Islands, which are tips of volcanic mountains, that rise precipitously from the ocean floor. There's no continental shelf or barrier reef to dampen the force of the powerful swells that come thundering out of the North Pacific and slam into the world's most famous surf zone — the 7 miles of coast between Haleiwa and Velzyland on Oahu's beautiful North Shore.

Off The Wall

ROB GILLEY

The North Shore coast faces north-west, and early season W swells tend to break cleaner at many spots than N or NE swells. Whatever the swell direction, the surf here can jump from 2ft to 15ft (0.6-5m) within a few hours and sneaker sets are common. On smaller swells, most spots break on lava reef close to golden sand beaches with deep channels, which make paddling out easier but also create some strong rips in larger surf. From mid Nov-Jan, all the professional surfers in the world flock to Hawai'i, and it becomes a major achievement to snag a wave in the hungry pack. The town of Haleiwa, with a variety of facilities and amenities, is the commercial centre of the North Shore, plus its Ali'i Beach Park has a consistent right break on most swells (W is best). It's a fast, walled-

TRAVEL INFORMATION

Local Population:
Oahu – 762,000
Coastline: 204km
(128mi)
Time: GMT-12hr
Contests: Nov-Feb
(6 major events)

Getting There – Three month visas are needed for most nationalities. Honolulu airport is a major Pacific stop off. It's a 45mins drive from Honolulu airport to the North Shore on either Highway 99 or 2. Many hotels or backpackers' hostels will pick you up at the airport.

Getting Around – The North Shore spots are close together, so you could rent a bike or take the Kam bus. Most people rent a car for ±$25/d. Fuel is 25% more than the US mainland.

Lodging and Food – The only North Shore hotel is the Turtle Bay Hilton ($150/dble). Most people stay at Waimea Backpackers ($25/d), B&B's in Hale'iwa ($20/d), or rent a flat ($600/w for 4 people). Surfers are the main tourist group, so high season is winter. Food isn't cheap ($15/meal); most shop at Foodland, one of the most expensive supermarkets in the US.

Weather – The stability of the temps is amazing. Between day and night, winter and summer, temps vary little from a near perfect 25°C (77°F). It's the same story in the water, which hovers around 24°C (75°F) year round. The winter surf season has rainy periods, especially on S winds. When NE-E trades blow, skies are usually clear. The west shore is much drier than the easterly windward coast.

Nature and Culture – Hike to Kaena Point or hit the Kahuku Sugarmill disco. One hour away, the south shore has plenty of popular tourist attractions, like Waikiki.

Hazards and Hassles – Drowning, collisions with the reef, heavy rips, flying boards and angry locals will all keep you on your toes! Minimise the risks by surfing the low key spots or by surfing very early and being patient and cautious in the line-up. Car rip-offs are common.

Handy Hints – The yellow pages of the phone book are loaded with surf shops, both in town and out in the country (North Shore).

WEATHER STATISTICS	J/F	M/A	M/J	J/A	S/O	N/D
total rainfall (mm)	90	55	17	18	35	65
consistency (days/mth)	8	7	5	6	6	9
min temp (°C/°F)	19/66	19/66	21/70	23/74	22/72	20/68
max temp (°C/°F)	26/79	27/81	29/84	29/84	30/86	27/81

up performance wave that ends up in a shallow 'Toilet Bowl' section. On huge swells, an outside reef heaves up waves at a place called Avalanche. For less challenging waves, the rights of Puaena Point (Puni's) break into the boat channel. A couple of miles north on Kam Highway, Laniakea is rare righthander that can be perfect (picture 15ft Malibu) on a NE swell. Jockos (just north around the point) is more consistent and the lefts have a sucky take-off that subsides into a long wall, but beware of really strong rips. On the opposite side of the next cove is Chuns Reef, a good, fun small wave. Around the next point is another mellow spot, appropriately called Marijuanas. Halfway up the North Shore, the Kam Highway swings wide around the bay called Waimea: the spot that has set the standard for big-wave surfing for over 40 years. Although somewhat eclipsed by outer reef tow-in breaks, mere mortals will find the 20-25ft (6.6-8.3m) swells that Waimea can handle, more than enough of a challenge. On smaller days, when 'The Bay' proper isn't working, a sandbar section called Pinballs can reel off some juicy little pockets right along the lava rock point. Waimea's shorebreak is a gnarly mix of crashing lips and powerful pockets; once avoided, today it's packed with suicidal bodyboarders and even a few stand-up surfers.

Log Cabins is an underrated right breaking over a treacherous lava bottom; its outer reef is a tow-in classic. Rockpile can present a decent peak, but Off-The-Wall (a.k.a. Kodak Reef) is the classic high quality, super crowded, right sprint, a favourite with photographers. Just a bit further up the beach is the righthand Backdoor section of the most famous wave in the world, Pipeline, and then the incredible Pipe left, tapering into the channel at Ehukai Beach. No other spot on earth quite matches the full Pipeline experience – the power, the barrels, the crowds, the glory, the humility ... this is quintessential North Shore! If you're looking for breathing room, check out the beach between Ehukai and Rocky Point – Pupukea, Gas Chambers, Monster Mush – can have good peaks worth checking out. The modest lava jut of Rocky Point is a swell magnet and a jam-packed theatre of progressive new school surfing. Past Kammieland, Sunset Beach curves out to Sunset Point. The long, unpredictable rights, hollow inside bowl, and occasional lefts are as good as they've ever been, but the shift in media attention has mellowed the vibe a little, however it's still a long swim in if your leash breaks. About a mile north, past Val's Reef and Phantoms, is Velzyland, perhaps the most localised spot on the strip.

Sunset

ALEX WILLIAMS

From Oct to March expect numerous, very powerful 10-30ft (3.3-10m) swells coming off deep lows travelling east across the North Pacific, with wave periods of around 15-20 seconds. From Apr to Sep, the North Shore is generally flat, but other sides of the island see frequent 3-8ft (1-2.6m) NE windswell and 2-8ft (0.6-2.6m) SE-SW summer groundswell. Trade winds are very stable year round, blowing from the E for 27% of the time in Dec to 58% of the time in Aug. This is sideshore at most North Shore spots, so if it gets too strong, it will mess up the waves. Southerly (or Kona) winds occur periodically in winter. This can bring offshore winds to places like Hale'iwa and Laniakea. Tidal range is slight, but shifting combinations of wind, tide and swell can turn conditions from junky to epic in a very short time.

Chun's

ALEX WILLIAMS

SURF STATISTICS		F M	A M	J J	A S	O N	D
dominant swell		NW-NE	NW-NE	NW-N	NW-N	NW-NE	NW-NE
swell size (ft)		8-9	6-7	3-4	1-2	4-5	7-8
consistency (%)		90	70	40	30	60	80
dominant wind		NE-SE	NE-E	NE-E	NE-E	NE-E	NE-SE
average force		F4	F4	F4	F4	F4	F4
consistency (%)		63	66	76	88	77	77
water temp (°C/°F)		24/75	24/75	25/77	26/79	27/81	25/77
wetsuit							

53. North-West Maui

HAWAI'I

Kauai
Oahu · Molokai
Lanai · **Maui**
Kahoolawe
Hawai'i

Summary
+ THINNER CROWDS THAN OAHU
+ WORLD CLASS SPOTS
+ WINDSURFING HEAVEN
+ AMAZING VOLCANIC SCENERY

– SWELL SHADOWS
– STRONG TRADE WINDS
– DIFFICULT ACCESS TO SOME SPOTS
– HIGH PRICES

Honolua Bay

SYLVAIN CAZENAVE

While Oahu's North Shore has dominated media coverage of Hawai'ian surf, each island in the chain gets its share of waves, and Maui has some of the best, if not the most. An island of contrasts such as lush green valleys and arid coastline, tropical fruits and flowers and barren lava and cactus, low plains and towering peaks, but most importantly, the whole of Maui is fringed with surf. The legendary rights of Honolua and Maalaea are part of the offerings, which now include the biggest name of all – Jaws!

On a major NE swell (NW swells are blocked by Molokai), a classic, long, hollow righthand point peels into Honolua Bay. The first section, Coconuts, breaks in front of cliffs, then wraps into the bay where it hits a very hollow section. It'll either result in a classic barrel or the lip will slam down and propel the unlucky towards the infamous cave, where many a surfboard met an untimely end in the pre-leash days! Honolua is

LAURENT MASUREL

Lahaina Harbour

SYLVAIN CAZENAVE

definitely a wave for only the most experienced of surfers. Although the intensity of the crowds cannot match the North Shore, the place gets packed when it's on with half the island's best surfers eager to get a piece of the action. Beware of urchins on the shallow reef in the bay! North-east of Honolua Bay is the small town of Honokohau, where a track runs down to a good righthand reef. Further east the road deteriorates and is dangerous (some car rental outfits won't insure you on this stretch). A better

TRAVEL INFORMATION

Local Population:
Maui – 120,000
Coastline: Maui –
218km (136mi)
Time: GMT-12hr
Contest: Nov. 2 (Junior)

Getting There – (See 52. North Shore, Oahu). Almost all flights connect in Honolulu. Flights from there to Kahului (the capital of Maui County) are plentiful at ±$70/rtn. Pre-booked package deals are the cheapest way to go.

Getting Around – A car is essential - basic rental costs around $25/d. Fuel costs 40c/l. It takes 45mins to drive from the airport to Honolua. Rental cars are a popular target with thieves.

Lodging and Food – Accommodation prices are higher than on Oahu. Good bases are Haiku or Paia near Hookipa in the winter; in summer, the Nani Kai Hale condos in Lahaina are good. Double rooms cost about $50. Try to avoid the touristy south-west coast (centred around Kihei) if you're after a mellow trip that's more in tune with the Hawai'ian lifestyle. A decent meal will be around $30; cooking your own or living off fast food will help keep costs down.

Weather – (See 52. North Shore, Oahu). The water hovers between 24°-27°C (75°-80°F), so boardshorts and a rash vest, or a shorty on windy afternoons.

Nature and Culture – Haleakala Crater is the world's largest dormant volcano and, according to legend, is the soul of Maui. It has

been a place of pilgrimage for centuries, check out the sunrise from the summit. Other flat-day activities include mountain biking, windsurfing, diving, and whale watching (March and April are best for the Humpbacks). For nightlife, head to Lahaina or Kaanapali.

Hassles and Hazards – To avoid trouble with the locals, don't surf the big name spots at the busiest times of the day. Don't leave valuables visible in your car.

Handy Hints – There are plenty of surf shops like Maui Tropics in Paia, or Ole's in Lahaina. You will need a big board for some of the points, but nothing like you would need on Oahu's North Shore. Honolua and others are real board snapping spots. Beginners should head to Nancy Emerson's surf school.

WEATHER STATISTICS	J/F	M/A	M/J	J/A	S/O	N/D
total rainfall (mm)	90	55	17	18	35	65
consistency (days/mth)	8	7	5	6	6	9
min temp (°C/°F)	19/66	19/66	21/70	23/74	22/72	20/68
max temp (°C/°F)	26/79	27/81	29/84	29/84	30/86	27/81

option is to drive south towards Lahaina, checking out spots like Little Makaha, the mellow lefts of S-Turns, or Kaanapali Point (KPs).

From Lahaina east, the S coast is better exposed to SW summer swells, which produce more lefts than rights, the opposite of Maui's north shore. This coast is sheltered from the NE trades and is consistently offshore. Lahaina is a surfing hub with plenty of consistent spots, from Mala Wharf on the north end of town, to Lahaina Harbour and the Jetty, which throws out an insane barrel. To the south are a series of fickle reefbreaks, where small but nice waves can be found. One of Hawai'i's most famous summer spots is Maalaea, where a harbour breakwall has created a righthand wave that's considered to be the fastest in the world, but it needs a huge SW swell to break and is notoriously fickle. Local activists and environmental groups have so far successfully blocked several proposed extensions of the Ma'alaea jetty, which would destroy this world class gem.

On Maui's north shore, good waves can be found around town of Kahului, especially at Waiehu (in a built-up urban area with water quality and population issues) and Kanaha (a windy windsurfing Mecca near the airport), so you may want to head further out into the countryside. A drive out towards Palm Point will reveal a few short, wedgy lefts and some rarer rights that tend to be longer and mellower, but all the waves around here are very wind sensitive. This area is home to some of the best wavesailing in the world, so expect strong cross-shore winds on most days. Hookipa is the centre of windsurfing

SYLVAIN CAZENAVE
Dave Kalama, Jaws

The Hawai'ian Island chain is the most isolated archipelago in the world and swell exposure is second to none. Unfortunately, Maui is sheltered from many of the big SW, W, and NW swells by the smaller neighbouring islands of Molokai, Lanai and Kahoolawe and the Big Island creates a very large shadow on the rare SE swells generated by cyclones pinwheeling into the Pacific from Mexico. Generally, Maui receives less swell and more wind than Oahu. NE trades are strongest from May to Aug but winds can be much lighter in the mornings. The south coast is usually offshore, however it only gets surf on the rarer SW swells. The best winds for the N shore are the SSE Kona winds. Tidal range is small, but can have a drastic effect on shallow spots. Tide tables are widely available in surf shops.

SURF STATISTICS	J F	M A	M J	J A	S O	N D
dominant swell	N-NE	S-NE	S-SW	S-SW	S-NE	N-NE
swell size (ft)	7	5	3-4	2-3	4-5	6
consistency (%)	80	60	50	60	50	70
dominant wind	NE-SE	NE-E	NE-E	NE-E	NE-E	NE-SE
average force	F4	F4	F4	F4	F4	F4
consistency (%)	63	66	76	88	77	77
water temp (°C/°F)	24/75	24/75	25/77	26/79	27/81	25/77
wetsuit						

Jaws

activity in Hawai'i, but on windless days this good quality reefbreak is a very popular surf spot. Baldwin Beach, in nearby Paia, has mellow beachbreak waves, but Pavilions (the peaky point wave off the eastern end of Hookipa Beach Park) is the most consistent.

The most notorious spot on Maui is a wave most surfers are extremely unlikely to ride. With the development of tow-in surfing in the early 90's, Jaws burst onto the scene, amazing the world with the sheer magnitude of the waves that were being ridden there by a select group of windsurfing and surfing hellmen. If a huge swell hits Maui, drive out to Peahi, find a comfortable spot on the cliff and watch the show below. Remember to bring binoculars!

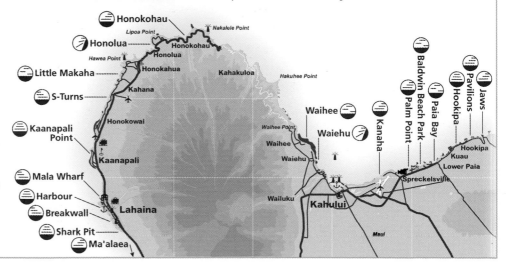

Honokohau
Lipoa Point
Nakalele Point
Honolua
Honokohau
Honolua
Hawea Point
Honolua
Honokahua
Kahakuloa
Hakuhee Point
Little Makaha
Kahana
Paia Bay
Baldwin Beach Park
Pavilions
S-Turns
Honokowai
Waihee
Palm Point
Hookipa
Jaws
Kaanapali Point
Waihee Point
Kanaha
Waiehu
Waihee
Kaanapali
Waiehu
Waiehu
Hookipa
Kuau
Mala Wharf
Wailuku
Lower Paia
Harbour
Spreckelsville
Breakwall
Lahaina
Kahului
Shark Pit
Maui
Ma'alaea

Team O'Neill Cory Lopez

SURFBOARDS
ONLY
•NO SWIMMING
•NO WADING
•NO BODY BOARDS
•NO KAYAKS
L.A. CO. CODE 17.12.510
M.C.C. CODE 17.12.510

FIND YOUR SPOT ON EARTH AND RIDE IT

Jack O'Neill
Inventor of the wetsuit in 1952

Malibu

North America

Meteorology and Oceanography

North America is a tale of two oceans, dividing the mighty North Pacific to the west and the stormy North Atlantic on the east. Whilst the two coastlines are fairly evenly balanced in length, the swell distribution is heavily biased towards the West Coast and in particular the famous breaks of Central and Southern California. This part of the USA is the cradle of modern surfing and is particularly fortunate to receive swells from 4 major surf producing sources. The North Pacific Aleutian lows are responsible for serving up some of the biggest waves on the planet and after bombarding Hawai'i, they continue on to influence the surf from Alaska to South America. These storms will form anywhere between 30° and 60°N, tracking from west to east, with a more northerly trajectory in the summer. When the low pressures drop down lower in the winter, they can bring more of a W swell scenario, but it is the NW swell which dominates the west coast of North America. The latitude of the storms is crucial in determining the associated wind patterns. For instance, British Colombia, Washington and Oregon receive tons of swell but as the depressions make landfall, these areas are blighted by strong SW-NW onshores. Storms tucked up in the Gulf of Alaska may produce swell for these areas (while California misses out) but the trade off is, this northern coast doesn't receive much, if any, of the S and SW swells that California scores in the summer. The S swells are courtesy of the hurricanes (chubascos) off the coast of Mexico and the SW swells are long distance travellers from the band of low pressures in the South Pacific. The fourth wave producers are remote western Pacific swells and local windswells, which can push up some small, fun surf from a due W direction.

The predominant NW winds moderate towards the south, where morning land breezes are replaced by the onshore sea breezes around midday. Santa Ana is the name given to the hot, dry E winds that blow off the desert in late summer. Southern California and the Baja Peninsula experience the west coast desert syndrome that indicates an area of upwelling. The cool California Current parallels much of West Coast USA, flowing towards Mexico, and is instrumental in providing the sea fog that is so common right along the western seaboard.

Tides grow in range as you travel north and are uniformly semi-diurnal.

Air and Water Temperatures

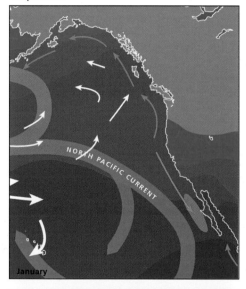

January

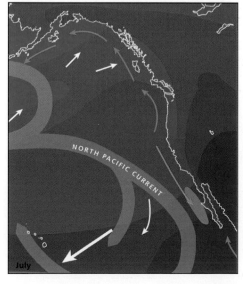

July

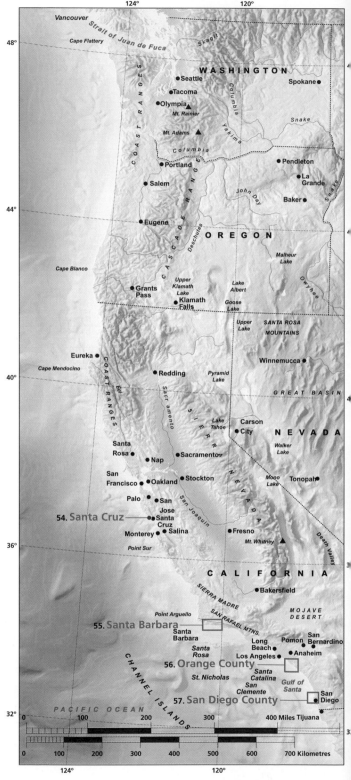

Across the continent on the East Coast, a new ocean brings a whole new set of weather systems. Firstly, and most importantly (from a surfer's perspective), the entire East Coast is affected by hurricane activity during summer and fall (June-Nov), which bring the biggest, most powerful and organised swells. These Atlantic swells, no matter how good, are notoriously infrequent and some hurricane seasons pass without producing any epic surf. August to October are the prime months when half a dozen storms should track from West Africa towards the Caribbean before swinging N to NE. Hurricane paths are very unpredictable, but generally, they do the Atlantic offshore arc or else keep tracking west over the Gulf of Mexico. This means that low pressure systems from the west are the main source of regular, swell producing weather. Cold fronts associated with these areas of low pressure, travel across the continental land mass, until they hit the ocean and start winding up again. Depending on where they pop off the coast, they can provide up to a few days swell for nearby states, but because they are travelling away from the coast, most of the swell is as well. The best winter source of swell are low pressure systems which form off the coast of Nova Scotia and are capable of sending NE lines all the way down to Florida. Unfortunately, these lows rarely remain in position for long, quickly spinning off towards Europe and consequently the swells lack duration. Another East Coast surf reality is the reliance on wind chop, which is usually from the SE, giving surfers some respite from the extensive flat spells. Morning land breezes followed by afternoon onshores are the summer rule of thumb, while winter sees a lot of NE winds followed by SW-NW offshores.

The Gulf Stream begins its Atlantic migration at the southern tip of Florida, hugging the coast up to Palm Beach County, before swinging NE towards the Outer Banks and then westwards to Europe. On the rare occasions that Southern Florida experiences a bit of cold weather, steam can be released from this blissfully warm ocean flow. Once its influence leaves the coast, drastic drops in winter water temperature occur, until the water starts slushing in New England and Nova Scotia, where the icy Labrador Current creeps down the north-east coast.

Tides are small and predictable in the south, but the further north you go, the greater the range.

Temperatures, Winds and Currents

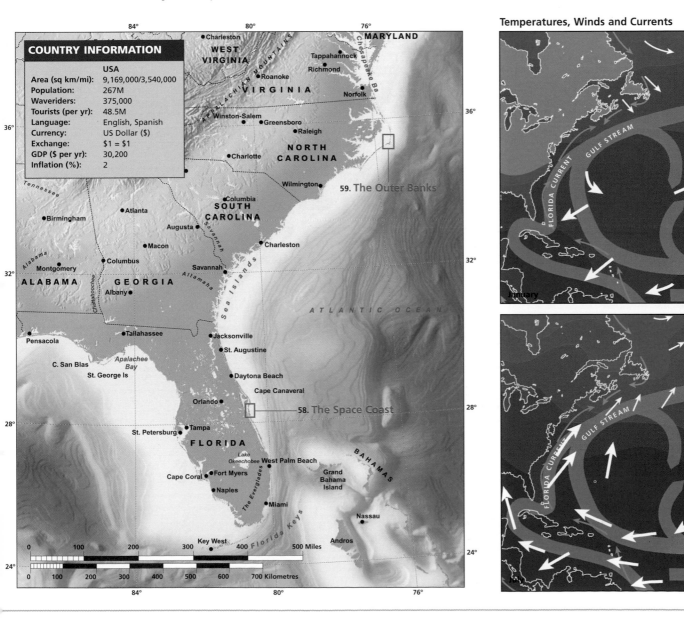

COUNTRY INFORMATION

USA
Area (sq km/mi):	9,169,000/3,540,000
Population:	267M
Waveriders:	375,000
Tourists (per yr):	48.5M
Language:	English, Spanish
Currency:	US Dollar ($)
Exchange:	$1 = $1
GDP ($ per yr):	30,200
Inflation (%):	2

54. Santa Cruz

The Point – Steamer Lane

DAN HAYLOCK

Summary

+ WIDE SWELL WINDOW
+ SPOT VARIETY
+ DOMINANT OFFSHORES
+ LAID BACK SANTA CRUZ
+ EASY ACCESS AND LODGING

− COLD WATER YEAR ROUND
− CHILLY WINTER TEMPS
− COMPETITIVE CROWDS
− SHARKS

Two California beach towns are forever squabbling over the right to call themselves "Surf City." Huntington Beach has miles of beachbreak surf and plenty of people, but Santa Cruz has a huge variety of surf spots and perhaps the finest set-up of any zone on the West Coast and plenty of people. Situated just inside the northern point of the half circle of Monterey Bay, Santa Cruz enjoys all the benefits of a southern exposure, yet W, NW, and N swells wrap into the town and fire on dozens of reefs, points, and beachbreaks. For surfers, the rugged green coastline around Santa Cruz is a cold water paradise that more than deserves the title Surf City. Situated about 120km (75mi) south of San Francisco, Santa Cruz has a unique laid-back style and an increasing large population.

RUSSI

Third Reef – Steamer Lane

RUSSI

Coming down the coast from San Francisco, you'll want to check out Pillar Point at Half Moon Bay and the wave now internationally known as Mavericks. If it's winter and the swell's huge, you can watch the local lads tow-in on some genuine giants. Down the coast, you'll find Año Nuevo, a seal reserve and a wedging wave

TRAVEL INFORMATION

Local Population: Santa Cruz Co. – 250,000
Coastline: Santa Cruz Co. – 51mi (82km)
Time: GMT-8hr
Contests: WQS (March)

Getting There – No visa. Most international flights land in LAX (7hrs drive to Santa Cruz), or San Francisco (2hrs drive).

Getting Around – Public transport is bad. If you can't rent a car, stay in Santa Cruz on the West Side. Rental cars start about $160/w but can be as low as $50 for a local rent-a-wreck! You need to be over 21. Fuel is cheap ($1.70/gal, 40¢/l). The road systems can be confusing, but are fairly efficient.

Lodging and Food – There are cheap dorm rooms (Carmelita Cottage) for around $15, but a motel double by the beach is $60-80 (The Super 8, Sea & Sand Inn, or Jewel of the Sea). Fast food is cheap ($5/meal), but restaurants are expensive.

Weather – Santa Cruz is wetter than Southern California, but it's not fully exposed to the oceanic patterns of Northern California. Facing south and sheltered from N winds, Santa Cruz has a warmer micro-climate. Winters are mild and freezing temperatures are rare unless the bitter N winds blow. Rainfall is fairly low. Spring is a weird time, it's often hazy (due to the difference between air and sea temperatures) with lots of wind but, like summer, it's sunny and dry. Autumn has perfect weather and plenty of swells. Because of the Monterey submarine canyon creating upwellings, the water remains cold year-round, always requiring a light steamer and occasionally a winter 4/3mm. O'Neill wetsuits were born in San Francisco in 1952 and moved to Santa Cruz in 1959.

Nature and Culture – Visit the Lighthouse Surf Museum or the Shakespeare Santa Cruz Museum. Take a stroll along the Wharf or the beach boardwalk. The drive down Highway 1, south of Carmel through Big Sur is awesome. Santa Cruz has some cool nightlife; check out the Catalyst and Palookaville bar/clubs.

Hazards and Hassles – To avoid crowds, surf the less accessible spots that locals tend not to bother with. To the south in Monterey Bay there is usually less crowd pressure and also north of town but beware of Great Whites. If it rains much, rivermouth beaches can become polluted, but the sandbanks will be good!

Handy Hints – There are plenty of surf shops like the O'Neill HQ on 41st Ave. A new board is around $400; you'll need a gun in the winter for tackling juicy rights. As a beginner go to Richard Schmidt or Club Ed surf schools. Longboarding is popular.

WEATHER STATISTICS	J/F	M/A	M/J	J/A	S/O	N/D
total rainfall (mm)	95	52	8	0	11	72
consistency (days/mth)	8	6	2	0	2	7
min temp (°C/°F)	5/41	7/44	10/50	12/54	11/52	7/44
max temp (°C/°F)	14/57	17/62	20/68	22/72	22/72	15/59

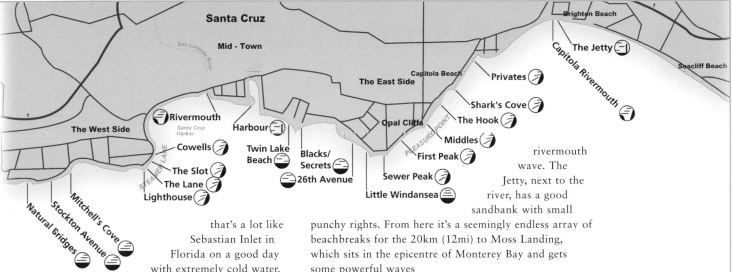

Santa Cruz

Mid - Town

Brighton Beach

The Jetty

Capitola Rivermouth

Seacliff Beach

Capitola Beach

Privates

The East Side

Shark's Cove

Opal Cliffs

The Hook

PLEASURE POINT

Middles

First Peak

Rivermouth

Santa Cruz Harbour

Harbour

Twin Lake Beach

Blacks/ Secrets

26th Avenue

Sewer Peak

Little Windansea

The West Side

Cowells

The Slot

The Lane

Lighthouse

STEAMER LANE

Mitchell's Cove

Stockton Avenue

Natural Bridges

rivermouth wave. The Jetty, next to the river, has a good sandbank with small punchy rights. From here it's a seemingly endless array of beachbreaks for the 20km (12mi) to Moss Landing, which sits in the epicentre of Monterey Bay and gets some powerful waves due to the energy-focusing of the Monterey Trench.

that's a lot like Sebastian Inlet in Florida on a good day with extremely cold water. Beware the abundant Great White sharks, which occasionally mistake surfers for seals – this is the centre of 'The Red Triangle' (a triangular shaped Great White breeding ground) which skirts the coast from Monterey to San Francisco! Further south, check out Waddell Creek, Greyhound Rocks, and Scott Creek, then Four Mile, Three Mile and – bam! – you're in town.

The West Side of Santa Cruz forms a series of points with a number of quality right reefs and a few pockets of beachbreak. The waves are usually punchy and can hold real size. Many spots have thick kelp beds that dampen the prevailing NW wind and smooth out the waves. From Natural Bridges and Stockton Avenue, past Mitchell's Cove and down to Lighthouse Point and Steamer Lane, there's plenty of raw power and great surf on this stretch of coast. 'The Lane' is a classic reefbreak that moves farther out as the swell gets bigger (Second Reef works from 10-12ft (3.3-4m), Third Reef from 15ft (5m) on up). Lefts are rarer and shorter, but the right can be very long. On a big W swell at mid tide rides can be had all the way around the point and into Cowells Beach and on towards the Municipal Pier – almost a mile! Steamer Lane is the site of O'Neill's annual 'Cold Water Classic,' and Cowells is a beginners' favourite. The San Lorenzo Rivermouth is in the centre of town near the amusement park and, (depending on the rain and thus sandbar build-up) can turn on magic peaks. Beachbreaks east of the rivermouth can be classic. The Harbour too, gets a sand build-up that creates a sucking, savage barrel right off the breakwall and into the boat channel, usually posted 'No Surfing', but surfers will be surfers.

The East Side scene is concentrated around the long, peeling, righthand points of Pleasure Point, apart from the fast lefts of Little Windansea. Sewer Peak, through First Peak, Middles, and down to The Hook, then on to the pleasant reefs at Shark's Cove and Privates. These rights wall up and peel down the rocky inlets on both summer S swell and big winter N swell. After that, if there has been sufficient rainfall, Capitola can provide a decent

NW swells come from lows off the Aleutian Islands (Oct-Mar), ranging in size from 3-15ft (1-5m). Early and late summer will see frequent 2-6ft (0.6-2m) W swells originating far out in the western Pacific or as short distance wind swells developing just offshore. Summer (July-Oct) surf can originate from either SW groundswells or hurricanes off Mexico. Waves can occasionally reach 10ft (3.3m), but average 2-6ft (0.6-2m). Check the Harbour Buoy or NOAA 46042 on the internet for the latest swell size. Dominant winds are NW-N year round, varying from 40% of the time in Jan to 70% of the time in June; it blows the strongest in spring. Because Santa Cruz faces south, prevailing winds are frequently offshore or cross-off. Tides are significant, with different spots favouring different tides.

SURF STATISTICS	J F	M A	M J	J A	S O	N D
dominant swell	W-NW	W-NW	S-SW	S-SW	W-NW	W-NW
swell size (ft)	6	4-5	4	4-5	5	6
consistency (%)	80	75	60	60	70	80
dominant wind	NW-N	NW-N	NW-N	NW-N	NW-N	NW-N
average force	F4	F4	F5	F4-F5	F4	F4
consistency (%)	44	57	69	66	62	47
water temp (°C/°F)	13/55	13/55	14/57	15/59	15/59	14/57
wetsuit						

ROB GILLEY

The view from Capitola to Four Mile)

55. Santa Barbara and Ventura

OREGON

CALIFORNIA

MEXICO

Summary
+ MANY RIGHT POINTBREAKS
+ GOOD WIND PATTERNS
+ GREAT WEATHER
+ ENTERTAINING AREA

− SWELL SHADOWS
− CONSTANT COMPETITIVE CROWD
− RELATIVELY COOL WATER
− POLLUTION
− URBAN ATMOSPHERE

Rincon

ROB GILLEY

Although the Santa Barbara area is on a south-facing coastline, the swell window to the S and SW is entirely blocked by the presence of the four large Channel Islands. Point Conception further narrows the window of opportunity to W and NW swells that wrap around the cape and bend into Santa Barbara. When this happens, what's lacking in quantity is made up in quality at an unrivalled series of right pointbreaks. This set-up is the best in California on a medium to large SW-W swell. Straddling both Santa Barbara and Ventura counties, this south facing coast is tricky; you can burn a lot of miles chasing a wave. The east part of Ventura from 'C' Street to Oxnard is clear of island shadows on direct S swells but blocked from W swells. On the extreme west end of the area, the Hollister and Bixby ranch areas near Point Conception are clear of the islands and pick up

Josh Farkerow, Rincon

RUSSI

RUSSI

swells from due S to full N, depending on the spot. North of Conception, the west facing coast is exposed to prevailing winds and more swell, making spots like Jalama, Surf Beach, and Point Sal classic for S wind or early morning sessions.

Moving east down the Santa Barbara Channel, a series of points catch fall, winter and spring W and NW swell

TRAVEL INFORMATION

Local Population:
Santa Barbara – 100,000
Coastline:
Santa Barbara –
41km (25mi)
Time: GMT-8hr
Contest: National

Getting There – (See 54. Santa Cruz). From LAX, drive I-405 N to Hwy 101 N. Sta Barbara is 1h30 from LAX not counting gridlock. You can use train ($20o/w) or bus ($15o/w). Connecting flight to Sta Barbara takes 45 min.

Getting Around – (See 54. Santa Cruz). Public transport exists but is not convenient with boards. Beach access is easy unless private property blocks the spot. If you can't rent a car, stay in Carpinteria.

Lodging and Food – (See 54. Santa Cruz). Carpinteria has 2 Motel 6's at $40-$50. Santa

Barbara (SB) has 34 beachfront hotels from deluxe to budget (Beachcomber: $60-$90). Camping at Carpinteria State Beach. Fast food is cheap ($8/meal), restaurants are expensive. Good value at various Mexican & the Sojourner in SB.

Weather – Southern California is famous for its idyllic sunny weather. It seldom rains from spring to fall, but morning fog is common. Spring-early summer dense fog and low clouds are common, often cleared by light afternoon onshores. The driest and sunniest time occurs when the easterly Santa Ana winds blow from the desert, usually in late summer. Winter is mild with a few rainy days, but bigger swells and favourable winds common. Water temp is cool, requiring a fullsuit year round, even hoods in the winter. El Niños bring warmer water, lots of swells (maybe too much), along with flooding rain.

Nature and Culture – Arrange a trip to the Channel Islands for surfing (there are spots), fishing or whale watching. Inquire at SB Harbour. SB entertainment includes zoo, theme restaurants, beach volleyball, hiking trails to mountains & nightlife.

Hazards and Hassles – Most pointbreaks visible from Hwy101 will be packed if breaking. Oxnard beachbreaks less crowded but some highly localised. Mind private properties. Granite boulders can hurt. Sharks cruise only in Nth SB County.

Handy Hints – Don't bother bringing a gun. A shortboard costs ±$350. Heaps of shops offer cheap gear: Al Merrick's Channel Island boards and Yater is in SB downtown.

WEATHER STATISTICS	J/F	M/A	M/J	J/A	S/O	N/D
total rainfall (mm)	85	49	3	0	11	52
consistency (days/mth)	4	3	1	0	1	3
min temp (°C/°F)	6/43	8/46	11/52	14/57	12/54	6/43
max temp (°C/°F)	18/64	19/66	21/70	24/75	23/74	20/68

action. These include Refugio (pronounced Refuffio), El Capitan, and Campus Point (Uni. of Calif). Leadbetter Cove is just north of the Santa Barbara marina and is a fun, right pointbreak with many peaks. The crowd is friendly, which makes it ideal for longboarders. The Sandspit, tapering between the harbour seawall and Santa Barbara Municipal Pier is another story: it's rare, but when it's on, it's a zippery, churning righthander that requires perfect trim and a fast board. A huge backwash stalks the take-off, compounding the hollowness that always exceeds the height. Sandspit only fires on large W swells. A mile south of the pier, several left and right beachbreak peaks eventually connect to Hammonds Reef, a reliable right wrapping around a semi-point. These spots are usually not protected by kelp and blow-out by midday. Past seldom good but tempting Fernalds Point at Summerland, the town Carpinteria offers an average beachbreak at the state park, then a little further on (at Ventura County line) is Rincon, the "Queen of the Coast." The views from Hwy 101 of lines wrapping around the point into the bay are breathtaking, as waves peel forever through 3 sections. Indicator is the outside point, not too crowded since it's very fast. Crowds increase as you move into the Second and First points. Rarely all three connect although the section between First and Second is makeable at mid tide, depending on sand at the stream mouth and swell direction. The ultimate right point machine, mind the boulders near shore. Continuing east on Hwy 101, much of the coastline is surfable and visible. La Conchita 'straits' offers several peaks, while Little Rincon produces long, right walls with rock hazards. Oil Piers is a great morning/evening patrol and Hobsons State Park has a slow peak that occasionally speeds up. There are several other reefs heading down to Pitas Point, another long, sectiony pointbreak wrapping into the slow-mo beginners' spot called Mandos. Goofys will notice the lefts at Johns on the other side of the point. Try Solimar Reef (way outside) if you're experienced enough, otherwise ride the inside beachbreak. Next spot before you head up over the bridge is the Overhead – a chaotic beachbreak, which the locals have somehow got wired – and a big reef wave way outside that's as symmetrical a peak as you're likely to find (can hold 15ft/5m plus). The big spot in Ventura

is between the point and the pier, an area that includes Pipes, Stables, Fairgrounds, and California (or 'C') Street. Beware concrete and rebars. Try South Ventura and the Santa Clara rivermouth down to Oxnard and Port Hueneme (pronounced 'why-knee-me').

The primary source of swell comes from the NW lows out in the Aleutian Islands in winter (Oct-Mar). Waves can reach 12ft (4m) but average 3-8ft (1-2.6m) on W to NW swells; Point Conception blocks NNW-N swells. SW groundswells and hurricanes off Mexico are mostly blocked by the Channel Islands (San Miguel, Santa Cruz, Santa Rosa and Anacapa), especially in Santa Barbara County. Either side of summer, frequent 2-6ft (0.6-2m) W groundswell or windswell can occur. Calm days and offshores are more common in winter even though the E Santa Ana winds tend to blow in late summer. Dominant winds are NW-W, NW – 28% (Dec) to 39% (Aug) – bringing choppy conditions from noon till dusk and sometimes earlier. Glassy days are more common here than elsewhere on the West Coast, with a noticeable difference between Santa Barbara and the frequently strong winds in the Point Conception area. Tides vary gently from 4ft-7ft (1.3-2.3m), getting a tide table is easy.

SURF STATISTICS	J F	M A	M J	J A	S O	N D
dominant swell	W-NW	W-NW	S-SW	S-SW	W-NW	W-NW
swell size (ft)	4	3-4	1-2	1-2	4	4
consistency (%)	60	50	20	20	60	60
dominant wind	W-N	W-NW	W-NW	W-NW	W-NW	W-N
average force	F3	F4	F4	F4	F4	F3
consistency (%)	63	60	65	66	66	66
water temp (°C°F)	14/57	14/57	16/61	17/62	16/61	15/59
wetsuit						

Ventura

OREGON

CALIFORNIA

MEXICO

56. Orange County

Huntingdon Beach Pier

RUSSI

Summary

+ VARIETY OF SPOTS
+ LOTS OF CLEAN WAVES
+ GREAT WEATHER
+ ENTERTAINING AREA

– CONSTANT COMPETITIVE CROWD
– RELATIVELY COOL WATER
– POLLUTION
– URBAN ATMOSPHERE

S outhern Californian surfing started in 1907 when Hawai'ian George Freeth performed for a huge crowd at Redondo Beach. Since then Southern California has remained the urban heartland of American surf culture. By the early 1960's people were taking to the waves in numbers as the 'SoCal' beach lifestyle rapidly developed. Today the place is more crazy and crowded than ever, but despite the chaos, surfing in LA can still be a pleasurable experience. Orange County is an extremely populated area south of the steep coves of Palos Verdes peninsular. North Orange County has mainly long, straight beaches, while the southern border reverts back to cliffs and coves again.

Seal Beach Pier is often a big close-out although it can have a good, bouncing wedge favouring a 4-6ft (1.3-2m)

Shaun Sutton, Salt Creek

ROB GILLEY

The Wedge

LAURENT MASUREL

swell and mid tides. Surfside is inconsistent but the jetty can offer punchy rights and juicy walls. The point is private property, so you have to park at Sunset Beach and walk north.

From Sunset Beach to Huntington there are several miles of long, rolling and rarely crowded waves. Access to the beach is difficult in places thanks to private land and

TRAVEL INFORMATION

Local Population:
Nth Orange Co. – 2M
Coastline: Orange Co. – 67km (41mi)
Time: GMT-8h
Contests: WQS (July)
WCT (July)
WQS (Sept)

Getting There – Most international flights land in LAX, 45min to the north. Rent a car, drive Freeway 405 south until you reach the Pacific Coast Highway (PCH). Connecting flights to John Wayne Airport take 25min.

Getting Around – Public transport sucks. If you can't rent a car, stay in one place. Rental cars start about $160/w but go as low as $50 for a local rent-a-wreck. You must be over 21 to hire. Gas is cheap (30¢/l). PCH traffic is intense at peak times.

Lodging and Food – A comfy double in a motel by the beach is $50-90 (Huntingdon Beach –

Shore Motel or Newport Beach - Channel Inn). Youth Hostels cost $20 a night. Camp at Bolsa Chica or Newport Dunes Resort. Fast food is cheap ($8/meal), restaurants are expensive.

Weather – California is famous for its ideal climate. It hardly ever rains, especially from spring to fall (autumn) when there are frequent morning fogs which disperse by noon. In summer the light onshores tend to crumble the waves, starting late in the morning. The driest, sunniest time occurs with 'Santa Ana' conditions when E winds blow from the desert. Winter is mild with occasional rainy days. Swells are bigger and the winds often favourable during these months. Though this area has the warmest water in California you still need a 3/2 steamer most of the time.

Nature and Culture – Great skate parks everywhere. Plenty of interesting surf and junk shops to browse. There's Disneyland if that's

your thing. Also check Knott's Berry Farm, Soak City and Wild River Water Park. Hollywood and LA's mean streets aren't far away.

Hazards and Hassles – The best way to avoid fierce crowds is to surf the less accessible spots. Park close to gated communities and walk. Watch out for metered parking (tickets are sent onwards by car rental agencies). There are a few stingrays and sea urchins but not many sharks. Watch out for murky waters after heavy rain - sewage and stormwater run-off is a big problem.

Handy Hints – Don't bother with a big wave gun. A shortboard costs ±$350, ($450 for a longboard). There are plenty of shops to buy cheap gear from - check Jack's, Robert August and HSS in HB. Newport Beach has plenty more surf shops. Watch out for lots of longboarders and people ripping everywhere.

WEATHER STATISTICS	J/F	M/A	M/J	J/A	S/O	N/D
total rainfall (mm)	72	37	3	0	7	45
consistency (days/mth)	4	3	1	0	1	3
min temp (°C/°F)	9/48	10/50	14/57	17/62	13/55	10/50
max temp (°C/°F)	18/64	19/66	22/72	25/77	24/75	21/70

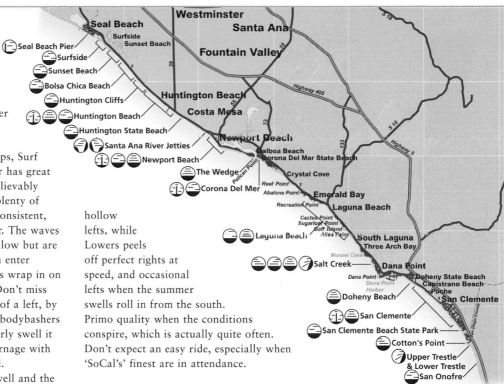

steep cliff paths and parking is metered. Check spots around Bolsa Chica State Park and Huntington Cliffs. The waves up here generally have less power than the spots to the south but the reduced crowd factor makes them an attractive option.

Huntington Beach is "Surf City" and its pier is both a loved and despised symbol of Californian surfing. Nearby there's a Surf Museum, a Walk of Fame, legendary surf shops, Surf Bars and Surf Theatres. Either side of the pier has great waves when they're working, but it gets unbelievably crowded. The State Park to the south offers plenty of slightly less busy peaks. All these waves are consistent, but they blow out at around 11am in summer. The waves at Santa Ana River Jetties are notoriously hollow but are also crowded and polluted. South of here you enter Newport Beach's rock jetties where killer lefts wrap in on S swells. Expect heavy, competitive crowds. Don't miss The Wedge, the infamous backwashed, beast of a left, by the long jetty. Only ridden by bodyboarders, bodybashers and masochists. With a 6-8ft (2-2.6m) southerly swell it can be 12-15ft (4-5m) - a fine spectacle of carnage with crowds, TV crews and ambulances all around.

Corona Del Mar loves a medium sized S swell and the jetty provides good wind protection. Further south, access becomes a problem until the reef peaks around Laguna Beach and Brooks St sometimes provide coveted summer action. Salt Creek has the best waves in the area, comprising of The Point, a fast left, the ultra consistent peaks of Middles and some hollow shories towards Dana Strands. Past the wave destroying breakwalls of Dana Point Harbour lies Doheny Beach State Park, a great place for beginners to ride mellow S swells. The Surfrider Foundation has made its home in San Clemente where a mixture of average beachbreaks and better reefbreaks like T Street feed the hordes of locals in the area. Designated surfing areas in summer can condense the inevitable crowds. San Clemente State Park is a small swell haven with camping facilities. It's also the northern access points for the sucky, left tubes of Cottons, which gets hollower as the swell gets bigger. Everything about this wave is difficult, not least the access, and it is here that San Diego County starts. Just over the county line is that hallowed turf of 'SoCal' surfing – Trestles. Consisting of Uppers and Lowers, Trestles handles all swell directions, all tides, most winds and huge crowds. Uppers favours rights on winter NW swells but can still churn out

hollow lefts, while Lowers peels off perfect rights at speed, and occasional lefts when the summer swells roll in from the south. Primo quality when the conditions conspire, which is actually quite often. Don't expect an easy ride, especially when 'SoCal's' finest are in attendance.

Laguna Beach

The primary source of surf in summer comes courtesy of S-SW groundswells from April to September, including hurricane swells off Mexico between July and October. At this time of year, waves can reach 12-15ft (4-5m) but average 3-8ft (1-2.6m). In winter (Oct-Mar), low pressures to the NW send down swells of 2-12ft (0.6-4m). In general Orange County's swell exposure is not as good as San Diego's but on any given day in spring or autumn there might be 2-6ft (0.6-2m) of W swell coming from groundswell in the western Pacific or nearshore windswell. Prevailing winds are NW-W, most common in December and least so in August. The magical 'Santa Ana' E winds blow in late summer. Offshore days are more common in winter, but all year the winds are rarely strong and glassy days are one of California's finer features. Tides vary from 4-7ft (1.3-2.3m) - finding a tide table is easy.

SURF STATISTICS	J F	M A	M J	J A	S O	N D
dominant swell	W-NW	W-NW	S-SW	S-SW	S-SW	W-NW
swell size (ft)	4-5	4	2-3	4	5	4-5
consistency (%)	70	60	50	50	70	70
dominant wind	W-N	W-NW	W-NW	W-NW	W-NW	W-N
average force	F3	F4	F4	F4	F4	F3
consistency (%)	63	60	65	66	66	66
water temp (°C/°F)	14/57	14/57	16/61	17/62	16/61	15/59
wetsuit						

Trestles

57. San Diego

Looking south from Blacks to Scripps Pier

ROB GILLEY

Summary

+ VARIETY OF SPOTS
+ LOTS OF CLEAN WAVES
+ GREAT WEATHER
+ FLAT DAY ENTERTAINMENT

- CONSTANT COMPETITIVE CROWDS
- RELATIVELY COOL WATER
- POLLUTION
- URBAN ATMOSPHERE

From the long sandy beaches in the north of the county to Sunset Cliffs and Point Loma, every inch of this coastline has been thoroughly scoured by generations of surfers. Its line-ups have featured in countless magazine spreads and these days dozens of web-cams spy on the waves, 24/7. With at least 80 spots from Camp Pendleton to Silver Strand, there are plenty of good waves and, of course, plenty of amped locals to share them with.

There are so many good breaks, between Camp Pendleton and Cardiff, it's impossible to list them all here. Oceanside always has something to offer from its assortment of jetty, pier and beachbreaks. A stretch of undemanding waves extends from Carlsbad to Encinatas before the impressive peak of Swami's livens things up. Long, lined-up rights hold as big as it gets while the shorter lefts disappear with size, but the crowds never will! Fun, well-mannered

Blacks

ROB GILLEY

Looking north from Point Loma to La Jolla

DON BALCH

peaks grace Cardiff Reef making it a longboarders' favourite. At Seaside Reef, any swell direction will make for hectic, dredgy, hollow waves. From Seaside to Del Mar is a stretch of average, uncrowded beachbreaks, inbetween the flagged swimming areas, where lifeguards dish out fines for breaking the rules. Del Mar also has relatively uncrowded peaks...park at 15th or 11th Street and walk across the railway line. 15th Street works best on a south swell, up to 8ft (2.6m) max. Torrey Pines State Park offers another long, uncrowded shoreline with Bathtub Rock and Glider Field being the most consistent, quality waves.

TRAVEL INFORMATION

Local Population:
San Diego County – 2.9M
Coastline: San Diego County – 122km (76mi)
Time: GMT-8hr
Contests: WQS (April) WCT

Getting There – (See 56.Orange County). From L.A. connecting flights to San Diego take 35mins, driving takes 2hrs, or it's a 3hr train ride.

Getting Around – (See 56.Orange County). Public transport is bad. If you can't rent a car then stay in La Jolla for good access to the most number of spots.

Lodging and Food – You can get cheap dorm rooms for around $15/d (Banana Bungalow,

Ocean Beach Backpacker). A beach motel is $70/d (Surfer Motor Lodge). The best campground is Silver Strand.

Weather – (See 56.Orange County)

Nature and Culture – Visit Sea World and the Wave House Flowrider in Mission Beach. Baseball (The Padres) or football (The Chargers) play at the Dome. There are lots of bars and restaurants along Garnett Avenue in Pacific Beach. If America freaks you out and you want something even crazier, head south of the border to Tijuana and beyond.

Hazards and Hassles – The best way to avoid crowds is to surf the less accessible spots as local surfers tend to populate the most famous

places. Either way, stay low key. North County usually has less pressure and local people are generally extremely friendly. If it rains, watch out for polluted beaches. Respect lifeguard's beach restrictions, and local heavies.

Handy Hints – A big wave gun will be used only rarely, usually at the Cove although Blacks gets big and extremely powerful. There are plenty of shops to buy cheap gear. Harry's (home of Skip Frye and Hank Warner's legendary boards, at Pacific Beach), Emerald City (Mission Beach) are two well known shops. You can also rent gear from South Coast SS (Pacific Beach). The standard of surfing is extremely high. Easy access to the border for Mexico runs.

WEATHER STATISTICS	J/F	M/A	M/J	J/A	S/O	N/D
total rainfall (mm)	50	28	5	3	6	37
consistency (days/mth)	6	3	2	1	2	5
min temp (°C/°F)	8/46	11/52	16/61	17/62	15/59	10/50
max temp (°C/°F)	17/62	19/66	22/72	23/74	23/74	20/68

One of many reefs, Sunset Cliffs

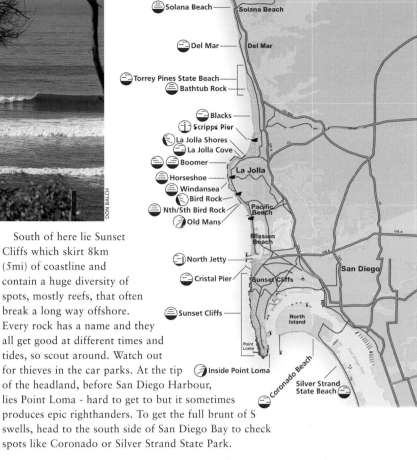

Reaching the excellent peaks of Black's Beach involves a 15 minute, slippery cliff climb down to hard breaking barrels. Big Blacks is a class act but the punishing paddle-out and long hold-downs sort the men from the boys. A submarine canyon invites and amplifies the swell, making Blacks a couple of feet bigger than everywhere else. Next door is Scripps Pier, home of the renowned Institute of Oceanography, where classic winter swells break. The Cove area has several fickle, but powerful waves, the main one only working under the biggest winter conditions. Lost boards (and bodies) will get pushed into the caves and cliffs directly in front of this meaty lefthander. The Cove usually works best with N swells and S or SE winds.

Look out for good days at Boomer, Horseshoe, Windansea or Big Rock. These reefs are south of the Cove, down Coast Boulevard. The swell sucking Windansea can be rideable up to 12ft (4m). Its grinding shorebreak can be too heavy for many as can the most protective locals you'll ever encounter. Be low key, or wait for an invite.

Nearby lie Bird Rock and Rockpiles. These work better with S swells and are heavy, difficult waves, suited to advanced riders. Pacific Beach is next, with numerous reefs at the foot of the cliffs that are easy to ride and easily blown out. Mid-tide with a medium swell is recommended for the cruisey peaks of Old Mans or Crystal Pier. At Mission Beach there's less crowding and more wind protection closer to the south jetty. Ocean Beach is a popular place for San Diego-based surfers with numerous surf shops and lively beachfront action. The waves around the pier are average beachbreaks that can, of course, get very good.

South of here lie Sunset Cliffs which skirt 8km (5mi) of coastline and contain a huge diversity of spots, mostly reefs, that often break a long way offshore. Every rock has a name and they all get good at different times and tides, so scout around. Watch out for thieves in the car parks. At the tip of the headland, before San Diego Harbour, lies Point Loma - hard to get to but it sometimes produces epic righthanders. To get the full brunt of S swells, head to the south side of San Diego Bay to check spots like Coronado or Silver Strand State Park.

Plenty of surf comes from NW swells generated by low pressures off the Aleutian Islands in winter (Oct-Mar), with waves breaking from 3-15ft (1-5m). Spring and autumn can pick up any wind or groundswells generated in the western Pacific. Summer surf originates from either SW groundswells or hurricanes off

La Jolla Cove

Mexico between July and October). Waves can reach 10ft (3m) but average 2-6ft (0.6-2m). Winter is more likely to be offshore or pray for the late summer 'Santa Ana.' Dominant winds are NW-W. Light sea breezes from these directions create choppy conditions from noon till dusk, particularly in summer and sometimes before noon. Kelp beds help to smooth out the surface at some spots. Tides range from 4-6ft (1-2m). Surf shops have tide tables.

SURF STATISTICS	J F	M A	M J	J A	S O	N D
dominant swell	W-NW	W-NW	S-SW	S-SW	S-SW	W-NW
swell size (ft)	5	3-4	3	4-5	5-6	5
consistency (%)	70	70	60	60	80	70
dominant wind	W-N	W-NW	W-NW	W-NW	W-NW	W-N
average force	F3	F4	F4	F4	F4	F3
consistency (%)	63	64	63	64	77	74
water temp (°C/°F)	15/59	15/59	17/62	19/66	18/64	17/62
wetsuit						

Windansea

58. Space Coast

Anny Mechado, Sebastian Inlet

Summary

+ ENDLESS MILES OF BEACHES
+ EASY WAVES
+ CLASSIC HURRICANE SWELLS
+ THE SUNSHINE STATE
+ TOURISM HEAVEN

– SMALL WINDCHOP WAVES
– SUMMER FLAT SPELLS
– MAJOR SPOTS CROWDED
– PAY TO PARK
– HIGH SHARKBITE FACTOR

Florida receives a lot of attention as the focus of the surf scene on the US East Coast but unfortunately it doesn't receive as much swell! A semi-tropical year round climate and a culture dedicated to leisure doesn't offset the generally poor sandbanks and mushy conditions that occur most of the time. Hurricanes are the exception to the rule when powerful lines of swell will turn on classic waves at a few spots, but the wait can be misery. Florida's long Atlantic coastline consists of barrier islands, separated from the mainland by the Intracoastal Waterway. To the west, there's the equally long Gulf Coast, which has erratic surf at best. The beaches near Miami suffer from the swell blocking shadow of the Bahamas but Palm Beach County has the best aspect for NE swells and has a few breaks that handle the biggest swells. The north coast from Jacksonville to New Smyrna Beach features a stretch of flat beaches which you can drive along to choose one of the endless peaks between the occasional jetties and inlets.

Matt Kechele

However, it is the centrally located 'Space Coast' that is the surf industry cradle and home to such famous locations as Cocoa Beach and Sebastian Inlet.

The north of Brevard County is part of The Canaveral National Seashore, a pristine area of 'gator infested swamps, bird filled lagoons and the John. F. Kennedy Space Centre. Playalinda is a long NE facing beach, which will pick up the best of a NE swell and pitch at low tide. The beach is closed 3 days before every shuttle launch. Cape Canaveral itself would provide some excellent waves but it's off limits and poachers run the risk of arrest. Whenever big winter NE swells roll in, Cocoa Beach Pier

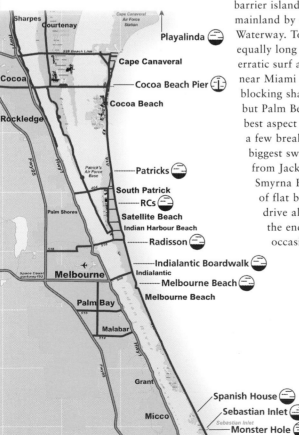

Bill Nailer, Sebastian Inlet

can provide shelter from the accompanying winds, at a more manageable size. Down through the Cocoa Beach blocks with their dead-end access streets, there are plenty of waves to choose from, that are usually longer and mushier at low tide and tend to become a shorebreak at high tide. This is Kelly Slater's home turf and some clues to his brilliance can be found among these sluggish, uninspiring beachbreaks. Patrick's Airforce Base, picks up more of the NE swell with some consistent sandbars near the few parking opportunities. Between Patricks and Indialantic is RCs, one of the few big wave spots that breaks with some power. This is because it breaks over 'coquina': a soft limestone containing crushed shells and coral, which gives the predominant lefts a permanent base to break on. Indialantic Boardwalk has a steeper beach profile, which in turn provides a steeper, hollower wave. Jacking close-outs are interspersed with some makeable barrels, but the competition is heavy for these pits as well as the few meter parking spots. Melbourne Beach area is residential, so parking is even trickier and locals take advantage of it to improve their knowledge of these shifty but average sandbanks. Florida's most famous wave is a straight cruise down the A1A, before paying Sebastian Recreation Area's charge ($3) to park under the inlet bridge. Sebastian Inlet is Florida's most extraordinary wave, where a crosswash bounces off the huge, curving jetty into First Peak, throwing up wedging rights, allowing hot waveriders plenty of impetus to launch major airs or pull-in. Further north is Second Peak, which can offer a left depending on the swell direction, while Third Peak provides fast, hollow lefts when the swell shows some north in it. Further up the beach are Chernobyles and

Cocoa Beach

Canaveral Pier

Spanish House, which need more swell to get the left tubes happening. All these peaks prefer low to mid tide incoming, but will break through to high, unless it's small in which case the backwash takes over. Expect intense crowds and weekend contests. On a bigger swell, brilliant pointbreak lefts and shorter rights can be ridden south of the inlet channel at sharky Monster Hole.

The bulk of rideable swells originate thanks to winter North Atlantic lows from October to March. These NE swells vary from 3-10ft (1-3.3m), but usually more like 2-6ft (0.6-2m). Summer can see waves generated by the sea breeze, resulting in sloppy NE or SE wind chop. The best waves are produced by an average of 10 hurricanes tracking from West Africa to the Caribbean mostly from August to October. Half of these hard-to-forecast hurricanes produce quality waves rarely exceeding 8ft (2.5m). Winds are predominantly onshore with NE-E winds in winter and W-SE in summer, but the offshores rarely coincide with decent swells. Expect of lot of 2-3ft (0.6-1m) wind chop conditions. Tidal range can reach 9ft (3m) and because the beach slope is gentle, it will affect most spots. Tidal info is often shown on noticeboards at the beach.

SURF STATISTICS	J F	M A	M J	J A	S O	N D
dominant swell	N-NE	N-NE	N-NE	E-SE	E-SE	N-NW
swell size (ft)	3-4	3	1-2	1-2	3	3-4
consistency (%)	70	50	40	20	40	70
dominant wind	N-SE	NW-SE	NW-SE	E-S	N-SE	N-SE
average force	F4	F4	F3	F3	F4	F4
consistency (%)	67	64	63	64	77	74
water temp (°C/°F)	16/61	20/68	24/75	26/79	24/75	21/70
wetsuit						

TRAVEL INFORMATION

Getting There – Most international flights will land in Miami, 2hrs away. Nationals will favour Orlando, 1hr away. It's easy to get cheap flights from all over the Americas or Europe. It'll take 24hrs to drive to New York and 12hrs to the Outer Banks.

Getting Around – Public transport sucks but car rentals are super cheap, starting ±$160/w but as low as $50 for a local rent-a-wreck. The road network is fantastic, the A1A being the ultimate surfroad. Many private property areas have prohibited beach access above the high tide mark.

Lodging and Food – Choose from ocean front hotels, spacious condos, beachside cottages, multi-bedroom bungalows to campground and RV sites. The Surf Motel in Cocoa Beach from ($25/dble). Heaps of raw bars, eclectic eateries and gourmet restaurants.

Weather – The Sunshine State's subtropical climate is ideal for surfing apart from summer's heavy rains, intense heat and lack of swells. Most of the year is warm aside from the coldest winter days. September-October, the best surf months, are still rainy with short, pouring showers and thunderstorms which force surfers out of the water to avoid the constant lightning! Although you're most likely to wear a springsuit, you may have to use a 2mm fullsuit from December to March whenever the water gets around 16°C-18°C (60°-64°F). South of Fort Pierce, the water remains warm year round, courtesy of the Gulf Stream.

Nature and Culture – Orlando's Disneyland is notable for Typhoon Lagoon, the best wavepool in the US. The Orange Avenue nightclubs are lively. Check the Kennedy Space Centre in Cape Canaveral.

Hazards and Hassles – With 25 attacks (2 fatal), Florida is the world's shark bite leader. Sebastian Inlet gets crowded but miles of beaches spread the masses. Mosquitoes, sealice and sand sea-ums are a summer bummer. Respect the lifeguard's beach restrictions, which often prevent surfing between 9am-5pm.

Handy Hints – Ron Jon's, the world's largest surf shop (or 9 acre tourist stop), is one of many in Cocoa Beach or Indialantic. There are many fine shortboard shapers (Natural Art, Quiet Flight) costing ±$350. With Disneyland so close, it's an easy family trip.

Local Population:
Florida – 15M
Coastline: Florida – 2,170km (1,356mi)
Time: GMT-5hr
Contests: Festival (Apr) Pro-Am (Sept)

WEATHER STATISTICS	J/F	M/A	M/J	J/A	S/O	N/D
total rainfall (mm)	50	80	175	175	225	57
consistency (days/mth)	5	6	10	13	14	6
min temp (°C/°F)	14/57	17/62	22/72	24/75	23/74	16/61
max temp (°C/°F)	25/77	28/82	31/88	32/90	30/86	26/79

VIRGINIA

NORTH CAROLINA

SOUTH CAROLINA

59. Outer Banks

Cape Hatteras

Summary

+ WIDE SWELL WINDOW
+ POWERFUL BEACHBREAKS
+ UNCROWDED AREAS
+ WILD SCENIC AREA

− WINDY CONDITIONS
− BEACHBREAKS ONLY
− COLD WINTERS
− COSTLY ACCOMMODATION

The Outer Banks are a bow-shaped string of barrier islands sitting in offshore isolation from the North Carolina coast. These low lying strips of sand appeared less than a 1000 years ago, a result of the merger of the cold Labrador Current from the north and the warm Gulf Stream from the south. This fusion has produced miles of shifting beachbreaks on these migrating islands whose width never exceed 5km (3mi).

Ken Hunt, Cape Hatteras

The constant movement of both the islands and the offshore sandbanks of the Diamond Shoals, has earned the Outer Banks a reputation as "The Graveyard of the Atlantic" with more than 2000 ships sunk in these waters since 1526. The Outer Banks are well exposed to all types of East Coast swell and the dozens of piers provide

Shark Fishing

some protection from wind and cross-shore drift. When it's happening, there are full on beachbreak barrels to be had, which are not short of power.

The populated northern end of the Outer Banks is an area of concentrated fishing piers that hold sandbanks

TRAVEL INFORMATION

Local Population:
Hatteras – 5,000
Coastline: Nth Carolina –
480km (300mi)
Time: GMT-5hr
Contests: ESA (Sept)

Getting There – It's an 8hr drive from New York or 15hrs from Miami. North Carolina's capital, Raleigh, is 4hrs away or Norfolk, Virginia, is 2hrs. The Cedar Island-Ocracoke Ferry from the south, cuts out miles of driving, but may need a reservation in summer.

Getting Around – A rental car is essential ($180/w), preferably a 4WD, because if you're not on the tarmac, there is nothing else but sand. Beach driving is forbidden in some places. Parking near all the piers is tricky unless you are a fisherman, and many of the small towns in summer have nowhere to park.

Lodging and Food – Buxton is central but not right on the surf like Avon or Rodanthe.

Motels/hotels are pricey (Salvo Inn: $40-$60; Surf Motel: $50-$90), B&B ($80-$100) but campgrounds are cheap (Ocean Waves: $15-$20) with more discounts off-season. Expect to pay $10 for a fast food meal.

Weather – The conflicting temperatures of the Labrador Current and the Gulf Stream can bring very unstable weather. Winters are cold and stormy while summers are wet and warm. Mid-seasons can be anything in between. Be prepared with a full range of clothing and stay alert whenever a huge storm comes by or when hurricanes get close. Storms can wash right over the lowest parts of the islands, cutting road access when they breach the sand dune defences that are built up on the Atlantic side of Hwy 12. Weather changes are radical and statistics show some of the greatest contrasts seen in the atlas, especially water temps, which get as low as 5°C(41°F). From boardshorts in the late summer, to 5/4/3, boots and hood in the winter, with everything in between.

Nature and Culture – Great fishing potential! Climb the 248-step lighthouse to check the sandbanks. Visit the Wright Brothers Museum at Kitty Hawk, the birthplace of modern aviation. Bars and nightclubs get very lively in summer, but winter is ghostly quiet in the small towns, full of empty holiday accommodation.

Hazards and Hassles – As with most of the USA, there are plenty of laws to abide by! Straying too close to a pier may see the grumpy, surfer hating fisherman casting their biggest lead toward you. On town beaches you must wear a leash! Respect the swimming only zones. Mosquitoes and sea-lice in summer. Shark sightings, no bites. There are always strong rips.

Handy Hints – There are dozens of shops, including Whalebone, Secret Spot, Wave Riding Vehicles and Natural Art. You shouldn't need a gun. Biggest towns are Nag's Head and Kill Devil Hills. Crowds from Virginia come down during summers and on weekends.

WEATHER STATISTICS	J/F	M/A	M/J	J/A	S/O	N/D
total rainfall (mm)	122	99	101	142	134	119
consistency (days/mth)	10	9	10	12	8	8
min temp (°C/°F)	3/37	8/46	17/62	22/72	17/62	7/44
max temp (°C/°F)	11/52	17/62	25/77	29/84	24/75	15/59

Nags Head Pier

either side and provide a great forum for the bulk of the local surfing community that live in this area. Piers like Kitty Hawk, Avalon, Nags Head, Jeanettes and Outer Banks get hollow peaks on both sides of them. Summer surfing restrictions between 9am and 5pm, plus no surfing within 200ft of most piers, are both enforced. Heading south out of town onto Pea Island, a short hike across the dunes to Boilers should reveal some good sandbanks around a shipwreck. Just north of Rodanthe is the over crowded, over rated barrels of S-Turns.

Rodanthe Pier is the most eastern point on the islands, which focuses much of the NE swells and a lot of the surfing action. Crowds can get intense around the pier where parking is a real problem. The last 100ft of this wood pier got swept away by a storm in 1989. The long stretch of sand down to Buxton holds endless promise of an unsurfed peak. With various 4WD ramps to the beach, it's always possible to escape the crowds. Through the small towns of Waves, Salvo and Avon, lefts will run in a NE swell and rights will bowl on anything out of the south. Avon has a pier that holds fun waves at smaller sizes. At Cape Hatteras is Lighthouse, the famous break in front of

the tallest lighthouse in the US, which was recently moved inland because of rampant erosion. This erosion is constantly changing the waves, which pick up most swells, with NE usually the best. The ends of the battered jetties can get dredgy but it all depends on where the sand is – barrels one week, mushy the next. Big NE swells can wrap around the Cape for cleaner and smaller conditions on the south-east facing shoreline, but a S swell is needed to turn on Frisco Pier. It's inconsistent but capable of producing the goods when NE winds blow offshore. Take the ferry to reach Ocracoke Island and miles more deserted beachbreaks that are usually passed up by the hordes of wave-hungry surfers traversing the islands on Highway 12.

Although hurricanes usually provide the best days, NE swells travel full speed to shore and offer the best consistency producing 2-12ft (0.6-4m) waves from September to May. Winters are very consistent but once the water temp gets below 12°C (53°F), messy beachbreak conditions become tough. Classic conditions come from late summer-early fall hurricanes producing perfect lines of 4-10ft (1.3-3.3m) swell. The open beachbreaks don't hold too much size but around the piers, triple overhead is a possibility. The Outer Banks are often swept by gusty winds but the islands'

SURF STATISTICS	J F	M A	M J	J A	S O	N D
dominant swell	N-E	N-NE	N-NE	SE	SE	N-E
swell size (ft)	5-6	4-5	3	2-3	4-5	5-6
consistency (%)	70	70	60	40	70	80
dominant wind	SW-N	SW-N			N-E	SW-N
average force	F4	F4	F4	F4	F4	F4
consistency (%)	66	54	51	55	52	64
water temp (°C/°F)	9/48	11/52	19/66	25/77	20/68	14/57
wetsuit						

curve means it's always possible to get offshore apart from a straight E wind. Dominant wind is NE in winter plus some cold offshore westerlies between storms and summer wind blows SW with NE sea breezes. Tidal range rarely exceeds 6ft (2m), but high tide in a small swell will fatten things out.

Central America
and The Caribbean

Meteorology and Oceanography

Central America and the Caribbean form the link between North and South America, showing characteristics of both continents plus a character all of its own. The imbalance of swell distribution is still apparent with the Pacific easily upstaging the Atlantic for size and consistency but the Caribbean islands are an improvement on the North American East Coast plus there is always the Gulf of Mexico swells to consider. Most Pacific shores from Mexico to Panama rely on the dependable, year round, long distance, SW swells from the South Pacific. Low Pressures just to the east of New Zealand seem to produce the most epic waves, despite a journey of up to 10,000km (6,000mi). This is because the bulk of the swell is pushed off the weather system's leading edge as it travels west and the clockwise rotation aids a SW direction of origin. The southern regions of the

Central American Pacific coast receive more of these southern swells but misses out on a lot of the North Pacific swells that Mexico enjoys. These NW swells rarely produce large waves, which will best strike the few WNW exposed regions like Nayarit, Jalisco or Guanacaste in Costa Rica. The tropical storms that form off the Mexican mainland from July to October always take a northern trajectory, so S swell is produced for the northern regions of Mexico, Baja and California. Rarely will these hurricanes (locally known as chubascos or cordonazos) produce much for El Salvador, Costa Rica or Panama, and often just close-out on the Mexican beaches. Whenever Central America's Pacific shores go flat, which isn't very often, a short journey to the other side, opens up the possibilities offered by the Gulf of Mexico and the Caribbean Sea. The Gulf of Mexico produces wind swell

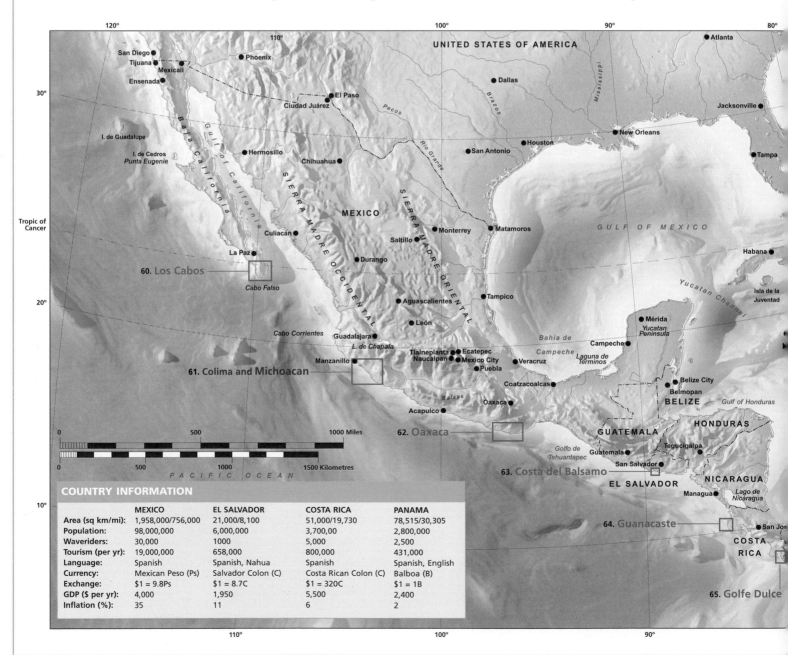

COUNTRY INFORMATION				
	MEXICO	**EL SALVADOR**	**COSTA RICA**	**PANAMA**
Area (sq km/mi):	1,958,000/756,000	21,000/8,100	51,000/19,730	78,515/30,305
Population:	98,000,000	6,000,000	3,700,00	2,800,000
Waveriders:	30,000	1000	5,000	2,500
Tourism (per yr):	19,000,000	658,000	800,000	431,000
Language:	Spanish	Spanish, Nahua	Spanish	Spanish, English
Currency:	Mexican Peso (Ps)	Salvador Colon (C)	Costa Rican Colon (C)	Balboa (B)
Exchange:	$1 = 9.8Ps	$1 = 8.7C	$1 = 320C	$1 = 1B
GDP ($ per yr):	4,000	1,950	5,500	2,400
Inflation (%):	35	11	6	2

coming out of the north but is less reliable than the sizeable and powerful waves that lash the Caribbean side of Costa Rica and Panama from Dec to March and July/August. Cold fronts and depressions north of Colombia are responsible for the unexpected winter waves, while rogue hurricanes can throw up swells through the June to Nov season. The wind set up for Central America is nearly ideal with plenty of glassy or light wind conditions. In summer, after the early offshores, a light SW sea breeze will spring up, but when the swell is big, there are always some sheltered coves to check along the contorted coastline. Winter is blessed by near constant northerly offshores, which can be a problem for the Caribbean coasts during the prime swell months.

Caribbean islands facing the North Atlantic accept swells travelling south from the high latitude band of low pressures that spin from Nova Scotia to Europe. These swells often bypass the North American East Coast, before reaching the exposed northern coasts of the Greater Antilles. Puerto Rico benefits from the maximum impact, with a swell focusing 8km (5mi) deep trench just offshore, helping to create reliable and occasionally huge waves from October to March. West of the Dominican Republic, the western Greater Antilles (Haiti, Cuba) are sheltered by the Bahamas; a string of islands which hide some good waves. The Lesser Antilles also attracts a decent share of North Atlantic N/NE swells but mainly rely on trade winds swell, hence the nametag of The Windward Islands. This area is also where the word hurricane originated from, and the West Indies are always in the firing line of hurricane alley, so surfers pray for the swell without the devastation. If one of these storms crosses over the islands and into the Caribbean Sea, then the west coasts may come to life with perfect waves at breaks that are usually dead flat.

Overall, the Caribbean is windy, dominated by an E/NE sea breeze which can produce cross/offshore conditions on NW facing spots or consistent wind mush on windward coasts. This wind is almost always blowing, so it stands to reason that there are always going to be rideable waves on islands like Barbados.

The whole region is mainly fed by the North Equatorial Current on both the Pacific and Atlantic sides, meaning just one thing – boardshorts!

Tidewise, the only major change in height affects Panama and Costa Rica, while most of the region experiences less than 4-5ft (1.3-1.6m) tidal range. Most of the Gulf of Mexico and the Caribbean Sea get mixed or diurnal tides.

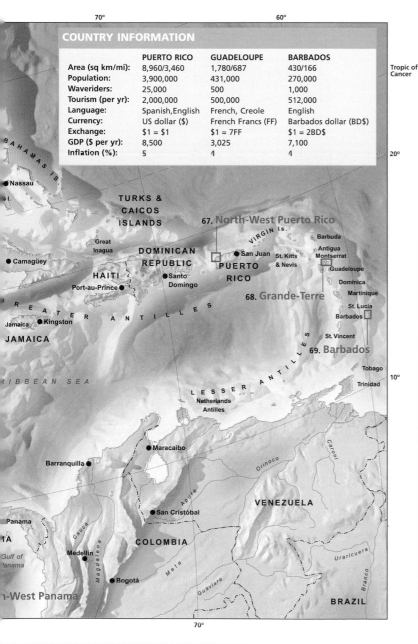

COUNTRY INFORMATION			
	PUERTO RICO	GUADELOUPE	BARBADOS
Area (sq km/mi):	8,960/3,460	1,780/687	430/166
Population:	3,900,000	431,000	270,000
Waveriders:	25,000	500	1,000
Tourism (per yr):	2,000,000	500,000	512,000
Language:	Spanish, English	French, Creole	English
Currency:	US dollar ($)	French Francs (FF)	Barbados dollar (BD$)
Exchange:	$1 = $1	$1 = 7FF	$1 = 2BD$
GDP ($ per yr):	8,500	3,025	7,100
Inflation (%):	5	4	4

Temperatures, Winds and Currents

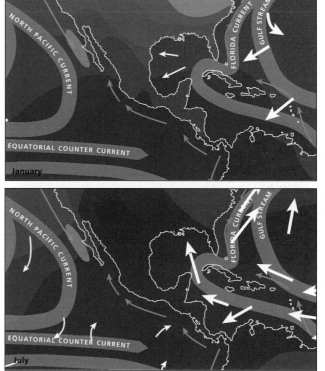

60. Los Cabos

Cabo

GEOFF RAGATZ

Summary
+ WARM WATER AND WEATHER
+ RIGHT POINTS
+ GOOD SWELL AND WIND PATTERNS
+ PLENTY OF SUNSHINE

– LACK OF POWER
– JELLYFISH AND DESERT BUGS
– CROWDS AROUND CABO
– SOME BAD ROADS

Baja California is a 1,200km (750mi) long finger of rugged coastline with hidden coves, white sandy beaches, rocky bluffs and crystal-blue waters teeming with wildlife. The west coast of Baja is exposed to Pacific swells whilst the Sea of Cortez, dividing the Baja Peninsula from the Mexican mainland, remains relatively calm. The 1200km (750mi) long Pacific side of this peninsula is a major surf destination for Californian waveriders, who follow the MEX1 as far south as they can go to Cabo San Lucas. The north part of this zone, up to five hours drive from the California border, is a well-travelled area that produces major big waves like Todos Santos. These break on N swells in cool water, due to the upwelling currents. The middle of the zone, around the epic Seven Sisters, swarms with good

ROB GILLEY

Shipwrecks

GEOFF RAGATZ

righthand points, but these have difficult road access. In the south, the tip of Baja is washed by warm seas and offers a 200° swell window from the NNW around to the SE. It also has a better road system and a few well developed seaside resorts. Los Cabos favours S swells from either long distance lows or nearby hurricanes, but the west coast also receives a fair amount of N swells.

TRAVEL INFORMATION

Local Population:
San José del Cabo –
25,000
Coastline: Baja –
3,200km (2,000mi)
Time: GMT-7hr
Contests: GOB (August)
WQS (July)
National

Getting There – Visa: 90 day tourist cards on entry. Daily flights from California with Mexicana, Alaska or Aero California. There is normally a ±$50 board tax. Surfers arriving in Mexico City can fly to San José del Cabo, but it's expensive. It's a 1600km (1000mi) drive from the US border.

Getting Around – Not many people drive all the way down here, unless they plan on catching the ferry from La Paz to Mazatlan on the mainland. Despite the 'Green Angels', and their none too reliable rescue service, it is not advised to break down between Pemex stations. Renting a VW Beetle costs $25/d. 4WD territory northeast of Shipwrecks. Buses are reliable for travel between cities.

Lodging and Food – Nov-Feb is the high season. The Los Cabos corridor is a set of hotels and resorts. San José is probably a better bet, the El Presidente Hotel faces a surf spot, but it's expensive. Expect to pay $40/dble for a good hotel. R.V. parks and campsites are cheap ($5-$10/d) and convenient: San Pedrito, Pescadero, Cerritos, Surfcamp Club Cabo and Cabo Cielo. A good meal costs up to $15.

Weather – This is the desert with very few trees and little shelter from the sun. The climate is hot and dry for most of the year with cacti and stunted bushes making up the vegetation. The summer gets steaming hot and with no A/C can be unpleasant at night. Rain only comes from summer cyclones, the 'chubascos'. These occur rarely, but provoke flash floods, lightning and gusty winds. Don't camp in dry riverbeds, more people die from doing this in the desert than anything else, September seems to be the most risky month. Unlike northern Baja, the water is

warm, it is only in Jan-April that you may need a thin wetsuit.

Nature and Culture – Cabo San Lucas has become a major tourist area. The Squid Roe Strip goes off at night. Whale watching is a flat day alternative. The surrounding environment is arid desert with stiflingly hot temperatures.

Hazards and Hassles – Hurricanes, floods, jellyfish stings, scorpions, desert bugs and intense heat are all threats. Localism has got pretty bad around Monuments and Zippers. If you get pulled over by the Federales (Police) or military don't try to bribe them, just be cool.

Handy Hints – You can rent beginners boards on the beach at Costa Azul. Guns not needed. Longboarders love Cabo. The west coast is a cool place to hangout. Los Cabos is the long-weekend surf destination for Californians.

WEATHER STATISTICS	J/F	M/A	M/J	J/A	S/O	N/D
total rainfall (mm)	15	0	2	25	150	20
consistency (days/mth)	1	0	0	2	6	2
min temp (°C/°F)	12/54	13/55	17/62	22/72	21/70	15/59
max temp (°C/°F)	24/75	29/84	33/91	35/95	33/91	27/81

Backwash, Cabo San Lucas

GEOFF RAGATZ

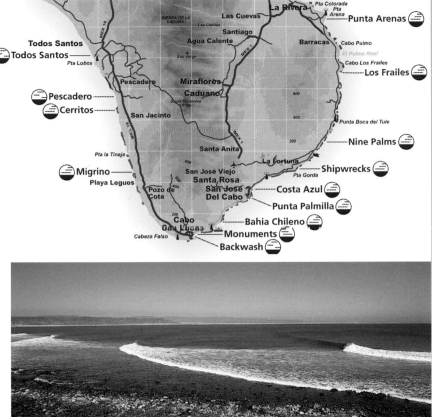

RUSSI

On the Tropic of Cancer, the small village of Todos Santos (not the famous island break) gives access to 2 beaches, Palm Beach (which tends to be better) and San Pedrito. There is a small artist community here who have given birth to a lively resort area. The Pescadero reefs are close to shore and get the maximum out of the swells. These beaches are crowd free and have plenty of campsites and surf condos. Longboarders love Cerritos; a beautiful headland with a nice and easy right point where humpback whales can sometimes be seen. Migrino is a consistent right point. Cabo San Lucas itself has the stupendous Backwash close-out, while the best nearby break is Monuments, a spectacular left that picks up any swell thanks to a submarine canyon. It's a short wave that doesn't handle crowds. Bahia Chileno is a less powerful version of the main Costa Azul wave zone but the crowds are thinner. Punta Palmilla is a bay that is full of resorts and condos. There are several breaks here, including La Punta, a big wave right. The 3 sections of Costa Azul are the main surf focus on the south shore: the Acapulcito section breaks on larger swells, giving longer rides into The Rock section, which is rocky and crowded. Further on the inside, a super fast right called Zippers, peels into the beach and huge swells will sometimes connect all three. From here a wild trail leads through the desert to numerous right pointbreaks on the edge of the Sea of Cortez. The further east you drive, the less consistent it becomes, and the more important it is to time your trip with a big cyclone swell. Shipwrecks is a major landmark, although Nine Palms is a better bet, which is well sheltered from the wind. Los Frailes is a harbour with a reef worth checking. The Punta Arenas area is a long, sand point and there is decent accommodation in the area.

Baja's southern tip is pretty consistent because of 3 sources of swell that provide waves for the exposed south and west shores. The summer (May-Oct) swell producers include southern hemisphere lows and deep tropical storms spinning off the Baja coast called 'chubascos'. They provide raw swells for the SE facing breaks in the Sea of Cortez, however, the most consistent swells are the long distance, clean S-SW swells from the southern Pacific. In winter, the North Pacific swells hit the west coast around Pescadero, but the exposure isn't great, so only the major swells will send rideable surf to this area. The west coast blows onshore in the afternoons, while the south coast is mainly offshore with the dominant NW winds. In the winter, the wind shifts more to the N and in the summer towards the W. Tide range is not a problem.

SURF STATISTICS	J F	M A	M J	J A	S O	N D
dominant swell	NW	NW	SE-SW	SE-SW	SE-SW	NW
swell size (ft)	3-4	2-3	3-4	4-5	4-5	3-4
consistency (%)	70	75	80	80	80	60
dominant wind	NW-N	NW-N	W-NW	W-NW	W-N	NW-N
average force	F3-F4	F3-F4	F3-F4	F3	F3	F3
consistency (%)	71	69	77	49	60	68
water temp (°C/°F)	23/74	23/74	25/77	28/82	28/82	26/79
wetsuit						

RUSSI

61. Colima and Michoacan

MEXICO SOUTH

• Acapulco

Pascuales

MEZ/ESM

Summary

+ BIG SWELL CONSISTENCY
+ CALM WIND PATTERNS
+ UNCROWDED, BARRELLING WAVES
+ CHEAP AND EXOTIC

− SUMMER SWELL EXCESS
− WET SUMMER CLIMATE
− MUDDY ROAD ACCESS
− MOSQUITOES AND BANDIDOS

With almost 4,000km (2,500mi) of Pacific coastline facing directly into SW swells, and a deep water trench to funnel this swell energy, mainland Mexico is a classic surf destination. It receives ample swell from both the North and South Pacific, whilst the Inter-Tropical Convergence Zone produces some of the strongest hurricane swells on earth. These slam into the numerous beaches, rocky headlands, rivermouths and points of Mexico, providing the biggest surfable waves in Central America. Colima and Michoacan State have their fair share of waves, which can be as heavy as the bandits and corrupt Federales (police) who are always ready to relieve travellers of their money and possessions.

Manzanillo Airport is the usual arrival point for surfers but the

Rio Nexpa

LAURENT MASUREL

David Dixon, Pascuales

MEZ/ESM

waves at nearby Cuyutlan are usually a huge, close-out shorebreak and not worth bothering with. A much better bet is El Paraiso, a fast A-Frame barrel, which is a good alternative especially if the crowded waves of Pascuales are maxing out. Pascuales is to this zone, what Puerto Escondido is to Oaxaca - a super powerful, top to bottom barrel, often double overhead and occasionally

TRAVEL INFORMATION

Local Population:
Manzanillo – 100,000
Coastline: 9,330km
(5,799mi)
Time: GMT-7hr
Contest: No

Getting There – 90 day tourist cards are issued for most nationalities on entry. International flights usually land in Mexico City. With 20M inhabitants, it is a daunting place to be introduced to Mexico. Fly from Mexico City with Mexicana to Playa de Oro, (Manzanillo), from where it's 45km (30mi) SE to Manzanillo City. Pay a ±$50 board tax. It's a 1hr30min drive to San Juan.

Getting Around – Hardcore Surf Tours are a surf tour company who take surfers to various secret spots that are otherwise hard to reach. They charge from $75-$100/d full service. With your own vehicle, the MEX200 goes through

Pascuales, Ticla and Nexpa. Avoid driving at night and be careful of bandidos and the Federales.

Lodging and Food – San Juan has the 'Wavehunters' villa. If this doesn't appeal then there are 4 hotels. You can rent dirt-cheap basic "palapas" in Pascuales - Edgar's $15/d, Ticla $3/d or Nexpa (bungalows available). For better accommodation head to Caleta de Campos. Food is basic and very cheap at around $3/meal.

Weather – Mexico's Sierra Madre is a high mountain range, which prevents cloud cover from reaching the coast. During the wet season (May-Sept) night-time thunderstorms can be torrential. At this time of year the temps are at their highest and, combined with the humidity, make for constantly hot and sticky conditions. A fan or A/C is advisable at this time. Winter is a far more pleasant time to visit, (±26°C/78°F), and the waves will be

smaller. El Niño years are hotter and rainier than normal. A rash vest and boardshorts is all that is required.

Nature and Culture – This area is very green with jungle all around and a lush mountainous shoreline cut by large rivermouths. Wildlife is plentiful, but sharks are only a worry close to harbours. Tecoman is the main town and Colima has a nearby volcano.

Hazards and Hassles – (See 62.Oaxaca). Although thieves are a problem, it's not as bad as the Escondido area. Montezumas Revenge is a particularly nasty stomach bug indigenous to Mexico.

Handy Hints – There is a surf shop in Tecoman. Bring spare boards, including guns if you feel like going big. Come in the winter for good weather and clean, easy beaches and points. Choose the summer if you're a charger.

WEATHER STATISTICS	J/F	M/A	M/J	J/A	S/O	N/D
total rainfall (mm)	4	1	158	254	254	18
consistency (days/mth)	1	0	8	13	12	2
min temp (°C/°F)	22/72	22/72	25/77	25/77	24/75	22/72
max temp (°C/°F)	31/88	32/90	33/91	33/91	32/90	32/90

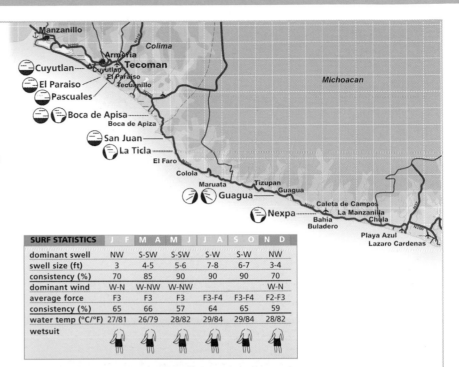

more. It breaks both left and right and is either perfect or a ferocious double-up close-out. On small to medium sized swells it might be better than Puerto, but when it gets huge it's only for experts. It's generally blown out by noon. Boca de Apisa is Colima's last option for a quality beachbreak and in the winter, with NW swells, can produce long rivermouth lefts. South of here is a Sunset-like reef which works only on large swells. After crossing the county border, you'll reach Punta la Playa at San Juan de Alima. Wavehunters operates a villa here, with a view of the surf from the top floor. There are also 4-5 other hotels in the vicinity. The wave here is a long right point sheltered from afternoon sea breezes. It needs a big swell to turn it on but even so, it's pretty consistent. If this isn't on then there are plenty of beachbreaks out in front of the town, all good quality and best ridden at high tide with light winds. To the east are 3 reefs with easy channels. La Ticla requires a bit of off-road driving to reach but it's worth the effort to ride this epic wave. When it's small, it's a good fun beachbreak favouring lefts but, with a bit of swell, La Ticla becomes an awesome rivermouth left. It is a dangerous area due to drug traffickers hiding out in the bush and people have been shot in the past, so don't hang around in this vicinity. On the MEX200 road to Nexpa, there are quality rights and lefts with no crowds at Guagua rivermouth. Finally, Barra de Nexpa 'palapas' (Mexican beach huts) face the long, tubing lefts of Rio Nexpa, an unusual rivermouth set-up, which is usually crowded. There can be rights off the peak, which break back into the rivermouth while the lefts break down a point on the west side of the river flow. The rights are much shorter and consequently less crowded. The lefts can handle solid size, get some strong currents and will dish out some poundings to the unwary. For reasonable quality rooms stay in Caleta de Campos.

SURF STATISTICS	J F	M A	M J	J A	S O	N D
dominant swell	NW	S-SW	S-SW	S-W	S-W	NW
swell size (ft)	3	4-5	5-6	7-8	6-7	3-4
consistency (%)	70	85	90	90	90	70
dominant wind	W-N	W-NW	W-NW			W-N
average force	F3	F3	F3	F3-F4	F3-F4	F2-F3
consistency (%)	65	66	57	64	65	59
water temp (°C/°F)	27/81	26/79	28/82	29/84	29/84	28/82
wetsuit	🏄	🏄	🏄	🏄	🏄	🏄

MEZ/ESM La Ticla

There is no definite best time of year for Mexico because there is always something going on. From Mar to Nov there are plenty of lined-up southern hemisphere groundswells plus the June to Oct hurricane season, which provides the biggest swells. The SW groundswells will be super clean but if the hurricane moves too close to land, instead of pounding SE-SW lines, the surf will be blown-out and messy with heavy rain. The beachbreaks are often too big for most surfers, reaching face heights of 25ft (8m) on the beaches, whilst the pointbreaks will be firing at 6-12ft (2-4m). A good time to visit is winter, when there are still some clean 3-8ft (1-2.6m) swells and a good variation of winds, from light W to N (offshore) and many glassy days. From Feb to May, the dominant wind is NW in the morning turning W in the

afternoon. The main changes occur during the rainy period when winds shift from the dominant N-NW to E-SE, which tend to be ok for many of the lefts. Tidal variation is slight and has little effect on most spots.

MEZ/ESM David Dixon, La Ticla

MEXICO
SOUTH

● Acapulco

62. Oaxaca

Carlos Cabrero, Puerto Escondido

STEVE FITZPATRICK

Summary
+ CONSISTENT YEAR ROUND
+ BIG, BARRELLING WAVES
+ FAIRLY CHEAP

− LOTS OF CLOSE-OUTS
− CROWDS AND DROP-INS
− CRIME
− INSECTS

Puerto Escondido, one of the best beachbreaks in the world, is a vicious, huge and spectacular barrel that breaks almost straight onto the shore with Hawaiian-style power. Frequent tropical storms and hurricanes pass by this coast in the summer time (April-Oct) and thanks to a deep water trench just offshore, the strong swells they produce hit the shore with little loss in size or power. These swells hit the sandbars at Zicatela Beach in such a way that the waves jack up in size, which is emphasised by a backwash. Magazine photos of this place are misleading – the waves often close-out and the paddle-out can be severe. Usually the rights break best. The wave is fickle, and will often be blown out by 11am. When this occurs, the best bet is to head south to the mellower, but busy lefts of La Punta, which will be

Roger Ramirez, Puerto Escondido

STEVE FITZPATRICK

Overview from MEX200

LAURENT MASUREL

offshore. It's easier to take a bus rather than endure the long, hot walk. Late afternoons should see the wind drop away and Puerto Escondido should clean up.

Whilst Puerto Escondido is Mexico's biggest drawcard, there's much more to explore in this area. Chacahua to the west is well worth a visit accessed either by catching a boat from Escondido or travelling by 4WD along the muddy tracks of a national park. The reward is a fast,

TRAVEL INFORMATION

Local Population:
Puerto Escondido –
50,000
Coastline: 9,330km
(5,800mi)
Time: GMT-7hr
Contests: ISA (May)
Open (Nov)
National

Getting There – (See 61.Colima and Michoacan) There are five flights a week between Mexico City and Puerto Escondido at a cost of $70/o-w. By bus is a long 15hr journey costing $14.

Getting around – Most surfers stay in Puerto Escondido and travel by taxi to La Punta or boat to Chacahua. Buses along the MEX200 are reliable and cheap. It takes 2hrs to get from Puerto Escondido to Huatulco. If you have a 4WD, then you can search out many good spots that can be found down the dirt roads.

Lodging and Food – Accommodation-wise, Puerto Escondido has everything from the cheapest, right up to the top hotels. Calle del Moro is a good place to be based giving you convenient access to the beaches and amenities. Art & Harry's is reasonable at $8-$10/dble. La Bamba surfcamp costs $50/d. For food Brunós has cheap and filling meals for around $3.

Weather – (See 61.Colima and Michoacan)

Nature and Culture – Visiting the archaeological site of Monte Alban or the city of San Cristóbal de las Casas requires a real effort, but they are worth the time and expense. The nightlife in Puerto Escondido is very lively. A horse ride out to the Atotonilco hot wells is a good afternoon trip.

Hazards and Hassles – Muggings and petty theft are on the increase, sometimes accompanied by violence - don't carry valuables around with you. Gun-toting Bandidos are also a growing problem. Don't camp on beaches or drive down quiet roads at night. Some of the spots get crowded. When it's big, Puerto Escondido is a wave for advanced surfers. Insects will be constant companions!

Handy Hints – Bring a couple of boards, including a gun and be prepared to snap them. A helmet is a good idea. Cheap boards can be bought at Central Surf ($250/gun) or rented from the Cabañas Las Olas or Rockaway ($3/d). Mexican surfers are hardcore and charge on the biggest of days - show them some respect. The Federales (police) are worth avoiding!

WEATHER STATISTICS	J/F	M/A	M/J	J/A	S/O	N/D
total rainfall (mm)	4	0	147	177	180	8
consistency (days/mth)	1	0	7	10	8	1
min temp (°C/°F)	22/72	23/74	25/77	25/77	24/75	22/72
max temp (°C/°F)	29/84	31/88	32/90	32/90	31/88	30/86

tubing, right pointbreak but unfortunately it requires a strong swell. To the east of Puerto are the beachbreaks of Colotepec, which can be easily checked from the road. Further east, Topleca is an isolated, peaky reefbreak about 30 minutes drive from the renowned hippie community of Zipolite. It's a popular rest stop on the backpacker circuit, but the powerful waves lack any decent shape and straight-handers are the norm. Bandits operate on the small coastal roads in this area, robbing people at night. Back on the main coastal road, the MEX200, there's a turn off down a dirt track in Rio Coyula that will lead to some sandy points and scattered reefs. It's a rarely surfed area with lots of good potential. A final place to check in this zone is Bahias de Huatulco (around the K252) with its pleasant tourist bays. Most of the beaches offer little in the way of good waves but Playa Manzanilla is a jewel of a right point found in Bahia Tangolunda. The Huatulco beaches of Bahia Santa Cruz and Playa Chahue are known locally as Olas Altas – translated it means high waves.

Oaxaca has consistent, year round surf, but many consider summer (April-Oct) as the prime surf season. Quality swells are generated from lows off New Zealand and these provide regular 3-10ft (1-3.3m) SW swells. Add the heavy action of the tropical storms or 'chubascos', generated off mainland Mexico, which churn up swells of 6-15ft (2-5m) between June-Oct. Many of these hurricane swells are just too unruly and close-outs are common. Double overhead days are far from rare and during the height of the swell you will often see waves getting to triple overhead. Some of the time the combination of wind and swell is far from ideal. Between Nov and Feb, there will be lots of glassy or N wind days, but less of the strong swells. When the summer swells are pumping, there's more chance of onshore, due W winds, blowing from 39% of the time in April to 17%

in July. Afternoon sea breezes are an almost daily occurrence. The summer rainy season brings winds from all directions, but mainly a mild W-NW or a better E-SE. Tidal range is minimal and has little effect on most spots.

SURF STATISTICS	J F	M A M	J J	A S	O N	D
dominant swell	NW	S-SW	S-SW	S-W	S-W	NW
swell size (ft)	3	4-5	5-6	7-8	6-7	3-4
consistency (%)	70	85	90	90	90	70
dominant wind	W-NE	W-NW	SW-NW	W-NW	W-NW	W-NE
average force	F3	F3	F3	F3	F3	F3
consistency (%)	64	57	56	34	39	61
water temp (°C/°F)	27/81	27/81	28/82	28/82	28/82	27/81
wetsuit						

Lifeguard tower – Puerto Escondido

SYLVAIN CAZENAVE

Puerto Escondido

LAURENT MASUREL

63. Costa del Balsamo

La Libertad Pier and Punta Roca

PUNTAMANGO.COM.SV

Summary

+ PERFECT RIGHT POINTBREAKS
+ MELLOW, WARM WAVES
+ MANY VIRGIN SPOTS
+ GOOD WIND PATTERNS
+ CHEAP LIVING

− RARELY BIG
− S SWELLS ONLY
− RAIN THROUGH BEST SWELL SEASON
− QUESTIONABLE SECURITY
− LACK OF NIGHT ENTERTAINMENT
− EARTHQUAKES

El Salvador hides an insane array of long, right pointbreaks making it a natural-footer's dream destination. Whilst its reputation has been built on the J-Bayesque waves of Punta Roca in La Libertad, El Salvador has more than just one wave, and the whole country is literally swarming with awesome right pointbreaks. Considering its small size, El Salvador could easily claim the highest density of quality pointbreaks in Central America. The western La Libertad area is the focus of attention but there's no doubt that future interest will turn towards the 'Oriente Salvaje', the eastern side of the country. The good news is that the civil war of the 80's is over and aside from some slight political unrest, it's a safe place to visit. With only 1.5 million people in El Salvador, crowds are kept to a minimum, except around the bigger centres. The area to the west of La Libertad is an excellent place to search for totally empty waves.

La Libertad

CHUCK GRAHAM

Near Atami

PUNTAMANGO.COM.SV

TRAVEL INFORMATION

Local Population: Libertad Province – 600,000
Coastline: 307km (190mi)
Time: GMT-6hr
Contest: national

Getting There – Visa: Most nationalities need a visa prior to travelling. For US citizens a $15 entry fee is required. Despite its small size, El Salvador has flights to many US cities with the national airline, TACA, or US airlines. The airport is conveniently located 20mins outside of La Libertad. Cross border buses also arrive from Guatemala. Dep tax $25.

Getting Around – Despite the war being over, it's still a wild area that is more suited to surf camps and guided tours. Renting a car is expensive. Buses and taxis between San Salvador and La Libertad are frequent and reliable. Renting a boat to reach some of the more remote breaks can be a good idea.

Lodging and Food – La Libertad is set around a small, stinking harbour but it's a cheap and popular local getaway. Punta Mango is a reliable tour operator in this area. Don Lito is a good hotel as is Posada with A/C rooms which face out onto Punta Roca. Rick's is a basic cheap place. There's also the new Horizonte Surf Camp in Zunzal which charges $9/p. A meal will be between $5-$8.

Weather – The difference between the two seasons is pretty dramatic. The dry season (Dec-April) is dusty and hot with extreme temperatures in March-April. Despite the heat, this is considered the best time to travel. The rest of the year receives heavy rainfall, which usually falls as afternoon and night-time downpours and can make the roads impassable. However the cooler rainy nights make it easier to sleep. Apart from in Zunzal, the insects (zancudos), aren't that bad. The coast is much warmer than the cloudy, misty mountains. San Salvador city offers a respite from the coastal heat.

Nature and Culture – A city tour should include the San Salvador churches and a visit to the national forest reserve WT Deininger or 'Evil's Doorway'. Volcano trips and Tazumal Mayan ruins take a couple of days to visit but are worth the effort. Don't expect a raging nightlife, a night curfew has been in force for a while.

Hazards and Hassles – Boulders underlie many spots, which aren't as sharp as the millions of urchins. Occasional crowds occur, wake up early and the line-up will be quiet. Pollution, sea lice, thefts, hepatitis, malaria and typhoid are all potential problems while decent medical attention is difficult to find.

Handy Hints – There are surf shops in San Salvador, but it's better to take your own gear. The points will require a fast board and a semi-gun for big days. The waves are predictable and soft-breaking. Take booties for use on rocky points. El Salvador suffers from major environmental problems: deforestation and lack of water treatment are two obvious examples.

WEATHER STATISTICS	J/F	M/A	M/J	J/A	S/O	N/D
total rainfall (mm)	4	34	255	260	272	22
consistency (days/mth)	1	3	16	20	18	3
min temp (°C/°F)	20/68	21/70	23/74	23/74	24/75	21/70
max temp (°C/°F)	30/86	31/88	29/84	29/84	28/82	27/81

East coast secret spot

RODRIGO BARRAZA

The coastline of El Salvador faces pretty much south so it only receives S-SW swells. Exposure to these swells is excellent making El Salvador a very consistent destination with plenty of small clean lines wrapping perfectly around the headlands. Big swells will produce 8-10ft (2.6-3.2m) conditions, which will remain rideable at most spots. The main swell season is March-October, but it could be considered a year round destination as any small swell will produce surfable waves. Another plus for the off-season is that it is blessed by E-NE winds which means that it's offshore most of the time, giving excellent water conditions. During the rainy season the winds will be offshore in the morning, then switch to sideshore around 10am and eventually onshore when the thunderstorms break out. As for tides, the range never goes over 6ft (2m) but it does affect the rocky points.

Starting in the east, Punta Roca is the world class pointbreak in La Libertad. It's a very long right, with hollow tubing sections breaking onto shallow, black boulders. It needs to be at least 3ft (1m) to break off the rocks, but it holds surf of up to 12ft (4m). Closer to town is La Paz, a less critical, fun point that's rocky but nevertheless popular with the locals. Another peak in town offers good lefts at The Pier but it's usually full of kids who don't mind the close proximity of the sewage pipe! Beginners may want to try the small swell beachbreaks at Playa Conchalio, even though it's a fast and barrelling wave, best in the dry season. Rio Grande is a rivermouth with long, mushy lefts and rights but it needs a decent size swell. Next wave west is Zunzal, another righthand point which seems to have waves every single day. It looks a lot like Punta Roca with many tube sections, but it has less power. It's a very consistent spot and as such it attracts local crowds on weekends and holidays. The rides are long, fun and safe. El Zonte is yet another right point but this one is dominated by heaps of rocks and should only be surfed at high tide. When the swell's big enough, there are some lefts that can be ridden on the other side of the bay. Driving west, the scenery gets dramatic with steep cliffs, mountain tunnels and winding roads. Most of the capes are inaccessible, but a boat trip around this area would undoubtedly be rewarding. The road leading to Mizata reveals a few points, while Mizata itself works like Zunzal: on any small swell at low tide, to avoid the high tide backwash. Lastly, there's the west facing Los Cabanos beachbreaks, just before Acajutla.

SURF STATISTICS	J F	M A	M J	J A	S O	N D
dominant swell	S-SW	S-SW	S-SW	S-SW	S-SW	S-SW
swell size (ft)	2	3	4-5	5	4-5	2
consistency (%)	70	80	90	80	80	70
dominant wind	NE-E	NE-E	NE-E	NE-E	SW-W	NE-E
average force	F4	F4	F3-F4	F4	F3	F4
consistency (%)	73	63	41	58	32	63
water temp (°C/°F)	27/81	27/81	28/82	28/82	28/82	27/81
wetsuit						

PUNTAMANGO.COM.SV

Km59 and Km61

64. Guanacaste

Portrero Grande (Ollie's Point)

KIKI COMMADIEU

Summary

+ CONSISTENT YEAR ROUND
+ FUN SIZED WAVES
+ POINTBREAK HEAVEN
+ RICH IN WILDLIFE
+ POLITICALLY STABLE

– LACK OF SIZE AND LEFTS
– OPPRESSIVELY HOT WEATHER
– MILLIONS OF INSECTS
– TOURIST PRICE INFLATION

SYLVAIN CAZENAVE

Costa Rica is one of those rare destinations that has a choice of two coastlines influenced by two different oceans. The Caribbean side produces big, wild waves during two short seasons, while the Pacific side gets pounded by medium sized swells all year long. With a nearly 180° swell window, the northern province of Guanacaste is very consistent with long distance Pacific swells arriving from the north and south. The area around Tamarindo is best during the dry season when clean, offshore conditions, sunshine and easy access make it a veritable tropical paradise. This is the nicest time to travel but you certainly won't be alone. May-Oct is the testing wet season, but this is a surf rich time, when perfect, SW groundswell, provides bigger waves. Costa Rica itself is a well-grounded place with political stability achieved without an army. It has good hospitals (in case of need) and

Tamarindo

SYLVAIN CAZENAVE

you can drink the tap water almost everywhere. All these things are rare in Central America.

Located on the Pacific coast near the Nicaraguan border is the famous, perfect, right rivermouth pointbreak of Potrero Grande, aka 'Ollie's point'. It was so named because an airstrip nearby was used by US

TRAVEL INFORMATION

Local Population: Guanacaste – 250,000
Coastline: 1,290km (805mi)
Time: GMT-6h
Contest: National

Getting There – No visa, but a 30 day limit for many nationalities. San José is the main airport, although flights from Miami land straight in Liberia (Guanacaste). The national airline is Lacsa, who usually charge for boards. There are daily flights to Tamarindo with Sansa and Travel Air.

Getting Around – The road system has improved dramatically over the years, but can still be challenging from the coast. San José is a 5h drive. Rental cars cost at least $35/d. During the rainy season, most spots can only be reached by 4WD (<$60/d). Don't drive at night. The bus system is efficient and cheap.

Lodging and Food – Costs have risen fast over the years, stay in one of the many Tamarindo hotels ($70+/dble) or in cheaper cabinas ($25/dble). Avellanes, Junquilla and Nosara are good places to stay. A typical restaurant bill is $8-$10.

Weather – Guanacaste is the driest part of Costa Rica with lots of sunshine and hot temperatures, often accompanied by oppressive 100% humidity. A fan or A/C is a must for sleeping. The dry season runs from December to April, but the rest of the year is not excessively rainy anyway, unlike the Caribbean side. Expect evening rain pretty much every day and clear mornings. San José, at 1100m escapes the worst of the heat. The water is warm year round; a rash vest will protect you from the sun and the occasional strong NE wind raising the wind chill factor in the dry season. A shorty may be useful.

Nature and Culture – National parks (e.g. Santa Rosa) swarm with monkeys, toucans, crocodiles and snakes. Lots of the beaches are prime turtle nesting sites. On the odd flat day the volcanoes (Arvenal) are spectacular. Try Tamaquad.

Hazards and Hassles – Sharks and sea crocodiles cruise around the Potrero and Naranjo spots but no attacks have been reported. Although it's almost malaria-free, there are tons of zancudos (insects). Sea-lice will bite you in the line-up, and occasionally the jellyfish harvest is striking. Rip-offs (cameras, cash etc.) occur but unlike San José this is a friendly place and you shouldn't get hurt.

Handy Hints – Reading the Tico Times can reveal some bargains for rental cars and hotels. High Tide surf shop (Tamarindo) is well supplied and many hotels rent out boards. Costa Ricans are well educated and often speak good English.

WEATHER STATISTICS	J/F	M/A	M/J	J/A	S/O	N/D
total rainfall (mm)	4	18	205	202	270	70
consistency (days/mth)	1	2	16	18	20	7
min temp (°C/°F)	23/74	23/74	22/72	23/74	23/74	22/72
max temp (°C/°F)	35/95	35/95	33/91	32/90	32/90	31/88

Langosta

PHILIPPE CHEVODIAN

Colonel Oliver North to land weapons for the Nicaraguan Contras. This is the wave featured on 'Endless Summer II'. Next door, Playa Naranjo is another world class wave. This hollow beachbreak faces a huge rock called Roca Bruja meaning Witches Rock which was deposited in the sea by an angry volcano 50km (30mi) away. The only effective way to reach these spots is by boat from Playa del Coco or by 4x4, but like most national parks, there's no accommodation and camping is a possibility but sketchy.

Moving down the coast is Tamarindo, which has been catching the attention of surfers for years, both for its waves and its laid-back vibe. Tamarindo is a wide bay with a rivermouth in the middle. At the northern end is Playa Grande, which is an excellent beachbreak and famous turtle breeding ground (these beautiful, friendly locals are often in the line-up). Playa Grande is a twenty minute walk or twenty minute drive (around the river) from Tamarindo (and the splendid Hotel Las Tortugas is worth a visit). With a decent swell, several good spots break in Tamarindo itself, these vary from a rivermouth (Estero's consistent fast lines) to beachbreaks (variable) and several reefbreaks (Pico Pequeño, Diria, Henry's), all well situated for NW-W swells. Heading south, Langosta is the next bay with a rivermouth and some decent reef set-ups. On small swells keep heading south towards Avellana which has a gnarly reefbreak, imaginatively named Little Hawai'i. Avellana also has good access to the crystal-blue rights of Playa Negra. Staying in Playa Junquilla or in Pablo Picasso's Cabinas will put you very

close to the waves. The coast leading to Nosara is full of secret spots, only accessible in the dry season with a 4WD. Nosara is a bigger centre with some beachbreak lefts and some good lodging. For the more hardcore, nearby Playa Ostional can be a good place to stay, whilst further south still, potential spots can be found around Punta Guiones. The reefs here pick up any swell and can get big. Stay at Playa Guiones Lodge or the campsite.

The major swell season is April to Oct, when swells hit from a variety of angles. S-SW swells coming off the Roaring Forties produce numerous 3-10ft (1-3.3m) swells - lows located off New Zealand give the best direction. Tropical storms off Mexico produce NW swells. Dec to April sees NW arctic swells, which, when combined with frequent offshores and no rain, makes this the best season for clean 3-4ft (1-1.3m) waves almost every day. Winds are not usually a factor, however there is a wet but gentle SW-W monsoon period from May to December. Typically, mornings are offshore, afternoons onshore. Winter sees a dry period with a lot of light winds from any direction, but predominately from the NW-NE. Tides can reach 12ft (4m), drastically changing the waves. Tide tables are hard to come by, and binoculars are useful for checking spots.

Playa Naranjo and Roca Bruja (Witches Rock)

PHILIPPE CHEVODIAN

SURF STATISTICS	J F	M A	M J	J A	S O	N D
dominant swell	NW	S-SW	S-SW	S-SW	S-SW	NW
swell size (ft)	2	3	4-5	5	4-5	2
consistency (%)	60	75	80	80	70	60
dominant wind	W-NE	S-NE	S-W	SW-W	SW-W	SW-NW
average force	F3	F2	F3	F3	F3	F3
consistency (%)	64	72	63	57	65	68
water temp (°C/°F)	26/79	27/81	28/82	27/81	27/81	26/79
wetsuit						

65. Golfo Dulce

Pavones

Summary

+ PAVONES LONG POINTBREAK
+ CALM WINDS
+ WILD, EXOTIC AREA
+ RAINFOREST WILDLIFE

− SEMI-CROWDED
− INCONSISTENT
− INTENSE RAINY SEASON
− LACK OF ROADS
− TROPICAL DISEASES AND INSECTS

C osta Rica is best known for the perfect small waves found around the Guanacaste area but it was actually the Pavones area that made the country famous, thanks to photos of some of the longest lefts in the world. Add in the wonderful tropical scenery and plenty of great waves to choose from and you have the makings of a good surf trip. Another major surprise comes from the Caribbean, which has revealed some unexpectedly powerful waves. The Osa Peninsula close to the Panamanian border is the place where surf trip fantasies become a reality, with spots hidden away behind lush

Matapalo

curtains of rainforest. The Golfo Dulce provides a watery divide between Pavones' lefts and Matapalo's rights, whilst the surrounding jungle hides many other spots.

Playa Zancudo is a beautiful beach far inside the Golfo Dulce but as it's so sheltered, waves will rarely break.

TRAVEL INFORMATION

Local Population:
Golfito area – 40,000
Coastline: 1,290km
(805mi)
Time: GMT-6hr
Contest: local

Getting There – No visa is necessary but there is a 30 day limit for many nationalities. San José is the main airport. The national airline is Lacsa, (board charge). Two airlines fly to Golfito, but some planes are too small to carry bigger boards. ($70/o-w). Tracopa has a bus service from San Jose to Golfito for $5 for the 8hr trip. An epic 3hr drive follows to reach Pavones from Golfito. Boats are a much faster way of getting around.

Getting Around – Apart from the main highway, roads are rare and are frequently washed out during the rainy season, so you will need a 4WD. You don't actually need a car, as it's easier to use the dirt-cheap public transport, pricey pangas (dugouts) or to hire rides to Matapalo and Punta Banco.

Lodging and Food – Costs have risen fast over the years. The basic Esquina del Mar in Pavones ($7) has a killer view. Pavones Surf (1km south - $15) and Tiskita Lodge (5km away - $65) offer better services. In Punta Banco a basic room costs $8/d. Matapalo has many private properties with upmarket bungalows (Bosque del Cabo, Bahia Esmeralda; ±$50)

Weather – This area has a wet, tropical climate with high temperatures and humidity year round, which is even more pronounced on the Caribbean side of the country. Rainfall rather than temp changes determine seasons. There is a prolonged rainy season between May and Dec with intense downpours, especially in the afternoons. The short dry season occurs when the wind turns to the N between Dec and April. The water remains very warm year round; take boardshorts and a long sleeve rash vest for the strong sun.

Nature and Culture – National parks (e.g. Corcovado) swarm with monkeys, Scarlet

Macaws, crocodiles and snakes. Wildlife and flora in the rainforests are stunning! Only Golfito and Puerto Jiménez offer some night action.

Hazards and Hassles – Most breaks are easy, walled-up waves, just mind the rocks. Crowds at Pavones get thick and locals get angry at times. Matapalo is private land and is much less crowded. Gringo property owners have had problems with surfers in the past. Malaria tablets are necessary. There are a few cases of Dengue Fever, swarms of mosquitoes, jellyfish and sea lice aplenty.

Handy Hints – If you end up spending time here, read the Tico Times for bargain rental cars, hotels etc. The local name for men is 'Ticos,' for women it is 'Ticas'. The people are really nice and most speak English. Pura Vida (Pure Life) means hello. Cases of muggings and thefts on foreigners are growing, be careful.

WEATHER STATISTICS	J/F	M/A	M/J	J/A	S/O	N/D
total rainfall (mm)	4	18	205	202	270	70
consistency (days/mth)	1	2	16	18	20	7
min temp (°C/°F)	23/74	23/74	22/72	23/74	23/74	22/72
max temp (°C/°F)	35/95	35/95	33/91	32/90	32/90	31/88

Being located in a bay, Pavones also needs a large swell to turn on. When it does it usually breaks for 100-150m on cobblestones at low tide in the rivermouth. At high tide the La Esquina del Mar section starts breaking. Occasionally the wave connects up at high tide, breaking so close to shore that surfers don't paddle back out, but instead walk back to the line-up. Rides of up to a kilometre are possible but you have to be quick to beat the longer sections. If Pavones is too small or crowded, then Punta Banco is a short 3km (2mi) hike away, and has some good coral reefbreaks offering empty rights and lefts. Places to stay and eat have recently sprung up around here. A walk or even a horse ride southwards towards Punta Burica will take you past Eclipse, a small rivermouth break. Punta Burica itself produces large surf breaking on many different reefs in a still largely unexplored area.

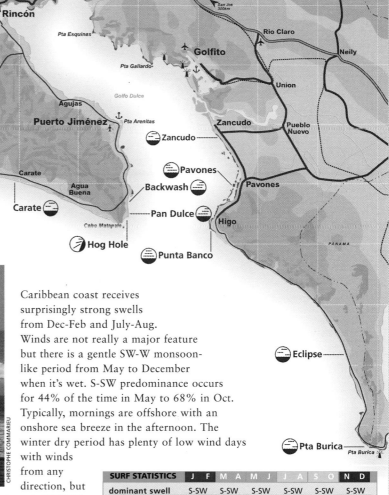

Matapalo

Matapalo on the other side of the Golfo Dulce has three quality right pointbreaks favouring low to mid tide. The most consistent is called Hog Hole, which produces very steep, fast walls. This is a challenging break, getting wild and heavy when it's big. If the swell gets to a decent size, Pan Dulce becomes a truly world class, right pointbreak which has been compared to Rincon. Long, mellow waves break as two separate sections on a rocky bottom in front of a large white beach. The last right (the closest wave to accommodation) is Backwash, so named because the waves tend to wedge off the cliff walls of the small cove it breaks in and jack up in size. Hollow sections make this a fun wave. If it's flat around Matapalo, try Playa Carate, just before the Corcovado National Park, which has good waves and picks up any S or W swell. If there's a W-NW swell, Drake's Bay has wild and empty surf.

The best swell season is April to Oct, which is blessed by two swell sources. The most important is the S swell from the Roaring Forties which produce numerous 3-12ft (1-4m) swells, with the best lows located around New Zealand. Secondly are the NW tropical storm or hurricane swells off Mexico. The

Caribbean coast receives surprisingly strong swells from Dec-Feb and July-Aug. Winds are not really a major feature but there is a gentle SW-W monsoon-like period from May to December when it's wet. S-SW predominance occurs for 44% of the time in May to 68% in Oct. Typically, mornings are offshore with an onshore sea breeze in the afternoon. The winter dry period has plenty of low wind days with winds from any direction, but predominantly NW-NE. Tides can reach 15ft (5m), which has a great effect on where you will surf. Some breaks are non-existent at low, then overhead at high!

SURF STATISTICS	J F	M A	M J	J A	S O	N D
dominant swell	S-SW	S-SW	S-SW	S-SW	S-SW	S-SW
swell size (ft)	2	3	4-5	5	4-5	2
consistency (%)	60	75	80	80	70	60
dominant wind	W-NE	W-NE	SW-W	SW-W	SW-W	SW-W
average force	F3	F2	F3	F3	F3	F3
consistency (%)	67	49	49	57	65	56
water temp (°C/°F)	26/79	27/81	28/82	27/81	27/81	26/79
wetsuit						

Jeremy Saukel, Pavones

66. South-West Panama

HONDURAS
EL SALVADOR
NICARAGUA
COSTA RICA
PANAMA

Sebaco

PHILIPPE CHEVODIAN

Summary
+ WORLD CLASS POINTBREAKS
+ CALM WIND CONDITIONS
+ CLOSE TO CARIBBEAN COASTLINE
+ UNCROWDED SPOTS
+ WILD EXOTIC AREA

– SANTA CATALINA IS CROWDED
– INTENSE RAINY SEASON
– LACK OF ROADS
– TROPICAL DISEASES

Panama joins Central America to continental South America via a thin isthmus of land blanketed in wild jungle and marshlands. It is severed by the amazing engineering feat that is the Panama Canal, which leads from the surf drenched Pacific coast to the great potential of the Caribbean coast. Panama feels like an uncrowded version of its neighbour, Costa Rica, plus there's the added bonus of offshore islands to explore.

It's slightly less exposed to the North Pacific swells than Costa Rica but Panama does have a good window for W and S swells along with calm wind patterns. Although the country is not as easy for the travelling surfer as Costa Rica, there is an untapped selection of pointbreaks and the

Chino, Santa Catalina

KIKI COMMARDIEU

Margo Montovani, Morro Negrito

HEATHER HOLIES

option of driving from coast to coast within 2 hours. The known spots in the Caribbean are around Colon or Bocas del Toro, with the western part of the country offering the best orientation for Caribbean swells.

On the Pacific side, several surf camps have opened in the Panamanian wilderness around Santa Catalina, where the peeling rights break almost every day, especially from

TRAVEL INFORMATION

Local Population:
Sta Catalina – 200
Coastline: Pacific coast –
1,690km (1,050mi)
Time: GMT-5hr
Contest: WQS (March)

Getting There – Visa: Brazil, Japan and most European nationals. Most flights go to Panama City, which is about 6-8 hours away. Miami is the main hub for international flights to Panama. Crossing the border overland from Costa Rica is another option. Copa is the national airline. Dep tax is $20.

Getting Around – It's not necessary to rent a car, as everything is easily accessible by public transport. The best way to get from Panama City (the capital) to the coast is to take a bus along the Pan American Highway to Sona (5hr, $7) or Remedios (8h, $10). From Sona, it takes 2hr to Santa Catalina, whilst from Remedios,

you need another bus, then a boat. To reach the really remote spots, a boat is needed.

Lodging and Food – You can rent a basic room in Santa Catalina but it's more of a surf camp option. Top local surfer, Ricardo Icaza (Ponky) has basic but decent cabins at the Casablanca Surf Resort ($50/p/d) or try Itolo ($35/d). Morro Negrito is ±$450/w full board. Food is basic.

Weather – Expect a wet, tropical climate with high temperatures and humidity year round, especially on the Caribbean side of the highlands. The seasons are determined by rainfall rather than temperature changes. There is a prolonged rainy season between May and Dec with intense downpours, especially in the afternoons. The short dry season occurs when the wind turns to the N between Dec and April. The water remains very warm year round so take boardshorts and a long sleeve rashy for sun protection.

Nature and Culture – The forest swarms with monkeys, birds, crocodiles and snakes. The closest city is Santiago. Since the USA pulled Noriega out of the country there have been very close links between the two nations.

Hazards and Hassles – Due to large tidal ranges, hitting the shallow reef is a real possibility. The surf doesn't get all that crowded, although Santa Catalina has some busier days. A Yellow Fever injection and malaria tablets are necessary. The heat can get very intense at any time of year.

Handy Hints – This is a remote area so take everything you need with you. Panama uses the US dollar. Political unrest is pretty much over now. The Canal now belongs to Panama.

WEATHER STATISTICS	J/F	M/A	M/J	J/A	S/O	N/D
total rainfall (mm)	110	67	315	387	365	510
consistency (days/mth)	7	7	15	17	16	15
min temp (°C/°F)	24/75	25/77	24/75	24/75	24/75	24/75
max temp (°C/°F)	29/84	30/86	31/88	31/88	31/88	29/84

PHILIPPE CHEVOD-AN

April to October. It's a very long pointbreak with 3 sections, the La Punta section being the best, which works better at high tide. When the tide is low, the place to go is the nearby lefts of Punta Brava. Weekends see a maximum of 15-25 waveriders but this rarely makes a heavy crowd. The waves are long and plentiful and winds are favourable all day long. Many nearby secret spots include Coiba or Sebaco Island, which has a reef that produces a square tube that has been compared to The Box in Australia.

The second surf zone is quite a long way north-west, located off Remedios, at Morro Negrito. Again, there is a surf camp here with 9 or 10 breaks in the vicinity. The main point of Morro Negrito is a speedy, pitching barrel, but for length, check the awesome lefts at Rivermouth, which on a good day, break as far as the eye can see (200-400m rides). The tiny, circular shape of Silva Island is home to an exploding cloudbreak called Nestles, which has the potential to hold 20ft+ (6.6m+) lefts and rights. Also on the island is P-Land, a fast, tubing left that starts breaking on a dangerous tabletop reef and wraps around the island. Rumours suggest that it can connect with another impressive break called Leftovers.

The major swell season is April-Oct, relying on the two usual swell generators for Central America at this time of year. The Roaring Forties produce numerous 3-12ft (1-4m) swells, the lows located around New Zealand being the best angled. Secondly are the NW hurricane swells off Mexico. Be aware that the Caribbean receives surprisingly strong swells from Dec-Feb and July-Aug. Wind-wise, there's little to worry about, as it is almost always calm. There is a gentle SW-W monsoon period from May to December. S-SW predominance occurs for 44% of the time in May to 68% of the time in Oct. Typically, mornings are offshore and afternoons see a light onshore sea breeze. There is very little wind in the dry winter period. Winds come from every direction with a NW-NE dominance. Spring tides can reach a huge 18ft (6m), so get hold of a tide table.

SURF STATISTICS	J F	M A	M J	J A	S O	N D
dominant swell	S-SW	S-SW	S-SW	S-SW	S-SW	S-SW
swell size (ft)	2-3	3-4	5	5-6	5	2-3
consistency (%)	70	80	90	90	80	70
dominant wind	W-NE	W-NE	SW-W	SW-W	SW-W	S-W
average force	F3	F2	F3	F3	F3	F3
consistency (%)	67	49	49	57	65	56
water temp (°C/°F)	26/79	27/81	28/82	28/82	27/81	27/81
wetsuit						

PHILIPPE CHEVODIAN

67. North-West Puerto Rico

Secret spot

ALL PHOTOS STEVE FITZPATRICK

Summary
+ CONSISTENTLY OFFSHORE
+ QUALITY POINTBREAKS
+ WARM, POWERFUL WAVES
+ EASY ACCESS
+ GREAT WEATHER

– WINDY
– HEAVY CROWDS AND LOCALS
– LOTS OF TOURISTS
– CAR CRIME
– POLLUTION/SEWAGE PROBLEMS

Otto Flores, Indicators

Puerto Rico is to Florida what Hawai'i is to California. It gets big, it's exotic and it has fierce locals. Located in what is regarded as the best corner of the Caribbean for surf, Puerto Rico's premier surf spots are found on the north-west corner of the island. The eastern or windward side is blocked by the Virgin Islands, the south coast only breaks on rare hurricane swells and while the north coast is consistent, it's often onshore and right next to the capital, San Juan. A deep water trench offshore (the second deepest in the world) means N-NE swells hit the north shore with little loss in size and power. Although the waves can get very big, the average winter conditions are around 4-6ft (1.3-2m). Most spots break on flat reefs of coral and lava.

Surfing in Puerto Rico has traditionally centred around Rincón, but today the area gets extremely

La Fortaleza

busy. The standard of local surfing is high and the crowds have led most surf travellers to seek quieter spots further to the north, around Isabela. Dunes has many quality reefs that are usually crowd free. Playa Motones in Isabela itself, is a consistent, hollow wave – always worth a look. Jobo's is a long right breaking onto a sand-covered reef and it

TRAVEL INFORMATION

Local Population:
San Juan – 1.6M
Coastline: 501km (313mi)
Time: GMT-4h
Contest: Pro-Am
(early Jan, early Feb)

Getting There – Puerto Rico is the most accessible island in the Caribbean. Visas are not necessary for most visitors because it is an US territory. There are regular flights to San Juan from the US East Coast, London, Madrid and other Caribbean islands. It's also possible to fly from New York direct to Ramey Base. This will cut two hours of driving from San Juan.

Getting Around – Local airlines don't take surfboards. Rental cars cost around $30/d for the cheapest model and are often targeted by thieves. The traffic gets hectic and the roads are dangerous. Fuel is cheap at 30c/l. Use cheap 'publicos' (buses) for town to town travel.

Lodging and Food – The best surf season is also the main tourist season and this means higher prices. However, compared to other Caribbean islands, it is quite cheap. Quality accommodation options include La Cima in Isabella, ($60/d), Cielo Mar in Aguadilla, ($55/d), or Surf & Board Surfari in Rincon, ($45/sgle/d). A good meal can be had for $15.

Weather – Puerto Rico has an idyllic tropical climate, with winter highs of around 24°C (75°F) and night-time lows that never drop under 15°C (58°F) at the coast. It rains a lot, especially in the mountains and in Sept-Oct. On the coast there is no distinct wet and dry season. From June-Oct strong hurricanes occasionally hit the island and can cause considerable damage. Most of the time you will be fine surfing in board shorts, but a shorty may be needed for early, windy sessions.

Nature and Culture – Very American colonial feel to it, like Hawai'i. Great windsurfing and diving. On land there's the El Faro maritime museum or the Arecibo Observatory. San Juan is the second oldest city in the Americas - El Morro is the place to go if you want to check the historic old town. There's good hiking in the El Yunque rainforest national park. The nightlife is very lively.

Hazards and Hassles – Shallow reefs, urchins and some very crowded spots. Localism can be extreme. Car theft is a definite concern. Sewage can be serious around the major cities. There is a high crime rate and lots of guns.

Handy Hints – There are plenty of surf shops selling quality equipment cheaply. Try Ramey Surfzone, West Coast and Hot Wavz in Rincon. Wear sunblock in the water and mosquito repellent in the evenings.

WEATHER STATISTICS	J/F	M/A	M/J	J/A	S/O	N/D
total rainfall (mm)	65	75	132	137	150	127
consistency (days/mth)	13	10	13	16	15	16
min temp (°C/°F)	21/70	22/72	23/74	24/75	24/75	22/72
max temp (°C/°F)	28/82	29/84	31/88	31/88	31/88	30/86

Mike Trahan, Tres Palmas

works best on small swells. Shacks is considered a windsurfing spot because of the consistent cross-shore conditions, but on windless days it is a well-shaped reefbreak. Watch out for the jagged coral heads.

Close to the military base in Ramey, a popular break is Surfer's Beach, but the urchins, crowds and pollution may put you off. Table Top, next door is a heavy wave with dangerous rocks on the inside – experts only. Most spots around Aguadilla are only worth checking on big swells but under these conditions the waves get heavy and crowded. Wilderness lives up to its name with powerful waves under the right conditions. Gas Chambers and Crash Boat have been made famous through magazine photos, and they are incredible waves. Unfortunately they don't break that often.

North-west facing Aguada area offers consistent waves at spots like Table Rock – a long right barrel – or at the more consistent BCs in Aguada town. Punta Higuero is an average beachbreak (good for beginners) that was used as a world contest site in 1968. Rincon offers classic rights but you'll never surf here alone. Domes is the other

Cold fronts coming off the US East Coast send N swells down towards Puerto Rico. These give waves from 2-15ft (0.6-5m) on the north and north-western shores of the island, occasionally reaching 15-20ft (5-6.6m). The swells wrap onto the west coast giving clean, offshore conditions. Easterly wind swells and occasional hurricanes in the Caribbean will produce waves in other parts of the island but the NW tip is by far the most consistent. The wind blows predominantly from the E, varying from 46% of the time in Dec to 71% in July. A NE wind is the winter standard and SE is most common in the summer. The NE wind easily blows out the island's north shore, although not the west coast. Tidal ranges are minimal but will affect many of the shallowest reefs. Tide tables are available in surf shops.

SURF STATISTICS	J F	M A	M J	J A	S O	N D
dominant swell	N-NE	N-NE	N-NE	N-NE	N-NE	N-NE
swell size (ft)	4-5	3-4	2	1-2	4	4-5
consistency (%)	80	65	40	30	70	80
dominant wind	NE-E	NE-E	E-SE	NE-SE	NE-SE	NE-E
average force	F4	F4	F4	F4	F4	F4
consistency (%)	79	76	83	96	90	78
water temp (°C/°F)	25/77	26/79	27/81	28/82	28/82	26/79
wetsuit						

Wishing Well

prime break with perfect long rights and ideal wind/swell exposure. There are several other reefs around here that hold big swells. Tres Palmas is the best of the lot and can hold waves up to 20ft (6.6m). Finally, often worth checking out is Little Malibu, which has small, fast, tubey rights over a shallow, fire coral reef.

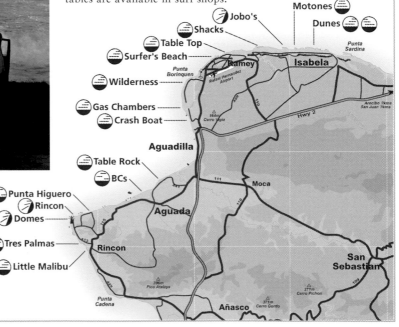

Motones
Dunes
Jobo's
Shacks
Punta Sardina
Table Top
Surfer's Beach
Ramey
Isabela
Punta Borinquen
Punta Hernandez Airport
Wilderness
Arecibo 7kms San Juan 7kms
Gas Chambers
164m Cerro Viela
Hwy 2
Crash Boat
Aguadilla
Table Rock
BCs
Moca
111
Punta Higuero
Aguada
Rincon
Domes
Tres Palmas
Rincon
110
San Sebastian
Little Malibu
110
Pico Atalaya
271m Cerro Pichon
Punta Cadena
198m
Cerro Gordo
Añasco

68. Grande Terre

Le Moule

PHILIPPE CHEVODIAN

Summary
+ SMALL, EASY WAVES
+ GOOD ALTERNATIVE WATER SPORTS
+ LAID BACK CARIBBEAN ATMOSPHERE

- SLOPPY ONSHORE WAVES
- SCHOOL CROWDS
- TOURIST DEVELOPMENT
- PRICEY

Tom Frager, La Chaise

FRÉDERIC LE LEANNEC

Together with Barbados, Guadeloupe is one of the east Caribbean's most consistent surf destinations. As well as regular trade wind swell it also receives N swell produced by cold fronts moving off the US East Coast in winter. However, Like Barbados the waves are often windy and rarely get bigger than 8ft (2.6m). French-governed Guadeloupe consists of two main islands joined in the middle, which viewed from above, reveal a butterfly shape. It is a 'département' of France, linked to the Paris government but retaining some regional autonomy. Compared to the rest of the Caribbean, thanks to the language, currency and French-influenced culture, Guadeloupe feels very much like the motherland, although it has its own unique 'Creole' style. Locals are generally proud to be both French and Guadeloupian.

Petite Havre

FRÉDERIC LE LEANNEC

Grande Terre has the majority of the surf spots while Basse Terre only gets surf from S and W hurricane swells. There are also the exposed islands of Marie Galante and La Désirade offshore, which have good potential for explorers.

Grande Terre consists of gently rolling scrubland and numerous

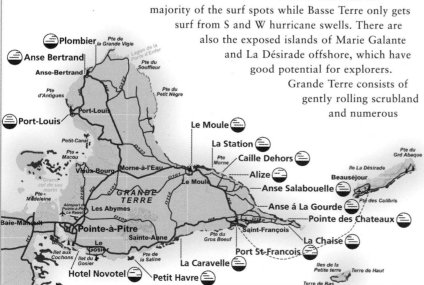

sugar cane fields. Le Moule, facing NE on the crescent-shaped coastline of Grande Terre, is the main surfers' hangout. It has the best exposure to swell and thus the most consistent waves. Normally this reef works as a 2-4ft (0.6-1.3m) onshore left with a juicy take-off right in front of the car park plus there is a rideable beachbreak nearby. Watch out for rocks and urchins when getting in and out of the water at Le Moule.

Heading south towards Anse Salabouelle is a set of dangerous reefs that include Caille Dehors and La Station. Alizé is an unchallenging, spot nearby. The peninsula around Pointe des Chateaux has reefs such as La Chaise and Anse à la Gourde providing meaty lefts when the swell gets big.

The southern shore is the most developed area of the coast, easily accessible from the capital Pointe-à-Pitre, but the surf spots are inconsistent and often onshore. Also, whenever they work, they attract crowds from the city. The coast from Saint-François to the fairly consistent and super-crowded peaks of Petit-Havre, has many easy surf spots. Heading back north from Le Moule towards Pointe de la Grande Vigie, there are a few spots but many are completely inaccessible due to high cliffs and a boat is the only way to reach them.

The last stretch of surfable coast faces north-west, which is almost always offshore but a moderate-sized

Anse Salabouelle

PHILIPPE CHEVODIAN

groundswell is needed to produce rideable waves. Port-Louis boasts the best wave on the island - a peak with long, mellow rights and a shorter left, but the swell needs plenty of size to get in here. Anse Bertrand is also a walled-up, easy right. The area conceals some excellent reefs like Plombier, Anse Laborde or Pointe d'Antigues, all of which break rarely and are for experts only.

The main swell season is from late October to March, with 2-10ft (0.6-3.3m) N-NE groundswells and consistent 2-5ft (0.6-1.6m) E wind swells. Onshore trade wind swell occurs year round but it will usually be small. Dominant E trades vary from 44% of the time in November to 70% in July. It tends to have a slightly more frequent NE pattern than SE, except during May-June and Sept-Oct. This is unfortunate as SE winds produce more offshores on Grande Terre. The hurricane season (June-Oct) offers a better chance to surf spots exposed to the Caribbean Sea, but at this time of year there is no regular groundswell. There is little tidal variation.

PHILIPPE CHEVODIAN

SURF STATISTICS	J F	M A	M J	J A	S O	N D
dominant swell	N-E	N-E	NE-SE	NE-SE	N-E	N-E
swell size (ft)	4	3	1-2	2	3-4	4
consistency (%)	70	60	40	40	60	70
dominant wind	NE-E	NE-E	NE-SE	NE-SE	NE-SE	NE-E
average force	F4	F4	F4	F4	F4	F4
consistency (%)	80	77	85	97	89	76
water temp (°C/°F)	25/77	25/77	27/81	28/82	28/82	26/79
wetsuit						

TRAVEL INFORMATION

Getting There – Visa: Same as France. Europeans can take a cheap charter flight from France. There are also flights from several American cities, Puerto Rico and nearby islands (LIAT). Ferries go here from Dominica (2hr) and Martinique (4hr).

Getting Around – There's a good public transport system but most spots require a rental car which is expensive ($40/d). The road system is well maintained but the east coast lacks paved roads. Driving can be a bit crazy - use the horn! Le Moule is the best place to base yourself.

Lodging and Food – Most of the hotels are on the south shore. If you can't stay in Le Moule, try St.-François. Renting a flat costs around ±$230/w and staying in a 2 star hotel is $40/dble. Creole cuisine is very tasty - try ti-punch, the local drink. A meal will cost around $15.

Weather – Like most tropical islands, the climate varies according to exposure to the trades. Grande Terre is the windward side of Guadeloupe, but being mainly flat it doesn't attract many rain squalls from out at sea. Most of the rain falls over the higher side, Basse Terre. The wettest season starts in June and sometimes lasts until December, with heaviest rains possible during the hurricane season of June-October. Temperatures remain around 26°C (79°F) all year with little variation.

Nature and Culture – Apart from visiting spice markets or sailing, Basse Terre offers enjoyable trekking around La Soufrière volcano. Diving is best at Îlets Pigeon, on the Caribbean side. There are mangrove swamps between the two islands.

Hazards and Hassles – Many of the spots break on limestone or coral, often in shallow water, so watch out for reef cuts. Some spots have many urchins. Avoid hurricane season because Guadeloupe is right in their paths and the surf is usually small at this time of year.

Handy Hints – Gear is expensive but available at Tong (Sainte-Anne). There is a surf school in Le Moule. There are lots of bodyboarders. The population is made up of local Guadeloupe and French expats. French is the official language though most locals speak Creole.

Local Population:
Pointe-à-Pitre – 145,000
Coastline: 260km (162mi)
Time: GMT-4hr
Contest: Local

WEATHER STATISTICS	J/F	M/A	M/J	J/A	S/O	N/D
total rainfall (mm)	75	95	152	197	245	175
consistency (days/mth)	13	11	14	17	18	17
min temp (°C/°F)	19/66	20/68	22/72	23/74	22/72	20/72
max temp (°C/°F)	28/82	29/84	30/86	31/88	31/88	30/86

69. Barbados

Summary
+ CONSISTENT SWELLS
+ FUN, PUNCHY WAVES
+ VARIETY OF SPOTS
+ PERFECT CLIMATE
+ CHILLED OUT ATMOSPHERE

– CONSTANT TRADE WINDS
– RARITY OF BIG SWELLS
– RELATIVELY EXPENSIVE
– AMERICAN MASS TOURISM

Wendell, Soup Bowls

ALL PHOTOS STEVE FITZPATRICK

Noah Snyder, Freights

Cattlewash

Barbados belongs to the Windward Islands, sitting east of the main Caribbean chain and about 350km (220mi) north-west of Venezuela. Famous for its holiday resorts, clear blue water and white sand beaches, it also has the eastern Caribbean's most consistent surf. Strong, constant trade winds make for consistent, year round swell on the east coast, while in winter, regular north swells light up the north and west coasts. Barbados offers some heavy waves but it is best suited to the surfer who enjoys chilling out on the beach and riding fun waves with an idyllic tropical backdrop. Most of the spots break onto flat coral reefs or beautiful sandy beaches.

TRAVEL INFORMATION

Local Population:
Barbados – 270,000
Bridgetown – 100,000
Coastline: 97km (60mi)
Time: GMT-4hr
Contest: Local

Getting There – Visas are not necessary but a return or onward ticket is essential to enter the country. From Europe, London is cheaper than other European cities. There are flights from most major cities in the USA. LIAT, the Caribbean airline, has connections between most of the islands. Departure tax is $12.50.

Getting Around – The bus service is very good and a much cheaper alternative to car rental. The big blue buses can carry boards but the smaller vans can't. Mini-mokes are the cheapest rental option at $35/d. Drive on the left.

Lodging and Food – Peak tourist season is from December-March and the price of decent accommodation can shoot up in these months. You should pay no more than $40/dble in a local guesthouse – ask at Smokey's or Bonito's Bar in Bathsheba. More upmarket places in Bathsheba include the Bajan Surf Bungalow

($60/dble), Atlantis ($45/dble) and the Edgewater ($95/dble). The food is great, with lots spice and plenty of fish. A meal usually costs less than $10 including beer or rum.

Weather – Barbados is blessed with a near perfect climate. The island receives 3000hrs of sunshine and up to 1m of rain a year and the constant trade winds help to keep the humidity and heat at bearable levels. The wettest season is from July-November when tropical fronts pass over the region. The wind is lightest at this time of year. February-May is the driest and windiest period. Hurricanes are not really a risk in Barbados - they tend to pass further to the north. In the water you will be fine in boardshorts and a rash vest for most of the year, although early morning sessions in the winter may call for a shorty.

Nature and Culture – Cruising around the island soaking up the scenery is an enjoyable way of filling a day. Stopping at small rum shops and village stores is the best way to meet the friendly local people. There is good diving and snorkelling on the west coast and windsurfing on the SE tip of the island. More organised

excursions like the Jolly Roger pirate ship or Sam Lord's coral castle can be fun but are usually packed with holidaymakers. For a good night out try either the Harbour Lights or Boatyards in town. In some night spots you pay a $15 cover charge after which all your drinks are free.

Hazards and Hassles – The onshore winds on the east coast are the biggest nightmare, even though they also provide extremely consistent waves. Take precautions against strong sun, mosquitoes and reef cuts. Popular surf spots get busy, but usually the atmosphere is cool as long as you're respectful. Drugs are frowned upon by the general community despite extensive use. Police will not hesitate to lock up tourists. Crack problems contradict the generally safe, easy-going reputation of the island, leading to robberies and occasionally violence.

Handy Hints – Surf gear is expensive so bring your own. Barbados line-ups are full of U.K. and east coast American surfers. Take a semi-gun for the bigger days in winter. Immigration will be particularly slow unless you have the name of a guesthouse or hotel where you are intending to stay.

WEATHER STATISTICS	J/F	M/A	M/J	J/A	S/O	N/D
total rainfall (mm)	47	34	85	147	174	150
consistency (days/mth)	10	8	12	17	15	15
min temp (°C/°F)	21/70	21/70	23/74	23/74	23/74	22/72
max temp (°C/°F)	28/82	30/86	31/88	31/88	31/88	29/84

Bathsheba, halfway up the east coast, is home to Soup Bowls, the island's most famous spot. It almost always has at least head-high surf, albeit often onshore. However, even when it's onshore, it's a powerful, hollow wave. With a couple of different take-off spots the crowds are fairly spread out, but the first peak is quite tight and gets busy. Respect the locals, who surf it extremely well and be careful of the rocks and urchins on the inside.

A 10 minute walk north is a mellow beachbreak called Sandbank - ideal for beginners. Just south of Soup Bowls is Parlors, similar to its famous neighbour, but with fewer crowds and a preference for bigger swells. Tent Bay, a powerful left, gets epic on a straight N swell. Conset Point is a rarely surfed mysto right needing a serious N swell to get classic. A particularly scenic spot nearby is Ragged Point – a fun, gentle beachbreak, best surfed from mid to high tide.

The south facing coastline only breaks on SE wind swells unless a hurricane is passing by. Long Beach is a dumpy, erratic beachbreak on the south-eastern side of the island, while South Point, Freights and Silver Sands work more consistently. They all show some good form, especially when the swell increases. South Point offers long lefts in front of the lighthouse, but at high tide gets a bad backwash. Close to Bridgetown is Brandons, which only works on big hurricane or wind swells.

The west coast only breaks on the biggest N swells so it's the least consistent part of the island but the E trade winds will provide the cleanest conditions. Sandy Lane, mid-way down the island, is a short, perfect left but it's either fantastic, or totally flat. Tropicana is a treacherous left for experts only. On the north-western tip of the island is Duppies, a consistent, powerful right that suffers from strong currents. Probably the best wave on the island after Soup Bowls, it is not for the faint hearted. It breaks some distance offshore, is reputed to be sharky, and the name refers to malevolent spirits and ghosts, so the vibe is heavy. If Duppies is closing out go to Maycocks nearby. It offers long, mushy, fun righthanders. Also check out the hard-to-reach North Point, and Morgan Lewis, which can be a good left pointbreak.

The best season for ground swells is from late October to March, when 2-12ft (0.6-4m) N-NE swells wrap around the north tip of the island to produce clean 1-10ft (0.3-3.3m) waves on the west coast and onshore 3-12ft (1-4m) waves on the east coast. The other main swell source is the E wind, which consistently kicks up 2-5ft (0.6-1.6m) swells. Sometimes they get big enough

to wrap onto the south coast where they clean up dramatically. This wind occurs year round so you're likely to find a rideable wave most days. Barbados is situated too far south to get hit by hurricanes, but their swell often reaches the east coast and when they're big can light up the southern tip as well. The prevailing wind comes from between the NE-SE for 50-70% of the time. NE is more common than SE, except in the summer months. Throughout the year, the mornings will often be glassy with residual wind swell offering superb conditions. Tidal variation is slight and has little effect on surf.

SURF STATISTICS	J F	M A	M J	J A	S O	N D
dominant swell	N-E	N-E	NE-SE	NE-SE	N-E	N-E
swell size (ft)	4-5	3-4	2-3	2-3	4	4-5
consistency (%)	80	70	50	50	70	80
dominant wind	NE-E	NE-E	NE-E	NE-E	NE-SE	NE-E
average force	F4	F4	F4	F4	F3-F4	F4
consistency (%)	93	91	92	86	92	86
water temp (°C/°F)	25/77	26/79	27/81	28/82	27/81	26/79
wetsuit						

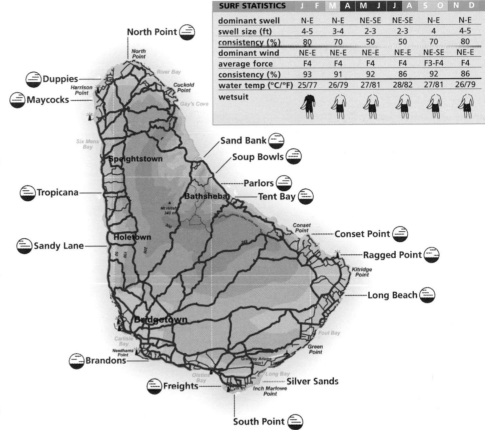

Parlors

South America

Meteorology and Oceanography

Following the trend set by the rest of the Americas, South America is also a clear case of split personality in terms of swell exposure. The Pacific coast from Ecuador to Peru and on to Chile is perfectly poised to soak up the best of the SW swells from the South Pacific surf factory. These low pressures trundle along a path from New Zealand to Cape Horn nearly all year round, marching out of the south-west onto the rocky shoreline of Pacific South America. These swells are helpfully guided by the Humboldt (or Peru) Current, which tends to drag more SW swells up the coast of Chile and into Peru. Some spots in Chile and Peru can be ridden every day, which is a rare privilege on Planet Surf's inconsistent shorelines. While Chile and most of Peru rely on generous SW swells, Northern Peru and Ecuador protrude enough to pick up the end of the wave train from the North Pacific Aleutian lows. These long-distance winter NW swells have to march for up to 10 days from their point of origin and consequently lose much in the way of height and power. Waves are seasonally erratic and water temps are balmy unless surfing the Galapagos Islands, where the end of the Humboldt Current deposits the coldest water found at equatorial latitudes. Central to Southern Peru, along with all of Chile, can get pounded by big waves through the southern hemisphere winter (April-Oct) and these swells don't necessarily stop in summer, rather they just decrease in frequency. Thousands of kilometres of desert fringe the coast where the constant S winds blow, bringing tailor-made offshores to the seemingly endless array of lefthand pointbreaks that nestle inside the protection of southern headlands. Northern Peru and Ecuador also feel the S wind but it's lighter and mornings can be windless.

The extensive Atacama Desert (the driest on earth) is sandwiched between the lofty peaks of the Andes to the east and the predictable massive upwelling that occurs off Southern Peru and Northern Chile. Compounded by the Humboldt Current, chilly year round water temps bring thick fog, yet a complete absence of rain in places. When the El Niño current crosses the Pacific, a warm layer of water can disturb the balance, causing chaos via heavy rain and mudslides in areas that usually receive no rain at all.

Tidal ranges never exceed 6ft (2m) on the Pacific coast, and semi-diurnal tides of even range are the rule of thumb.

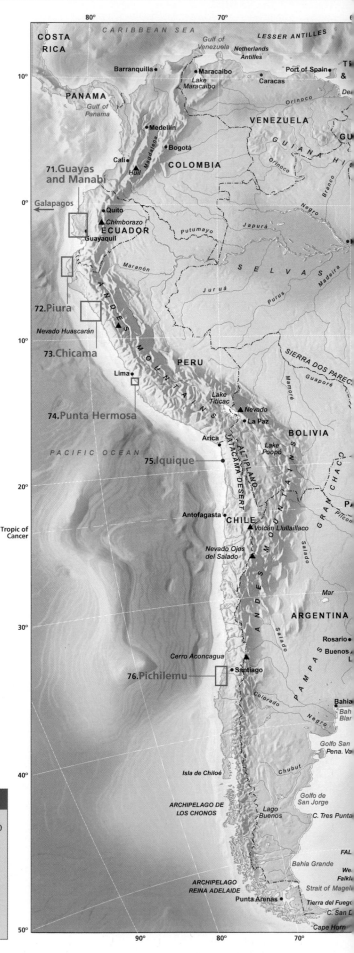

COUNTRY INFORMATION

	ECUADOR	PERU	CHILE	BRAZIL
Area (sq km/mi):	283,000/109,000	1,285,000/496,000	756,000/292,000	8,500,000/3,267,000
Population:	12,000,000	26,500,000	14,600,000	172M
Waveriders:	2,000	10,000	3,000	125,000
Tourists (per yr):	509,000	500,000	1,500,000	5.1M
Language:	Spanish, Quechua	Spanish, Quechua, Aymara	Spanish, Mapuche	Portuguese
Currency:	Sucre (Su)	New Sol (S)	Chilean Peso (Ch$)	Real
Exchange:	$1 = 25,000Su	$1 = 351S	$1 = 516Ch$	$1=2R$
GDP ($ per yr):	4,100	1,490	3,070	6,100
Inflation (%):	25	12	8	16

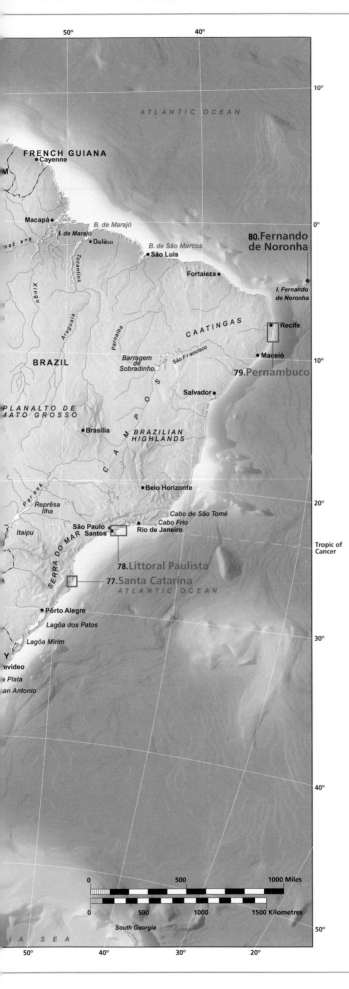

Across the continent, South America suffers the fate of most east facing coasts, namely a lack of decent groundswells. Most South Atlantic lows quickly travel eastward to Africa, sending out W and NW swell, but very little due N. This is compounded by the fact that the South Atlantic is the only ocean within tropical latitudes that does not receive any tropical storm action. The third detracting factor is the extensive continental shelf that robs the waves of height and power.

South America's east coast rarely gets epic big swells but its saving grace is the consistent and favourable windswell. Most of the surf in Argentina and Uruguay is too cold in winter and too small in summer but there are some classic days in between. Brazil accounts for the bulk of the eastern seaboard and not surprisingly gets the lion's share of consistently small onshore surf conditions. The southern surf regions from Rio Grande do Sul to Florianopolis provide the best chance of size from the southern hemisphere winter lows, which will send in S to SE swells. Rio de Janeiro also has S-SE facing shores, picking up winter swells or the windswell whipped up by the constant E seabreezes. Further north, the tropical part of Brazil gets SE trades in winter, producing windswell mush but very little to surf in summer. South America is almost devoid of islands, but Fernando do Noronha is a notable exception. This volcanic mountain rises from the ocean floor just south of the equator, and the waves have a similar power and pedigree to other volcanic islands in the Atlantic. Winter North Atlantic swells have Fernando do Noronha in their sights so the question must be asked if the NE facing coast of Brazil may conceal some classic, clean waves.

Currents are uninteresting on this side of South America although it is one of the few east facing coasts that provides a large area of coastal upwelling off Argentina's famous Patagonia coast. This area also experiences massive tidal range as does the NE equatorial coast of Brazil especially around the mouth of the Amazon.

Air and Water Temperatures

January

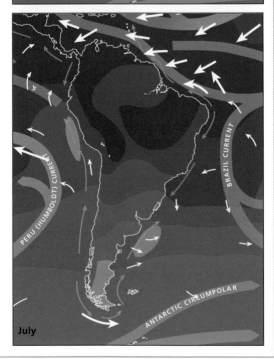

July

GALAPAGOS ISLANDS

70. San Cristóbal and Santa Cruz

El Canyon

Summary
+ POWERFUL REEFBREAKS
+ WAVES YEAR ROUND
+ UNCROWDED
+ WILDLIFE MECCA
+ RELATIVELY CHEAP

− INCONSISTENT
− COOL WATER
− FEW SPOTS
− TOUGH ACCESS

ALL PHOTOS MEZ/ESM

It was through observing the unique and diverse wildlife of the Galapagos Islands that led Charles Darwin to come up with the theory of evolution. These 17 isolated, oceanic oases have been declared a national park and even today, only 5 of the islands are inhabited. The archipelago is the result of fairly recent volcanic surges from the sea floor that remain very active, particularly Isabela Island. The coastal fringe is made up of lava reefs and boulders because the water is too cold for coral formation. The islands don't have that many good spots although further exploration may reveal more. Most of the reefs are sharp and the very clear water

Charlie Kühn, El Canyon

makes it hard to figure out exactly how deep it is. The water is actually the coldest equatorial water on earth, due to the Humboldt Current working its way up the coastline of South America and past the islands, bringing with it water from Antarctica. This water is nutrient rich, explaining the attraction for the prolific marine wildlife.

El Canyon

TRAVEL INFORMATION

Local Population:
Galapagos – 9,000
San Cristóbal – 2,500
Coastline: San Cristóbal – 127km (80mi)
Time: GMT-6hr
Contest: National

Getting There – No visa is required for most nationalities. Fly to mainland Ecuador first, either Quito or Quayaquil. There's only one flight daily direct to San Cristóbal with San/Saeta ($300-$350/rtn) or you can fly to Baltra/Santa Cruz with Tame. Flights are frequently full especially during peak season (Dec-Feb, July-Sept). Book early!

Getting Around – Unless you stay on a surf charter boat, hopping between islands involves the use of ferries. If you land in Baltra, you'll need to take a combination of buses and ferries to get to Puerto Ayora, then a ferry to Baquerizo. To get to most spots, you'll have to walk or take a taxi. Be careful of the sun, it's

strong and shade is rare, people have died getting lost!

Lodging and Food – Unless you stay on a boat, you have a choice of around 8-10 options in Baquerizo. The best hotel is Orca with AC ($30/d+breakfast). Or Cabanas Don Jorge, out of town, from $15/d. Food is generally fish & rice. Veggies and beers are expensive.

Weather – Despite its equatorial position, the Galapagos enjoys a relatively dry climate. The dry season, called 'garua', causes low clouds and drizzle from May to Dec but virtually no substantial rain. This is supposedly the cold season with constant SE winds. The water sometimes drops down to 18°C (64°F), due to the cold Humboldt Current, so a light steamer is needed at this time. Jan to May gets hotter and wetter, topping out at 23°-24°C (73°-75F), with lighter SE winds, so a springsuit should suffice. El Niño years are much warmer and wetter.

Nature and Culture – The Galapagos are a World Heritage Site due to the amazing wildlife, which shows little fear of people. From midnight to 6am all electricity is switched off - don't expect any nightlife.

Hazards and Hassles – In the case of an emergency, adequate hospitals are far away. Most lava reefs are shallow and the rocks have sharp edges. Sharks and male sea lions are swimming around but shouldn't pose a problem. There are a few cool locals (visit the Genoa Bar). Lack of shade leads to sunburn.

Handy Hints – Bring everything you may need with you. A couple of boards (a semi-gun may be needed), leashes, fullsuit and springsuit, booties, hats, sunscreen, insect repellent, flashlight and a conservationist attitude, because the Galapagos are a very special place. The National Park entry fee is $100, payable in cash at the airport. Credit cards are of little use.

WEATHER STATISTICS	J/F	M/A	M/J	J/A	S/O	N/D
total rainfall (mm)	57	60	9	4	7	6
consistency (days/mth)	7	4	2	3	6	8
min temp (°C/°F)	23/74	23/74	21/70	19/66	18/64	20/68
max temp (°C/°F)	30/86	30/86	28/82	25/77	25/77	27/80

The predominant S-SE trade winds mean that the most consistent, good quality spots are to be found on the north facing shores. Puerto Baquerizo (also named Wreck Bay), is the administrative capital of the islands, has the greatest concentration of decent surf spots in the Galapagos. It is also the second marine base of the Ecuadorian Navy and has the bulk of the island's accommodation. Carola is by far the most consistent wave, a right in front of the lighthouse. It's a long, tubular wave, rideable from 6-12ft+ (2-4m+) breaking on a lava rock reef close to shore and surrounded by dream scenery. To surf El Canyon, you have to enter a military zone, which is tolerated - so far! It is a left that breaks close to shore when small but holds waves up to 8-10ft (2.6-3.3m) on SW swells. Pay heed to the sets while getting in and out.

Charlie Kuhn, Puerto Baquerizo

Todd Holland, Loberia

Loberia is another good left and right but the problem here is the density of male sea lions that can get aggressive if you get too close to the females and pups. Seal bites are more of a threat than sharks, especially during mating season. Loberia also has a few nasty rocks sticking up out of the line-up. Tongo Reef is an excellent right; a 10 minute walk from El Canyon, but don't try to get there through the airport as it's forbidden! To reach Punta Pitt you need a boat. On the whole, the easiest way to surf the Galapagos is on a yacht charter, although recent park regulations may have made this impossible. The situation changes regularly, so try to find out the latest before departure.

Baltra Island is the main tourist hub, where there are two good spots near the airport. The main break is Seymour Norte, a top quality, long, right pointbreak. However, surfing has recently been banned because ecotourists have claimed that surfers cause visual contamination!

Busy Santa Cruz Island has big wave potential at Palmas Grandes, which is best on a south swell, and Cerro Gallina, a deep water spot more suitable for beginners.

The good news about being located right on the Equator is that the islands receive the cleanest swells from both N and S, but the bad news is that these swells are generated more than 5,000km (3,000mi) away and tend to be small and inconsistent. Small N and S swells can sometimes coincide and neutralise themselves! SW and NW swells are the most frequent, throwing up waves in the 2-8ft (0.6-2.6m) range, however, 12-15ft (4-5m) waves have been ridden. During May to Dec, SW swells are more consistent but it's colder (18°-20°C/64°-68°F) and windier (15 knots). Trade winds are from the SE but not too strong and, from Jan to April are lighter still, making this period the best call. Be aware of the tides, they vary from 3-8ft (1-2.6m), which can make for a difficult time at certain spots, especially on small to medium sized days when rocks can suddenly pop out of the water.

SURF STATISTICS	J F	M A	M J	J A	S O	N D
dominant swell	NW	NW	S-SW	S-SW	S-SW	NW
swell size (ft)	4	3-4	4	4-5	4	3-4
consistency (%)	60	50	60	70	60	50
dominant wind	SE-S	E-S	SE-S	SE-S	SE-S	SE-S
average force	F3	F3	F3	F3	F3	F3
consistency (%)	78	77	88	92	90	93
water temp (°C)	23/74	24/75	22/72	21/70	20/68	21/70
wetsuit						

Puerto Baquerizo

71. Guayas and Manabi

Montañita

GEOFF RAGATZ

Summary
+ TWO SURF SEASONS
+ CLEAN WARM WATER WAVES
+ CALM WINDS
+ TRIPS TO THE ANDES
+ VERY CHEAP

– LACK OF HEAVY WAVES
– SOME CROWDS
– RAINY WINTER SEASON
– PETTY THEFTS IN THE CITIES

Ecuador is small country that recieves plenty of small swells which is really unfortunate because there are many spots that only light up with a big swell. It's not all bad news though, because whereas most of the Pacific coast of South America is influenced by the cold Humbolt Current, Ecuador's waters are warmed by the Panama Current. Waves come from long distance swells, generated either to the south or the north and swells tend to roll in with moderate power and break onto forgiving reefs. There are many potential spots to the north of Salinas which are better exposed to N swells, but most of them only get good when it reaches double overhead. Spots to the south of Salinas, towards Playas, only break on S-SW swells. The coastline of Ecuador is made up primarily of an alluvial plain, irrigated by 2 major rivers, the Esmeraldas and Guayas.

The Guayas surf zone centres on several long, sectiony rights breaking over sand between Posorja and Playas. These include

GEOFF RAGATZ

Montañita

FRÉDÉRIC LE LEANNEC

Humboldt, Chabelas, Olas Verdes and Shark Bay, culminating in La Posada, the longest wave in Ecuador. Usually better, however, are the powerful, long rights of El Pelado which need a good swell to work, but not at high tide, as it breaks too close to the rocks to surf. Engabao is by far the most consistent break on the south shore with punchy, performance orientated small waves. Salinas is a

TRAVEL INFORMATION

Local Population:
Guayaquil – 150,000
Coastline: 2,237km (1,400mi)
Time: GMT-5hr
Contest: Int'l (Feb)

Getting There – No visa needed for most nationalities. It is cheaper to fly to Lima and take a connecting flight or a 24hr bus ride. If you do fly directly to Ecuador, then you will arrive in Quito, which is 11 hours by bus from Montañita, some airlines will take you to Guayaquil, 3hrs from Montañita.

Getting Around – National airlines, (San/Saeta, Tame) have cheap internal flights. Travelling by bus is very cheap. From Montañita there are plenty of 'chivas', (local public transport), that go to Manta, Salinas and Guayaquil; boards will travel on the roof or in the boot.

Lodging and Food – The hotel Baja Montañita is the best place to stay in the town, right in front of the peak ($15/dble). There is plenty of cheap accomodation, (Mitad del Mundo, Pelicano) and smaller villages will be cheaper ($5/dble). For upmarket accommodation stay at the Hotel Salinas or at the Imperial in Manta. Basic food costs are cheap, no more than $5 a meal. Try the 'ceviche' (raw fish).

Weather – As the name suggests, Ecuador has an equatorial climate, but the Andes have a big effect on the climate. The rainy season lasts from Jan-March. The north end of the country is hotter and wetter than the south. The 5-6000m snow-capped Andes see about 2500mm of precipitation a year. The mountain foothills and Quito have an eternal springtime climate that is fairly warm and dry. The Amazon Basin is constantly hot and sticky.

Nature and Culture – The rather dull coastline is best around Caraquez or Atacames. A visit to the high Sierras and the fabulous Andes Mountains is a must. Quito is a great place to hangout, whilst Otavalo, Banos and Vilcabamba are all unique places.

Hazards and Hassles – Dysentery, Hepatitis A and Cholera are all concerns. Only drink mineral water and be careful of what you eat. Malaria is a problem in Esmeraldas and in 'El Oriente' (The Amazon). Mosquitoes are abundant everywhere in the rainy season. Foreigners are targeted by pickpockets in the cities.

Handy Hints – There are no surf shops except Guayaquil in Manta. Bring your standard beachbreak board and a lycra vest. Faro is the cheapest place on earth to buy balsa wood boards. Crowds are only a problem near the cities and Montañita. Due to high inflation, change only a small amount of money at a time.

WEATHER STATISTICS	J/F	M/A	M/J	J/A	S/O	N/D
total rainfall (mm)	244	196	18	18	2	27
consistency (days/mth)	16	15	3	1	1	27
min temp (°C/°F)	21/70	22/72	20/68	18/64	19/66	20/68
max temp (°C/°F)	31/88	32/90	31/88	29/84	31/88	31/88

Salinas

busy, tourist peninsula that catches both N and S swells. Unfortunately most breaks are located in a military zone that requires a permit to enter - the Costa Surf Club may be able to help you get a ride in with someone who has a permit. FAE is a consistent left that needs perfect wind and swell direction to be classic, otherwise it's just a fun, workable wave. Close by is Chocolatera, a good but fickle right. La Bahia is well exposed with a great left by the rocks but again you will have to wait for the ideal conditions. There are a few other breaks north of Salinas that catch reasonable sized N swells. Punta Chulluype is the main spot with good potential but don't surf it at low tide as it's too shallow. Most of the breaks up towards Montañita have a really low consistency. Montañita itself is Ecuador's main surf break and is identified by a phallic shaped rock. It catches any N and S swells, holding up to 10ft (3.3m) sets and it's a juicy right even when it's only 2ft (0.6m). This world class wave is usually crowded and has become something of a surf centre where it's possible to get cheap, decent accommodation. If you get bored of Montañita's rights, then just to the north, inside Manabi Province, is Rio Chico where long, consistent, uncrowded lefts wrap into the rivermouth. The wave breaks in the property of a hotel, for which you must pay a fee to enter. Punta Mala, north of Salango, can only be reached by boat. The left you'll find there is worth the ride, as is the scenery. Puerto Cayo is considered the best beachbreak to head to on a medium sized swell although access is tough. San Mateo is a dreary fishing village with a remote but

classy left that breaks only around 10 times a season. It's sharky and fairly well-known by waveriders from Manta. Ecuador's surf city is Manta, full of bodyboarders who bust out some big moves on the hollow waves of Murcielago beachbreak.

E cuador is another one of those lucky countries that ís exposed to both North and South Pacific swells. N swells born in the Aleutians will take 5-7 days to reach Ecuador with plenty of decay in size. The prime surf season is from Nov to March with glassy conditions or light, onshore sea breezes. However it does rain a lot at this time of year. It will rarely be flat through this season, with many days in the 2-6ft (0.6-2m) range with occasional 8-10ft (2.6-3.3m) swells that will light up all the spots. SW swells in the southern hemisphere winter are consistent, but this is the time of the trade winds that make a mess of the surf, and it is also colder. S-SW is the main wind direction, which varies from 53% of the time in March to 87% in July-Nov, while the rainy season brings a period of calmer winds. Overall the wind patterns are good for the N swells. Most surf spots are not very tide sensitive but tide tables are non-existent for those that are.

SURF STATISTICS	J F	M A	M J	J A	S O	N D
dominant swell	NW	NW	S-SW	S-SW	S-SW	NW
swell size (ft)	4	3	3-4	4	3-4	3-4
consistency (%)	70	60	60	70	60	70
dominant wind	S-SW	S-SW	S-SW	S-SW	S-SW	S-SW
average force	F3	F3	F3	F3	F3	F3
consistency (%)	68	58	82	87	86	86
water temp (°C/°F)	24/75	24/75	22/72	21/70	22/72	23/74
wetsuit						

72. Piura

David Fioranni, Cabo Blanco

JAVIER FERNANDEZ

Summary

+ GREAT LEFTS, WITH GOOD WINDS
+ WARM WATER, PLENTY OF SUN
+ CLOSE TO S SWELL EXPOSURE
+ CHEAP

− SHORT SWELL SEASON
− FAIRLY INCONSISTENT
− BASIC LODGING AND FOOD

Most of the Peruvian coastline is chilled by the Humboldt Current and rocked by S swells, but the north-west corner of the country is an area that enjoys very different conditions. The waters in the north part of the Piura Province are warmed up by the southern extremity of the Panama Current. The swell pattern is also different on this stretch of Peru's coast as it favours swells coming out of the North Pacific. However it's not as consistent as the rest of Peru and is only worth visiting in the middle of the northern hemisphere winter.

At this time of year it can get quite busy with surfers from Lima coming up for Christmas. If it does go flat here, then it's only a short distance to the beaches exposed to the more consistent S swells.

Máncora, is a small fishing village with a gentle left pointbreak that has nice walls and, depending on how much

STEVE FITZPATRICK

Felipe Bernales, Organos

JAVIER FERNANDEZ

sand is covering the rocks, a few tube sections. It's generally a mellow wave that is consistent and busy. If Máncora is small, a walk of about 15 minutes to the north will reveal Punta Ballenas, a sandy, left point that picks up more swell - it's usually a messy, sectiony wave but it's fun. Los Organos is a beach resort whose rocky headland produces a fun left wrapping onto a rock ledge

TRAVEL INFORMATION

Local Population:
Talara – 90,000
Coastline: 2,414km (1,508mi)
Time: GMT-5hr
Contest: National

Getting There – Citizens of NZ and Spain need visas. There are plenty of international flights to/from Lima Airport. Flying from Lima to Talara/Tumbes costs around ±$100 with Aeroperu, the bus will cost you only $10, but the journey takes 22hrs. Another option is flying to Guayaquil in Ecuador and then taking a 6hr bus ride over the border (occasionally disputed).

Getting Around – Buses are cheap (from $0.50), reliable and plentiful - boards also present no problem. Hiring a 'collectivo' is a possibility if there's a group of you and you want to get to somewhere a little more remote. A travel pass is a good investment for

those intending to spend a long time in Peru. Talara is 60km (40mi) from Máncora.

Lodging and Food – Many surfers stay at 'Crillon', a rough pension in Máncora for $2/d but there are many small resorts springing up like the Máncora Beach Bungalows ($15/d). Talara has the best range of accommodation. There is lots of very cheap seafood (ceviche), fish & rice costs about $2.

Weather – Peru's semi-arid climate is ideal for travelling - it hardly ever rains, daily variations are minimal, temps are never too hot or too cold (except, maybe in deepest winter). This doesn't mean unbroken sunshine. The big difference between land and sea temps brings a near constant mist, called 'garua', which occurs regularly except from Dec-March. Most of the year is hot and sticky with plenty of sunshine. Wind patterns are light. You will only need

boardshorts and a vest for most of the spots but around Lobitos/Talara a light fullsuit is the go.

Nature and Culture – Much of coastal Peru is desert - a trip to the Inca ruins of Cajamarca is cool but it's a long journey. If you're into big game fishing, the ocean is full of big fish and is renowned for giant swordfish. During El Niño years all the fish vanish.

Hazards and Hassles – Be careful in popular tourist areas, as pickpockets are rife in such places. Eat only well cooked or boiled food.

Handy Hints – While Lima has some good shapers, there is little available in the Máncora area. This area is easily combined with a trip to Ecuador. Basic Spanish is essential if you're travelling here without a guide.

WEATHER STATISTICS	J/F	M/A	M/J	J/A	S/O	N/D
total rainfall (mm)	3	4	0	0	0	1
consistency (days/mth)	0	0	0	0	0	0
min temp (°C/°F)	23/74	23/74	21/70	20/68	20/68	21/70
max temp (°C/°F)	30/86	31/88	30/86	28/82	29/84	29/84

STEVE FITZPATRICK

Máncora

that's better at low tide. El Nuro is another left, 9km (6mi) to the south (you need a 4WD), facing a tiny fishing village, which with a bit of N swell can be a fun, high performance wave.

On a big N swell, world class Cabo Blanco will wake up. This is where Ernest Hemingway is supposed to have found the inspiration to write the novel "The Old Man and The Sea". It's an excellent barrelling sand point that breaks in front of rocks with plenty of fast tubes. The take-offs are usually late and you need to constantly fight the rip. Unfortunately it is a crowded wave and the atmosphere can become aggressive. It's also a challenging barrel that's for experts only. It's probably best not to stay in the village as the local fishermen hate surfers. This is due to the proposed building of a jetty being dropped after a group of surfers successfully protested against the plan. South of the village is another challenging left called Punta Panico. If Cabo Blanco is crowded, check other spots to the south, like Cabo Blanquillo or Punta Restin, both of which are classic lefts. You'll find the Panama Current's influence waning down here and the water will be 2°-3°C (5°-7°F) colder than in Máncora.

Lobitos, on the way to Talara is another barrelling left, breaking over sharp rocks. Water temps drop drastically in Talara – the water can be 2°C (5°F) colder on the south side of town than on the north. It rarely breaks, but when it does, Punta Lobo is a quality left point, as are Punta Arena and Negritos, best at low tide with a moderate swell.

The swells which hit NW Peru come from the North Pacific, being the same swells that pound Oahu's North Shore five or six days earlier. Only the heart of the season (Nov-Feb) will see reliable 2-8ft (0.6-2.6m) conditions. Being long distance swells, the waves will be perfectly lined up with long lulls between sets. If it's flat here then it's only a short drive to the south-westerly facing coastline beyond Bayovar and the consistent S swells. Winds are invariably from the S-SW, S is straight offshore for most of the left points and afternoons see a light SW sea breeze that can have a slight effect on the quality of some of the more exposed spots. Although the winds are light year round, they are lighter still in the prime swell season. Tidal ranges are up to 6ft (2m) with most spots breaking better at low tide.

SURF STATISTICS	J F	M A	M J	J A	S O	N D
dominant swell	NW	NW	–	–	NW	NW
swell size (ft)	4	3	1-2	1	1-2	3-4
consistency (%)	70	50	20	10	20	60
dominant wind	S-SW	S-SW	S-SW	S-SW	S-SW	S-SW
average force	F3	F2-F3	F3	F3	F3-F4	F3-F4
consistency (%)	66	58	82	86	86	86
water temp (°C/°F)	24/75	25/77	23/74	22/72	21/70	22/72
wetsuit						

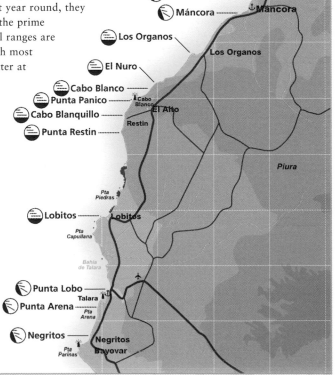

Pta Sal

Punta Ballenas
Máncora — Máncora
Los Organos
Los Organos
El Nuro
Cabo Blanco
Punta Panico
Cabo Blanco
El Alto
Cabo Blanquillo
Restin
Punta Restin

Piura

Pta Piedras

Lobitos
Lobitos
Pta Capullana

Bahia de Talara

Punta Lobo
Talara
Punta Arena
Pta Arena

Negritos
Pta Parinas
Negritos
Bayovar

JAVIER FERNANDEZ

Lobitos

73. Chicama

Chicama – the longest left in the world

JAVIER FERNANDEZ

Summary

+ PERFECT UNCROWDED LEFTHAND POINTBREAKS
+ EXCELLENT WIND PATTERNS
+ CHEAP LIVING COSTS
+ HISTORICAL SITES
+ CLOSE TO THE ANDES

– DULL COASTAL SCENERY
– CHILLY WATER
– PETTY THEFTS IN THE CITIES
– DIFFICULT, TEDIOUS ACCESS

In this crowded surf world, it is almost unbelievable to think that the longest left pointbreak on earth is reeling along right now with nobody surfing it. The reasons why nobody bothers with it are not entirely clear. It breaks mainly on sand, is relatively gentle, is very consistent and is surrounded by a bunch of other super long, quality waves. It is also consistently offshore. This utopian wave is Chicama, but amazingly, there's more to this part of Peru than just Chicama's endless walls.

To the north of Chicama is Puerto Eten, which can be found to the west of Chiclayo – it's a left and right peak, breaking over some dangerous rocks. Next is Pacasmayo, the first of many endless lefts, that catches loads of swell and peels forever. Chicama is to be found halfway between Lima and the border of Ecuador. Obviously there are some bad things about this place and they are the reasons why it has remained empty.

Tortora Reed Caballitos

JAVIER FERNANDEZ

Cesar Aspillaga, Puemape

JAVIER FERNANDEZ

The landscape around Chicama is extremely dull, the water quite cold and there's nowhere decent to stay, but this is not enough of a reason to fully explain its unpopularity. One of the main contributing reasons is the lack of media exposure, thanks to consistently bad light making inviting looking line-up shots very rare. This is a contradiction though – when you ask any surf traveller

TRAVEL INFORMATION

Local Population: Trujillo – 800,000
Coastline: 2,414km (1,500mi)
Time: GMT-5hr
Contest: National (May)

Getting There – Citizens of NZ and Spain need visas. Lima Airport has plenty of international flights. Flying from Lima to Trujillo (the nearest big centre) costs ±$50/o-w with Aeroperu, or there is a 9hr overnight bus trip for only $3/o-w. Stop at Paijan for Malabrigo/Chicama. Chiclayo is 4hrs away. Departure tax is $18.

Getting Around – Bus is the best way to get around. They're cheap, regular and surfboards don't present a problem. Journeys can be very long and tiring. If you travel in a group it may be worth hiring a 'collectivo' (minibus).

Lodging and Food – A cheap and popular pension in Chicama is El Hombre which costs $5/d. Another good option is the Huanchaco Hostel, facing a consistent left point. Seafood is excellent value at around $2 a meal.

Weather – Peru's semi-arid climate is ideal for travelling. Temps are never too hot or too cold, (except maybe in deep winter), and it hardly ever rains. This doesn't mean constant sunshine, the differences between land and sea temps creates a near permanent mist, which is depressing when combined with the bleak countryside. Dec-March is about the only time that you can expect clear skies. Do not visit this area during El Niño years. The water may be warmer but it will rain all day, every day, bridges and roads will be washed away and the water will turn a muddy brown. You'll require a 3/2 steamer from May-Nov and a springsuit the rest of the time.

Nature and Culture – The Huanchaco Festival with the 'Caballitos de Tortora' and some surf contests take place in May. Close by are the remains of Chan-Chan, an old Moche Indian site. For hiking and climbing, go to Huaraz, home of the famous Cordillera Blanca, a 6000m high mountain.

Hazards and Hassles – There aren't many hazards to be aware of. Petty thefts, especially on crowded buses are very common. Eat only boiled and cooked food.

Handy Hints – In Lima there are surf shops and good shapers, but there's nothing available around Chicama. Take booties for hopping over rocks, a light fullsuit and an everyday board. A longboard would be ideal for some of the long, slow waves. Basic Spanish is essential for independent travellers.

WEATHER STATISTICS	J/F	M/A	M/J	J/A	S/O	N/D
total rainfall (mm)	3	4	0	0	0	1
consistency (days/mth)	0	0	0	0	0	0
min temp (°C/°F)	21/70	20/68	18/64	16/61	16/61	17/62
max temp (°C/°F)	29/84	29/84	25/77	22/72	23/74	25/77

Walking back to the take-off, Chicama

JAVIER FERNANDEZ

Puemape, which catches more swell and also peels forever. This is also true of Punta Prieta, south of Chicama.

Another place worth checking out is Punta Huanchaco, home of the tortora reed caballito riders, maybe the world's first surfers. Fishermen have been riding the lefts back to shore at this spot since 2400BC. For today's surfer it offers easy and super consistent waves. Huanchaco is the only place around here with a bit of life and even some greenery. If Huanchaco gets big, the best bet is to either head back to Chicama or go to Salaverry Harbour, where between the jetties an A-frame peak breaks that holds big waves and has a handy channel on either side of it. None of these spots get N swells. The Bayovar Peninsula does though, and is also home to another perfect left pointbreak. If this doesn't appeal then further north are the warmer waters and N swells of the Máncora region.

where the longest wave in the world is, the answer is invariably Chicama. Whatever the reason, it doesn't alter the fact that the length of the ride can be truly amazing. The actual distance between the take-off point and the fishing jetty where the wave ends is 4km (2.5mi), although to be fair no one has actually ridden it for that distance. On good days most people end up catching 3-5 different waves on a journey down the point. It would be a rare day when it becomes necessary to paddle back to the line-up. It is far easier to keep surfing waves down the length of the point, get out and then walk back up to the take-off zone. The wave could happily handle a crowd of 100 surfers, but it would be unusual to see 10 or 20 out here at any time. Unbelievably, surfers get bored of this endless left and normally head north to

Regular 4-12ft (1-4m) S-SW swells come from lows deep down in the southern hemisphere. Due to the temperature differences between the cold water and hot land, the wind blows continually, dead S for 40-55% of the time and an even better SE for 30-45% of the time. This is offshore in the NW facing bays, where most of the lefthand points are located. A morning SE wind will turn more to the S in the afternoons. Tidal ranges are small.

SURF STATISTICS	J F	M A	M J	J A	S O	N D
dominant swell	S-SW	S-SW	S-SW	S-SW	S-SW	S-SW
swell size (ft)	2-3	3	4	4-5	4	2-3
consistency (%)	60	70	80	80	70	50
dominant wind	SE-S	SE-S	SE-S	SE-S	SE-S	SE-S
average force	F3	F3	F3	F3	F3	F3
consistency (%)	88	90	89	88	87	88
water temp (°C/°F)	21/70	21/70	18/64	17/62	17/62	18/64
wetsuit						

Punta Huanchaco

FRÉDÉERIC LE LEANNEC

74. Punta Hermosa

ALL PHOTOS JAVIER FERNANDEZ

Sandro Pestana, Pico Alto

Summary

+ CONSISTENT SWELLS
+ GREAT DENSITY OF SPOTS
+ BIG WAVE POTENTIAL
+ CHEAP AND EASY LIVING
+ PERUVIAN CULTURE

– LACK OF PERFECT CONDITIONS
– COLD WATER
– COASTAL FOG
– BARREN COASTLINE
– WEEKEND CROWDS

Peru has one of the oldest surf cultures in the world with totora reed horses (see caballitos – previous zone) being ridden since 2400BC. Surfing in Peru had its resurgence and redevelopment a little later than in Hawai'i. Peru was host to the World Championships in 1965 and the world was awoken to the potential of one of the most ancient of surfing countries. Since then, local guys like Felipe Pomar and Carlos Dogny have pushed Peruvian surfing further than it's been taken in almost every other developing country. The capital, Lima, sits on the shores of the Pacific and has become Peru's surf city. There are good waves in the districts of both Miraflores and neighbouring Costa Verde, where the world class Herradura left point can go off. However, due to both crowds and pollution most travellers prefer to keep away from the

Magoo de la Rosa

San Bartolo

city, and instead head 1hr drive to the north, to the Punta Hermosa area. This is a great area for a surfer to find himself in, as there are ample consistent spots within walking distance of each other. In the southern hemisphere winter, the waves around Punta Hermosa are typically big, mushy rights, with a lack of shape that can be ideal for longboarding. While a lot of the headlands favour the rights, there are also hollow lefts, plus a few offshore bomboras that handle serious size and power.

Starting in the north of this zone, you will find Pulpos, a beachbreak that usually closes-out and is rarely worth

TRAVEL INFORMATION

Local Population:
Lima – 7M
Coastline: 2,414km,
(1,510mi)
Time: GMT-5hr
Contests: WQS (May)
National

Getting There – (See 72. Piura). Punta Hermosa is only ±45mins away from Lima by taxi, and there are buses. Lima has a high crime rate - take care. Basic Spanish is essential for independent travel. Dep. tax is $18.

Getting Around – (See 72. Piura)

Lodging and Food – There are places to stay nearly everywhere (try Magoo's El Coco Pension at $15/dble and Pico Alto Surfcamp), with several

cheap lodging possibilities in Punta Hermosa or San Bartolo. Food is cheap; especially fast food (bembos) and the local seafood (ceviche) should be tasted. The local beers are good.

Weather – (See 72. Piura) The Andes often has superb visibility. The garua sea mist makes thick, damp clouds that make everything look depressing. A light fullsuit is needed from May-Nov and a springsuit for the rest of the year. Avoid El Niño years because it never seems to stop raining.

Nature and Culture – It's a cool place to hang out, with plenty of nightlife and some interesting wildlife. Take some time out from the surf and take a flight over the mysterious

Nazca lines. The cemeteries in Arequipa are worth a visit, as is the stunning Macchu Picchu site high in the Andes.

Hazards and Hassles – Buses are safe to use. There is the hassle of kids using razor blades to steal things from pockets or backpacks. Be especially vigilant in the popular tourist areas of the bigger towns.

Handy Hints – Lima has some very good board shapers (try Wayo Whilar). A new board costs about $200, a gun $250. Take booties for protection from urchins and rocks and a light fullsuit (Boz is a good local wetsuit brand). Try to combine this trip with a visit to the Chicama/Máncora area.

WEATHER STATISTICS	J/F	M/A	M/J	J/A	S/O	N/D
total rainfall (mm)	1	0	5	8	5	2
consistency (days/mth)	0	0	1	2	0	0
min temp (°C/°F)	19/66	18/64	15/59	14/57	14/57	16/61
max temp (°C/°F)	26/79	25/77	21/70	18/64	20/68	23/74

La Isla

Arica
Pulpos
El Silencio
Senoritas
Caballeros
Pico Alto
Playa Norte
La Isla
Punta Rocas
Huayaco
Peñascal
Santa Rosa
Punta Hermosa
Pico Alto
Surfcamp
San Bartolo
Santa Maria

riding. El Silencio is a headland with reliable lefts and rights breaking off either side.

Next to this is another headland with two spots called Señoritas and Caballeros, so named, because in the past men and women were segregated into their own beaches. Señoritas breaks left with power while Caballeros produces longer, fatter rights. This is a very popular weekend sunbathing spot. Pico Alto is the next spot, being a serious right that will require guns of at least 8ft, more if you want to ride it up to 25ft (8.3m) like some of the local chargers have! It's a 30 minute paddle just to get in position, only rideable when the wave face is clean and smooth and is likened to Hawai'i for its challenging power. Playa Norte is another popular beach with weekend visitors from Lima, causing the rights to be busy. The next headland is the reef peak of La Isla, where crowds are guaranteed at weekends and holidays. Punta Rocas is by far the most consistent and unfortunately most crowded spot. The line-up favours rights which work from 3-12ft (1-4m); this used to be a WQS contest site. Huayco is a secluded beach with scattered rocks lining the bottom; it's best checked on small swells. On bigger days the Santa Rosa headland produces lefts and rights – Peñascal is a long right with plenty of fun sections

and Santa Rosa is a fickle left. San Bartolo has two spots that are usually quieter than most of the other breaks; this is because it is located inside private property. A trip out to Puerto Viejo for long lefts or Cerro Azul for hollow, tubey rights off the jetty is definitely worth the effort. Don't miss the superb right on the beautiful San Gallan Island off the Paracas Peninsula.

Regular 4-15ft (1.3-5m) S-SW swells come pouring off the Roaring Forties lows. Also, the constant S winds that accompany the Humboldt Current produce swell of at least 2-3ft (0.6-1m) almost continuously and so with these two sources of waves it is

Alfonso Panochi, Punta Rocas

rare to find it totally flat. The prevailing S-SE winds are pretty much perfect. The wind blows dead S (sideshore) 30-40% of the time and SE 35-55% of the time – most of the prime spots face NW and so are usually offshore. SE morning winds will turn to the S after lunch. Tides have little effect on most spots, and tide tables can be obtained from the better surf shops in Lima.

Piti Block

SURF STATISTICS	J F	M A	M J	J A	S O	N D
dominant swell	S-SW	S-SW	S-SW	S-SW	S-SW	S-SW
swell size (ft)	3-4	4	5	6	5	3-4
consistency (%)	70	70	80	90	80	60
dominant wind	SE-S	SE-S	SE-S	SE-S	SE-S	SE-S
average force	F3	F3	F3	F3-F4	F3-F4	F3
consistency (%)	81	87	83	85	88	85
water temp (°C/°F)	19/66	20/68	16/61	14/57	15/59	17/62
wetsuit						

75. Iquique

Iquique

Summary

+ VERY CONSISTENT, ALL YEAR
+ BIG, POWERFUL WAVES
+ CHILLED, UNCROWDED ATMOSPHERE
+ PERFECT CLIMATE

− SHALLOW REEFS AND URCHINS
− NO MELLOW WAVES
− LONG JOURNEYS
− MONOTONOUS LANDSCAPE

ALL PHOTOS GEOFF RAGATZ

Chile is a super consistent surf country that is almost entirely untapped by surfers. North of the capital, Santiago, the landscape quickly changes to that of the Atacama, the driest desert in the world. The Pan American Highway skirts the edge of the Atacama and can be used to search for some of the perfect reefbreaks found there. Arica and Iquique are two cities in the Atacama, 400km (250mi) apart and both are the home of great waves. Most of the waves along this coastline break close to the shore as cylindrical barrels slamming down hard onto shallow reefs full of urchins. It's often big and gnarly and many of the spots are more suitable for bodyboarders or the most skilled of surfers. Fortunately, there are channels, which enable safe paddle-outs to most line-ups. The city of Arica is located on the magical Alacran Peninsula, which is packed with classic spots. Between here and Iquique are potentially dozens of world class spots that can only be reached by 4WD.

Liuta River Valley

TRAVEL INFORMATION

Local Population:
Iquique – 160,000
Coastline: 6,435km (4,020mi)
Time: GMT-4hr
Contest: Local

Getting There – Citizens of NZ, Brazil, South Africa and the US need visas, costing $20. Santiago is the usual entry point. Transfer flights to Iquique with Lan Chile or take one of the excellent buses (28hrs, $35/o-w). Another option is to fly to Lima (Peru), then get a bus to Tacna (36hrs), cross the border and travel the remaining 450km (280mi) to Iquique.

Getting Around – Cars can be rented for $300/w but it's not really necessary as buses are very cheap and efficient. Once in Iquique most spots are within easy walking distance. If you want to explore the desert then you will need a well-equipped 4WD. Lan-Chile air passes are good value for money.

Lodging and Food – The cost of living is rising but a double room goes for around $25. Cheap hostels will give you a bed for $10 - the cheapest option is to camp. At the other end of the scale are hotels like The Prat, $50/dble or the Cavancha, $40/dble. Seafood is cheap and widely available, the local brew is Pisco Sour.

Weather – The Atacama Desert is one of the driest places in the world with rain falling only once every 15 years on average, yet Iquique is a city with an eternal springtime climate. Its location at the base of some big canyons means that it collects what moisture there is from both the desert and from sea humidity. This makes it a surprisingly green place. Temps are stable year round at around 24°C (75°F) with very little variation. This is a near perfect climate for travelling in. Hazy mornings usually clear when the breeze picks up. Despite the influence of the cold Humboldt Current, the water is warmer than most of the country, especially in the summertime (Nov-March). A light 3/2 steamer is needed for most of the year, but in the summer you could make do with a shorty.

Nature and Culture – Check out an oasis in the desert or spend a few days in the Andes. The spectacular Lauca National Park is about an 8hr bus ride from Iquique. Other worthwhile sites include the Atacama Giant, Pintados and the ghost town of Humberstone.

Hazards and Hassles – In the water your main danger is from the shallow, urchin covered reefs and thick, heavy waves. The local surfers are almost all bodyboarders and there aren't many of them, but even ten people in a tight take-off zone can make for a crowded line-up.

Handy Hints – Iquique has a surf shop but its range is limited. It's better to bring your own gear, including big-wave guns, boots and a helmet. Many Chilean men work in mines out in the desert and so Iquique seems to be populated almost entirely by women.

WEATHER STATISTICS	J/F	M/A	M/J	J/A	S/O	N/D
total rainfall (mm)	0.5	0	0	0	0	0
consistency (days/mth)	0	0	0	0	0	0
min temp (°C/°F)	18/64	17/62	14/57	13/55	13/55	16/61
max temp (°C/°F)	27/81	25/77	21/70	19/66	21/70	24/75

Colegio

Intendencia
Punta Gruesa
La Urraca
Colegio
Punta Dos
Punta Una
Iquique
ISLA SERRANO
Caleta Morro
Iquitados Stadium
Hospital
Playa Cavancha
Punta Cavancha
Stadium

Iquique itself contains a handful of excellent reefbreaks in a kilometre long stretch. When looking at the waves from the shore it's easy to be deceived by the size, what appears to be 4ft (1.3m) is actually 6-8ft (2-2.6m)! All these waves face the main coastal road and, when the swells are big, crowds are guaranteed to gather and watch the show.

Coco

Intendencia is a challenging and very heavy left that has to be perfect in order to be makeable. Punta Dos is a barrelling wave that explodes on a gnarled reef. It is an uncompromising wave that will punish the hesitant and therefore is for experienced surfers only. When it's small, La Urraca is a reasonable left with a narrow channel. The most consistent spot is Colegio, a thick right facing the main high school. It holds waves up to 12-15ft, (4-5m). Punta Una is another barrelling wave that sucks hard off the reef with the end section going almost dry. Further down the seafront road are more reefs and Playa Cavancha, a beachbreak, which is usually just a big close-out. On a regulation 4-6ft (1.3-2m) swell, most of the reefs work, with the best waves usually being rights. Even further south are more exposed beaches, Huayquique is only worth checking on small swells with light winds. The main road skirts the coast for a further 70km (45mi), all the way up to Chanabaya, with loads of opportunities. If the surf does go flat (very rare), there's some great nightlife in Iquique.

Super consistent S-SW swells between 3-15ft (1-5m) come pouring off the Roaring Forties year round, although winter obviously sees much bigger and more regular swells. Storms frequently hit the south of the country, so the further north, the better the weather. The predominant wind is from the S-SE and blows up to 65% of the time (June). Usually it's a direct SE but in Oct-Nov it can vary a lot more. 10-12% of days has totally calm winds. Mornings are usually glassy, then a light offshore picks up, lasting until noon, after which a gentle S sea breeze creates a little bit of chop on the wave face. Most of the rights are very wind sensitive. Mid to high tide is the go for most spots. Tidal range never exceeds 6ft (2m) but it still affects many breaks.

SURF STATISTICS	J F	M A	M J	J A	S O	N D
dominant swell	S-SW	S-SW	S-SW	S-SW	S-SW	S-SW
swell size (ft)	4	4-5	5-6	6-7	5-6	4
consistency (%)	70	75	80	90	80	60
dominant wind	SE-S	SE-S	SE-S	SE-S	SE-S	SE-S
average force	F2	F2-F3	F2-F3	F3	F3	F2-F3
consistency (%)	65	66	60	62	67	65
water temp (°C/°F)	19/66	19/66	18/64	16/61	17/62	18/64
wetsuit						

La Urraca

76. Pichilemu

Punta Lobos

ALEX WILLIAMS

Summary
+ SUPER CONSISTENT
+ LOTS OF LONG LEFT POINTBREAKS
+ GREAT COUNTRYSIDE
+ LAID BACK PEOPLE

− COLD WATER YEAR ROUND
− RAINY WINTERS
− WINDY
− HARD ACCESS TO SPOTS

Chile is a strangely shaped country, twenty five times as long as it is wide. Its 4,300km (2,700mi) of coastline is the southernmost surf region on the Pacific coast of South America. South Pacific lows pushed along by the Humboldt Current generate the most consistent swells on the planet, resulting in a surf excess rather than the usual problem of flat days. Just off the coastline of Chile is a deep water trench, which plunges to depths of 8000m (26,240ft), and allows SW swells to hit the coast with speed and power. Together with the dominant S winds, perfect set-ups abound in the north facing bays for reeling offshore lefts to create a goofy footers heaven (with a distinct lack of goofy footers!) Pichilemu is probably the most famous name in this zone, which is called Region V and VI in the orderly numerical naming system of Chile.

GEOFF RAGATZ

Secret spot

GEOFF RAGATZ

Surfing started in Chile in the early 70's around Ritoque, which has powerful and super consistent beachbreaks that are clean on N winds. When the more normal S winds blow, surfers head to Maitencillo rivermouth on small swells. If it's big then El Claron has a left pointbreak, peeling over sand covered rocks.

TRAVEL INFORMATION

Local Population:
Viana Region – 760,000
Coastline: 6,435km
(4,020mi)
Time: GMT-4h
Contest: No

Getting There – Nationals of NZ, Brazil, South Africa and USA all need visas, at a cost of $20. Santiago Airport is well connected with North America, Europe and Australasia. The national airline is LAN. From neighbouring countries it's much cheaper to come by bus. Pichilemu is 5hrs by bus ($8/o-w) from Santiago.

Getting Around – Renting a car is not necessary, as the bus service is reliable. If you stay in Pichilemu, everything is actually within walking distance. To rent a car will cost around $300/w. Lan-Chile offer some good value travel passes.

Lodging and Food – Costs have risen over the years, but $25/d is still a feasible budget. Surfers hang at the Jamaica Inn ($7/dble). The best hotels are the Roos or España at $20/dble. There is lots of cheap seafood at Cafeterias - 'Curanto' is a must. 'Pisco' is the drink of choice. Expect to pay $10 a meal.

Weather – Looking at the vegetation reveals a mixed climate of mild Mediterranean and wet Oceanic. Due to the relatively low latitude, winter is a period to avoid because of cold temperatures, frequent showers and changeable weather. It is possible at this time to snowboard in the mountains, 4hrs away. Sunshine levels vary from 2-3hrs in winter to 8-9hrs in the summer. Summers are dry and quite warm, but the coast is sometimes shrouded in mist. The Humboldt Current cools the water year round and it rarely exceeds 17°C (62°F).

Nature and Culture – Pichilemu and other coastal resorts get crowded during the summer with visitors from the capital, Santiago. There are 3 nightclubs in Pichilemu (cover charge around $5) but Valparaiso and Cartagena are lively. Don't miss the Andes and the volcanoes.

Hazards and Hassles – Nothing really. Strong rips make getting to the line-up difficult when it's big. Otherwise the locals are cool, crowd pressure is low, rocks are well covered with seaweed and the numerous seals are curious, but harmless. The only trouble is smog and urban hassles in Santiago.

Handy Hints – You can have your board fixed in the main surf hubs and get a leash or wax, but don't expect too much. Bring all necessities. Locals will expect you to sell your gear. It seems that Chile is waking up now that the Pinochet era is over.

WEATHER STATISTICS	J/F	M/A	M/J	J/A	S/O	N/D
total rainfall (mm)	18	62	230	210	82	37
consistency (days/mth)	2	7	16	15	10	7
min temp (°C/°F)	12/54	9/48	7/44	5/41	7/44	11/52
max temp (°C/°F)	27/81	25/77	18/64	17/62	21/70	26/79

Another option is the Quintero/Papagayo long left set-up, which is often crowded.

North of Santiago's Viña del Mar beach, are the Reñaca beachbreaks, very popular waves, especially in the summer, with an excess of learners on bodyboards. All these beachbreaks are exposed, so whenever there is a swell it's best to head to the sheltered spots with their long lefts, such as the high tide breaking Las Salinas. Another major surf zone starts at Algarrobo, which is a short, powerful, left reefbreak close to a pier. It's not far from Cartagena; a busy summer resort that has another good left. La Boquilla is a notable rivermouth wave, also with good lefts. Navidad and Matanzas are rocky inlets that also produce quality lefts. Nearby is by far the longest left barrel in this region, however getting there requires a permit because it's private property. The wave is superb but when it's on there is always a strong rip that requires constant paddling to stay in position.

South of here is Punta Topocalma and then the breaks of the Pichilemu area. First surfed in 1983, Pichilemu quickly became a popular destination with surf travellers because of the endless pointbreaks and laid-back atmosphere. Pichilemu itself is a small village and home to what, when the sandbanks are aligned properly, may be the longest wave in Chile. When the swell is small, there is a short left within easy walking distance called Infernillo – with no wind and a high tide, it's another classic left barrel.

Lastly, 7km (4mi) south is Punta de Lobos, yet another long left pointbreak which handles considerable size and is by far the most consistent wave around. A French guy has built cabañas offering accommodation right on the point.

Secret spot
ALEX WILLIAN.S

S-SW swells from Antarctica lows are consistent with sizes varying from 2-18ft (0.6-6m) year round. The dominant wind comes from the S varying from 32% of the time in June to 55% of the time from Oct through to Feb. The winter period of May-July also gets a lot of NW-NE winds (30-40%). The remainder of the year sees a S or lighter SW pattern. This means that the north facing coves will often be offshore, favouring lefts. Mid to high tides are the go at most spots. The tidal range is significant, but it's hard to find a tide table.

SURF STATISTICS	J F	M A	M J	J A	S O	N D
dominant swell	S-SW	S-SW	S-W	S-W	S-W	S-SW
swell size (ft)	4-5	5	6	7-8	6	4
consistency (%)	80	80	90	80	90	60
dominant wind	S-SWE	S-SW	N-S	N-S	S-SW	S-SW
average force	F4	F4	F4	F4	F4	F4
consistency (%)	73	66	55	56	66	73
water temp (°C/°F)	16/61	15/59	14/57	13/55	13/55	15/59
wetsuit						

Pichilemu
FREDERIC LE LEANNEC
Maitencillo
ALFREDO ESCOBAR

Maitencillo
El Claron
Papagayo
Ritoque
Reñaca
Las Salinas
Quintero
Viña del Mar
Valparaiso
San Felipe
Los Andes
Quillota
F30
F90
Algarrobo
Casablanca
Mirasol
El Quisco F90
Cartagena
San Antonio
Santiago
68
Talagante
Cerro Bandurrias
Melipilla
La Boquilla
Matanzas
Navidad
Cerro Los Arboleras
Punta Topocalma
Cerro Tuneno
Rancagua
Pichilemu
Infernillo
Punta de Lobos
Pichilemu
Cañuil
PANAMERICAN HIGHWAY

77. Santa Catarina

Silveira

ALL PHOTOS FLAVIO VIDIGAL

Summary
+ GREAT CONSISTENCY
+ WIDE RANGE OF SPOTS
+ TROPICAL SCENERY
+ SAFE AND DEVELOPED AREA

– COOL WATER
– RELATIVELY CROWDED
– SOME BEACHES CLOSE DURING
  THE FISHING SEASON
– WET CLIMATE

It is the deep south of Brazil that offers the best surf in the country, with bigger swells and more coastal variations than the north. While Parana and Rio Grande do Sul States have good potential, Santa Catarina Island, facing ESE, is definitely the best option. This island destination is commonly referred to as Florianopolis, which is actually the capital city of Santa Catarina State, as well as a port on the west side of Santa Catarina Island. It is a great destination, with a concentration of 20 breaks covering a 225° swell window, plus, further south are the quality spots around Guarda de Embau, Garopaba and Imbituba.

Towards the north of Santa Catarina Island, Santinho produces good lefts,

Flavio Padaratz, Praia do Moçambique

but it needs a rare SE swell and NE wind. Moçambique is the longest beach with 12 access points – the north end is usually the best with fast, walled-up waves. The Galheta nudist beach is a bit of a hike, but it gets hollow waves with no crowds. If the wind is blowing from the S, Praia Mole is the spot for clean, consistent beachbreaks. World famous Joaquina beach provided classic conditions for a 1986 ASP World Tour contest. It's a thick, powerful beachbreak that favours lefts, making it more than popular. Campeche is a big beach with a rarely breaking but classic long, hollow right that needs a major S swell.

Roberto Perdigão, Praia da Vila

There are also some consistent rights to be found up towards Morro das Pedras. The lefts at Matadeiro rivermouth are rumoured to be epic but extremely fickle and inconsistent. Lagoinha do Leste is hard to reach, but well worth the mission, with powerful, empty waves as your reward. Another spot that is hard to get to is Naufragados, which requires a long hike or the hiring of a boat. It is a hollow wave, although one with a tendency to close-out, however the scenery alone can make the trip worthwhile. Guarda do Embau is a laid-back resort town with a lefthander that is the best rivermouth wave in Brazil. Even if the river doesn't turn on the goods, then there is still a punchy beachbreak set amongst some amazing rock formations. Prainha and Gamboa are both beachbreaks close by and are useful to escape from the crowds. Garopaba rivals Guarda as a surf travel town because of Silveira, a great right point that wraps around a rocky headland. The other swell magnet is Ferrugem – a super consistent beachbreaks that pack some punch. There are several good breaks hidden away on the coast near Imbituba, which are well worth a quick look, like Rosa, site of the 2000 World Longboard Championships. It is in Imbituba where the biggest waves in Brazil are to be found at Praia da Vila, which holds chunky rights in S to E swells.

Joaquina

This part of Brazil receives the most swell in the country from deep low pressures spinning past Cape Horn above Antarctica. Swells are reasonably powerful and frequent, especially from April to Oct. This source of S-SE swells provides 2-10ft (0.6-3.3m) waves with occasional 10ft (3.3m) conditions at the big wave spots like Praia da Vila. Unlike many surf destinations it seems that spring is better than autumn with many more E swells, coming mainly off deep lows passing to the SE and sometimes from hurricanes off Africa which send in short lived groundswells. Wind patterns are stronger than on the Littoral Paulista (São Paulo), blowing primarily from the E in the summer and from either the NE or SW in the winter. SW winds mean stormy weather, while 'lestadas' (easterlies) are the usual sea breezes, which blow with force after lunch. Tidal variation is minimal and has little effect on most spots.

SURF STATISTICS	J F	M A	M J	J A	S O	N D
dominant swell	S-SE	E-S	E-S	E-S	E-S	S-SE
swell size (ft)	2	2-3	3-4	4	3-4	2
consistency (%)	50	60	70	70	70	50
dominant wind	NE-SE	NE-SE			NE-SE	NE-SE
average force	F4	F4	F4	F4	F4	F4
consistency (%)	58	53	67	68	80	59
water temp (°C/°F)	23/74	22/72	20/68	17/62	17/62	21/70
wetsuit						

Jaqueline Silva, Praia Mole

TRAVEL INFORMATION

Getting There – Most nationalities need a visa. Brazilian Varig airlines charge $50 board tax. National flights are expensive (buy an air pass before you arrive in Brazil), but charter flights to São Paulo are plentiful. It's 12 hours by 'leito' (sleeper bus) from São Paulo ($20/o-w).

Getting Around – Rental car rates are similar to the US, from $180/week - fuel is 60c/l. The highway BR-101 has the unenviable reputation of having the worst crash rate in the world. Roads are generally dangerous throughout the country, with road layout sometimes extremely unpredictable. A good example is the road from Garopaba to the beach, which without warning goes from a multiple lane highway down to a single lane road.

Lodging and Food – In the summer many people descend on this area from all the big national cities, as well as plenty of Argentinians from across the border. Finding cheap accommodation at this time becomes difficult. Throughout the surf season you should be able to get accommodation within the $20/dble range. Ask about rooms at Larica's Café in Guarda.

Weather – The climate is wet/subtropical with as much rain in the winter as in the summer, (about one day out of three). Winter brings stormy weather while the summer has afternoon thunderstorms. Deep winter can be surprisingly cold. The water remains pretty stable year round, requiring a light fullsuit most of the time. Springsuits and boardies can be used at certain times of the year. Sometimes S winds in the winter feed warm water currents up the coast, whilst E winds and swells can bring in cold water currents.

Nature and Culture – The biggest party of the year is the Oktoberfest, in Blumenau and is definitely not what you would expect from Brazil. This is a cosmopolitan region but with a quiet, rural vibe based around the small fishing villages. There is sandboarding in Joaquina or windsurfing in Lagoa.

Hazards and Hassles – Although crowds are much thinner than in São Paulo, you're in Brazil and all Brazilians love to surf. During the fishing season from May-June some of the beaches ban surfing. Mussels and urchins occur at a few spots, notably Silveira.

Handy Hints – Boards are easily available and cost around $200. Garopaba is a good place to buy one. Inflation is running quite high, so don't change too much money at once. The currency's name has changed five times in the past 15 years. Cash points are plentiful.

Local Population:
Florianopolis – 300,000
Coastline: 7,491km
(4,680mi)
Time: GMT-4hr
Contest: WQS (Jan, Oct)

WEATHER STATISTICS	J/F	M/A	M/J	J/A	S/O	N/D
total rainfall (mm)	105	92	112	130	125	100
consistency (days/mth)	9	7	10	11	10	9
min temp (°C/°F)	22/72	19/66	14/57	13/55	16/61	20/68
max temp (°C/°F)	28/82	27/81	22/72	21/70	22/72	26/79

BRAZIL
SOUTH

78. Littoral Paulista

Pitangueiras

ALL PHOTOS TONY FLEURY

Summary
+ FAIRLY CONSISTENT CLEAN SURF
+ EASILY ACCESSIBLE
+ GOOD QUALITY FACILITIES
+ URBAN ENTERTAINMENT

− HEAVY CROWD PRESSURE
− LACK OF BIG WAVES
− POLLUTION
− BUILT UP COAST, HEAVY TRAFFIC

São Paulo is one of the world's largest cities and so it is of little surprise to discover that the sub-tropical shores of the Littoral Paulista (the city beaches), are teeming with hot surfers. This whole zone is basically a long stretch of average, sandy beachbreaks, located between two peninsulas, dotted with inlets, bays and points. The South Atlantic rarely pushes in swells big enough to make the pointbreaks fire, so most surfing here will be done on fickle reefs or hollow beachbreaks, which are always busy. If you're a beginner, happy to ride small, mushy waves, then the poorer quality peaks that can be found on the bigger beaches

Praia de Tombo

Camburi

will offer less intense crowds. Another way of avoiding the worst of the crowds is to take a long hike or a boat to some of the spots with harder access that can be found along the more rugged stretches of coastline.

The easiest place to begin searching for waves are the Santos beaches, the nearest to the city centre and beside Brazil's main harbour. Embaré is an old, stylish town with consistent waves. On the other side of the Balsa river is Ilha de Santo Amaro, where around the town of

TRAVEL INFORMATION

Local Population: São Paulo – 17M
Coastline: 7,491km (4,681mi)
Time: GMT-4hr
Contests: WQS (Nov), Nat (April)

Getting There – (See 77.Santa Catarina). There are plenty of international flights to São Paulo. There are plenty of charter flights from all major Brazilian cities to São Paulo. Brazilian Varig Airlines charges $50 board tax. The coast is 30mins away from São Paulo's Congonhas Airport.

Getting Around – Rental car rates start at $180/w and fuel is 60c/l. There is a good road network between São Paulo and Rio de Janeiro, but it still gets clogged up at rush hours. Roads to the secluded spots may be impossible for anything but a 4WD after rain.

Lodging and Food – There is the full range of accommodation possibilities in Guaruja. Surf season is the off-season for tourists, although July is still busy. Finding a room ($20/dble) in a 'pousada' or 'chales' (try the Villa Marini) in Maresias/Trindade is easy. Basic foodstuffs are cheap. When eating out, stick to the 'prato do dia' (dish of the day) or the pay by weight system in order to keep costs down.

Weather – Although it's a tropical area the Serra do Mar makes this area wetter and cooler than you would expect. São Paulo is at an altitude of about 800m, and can get cold and grey while the coast is warm and sunny. During the winter (May-Sept) surf period, temps average 23°C (74°F), rarely falling under 18°C (64°F). Summers are hot and humid. The bad air pollution can make it very

uncomfortable. Springsuits are generally sufficient, although, on some cooler winter mornings a light steamer may be the go.

Nature and Culture – Maresias is a packed beach, where people go to see and be seen. Ilhabela is a nice place to escape the crowds and enjoy some good scenery. Parati to the north, is an enjoyable colonial town.

Hazards and Hassles – The worst problems are the crowds in the water and bad pollution. Crime is not as high as in Rio but be careful in the outskirts of São Paulo.

Handy Hints – Boards and other gear are cheap and easily available. Maresia is a good place to pick up a new board (roughly $200). There's a female only surf school called "Hot Girl."

WEATHER STATISTICS	J/F	M/A	M/J	J/A	S/O	N/D
total rainfall (mm)	227	117	65	42	102	167
consistency (days/mth)	14	11	8	5	10	14
min temp (°C/°F)	23/74	22/72	19/66	18/64	19/66	21/70
max temp (°C/°F)	30/86	28/82	28/82	26/79	26/79	29/84

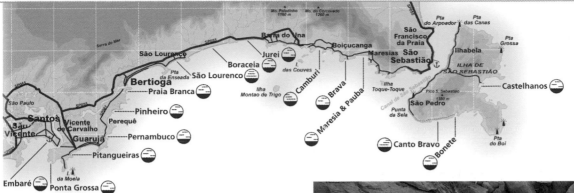

Praia do Tombo

Guaruja, the main breaks can be found. Ponta Grossa is a secluded beach with good rights and few crowds. Heading north towards Pitangueiras, there are a few hidden reefs and beaches that are well worth searching for. Pitangueiras itself is a very consistent spot, but it's popular and it's a fight for every wave. Heading northeast, Pernambuco is a well regarded beachbreak that is consistent, hollow and you guessed it – crowded! One of the few spots that handles a bit of S wind. The northern part of Guaruja Island is less developed, but like everywhere in this zone, it still gets busy. The waves can be good at either Pinheiro or Praia Branca, where the difficult access cuts the crowds a bit.

From Bertioga to Maresias, there is a 60km (40mi) stretch of variable quality surf that is accessed along the SP055. São Lourenco has rivermouth formed sandbars and Boraceia a large beach. The village of Barra do Una is close to the quiet beach of Jurei. Camburi can produce some excellent lefts on a major S swell and Brava is another out of the way break. Maresias is one of the most popular surf spots in the area and the beach of choice for São Paulo's most beautiful people, with 4km (2.5mi) of clean sand and clear water with some good, consistent beach peaks. There are also a few reefs here, a good one can be found at Canto do Moreira. Sometimes the beach peaks here can really turn on the goods and produce epic waves. If it gets big, then the little fishing village of Pauba has some decent waves. A final and often worthwhile option is to take a ferry over to the beautiful coast of Ilhabela. If it's dry then a dirt road will allow you to gain access to Castelhanos, which has hollow surf on an E swell. On S swells take a boat or walk for four hours to Bonete or try out the treacherous rights of Canto Bravo to the south of Veloso.

The Littoral Paulista is well exposed to frequent S-SE swells coming up from Antarctica. From April-Oct you can expect plenty of 3-8ft (1-2.6m) days. Unusual late winter E swells produced by lows tracking way off the coast or by the strong E winds sometimes caused by high pressures, will send short lived ENE groundswells onto Brazil's beaches. Swells rarely get very big and when they do there are few spots that can hold much size. The dominant wind blows from the E, varying from 16% of the time in June to 32% in Oct. Winters though, seem to produce more S-SW winds; this is most common when a cold front approaches the coast. It is usually offshore in the mornings, but by 10am the E sea breeze picks up. Tidal ranges are small and don't really effect most spots, a 'tabua de mares' (tide table) is easy to get hold of.

SURF STATISTICS	J F	M A	M J	J A	S O	N D
dominant swell	S-SE	S-E	S-E	S-E	S-E	S-SE
swell size (ft)	1-2	2	3	3-4	3	1-2
consistency (%)	40	50	70	80	70	40
dominant wind	NE-SE	NE-SE	NE-SW	NE-SW	NE-SW	NE-SE
average force	F3	F3	F3	F3	F3	F3
consistency (%)	62	63	71	73	80	65
water temp (°C/°F)	25/77	25/77	22/72	20/68	20/68	23/74
wetsuit						

Pauba

79. Pernambuco

FERNANDO DE
NORONHA

BRAZIL
NORTH-EAST

Maracaipe

ALL PHOTOS LAURENT MASUREL

Summary
+ EASY, UNCROWDED BEACHBREAKS
+ RARELY FLAT
+ PARADISE BEACHES
+ GREAT ATMOSPHERE

– SMALL SURF
– FREQUENT ONSHORES
– SHARKS
– PETTY CRIME IN RECIFE
– RELATIVELY EXPENSIVE

Nordeste is the Brazil of clichés... colourful, vibrant and always exciting. The 70km (43mi) coastal strip that makes up the seaboard of Pernambuco State is just a small area of this vast region. It's a low lying, fertile plain with a great mix of beaches and reefs. Most of the reefs lie within 200m of the shore and offer powerful waves on offshore days, whilst the beaches are better surfed on the more common onshore days. The main centre is Recife, a place that used to be a good base for surfers, but all this has changed. The construction of a huge harbour in Boca de Suape in the early 90's, along with irresponsible coastal development and some serious over-fishing, meant that the local eco-system experienced major changes. These changes were graphically illustrated at the top of the food chain where sharks began to go hungry and unsurprisingly, shark attacks on surfers increased dramatically. In the space of a few years there were six fatal attacks. The authorities, worried about dropping tourist numbers, responded by placing the blame squarely on the shoulders of surfers and banned surfing along a 60km (37mi) stretch of coast! Since 1998, the beaches where surfing has been prohibited include the following: Olinda, one of the most picturesque colonial towns in the country; Praia del Chifre, Recife; the resort area of Boa

Maracaipe

Viagem including the quality Acaiaca reefs; the hollow reefbreaks of Abreus; the reefs of Quebra Mar; the reliable SE facing beachbreaks of Paiva and finally Pedra Preta. Although the Gaibu Peninsula is located inside the prohibited zone, the authorities have allowed the locals access to the surf and there have been no attacks so far.

The first of the spots on the peninsula is to the south of the 1km (0.6mi) long jetty at Porto de Suape. It's a consistent beachbreak called Cupe and there's plenty of accommodation close by. As most people head straight to the reefs or Maracaipe, it would be rare to find this beach very busy. Porto de Galinhas is a well-known tourist resort with 10 hotels and 60 pousadas. There's a shallow, outside reef that can have good waves on glassy

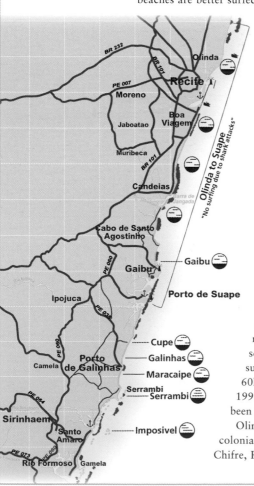

Galinhas reefs

here in recent years due to an increase in the amount of surfers coming down from Recife since the surfing ban. Occasionally, Serrambi's shallow reefs provide hollow, spitting barrels, but only on the rare days when the wind is offshore or it's glassy. There is a left that wraps around the reef into a channel and a right that holds some good size. To the north of Barra da Sirinhaem you will find outside reefs such as the hard to get to mysto left Impolsivel, off Ilha Santo Aleixo.

days. Close to Galinhas harbour is a punchy right and an occasional left, it takes about 10 minutes to paddle out to the waves. The most consistent beach in this zone is Maracaipe, which hosted the 2000 World Surfing Games. Although the middle of the beach is usually the best, there are dozens of other sandbanks to choose from. The wave tends to roll through from outside banks reforming several times on its journey to the close-out shorebreak. High tide tends to be better but on the whole the wave quality is poor. A 30 minute walk up the beach will bring you to Ponta de Serrambi, which is a quality spot surrounded by luxury apartments. Localism has increased

During the winter rainy season it's rarely flat due to a constant wind swell created by the E-SE tradewinds. Most waves are in the 2-5ft (0.6-1.6m) range and have a lack of shape and power on the beaches. Only the reefs will produce quality, clean surf and only then when the wind is offshore or glassy. Groundswells are rare and come from lows to the S, most frequently from May to Oct. Sometimes these swells can reach 8ft (2.6m). Most swells suffer from diminishing size having travelled such a long distance. In winter thunderstorms bring strong winds followed by a glass-off. This can happen several times in a day, so be on it. S-SE is the main wind, blowing from 90% of the time in Jan to 82% in Sept. It will be more SE than E in the winter. With a tidal variation of up to 8ft (2.6m), shallow reefbreaks can be unsurfable at low tide or too full at high.

Praia do Chifre, Recife

SURF STATISTICS	J F	M A	M J	J A	S O	N D
dominant swell	–	–	E-SE	E-SE	E-SE	–
swell size (ft)	0-1	1-2	2-3	2-3	2	1
consistency (%)	20	30	70	60	50	20
dominant wind	E-SE	E-SE	E-SE	E-SE	E-SE	E-SE
average force	F4	F4	F4	F4	F4	F4
consistency (%)	88	85	84	86	85	88
water temp (°C/°F)	27/81	27/81	26/79	25/77	24/75	26/79
wetsuit						

TRAVEL INFORMATION

Getting There – (See 77.Santa Catarina). Recife is Brazil's third biggest airport after Rio and São Paulo and so has many flight connections with the US and Europe. Porto do Galinhas is 60km (37mi) from Recife on either the BR101 highway or the good PE 38 road. Dep tax is $30.

Getting Around – Flooding can occur in the winter and the roads can get very muddy making beach access difficult. Renting a car will cost from $50/d, buses run from Recife to Galinhas. A local taxi ride shouldn't really cost more than $2. Use the 'jangadas' (dugouts) for $4/hr to reach the outside reefs.

Lodging and Food – Porto da Galinhas is a major resort but you may find Maracaipe a better and cheaper bet - try the Hotel Flat ($40/dble), Pousada dos Coqueiros ($45/dble) or one of the many cheap pousadas, such as Raio do Luz, $15/dble. The surf season is the off-season for

tourists, so bargain time. A meal shouldn't cost more than $8; try eating peixadas and macaxeira. The local drink is caipiriñha.

Weather – Pernambuco enjoys a semi-tropical climate. The rainy season lasts from May to Aug, when afternoons see heavy thunderstorms. Overall rainfall is 4-5ft (1.3-1.6m) per year. Winter temps hardly ever drop below 20°C (68°F), but the onshore E-SE trade winds prevent the air from getting too hot. No need to wear more than boardshorts and a rash vest.

Nature and Culture – The coastline is a beautiful blend of low sand dunes and palm trees. The waters are murky in the winter. Good diving off Santo Aleixo Island. Recife is a worthy cultural visit (check the jail), as is Olinda, the former capital of Brazil.

Hazards and Hassles – No shark attacks north of Boca de Suape for a while now, mainly because of the surfing ban. Big beaches like Maracaipe only get crowded at weekends, but if one of the good reefs turns on it will be busy whatever time it is. In Recife and Boa Viagem stay alert for pickpockets and muggings.

Handy Hints – Recife's shapers have suffered badly with a drop in business since the ban. Surfboards are cheap at $200. Katu surf shop is in Galinhas and there's a board repairer in Maracaipe. Brazil is an ethnically diverse country but the people are united through their love of Samba music and Forro dancing.

Local Population:
Recife – 1.5M
Coastline: 7,491km (4,680mi)
Time: GMT-3hr
Contest: WQS (Oct) National

WEATHER STATISTICS	J/F	M/A	M/J	J/A	S/O	N/D
total rainfall (mm)	70	190	270	203	45	26
consistency (days/mth)	11	15	22	20	10	6
min temp (°C/°F)	25/77	24/75	23/74	22/72	23/74	24/75
max temp (°C/°F)	30/86	29/84	28/82	27/81	28/82	29/84

FERNANDO DE NORONHA

BRAZIL
NORTH-EAST

80. Fernando de Noronha

Abras

Summary

+ POWERFUL TUBING BEACHBREAKS AND REEFBREAKS
+ CONSISTENTLY OFFSHORE
+ UNTOUCHED, WILD ENVIRONMENT
+ PEACEFUL ISLAND VIBE

– SHORT SURF SEASON
– DIFFICULT ACCESS
– VERY EXPENSIVE LIVING COSTS

ALL PHOTOS MARC FENIES

Looking at the location of Fernando de Noronha on a map, you will probably be surprised to find that the island's main source of swell is not from the south like most of Brazil, but from the North Atlantic lows that provide Europe with its surf. How the swells make it the thousands of miles south is a bit of a mystery – the most likely scenario is that they are pushed along by favourable winds and ocean currents.

The island has had a colourful recent history, having been used as a battlefield, jail, air base and weather station. It has now become a tourist heaven for divers and surfers. It is never under 2ft (0.6m) during Dec-Feb, and swells last for 5-6 days. Like Hawai'i, the island is the summit of a huge underwater volcano, rising 4.3km (2.7mi) from the ocean floor. The surrounding deep water and lack of continental shelf allows the swells to hit with unimpeded

Sergio Cavalcante, Cacimba do Padre

'Funny Buggy'

speed and power. It also causes the waves to jack up in size. The west side of the island is too mountainous for any surf, whereas the east side has perfect topography. The steeply sloping beaches make for some fast barrels, which tend toward the straight-hander category, but are perfectly suited to bodyboarders.

Starting from Vila dos Remédios, the main village, you can check many of the spots from different 'mirantes'

TRAVEL INFORMATION

Local Population:
Fernando – 1,500
Coastline: 32km (20mi)
Time: GMT-3hr
Contest: WQS (Feb)

Getting There – (See 77.Santa Catarina). There are three flights daily from Natal (350km /220mi away) and Recife (500km/310mi away) on the Brazilian mainland, for about $250/rtn. Book in advance with either Trip or Nordeste Airlines, as the busy tourist season corresponds with the surf season.

Getting Around – Fernando de Noronha is only 8km (5mi) long and 3km (2mi) wide, so instead of renting a car, go for a 'funny buggy' – they cost about $55/d. Fuel is expensive. Ask at the harbour about renting boats to get to the more remote spots.

Lodging and Food – There are 70 'pousadas' (guesthouses), Esmeralda is the best hotel ($90/dble), and the Pousada Morena is $50/dble. Most pousadas have full-board prices for $25/p/d. Food and drink wise you have a choice of either expensive imported items (like beer) and cheap repetitive seafood served in the 'launchonetes'.

Weather – Being located just south of the Equator, Fernando de Noronha enjoys a hot and humid climate split between a dry and wet season. SE trades bring the heaviest rain (nearly every day) from April to July and even into Aug. Temps are very stable, with the air and water being around 26°-27°C, (80°-82°F). In the dry season everything turns very brown and burnt, the wet season is much greener. For the best surf and weather come earlier in the season.

Nature and Culture – An appreciation of nature and hiking will greatly enhance your

enjoyment of the island. Aquatic life is very rich with fish, shark, dolphins, (swimming with them is not allowed, nor is spear fishing), and turtles as well as birds and big lizards. There is no nightlife on the island or urban entertainment, if there's no surf then occupy yourself by hiking or diving.

Hazards and Hassles – There are plenty of sharks, stingrays and Moray Eels around but they don't pose much threat. In the wet season there are lots of mosquitoes. Be careful of sunburn and reef cuts.

Handy Hints – The island has been a national park since 1988 with a ticket system that favours shorter visits ($80/7d, $210/14d). There are few real locals but Brazilians from the mainland stay here for weeks on end. Bring absolutely everything you need with you. Equipment is available but it's expensive.

WEATHER STATISTICS	J/F	M/A	M/J	J/A	S/O	N/D
total rainfall (mm)	70	190	270	203	45	26
consistency (days/mth)	11	15	22	20	10	6
min temp (°C/°F)	25/77	24/75	23/74	22/72	23/74	24/75
max temp (°C/°F)	30/86	29/84	28/82	27/81	28/82	29/84

Boboca

Boldro

the centre of the island's beach scene. Isla San José is on the way north to Baia da Rata, which have good rights and lefts respectively, that never get busy. If the swell is big enough then you may get to surf Abras, the best left on the island. It starts off as an open barrel before turning into a carveable wall that in turn becomes a fast section that you have to kick out of. Another spot worth checking on a big swell is the classic righthander at Baia da Rata, which wraps around the northernmost point of Noronha. It's better to go there by boat, rather than paddling as it's a long way and there are many sharks.

SURF STATISTICS	J F	M A	M J	J A	S O	N D
dominant swell	NW-N	NW-N	–	–	NW-N	NW-N
swell size (ft)	4-5	3-4	1	1	1-2	4
consistency (%)	80	60	10	10	20	70
dominant wind	E-SE	E-SE	E-SE	E-SE	E-SE	E-SE
average force	F4	F3	F4	F4	F4	F4
consistency (%)	82	77	85	92	93	94
water temp (°C/°F)	27/81	27/81	27/81	26/79	26/79	26/79
wetsuit						

Low pressures sitting off the east coast of North America generate plenty of 2-12ft (0.6-4m) N swells between Nov and March. South swells hit between April and Oct but due to onshore winds and steeply rising beaches, they don't produce good quality waves. Wind patterns are extremely stable, SE is the predominant direction varying from 41% in April to 70% in Sept, when it's not blowing SE it will almost certainly be due E. In fact for 94% of the time it blows from one of these two directions. This means perfect offshore conditions on the NW facing surf coastline. There are some slight variations at the end of the dry season, (Feb-April), when there may be NE and S winds. In spite of very little tidal action, low tide is usually too shallow on the reefs so head to the beachbreaks.

(viewpoints). The most consistent spot is Cacimba do Padre in the south, a heavy shorebreak that favours rights (like most of the beachbreaks on the island). The swell can be doubled in size here and reach heights of 12ft (4m) offering huge, cavernous barrels before closing out on the fine sand beach. With enough swell, it starts breaking outside and rolls through to the inside. At the west end of the beach are the 'Dois Irmãoes', two impressive rock formations. Boldro is a hazardous reef with some very good lefts and rights that barrel when it's small but it gets a little crazy when the swell is over 6ft (2m). From the nearby harbour you may be able to see some deep water reefs that break when the swell is over 8ft (2.6m). More good waves are to be found at Praia do Italcabe in Conceição, which is a fast beachbreak and is

Yannick Beven, Abras

Lost and Threatened Spots

The World's coastline is attracting an ever increasing share of the population. In the year 2000, it was estimated that 60% of the planet's population lives within 100km (60mi) of the coast. This population pressure is transferred to surf spots, which are being endangered by other human activities. These include harbour and jetty construction, tourism development, beach creation, nourishment and stabilisation and other water sports like jet-skiing and fishing plus the environmental issues of sewage, stormwater, oil spills, industrial water pollution, global warming and coastal access issues. Across the Earth, surf spots are disappearing because governments have not recognised waves as a natural resource worthy of preservation. This attitude is changing since the landmark legal findings in the case of Chevron's destruction of a break at El Segundo. The court declared that surf spots are recreational areas and should they be damaged, then compensation must be paid. This

Bundoran, Ireland
Since 1998, Bundoran authorities have launched a project to build a fishing harbour jetty right on 'The Peak', one of Ireland's outstanding spots. The protest has had great support from the surf media, the project is on hold.

ALEX WILLIAMS

La Barre, France
This great left was a big lure for 60's surftrippers before the Boucau jetty extension from 1970 to 1971. The spot improved then disappeared. The 2nd jetty construction completed in 2000 makes it even worse.

CARUSO

Rabo do Peixe, Azores
In São Miguel, fishermen extended the jetty in 1998 close to Rabo do Peixe harbour but they actually threw rocks in the wrong place and made the harbour entrance even more sketchy. Because of a narrower swell window, the former Pipe-like spot lost consistency. On nearby Terceira, 10km (6mi) of golden sand beachbreak were gone after Praia da Vittoria turned into a harbour in the 80's. A proposed oil refinery and water treatment plant threatens Santa Catarina, an excellent A-frame peak.

ALEX WILLIAMS

Akatei, Japan
One of the rare, quality, right pointbreaks in Chiba Prefecture was completely destroyed by a harbour jetty in 1993. That loss initiated the launch of Surfrider Japan.

KAMOGAWA MUSEUM

Malé, Maldives
Malé is the capital of the Maldives and the biggest island. 100,000 people live on 2sq/km! Coastal erosion is great and the Japanese have been building a seawall of Tetrapods. The only spot in town used to work all the time, but now there is a lot of backwash.

YEP

Reef 69, Bruce's Beauties, South Africa
Reef 69 was situated further up the point from the usual take-off spot at Bruce's Beauties, made famous in Bruce Brown's Endless Summer. Developers built a harbour right over it and a fantastic section of the awesome righthander was destroyed.

BRADLEY SEAMAN

NEW SPOT!
Narrowneck, Queensland, Australia
Narrowneck in Surfer's Paradise, on Queensland's Gold Coast has a long history of sand erosion problems. In spring 2000, 350 geotextile sandbags weighing 500 tons each have been laid down to help control further erosion. The V-shaped structure produces powerful rights and lefts, while protecting the coast and creating a natural habitat for fauna and flora.

has come in the form of $300,000 to build Pratte's artificial reef, which will start producing waves in 2001.

Some coastal structures do improve wave quality such as – California: Half Moon Bay jetty; Santa Cruz harbour; Sandspit; Huntington Pier; Newport groynes; The Wedge, Florida: Sebastian Inlet, France: Cavaliers, Australia: Kirra.

Jetties, breakwalls, groynes, piers and artificial reefs can help to provide shelter from the wind and stabilise good sandbanks. Environmental impact studies must be conducted but any new quality surf spots would help to atone for the extinction list below and help spread the ever burgeoning global crowd.

Environmental Causes

SURFRIDER USA: San Clemente, California – www.surfrider.org

SURFRIDER EUROPE: Biarritz, France – www.surfrider-europe.org

SURFRIDER BRAZIL: Itanhanga, Rio de Janeiro – www.surfrider.org/brasil

SURFRIDER JAPAN: Kamogawa, Chiba – www.surfrider.gr.jp

SURFRIDER AUSTRALIA: Currumbin, Queensland – www.surfrider.org.au

SURFERS AGAINST SEWAGE: St Agnes, England – www.sas.org.uk

SURFERS ENVIRONMENTAL ASSOCIATION: Durban, South Africa

SAVE OUR SURF: Honolulu, Hawai'i

Ma'alaea, Hawai'i
After 3 attempts (1955, 1959 & 1979) to create a safe harbour, the late 90's engineers have again proposed to build a 620ft breakwater and blast a new channel. Many opponents such as surfers, have managed to stop that project. Ma'alaea is one of the fastest peeling waves on the planet.

NEW SPOT!
Pratte's Reef, California, USA
Chevron constructed a groyne in 1984 to protect their oil pipes. They were successfully sued by Surfrider Foundation and a $300,000 fine was imposed. Surfrider and the California Coastal Commission have joined together to build the first artificial surfing reef in the US.

Dana Point, California, USA
This wave near San Clemente was one of the truly classic pointbreaks in SoCal. The magic righthanders fully disappeared after completion of a harbour in 1967.

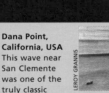

South Beach, Florida, USA
The South Point area of South Beach holds the finest waves in Miami Beach. Beachfront residential, hi-rise construction may affect public access and even lead to a ban on surfing.

Recife, Brazil
In the early 90's, the construction of a huge harbour at Boca de Suape, combined with massive coastal development and overfishing, started a period of concentrated shark attacks with 6 fatal cases. Authorities blamed surfers for the massive disruption to the food chain, and prohibit surfing on a 60km (38mi) stretch of beach and reefbreaks.

Petacalco, Mexico
In 1972, Lazaro Cardenas at the Rio Balsas rivermouth became a huge steel factory harbour allowing major ships to enter. Combined with a major hurricane in 1975, the Petacalco sandbanks, which used to rival Puerto Escondido, have never returned.

Seymour Norte, Galapagos Islands
Seymour Norte is a long wrapping right. Eco-tourists complained that surfers cause visual contamination when watching birds or marine iguanas. Since park officials don't like surfers, and eco-tourists bring in more revenue, surfing is prohibited there.

Cabo Blanco, Peru
In 1992, a small group of Peruvian surfers founded ACOPLO (Asociación para la COnservación de las PLayas y Olas) won a struggle against the Peruvian government to save Cabo Blanco's tubular lefts. With the support of US big game fishermen, local fishermen had planned a rock groyne, right on the spot. The surfers got it moved just north of the breaking wave, but rides get dangerous on big days. More projects threaten world class spots (La Herradurra, Pacasmayo). A law was passed in June 2000 to protect the best spots.

Copacabana, Brazil
In the early 70's, the government claimed the beach to build a new coastal road. This world famous beach used to hold 12ft (3m) surf with offshore conditions, but rarely works now.

Surf Schools, Camps and Charters

Main Worldwide Surf Travel Agents

The companies listed below represent about 80% of the world's surf camps, charter boats, tours etc. Contact your nearest agent or browse through their websites for information on what they offer. If you can't find the information you require please e-mail lowpressure.co.uk and we will try to provide information and further contacts. More information is also provided on the wavezones.com website.

OPERATORS	AGENCIES/COUNTRIES	TEL	FAX	WEB
Atoll Travel	Foster, Victoria	1 800 622 310	(0)3 5682 1202	www.users.bigpond.com/atolltvl
		61 (0)3 5682 1088		
	Albatros - ITALY	39 (0)544 363 34	(0)544 212 355	
	Maldives Scuba Tours - UK	44 (0)1449 780 220	(0)1449 780 221	
	Shanahan - NZ	64 (0)9 486 3091	(0)9 489 7660	
	Surf Travel - BRAZIL	55 (0)21 422 0425	(0)21 322 0756	
	Turquoise - FRANCE	33 (0)4 9113 9492	(0)4 9190 6011	
	VB Travel - SPAIN	34 (0)928 270577	(0)928 228020	
	Waterways - Cal, USA	See below		
Global Surf Travel	Wailuku, Maui, USA	1 808 244 1677	1 808 244 3226	www.globalsurftravel.com
	Queensland, AUS	61 (0)7 552 00 962		
Go Tours	Southport, Queensland, AUS	61 (0)7 559 12 199	(0)7 553 21 854	www.surftheearth.com.au
Low Pressure Travel	London, UK	44 (0)20 7792 7908	(0)20 7229 7132	www.lowpressure.co.uk
	Landes, FRANCE			travel@lowpressure.co.uk
Nias Tour	Sao Paolo, BRAZIL	55 (0)11 3105 6856	(0)11 3104 0059	www.niastour.com.br

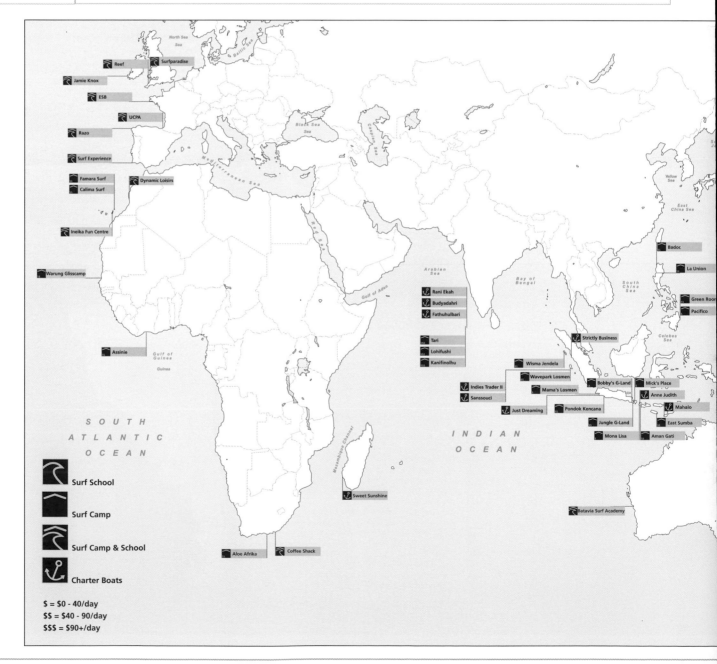

Surf School

Surf Camp

Surf Camp & School

Charter Boats

$ = $0 - 40/day
$$ = $40 - 90/day
$$$ = $90+/day

OPERATORS	AGENCIES/COUNTRIES	TEL	FAX	WEB
Surf Express	Satellite Beach, Florida, USA	1 321 779 2124	1 321 779 0652	www.surfex.com
The Surftravel Company	Cronulla Beach, AUS	1 800 68 SURF 61 (0)2 9527 4722	(0)2 9527 4522	www.surftravel.com.au
	STC - NZ	64 (0)9 473 8388	(0)9 473 8698	
	Waterways - USA	See below		
	STC - BRAZIL	55 (0)11 241 2637	(0)11 5092 3936	
	Travel Scene - JAPAN	81 (0)466 33 7083	(0466 33 6535	
	Marina - FRANCE	33 (0)5 5849 3141	(0)5 5841 8389	
True Blue Surf Travel	Cape Town, SA	27 (0)21 419 0618	(0)21 419 0638	www.truebluetravel.co.za
Waterways Travel	Van Nuys, Cal, USA	1 800 928 3757 1 818 376 0341	1 818 376 0353	www.waterwaystravel.com
Wavehunters	Santa Barbara, Cal, USA	1 888 899 TUBE 1 805 899 2885	1 805 899 0048	www.wavehunters.com
	Worldsurfaris - AUS	See below		
Worldsurfaris	Mooloolaba, Queensland, AUS	61 1 800 611 163 61 (0)7 5444 4011	(0)7 5444 4911	www.worldsurfaris.com
	Wavehunters - Cal, USA	See above		

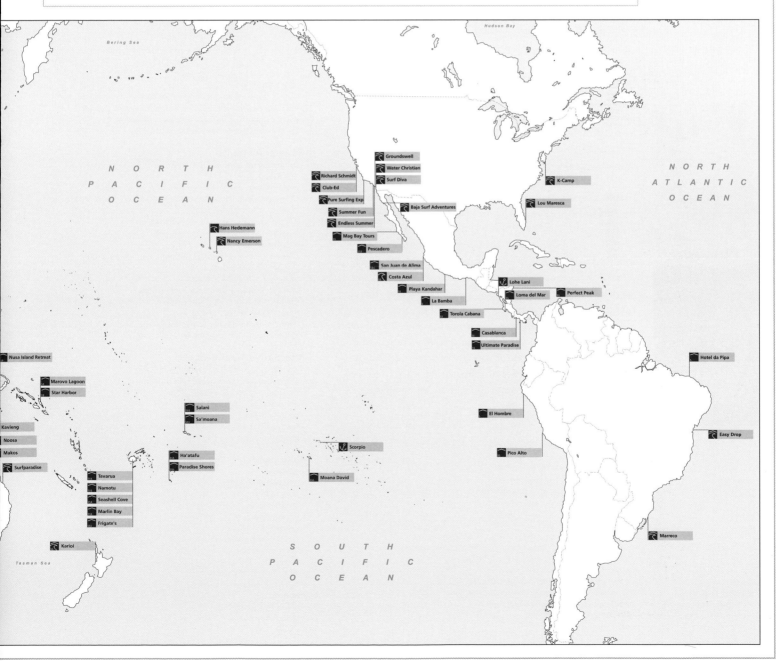

Travel Information

Airline Travel with Boards

There are no standardised rules when it comes to airline charges for boards. Some airlines have a fixed fee per boardbag but most are dependant on many factors such as the airport and what time you check-in, the plane's passenger and luggage capacity, your appearance and attitude and most importantly, the mood of the person at the check-in counter. Usually bodyboarders will not have to pay excess baggage, unlike longboarders, who sometimes don't get their boards on at all. As well as being oversized, surfboards are very fragile, prompting many airlines to insist you sign a damage waiver. Some companies view luggage per piece while some do it by weight, or both combined. Make sure you know the policy before departure. Some of the more crucial points to remember include:

– Arrive early, dress well, be polite and smile a lot.
– Ask your travel agent about the airline's policy and double check the information with the airline by ringing the check-in desk at the airport.
– Warn the airline to help them manage their luggage capacity.
– Some surf travel agents have already negotiated free board carriage.
– Most airlines charge per bag, so pack your boards in one boardbag.
– Ensure your board will be loaded on national or internal flights, especially if it's 8ft+.
– Always use a tough durable boardbag and give extra protection to the fins.

Very Friendly
BRITISH AIRWAYS
GARUDA
QANTAS
SINGAPORE
TAP

Friendly
AERO CALIFORNIA
AIR LANKA
AIR NEW ZEALAND
JAL
LACSA
LUFTHANSA
TACA
VARIG

Unfriendly
AERO MEXICO
AIR FRANCE
AMERICAN
AOM
CATHAY
HAWAIIAN
LAN CHILE
MALAYSIAN
MEXICANA
MEXICANA
TWA

Very Unfriendly
CONTINENTAL
DELTA
IBERIA
KLM
SAA
UNITED

Surf Travel First Aid Kit

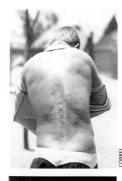

Surfers should always travel with some sort of first aid kit. Lacerations from your board are the most common type of injury (followed by lacerations from someone else's board) along with abrasions from contact with the ocean floor. Being able to treat reef cuts is a major priority, as well as having remedies for ailments commonly experienced when travelling. Further reading and increasing your first aid knowledge is recommended. Below is a list of essentials plus some heavy duty kit for the more medically experienced surf trippers. We have avoided brand names as these vary from country to country but the basic treatment/compound is generally the same. **P** items are available at a pharmacist. For **POM** items, a prescription is usually required. If an **A** follows the item it denotes an alternative to the conventional treatment. Always follow the manufacturers recommendations and use common sense when dealing with all medications. Make a record of all treatments. Never use out of date pharmaceuticals and use a hard case to protect bottles of solutions. Be open to local remedies, especially when dealing with localised ailments.

Cuts and Abrasions
Cleaning wounds
– hydrogen peroxide 3%
– povidone-iodine 10% solution
– hypericum and calendula solution (cuts, bites and stings) A
Treating wounds
– antibiotic powder
– antibiotic cream POM
– erithromycin 500mg (general bacterial infections) POM
– dioxycycline 100mg capsules (for specific bacterial infections) POM
– tea tree oil (natural antiseptic, anti-fungal) A
Wound dressings
– adhesive tape (1" wide and waterproof)
– band-aids/plasters (multi-sized waterproof)
– sterile gauze pads (multi-sized)
– steristrips/butterfly stitches
– bandages

Pain Relief
– aspirin, paracetemol, ibuprofen (pain, fever, inflammation)
– acetaminophen (with 30mg codeine for severe pain) P
– pseudoephedrine (nasal, sinus, ear conditions)
– oil of cloves (tooth pain and mouth sores) A

General Ailments
– sulfacetamide sodium 10% (eye drops) P
– eye drops
– antibiotic ear drops (for infected surfer's ear) POM
– silver sulfediazine cream 1% (burns, skin infections) POM
– lindane lotion (crabs, lice) P
– oral re-hydration kit (severe dehydration)
– laxative, cascara, senna, or castor oil
– anti-fungal cream
– diphynhydramine (itching, rash and allergic reactions)
– chamomile (itching, rash) A
– lopramide (acute diarrhoea)
– bismuth subsallcylate (nausea, diarrhoea)
– ginger root (chew for nausea, travel sickness) A
– antacid/heartburn tablets
– trimethoprim/sulfamethoxazole tabs (for bladder infections) POM
– cystitis and thrush treatments

Alternative Treatments all A
– echinacea (boosts the immune system)
– garlic capsules (prevent general illness)
– cayenne capsules (prevent colds/flu)
– aloe vera gel (sunburn)
– royal jelly/bee pollen (burns, wounds)
– tea tree oil (a natural antiseptic good for coral cuts)
– arnica (bruising and shock)

Equipment
– tweezers
– scissors/utility knife
– duct tape
– thermometer
– eyedropper
– safety pins
– safety razor blades/scalpel
– lighter/matches
– torch
– cotton applicators/buds
– tongue blades
– mirror
– water filtration straw
– soap (small bar)
– gloves, latex or vinyl

Useful Address
SURF AID: Gisborne, NZ
www.surf-aid.org

Planet Surf Hotspots

This is by no means all encompassing but the following waves are definitely world class.

GEOFF RAGATZ

10 Beachbreaks
Bay of Plenty, Durban, South Africa
Black's Beach, California, USA
Cacimba do Padre, Noronha, Brazil
Duranbah, Queensland, Australia
Hossegor, France
Kuta/Legian, Bali
North Narrabeen, NSW, Australia
Pascuales, Mexico
Roca Bruja, Guanacaste, Costa Rica
Supertubos, Peniche, Portugal

STEVE FITZPATRICK

10 Gnarly Waves
Cave Rock, Durban, South Africa
El Quemao, Lanzarote, Canary Islands
Padang Padang, Bali, Indonesia
Pipeline, Oahu, Hawai'i
Shark Island, New South Wales, Australia
Super Suck, Sumbawa, Indonesia
The Box, Western Australia
Teahupoo, Tahiti
Newport Wedge, California, USA
▸ Waimea shorebreak, Oahu, Hawai'i

LANCE SLABBERT

20 Lefts
Chicama, Peru
Cloudbreak, Fiji
Desert Point, Lombok
▲ G-Land, Java
Gnaraloo, NW Australia
Honkys, Maldives
Lance's Left, Mentawai, Indonesia
Mundaka, Spain
Nuusafe, Upolu, Samoa
One Palm Point, Java, Indonesia
Pavones, Costa Rica
Puertocillo, Chile
Raglan, New Zealand
Restaurants, Fiji
Rio Nexpa, Mexico
Scar Reef, Sumbawa, Indonesia
St-Leu, Réunion
Tamarin Bay, Mauritius
Ta'apuna, Tahiti
Uluwatu, Bali, Indonesia

20 Rights
Bells Beach, Victoria, Australia
Cloud 9, Siargao, Philippines
Cowaramup, Western Australia
Coxos, Portugal
Gas Chambers, Puerto Rico
Hollow Trees, Mentawaii, Indonesia
Honolua Bay, Maui, Hawaii
▾ Jeffrey's Bay, South Africa
Kirra, Queensland, Australia
Lagundri Bay, Nias, Indonesia
La Libertad, El Salvador
Ma'alaea, Maui, Hawaii
Malibu, California, USA
Rincon, California, USA
Safi, Morocco
Santa Catalina, Panama
Sultans, Maldives
Makaha, Oahu, Hawaii
Stent Road, New Zealand
Thurso East, Scotland

ROB GILLEY

CHRIS VAN LENNEP

20 Big Waves

Avalanche, France	Meñakoz, Spain
Dungeons, Cape Peninsula, South Africa	Nazare, Portugal
Easter Reef, Victoria, Australia	Outer Log Cabins, Oahu, Hawai'i
El Buey, Chile	Pico Alto, Peru
Jardim do Mar, Madeira	▲ (top) Puerto Escondido, Mexico
Jaws, Maui, Hawai'i	Revelations, Outer V-Land, Oahu, Hawai'i
King Island, Tasmania, Australia	Tangaroa, Rapa Nui
Sunset Beach, Oahu, Hawai'i	Tres Palmas, Puerto Rico
Margaret River, Western Australia	▲ Todos Santos, Baja, Mexico
Mavericks, California, USA	Waimea Bay, Oahu, Hawai'i

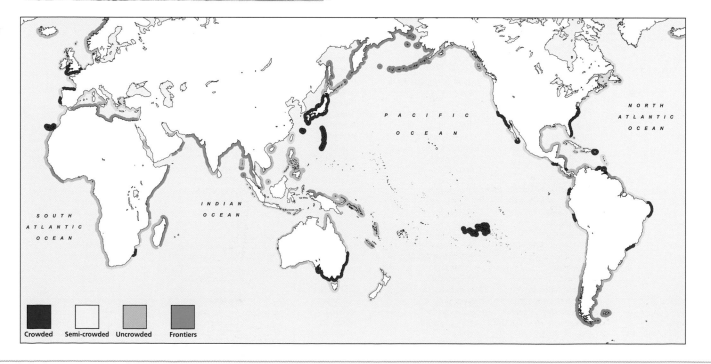

Crowded **Semi-crowded** **Uncrowded** **Frontiers**

NORTH ATLANTIC OCEAN
PACIFIC OCEAN
INDIAN OCEAN
SOUTH ATLANTIC OCEAN

Spot Index with Zone Numbers

THE WORLD
STORMRIDER GUIDE

THE STORMRIDER GUIDE
EUROPE

A LOW PRESSURE PUBLICATION

THE STORMRIDER GUIDE
NORTH AMERICA

available summer 2001

If you don't go,